W0245943

Intelligent Information Systems

Advances in Soft Computing

Editor-in-chief
Prof. Janusz Kacprzyk
Systems Research Institute
Polish Academy of Sciences
ul. Newelska 6
01-447 Warsaw, Poland
E-mail: kacprzyk@ibspan.waw.pl
http://www.springer.de/cgi-bin/search-bock.pl?series=4240

Mieczysław Kłopotek
Maciej Michalewicz
Sławomir T. Wierzchoń

Intelligent Information Systems

Proceedings of the IIS'2000 Symposium,
Bystra, Poland, June 12–16, 2000

With 94 Figures
and 24 Tables

Physica-Verlag

A Springer-Verlag Company

Dr.-Eng. habil. Mieczysław Kłopotek
Dr.-Eng. Maciej Michalewicz
Ass. Prof. Dr.-Eng. Sławomir T. Wierzchoń
Polish Academy of Sciences
Institute of Computer Sciences
ul. Ordona 21
01-237 Warsaw
Poland
E-mail: klopotek@ipipan.waw.pl
        michalew@ipipan.waw.pl
        stw@ipipan.waw.pl

ISSN 1615-3871
ISBN 978-3-7908-1309-8   ISBN 978-3-7908-1846-8 (eBook)
DOI 10.1007/978-3-7908-1846-8

Die Deutsche Bibliothek – CIP-Einheitsaufnahme
Intelligent information systems: with 24 tables / Mieczysław Kłopotek; Maciej Michalewicz; Sławomir T. Wierzchoń. – Heidelberg; New York: Physica-Verl., 2000
   (Advances in soft computing)
   ISBN 978-3-7908-1309-8

Physica-Verlag is a company in the BertelsmannSpringer publishing group.
© Physica-Verlag Heidelberg 2000

Softcover Design: Erich Kirchner, Heidelberg

SPIN 10769648   88/2202-5 4 3 2 1 0 – Printed on acid-free paper

Preface

This volume contains articles accepted for presentation during The Intelligent Information Systems Symposium IIS'2000 which was held in Bystra, Poland, on June 12-16, 2000. This is ninth, in the order, symposium organized by the Institute of Computer Science of Polish Academy of Sciences and devoted to new trends in (broadly understood) Artificial Intelligence.

The idea of organizing such meetings dates back to 1992. Our main intention guided the first, rather small-audience, workshop in the series was to resume the results gained in Polish scientific centers as well as contrast them with the research performed by Polish scientists working at the universities in Europe and USA. This idea proved to be attractive enough that we decided to continue such meetings. As the years went by, the workshops has transformed into regular symposia devoted to such fields like Machine Learning, Knowledge Discovery, Natural Language Processing, Knowledge Based Systems and Reasoning, and Soft Computing (i.e. Fuzzy and Rough Sets, Bayesian Networks, Neural Networks and Evolutionary Algorithms). At present, about 50 papers prepared by researches from Poland and other countries are usually presented. Besides, for several years now, the symposia are accompanied by a number of tutorials, given by the outstanding scientists in their domain.

Up to this year the proceedings were published as our local publication and they were distributed among the scientific libraries. We feel however, that the subject matter as well as the quality of papers is sufficient to present the proceedings to a broader scientific audience.

The main topics of this year symposium included:

- Logical and Methodological Foundations of AI
- Unsupervised Learning
- Rules and Decision Trees Acquisition
- Handling of Uncertainty
- AI for Database Systems
- Rough Sets
- Neural Networks and Evolutionary Algorithms

Out of a large number of submissions, the Program Committee has selected only 28 full papers for presentation. The remaining papers qualified as communications, will appear in the associated volume, edited by the local publishing house.

We were pleased to see the continuation of the last year trend towards an increase in the number of co-operative contributions and in the number and diversity of practical applications of theoretical research.

Application areas of presented methods and systems included medical and mechanical diagnosis, decision making. Practical issues were investigated from various theoretical points of view like automated and semi-automated learning procedures, evolutionary and rough set theoretic approaches to learning and knowledge representation, agent technology. As a result, interesting practical solutions were proposed and challenging new research issues were suggested. Questions of efficiency of proposed and existing algorithms were studied by means of logical analysis and simulation studies. Overlapping of diverse branches of AI research was strikingly visible.

On behalf of the Program Committee and of the Organizing Committee we would like to thank all participants: computer scientists mathematicians, engineers, logicians and other interested researchers who found excitement in advancing the area of intelligent systems. We hope that this volume of IIS'2000 Proceeding will be a valuable reference work in your further research.

Warsaw,
June, 2000

Mieczysław A. Kłopotek
Maciej Michalewicz
Sławomir T. Wierzchoń

Contents

Rule and Decision Tree Acquisition

Rough Sets

Unsupervised Learning

Logical and Methodological Foundations of AI

Neural Networks and Evolutionary Algorithms

Handling of Uncertainty

AI for Database Systems

IIS'2000 Programme Committee

- Prof. Dr. hab. Zdzisław Bubnicki, Instytut Sterowania i Techniki Systemów Politechniki Wrocławskiej
- Prof. Dr. hab. Eng. Ryszard Choraś, Akademia Techniczno-Rolnicza w Bydgoszczy
- Prof. Dr. hab. Piotr Dembiński, Instytut Podstaw Informatyki PAN - chairman
- Prof. Dr. hab. Ludosław Drelichowski, Akademia Techniczno-Rolnicza w Bydgoszczy
- Płk Dr. hab. Eng. Czesław Flanek, Akademia Obrony Narodowej
- Prof. Dr. hab. Eng. Zdzisław Hippe, Politechnika Rzeszowska
- Prof. Dr. hab. Eng. Olgierd Hryniewicz,Instytut Badań Systemowych PAN
- Prof. Dr. hab. Eng. Józef Korbicz, Politechnika Zielonogórska
- Prof. Dr. hab. Jacek Koronacki, Instytut Podstaw Informatyki PAN, Polsko-Japońska Wyższa Szkoła Technik Komputerowych
- Prof. Dr. hab. Witold Kosiński, Polsko-Japońska Wyższa Szkoła Technik Komputerowych
- Dr Eng. Maciej Michalewicz, Instytut Podstaw Informatyki PAN - scientific secretary
- Prof. Dr. hab. Zbigniew Michalewicz, University of North Carolina, Instytut Podstaw Informatyki PAN
- Prof. Dr. Ryszard S. Michalski, George Mason University, Instytut Podstaw Informatyki PAN
- Dr Eng. Paweł Nowacki, Polsko-Japońska Wyższa Szkoła Technik Komputerowych
- Prof. Dr. hab. Eng. Zdzisław Pawlak, Komitet Badań Naukowych
- Prof. Dr. Zbigniew Raś, University of North Carolina, Instytut Podstaw Informatyki PAN
- Prof. Dr. hab. Henryk Rybiński, Instytut Informatyki Politechniki Warszawskiej
- Prof. Dr. hab. Andrzej Skowron, Instytut Matematyki, Uniwersytet Warszawski
- Prof. Dr. hab. Eng. Ryszard Tadeusiewicz, Akademia Górniczo-Hutnicza w Krakowie
- Prof. Dr. hab. Eng. Alicja Wakulicz-Deja, Instytut Informatyki Stosowanej, Uniwersytetu Śląskiego
- Prof. Dr. hab. Jan Węglarz, Instytut Informatyki Politechniki Poznanskiej

- Prof. Dr. hab. Eng. Stefan Węgrzyn, Instytut Informatyki Teoretycznej i Stosowanej PAN
- Doc. Dr. hab. Sławomir Wierzchoń, Instytut Podstaw Informatyki PAN
- Prof. Dr. hab.Eng. Krzysztof Zieliński, Akademia Górniczo Hutnicza w Krakowie
- Prof. Dr. hab. Jan Żytkow, University of North Carolina, Instytut Podstaw Informatyki PAN

We would like to thank the Programme Commmittee Members for careful reviewing of the submitted papers.

Proceedings Editors

Optimization and Interpretation of Rule-Based Classifiers

Włodzisław Duch, Norbert Jankowski, Krzysztof Grąbczewski and Rafał Adamczak

Department of Computer Methods, Nicholas Copernicus University, Grudziądzka 5, 87-100 Toruń, Poland.
E-mails: duch,norbert,kgrabcze,raad@phys.uni.torun.pl

Abstract. Machine learning methods are frequently used to create rule-based classifiers. For continuous features linguistic variables used in conditions of the rules are defined by membership functions. These linguistic variables should be optimized at the level of single rules or sets of rules. Assuming the Gaussian uncertainty of input values allows to increase the accuracy of predictions and to estimate probabilities of different classes. Detailed interpretation of relevant rules is possible using (probabilistic) confidence intervals. A real life example of such interpretation is given for personality disorders. The approach to optimization and interpretation described here is applicable to any rule-based system.

1 Introduction

In many applications rule-based classifiers are created starting from machine learning, fuzzy logic or neural network methods [1]–[3]. If the number of rules is relatively small and accuracy is sufficiently high such classifiers are an optimal choice, because the reasons for their decisions are easily verified. Crisp logical rules are desirable since they are most comprehensible, but they have several drawbacks. First, using crisp rules only one class is identified as the correct one, thus providing a black-and-white picture where some gradation may be more appropriate. Second, reliable crisp rules may reject some cases as unclassified. Third, using the cost function based on the number of errors made by the crisp rule classifier leads to a difficult optimization problem, since only non-gradient optimization methods may be used.

These problems are overcomed if continuous membership functions are used, leading to fuzzy rather than crisp rules. Fuzzy rules have two disadvantages. First, they are not so comprehensible as the crisp rules, and second, they usually involve a number of parameters determining positions and shapes of the membership functions. To avoid overparameterization systems based on fuzzy logic frequently use a fixed set of membership functions, with predetermined shapes. Defining linguistic variables in such context-independent way amounts in effect to a regular partitioning of the whole input space into convex regions. This approach suffers from the curse of dimensionality, since with k linguistic variables in d dimensions the number of possible input combinations is k^d. Fuzzy rules simply pick up those areas in the input space that contain vectors from a single class. Without the possibility to adapt membership functions to individual clusters in a single rule fuzzy rules do not allow for optimal description of these clusters. Much better results may be obtained with context-dependent linguistic variables [4].

Another issue is the interpretation of the results obtained using rule-based classifiers. Although interpretation of crisp rules seems to be straightforward in fact it may be quite misleading. A small change in the value of a single feature may lead to a sudden change of the predicted class. Thus interpretation of crisp rules is not stable against small perturbations of input values. Fuzzy rules are better in this respect since estimation of probabilities of different classes change smoothly. Still a problem of tradeoff between the fuzziness and the degree of precision remains. If the membership functions are too fuzzy many classes have similar probability; if they are almost crisp perturbation of the input vector may significantly change classification probabilities, even if the size of the perturbation is within the range of accuracy of the measured input values. Believing the predicted results without exploration of alternative classes may in such cases be rather dangerous. Rough rules suffer from the same interpretative problems even to a greater degree, because rough classifiers produce a large number of unstable rules (cf. [5] on the importance of stability).

Thus although the biggest advantage of rule-based classifiers is their comprehensibility in practice reliable interpretation of sets of rules may not be so simple. A solution to these problems facing crisp and fuzzy rule-based classifiers applied to data with continuous features is presented in this paper. Neural and machine-learning methods of rule extraction from data were described in our previous publications [1]–[3]. Therefore we will assume that a small number of crisp logical rules has already been found. In the next section optimization and application of sets of logical rules is described. The third section deals with detailed interpretation of rule conditions and the fourth section illustrates optimization and interpretation of rules on a real-life psychometric data problem. The paper is finished with a short discussion.

2   Application and optimization of rule-based classifiers

Previously [1]–[3] we have described a complete methodology of rule extraction from the data. It is composed from the following steps:

- Select linguistic variables. In case of a continuos feature x linguistic variable s_k is true if the input value $x \in [X_k, X_k']$, i.e. linguistic variables are parameterized by interval values $s_k(X_k, X_k')$.
- Extract rules from data using neural, machine learning or statistical techniques.
- Optimize linguistic variables (X_k, X_k' intervals) using the extracted rules and exploring the reliability/rejection rate tradeoff.

- Repeat the procedure until a stable set of rules is found.

Optimization of linguistic variables is done by minimization of the number of wrong predictions $\min_M \left[\sum_{i \neq j} \mathcal{P}(C_i, C_j) \right]$ (where $\mathcal{P}(C_i, C_j)$ is the confusion matrix for a rule-based classifier M), simultaneously with maximization of the predictive power of the classifier $\max_M [\text{Tr } \mathcal{P}(C_i, C_j)]$ over all intervals X_k, X_k' contained in the model M. This is equivalent to minimization without constraints of the following cost function $E(M)$:

$$E(M) = \gamma \sum_{i \neq j} \mathcal{P}(C_i, C_j) - \text{Tr } \mathcal{P}(C_i, C_j) \geq -n \tag{1}$$

where the parameter γ determines a tradeoff between reliability and rejection rate (number of vectors in the "don't know" class). Sets of rules of lower reliability (making larger number of errors) have lower rejection rates than sets of rules of higher reliability that have larger rejection rate. If $\mathcal{P}(C_i, C_j)$ depends in a discontinuous way on the parameters in M minimization of this formula is difficult, requiring non-gradient minimization methods.

Real input values are obtained by measurements that are carried with finite precision, therefore it is natural to assume that instead of a crisp number X_i a Gaussian distribution $G_{X_i} = G(Y_i; X_i, S_{X_i})$ centered around X_i with dispersion S_{X_i} should be used. Performing a Monte Carlo sampling from the joint Gaussian distribution for all continuous features $G_X = G(\mathbf{Y}; \mathbf{X}, \mathbf{S}_X)$ an input vector $\mathbf{X}$ is selected and the rule-based classifier M is used to assign a class $C(\mathbf{X})$ to these vectors. Averaging results allows to compute probabilities $p(C_i|\mathbf{X})$. Dispersions $\mathbf{S}_X = (s(X_1), s(X_2) \ldots s(X_N))$ define the volume of the input space around $\mathbf{X}$ that has an influence on computed probabilities.

Assuming that uncertainties $s_i = s(X_i)$ are constants independent of the feature values X_i is a useful simplification. For a single feature $x = X_i$ to a very good approximation [2] a rule $R_{[a,b]}(x)$, which is true if $x \in [a, b]$ and false otherwise, is fulfilled by a Gaussian number G_x with probability:

$$p(R_{[a,b]}(G_x) = T) \approx \sigma(\beta(x - a)) - \sigma(\beta(x - b)) \tag{2}$$

where $\beta = 2.4/\sqrt{2}s$ defines the slope of the logistic function $\sigma(\beta x) = 1/(1 + \exp(-\beta x))$. For large dispersion s this probability is significantly different from zero well outside the interval $[a, b]$. Thus crisp logical rules for data with Gaussian distribution of errors are equivalent to fuzzy rules with "soft trapezoid" membership functions defined by the difference of the two sigmoids, used with crisp input value. The slopes of these membership functions, determined by the parameter β, are inversely proportional to the uncertainty of the inputs. In our neural network approach to rule extraction such membership functions are computed by the network "linguistic units".

For uncorrelated input features X_i the probability that $\mathbf{X}$ satisfies a rule $R = R_1(X_1) \wedge \ldots \wedge R_N(X_N)$ may be defined as the product of the probabilities of $X_i \in R_i$ for $i = 1, \ldots N$. Our rule extraction methods produce very simple rules that do not contain dependent features in a single rule, therefore taking the product is a good approximation. Another problem occurs when probability of $\mathbf{X}$ belonging to a class described by more than one rule is estimated. Rules usually overlap because they use only a subset of all features and their conditions do not exclude each other. Summing and normalizing probabilities obtained for different classes may give results quite different from real Monte Carlo probabilities. To avoid this problem probabilities are calculated as:

$$P(x \in C) = \sum_{R \in 2^{\mathcal{R}_C}} (-1)^{|R|+1} P(x \in \bigcap R) \tag{3}$$

where $\mathcal{R}_C$ is a set of all classification rules for class C, $2^{\mathcal{R}_C}$ is a set of all subsets of $\mathcal{R}_C$, and $|R|$ is the number of elements in R.

The uncertainty s_i of features may for some data dependent of the values of X_i. Classification probabilities may in such cases be based on a direct calculation of optimal soft-trapezoidal membership functions [6]. Linguistic units of neural networks with LR architecture provide such window-type membership functions, $L(x; a, b) = \sigma(\beta(x - a)) - \sigma(\beta(x - b))$. Relating the slope β to the input uncertainty allows to calculate probabilities in agreement with the Monte Carlo sampling. A network rule node (R-node) computes normalized product-type bicentral function:

$$R_j(\mathbf{X}; \mathbf{p}_j) = \frac{\prod_{i \in \mathcal{I}(R_j)} \sigma((X_i - t_{ij} + b_{ij})s_{ij}^L)(1 - \sigma((X_i - t_{ij} - b_{ij})s_{ij}^R))}{\sigma(b_{ij}s_{ij}^L)(1 - \sigma(b_{ij}s_{ij}^R))} \tag{4}$$

where $\mathcal{I}(R_j)$ is a set of indices of features used in a given rule R_j and $R_j(\mathbf{X}; \mathbf{p}_j) = R_j(\mathbf{X}; \mathbf{t}_j, \mathbf{b}_j, \mathbf{s}_j^L, \mathbf{s}_j^R)$. Combining rules for separate clasess C_j:

$$O_j(\mathbf{X}) = \sigma(\sum_{i \in \mathcal{I}(C_j)} R_i(\mathbf{X}; \mathbf{p}_i) - 0.5) \tag{5}$$

where $\mathcal{I}(C_j)$ is a set of rules indices for a given class C_j, probability of a class C_j for the given vector $\mathbf{X}$ is:

$$p(C_j|\mathbf{X}; M) = O_j(\mathbf{X}) / \sum_i O_i(\mathbf{X}) \tag{6}$$

and the probability of a class C_j for a given vector $\mathbf{X}$ and rule R_i is

$$p(C_j|\mathbf{X}, R_i; M) = p(C_j|\mathbf{X})R_i(\mathbf{X}; \mathbf{p}_i) \tag{7}$$

Optimization of model parameters: centers $\mathbf{t}$, biases $\mathbf{b}$ and slopes $\mathbf{s}$, may be done for example by the backpropagation gradient descend algorithm in the multilayer perceptron networks or by the Kalman filter approach in the IncNet neural networks [7]. Since probabilities $p(C_i|\mathbf{X}; M)$ depend now in a continuous way on the linguistic variable parameters of the rule system M the error function:

$$E(M, \mathbf{S}) = \frac{1}{2} \sum_{\mathbf{X}} \sum_{i} \left(p(C_i|\mathbf{X}; M) - \delta(C(\mathbf{X}), C_i) \right)^2 \qquad (8)$$

depends also on the Gaussian uncertainties of inputs $\mathbf{S}$ or on all parameters of the bicentral functions if full optimization of the membership functions is performed. Confusion matrix computed using probabilities instead of the yes/no error count allows for optimization of Eq. (1) using gradient-based methods. This minimization may be performed directly or may be presented as a neural network problem with a special network architecture. Uncertainties s_i of the values of features may be treated as additional adaptive parameters for optimization. Assuming that the uncertainty of s_i is a percentage of the range of X_i values optimization is reduced to a one-dimensional minimization of the error function.

This approach leads to the following important improvements for any rule-based system:

- Crisp logical rules are preserved giving maximal comprehensibility.
- Instead of 0/1 decisions probabilities of classes $p(C_i|\mathbf{X}; M)$ are obtained.
- Uncertainties of inputs s_i provide additional adaptive parameters.
- Inexpensive gradient method are used allowing for optimization of very large sets of rules.
- Rules with wider classification margins are obtained, overcoming the brittleness problem.

Wide classification margins are desirable to optimize the placement of decision borders, improving results on the test set. If the vector $\mathbf{X}$ of an unknown class is quite typical to one of the classes C_k increasing uncertainties s_i of X_i inputs to a reasonable value (several times the real uncertainty, estimated for a given data) should not decrease the $p(C_k|\mathbf{X}; M)$ probability significantly. If this is not the case $\mathbf{X}$ may be close to the class border and a detailed analysis of the influence of each X_i feature value on the classification probability should be performed.

3 Confidence intervals and probabilistic confidence intervals

Logical rules may be replaced by *confidence intervals* or *probabilistic confidence intervals* [8]. Confidence intervals are calculated individually for a given input vector while logical rules are extracted for the whole *training set*. These intervals allow for analysis of the stabilty of rules as well as the interpretation of a given case. Suppose that for a given vector $\mathbf{X} = [X_1, X_2, \ldots, X_N]$ the highest probability $p(C_k|\mathbf{X}; M)$ is found for the class k. Let the function $C(\mathbf{X}) = \arg\max_i p(C^i|\mathbf{X}; M)$, i.e. $C(\mathbf{X})$ is equal to the index k of the most probable class for the input vector $\mathbf{X}$. The confidence interval $[X_{min}^r, X_{max}^r]$ for the feature X_r is defined by

$$X_{min}^r = \min_{\bar{X}} \left\{ C(\bar{\mathbf{X}}) = k \ \wedge \ \forall_{X_r > \hat{X} > \bar{X}} \ C(\hat{\mathbf{X}}) = k \right\}$$

$$X_{max}^r = \max_{\bar{X}} \left\{ C(\bar{\mathbf{X}}) = k \ \wedge \ \forall_{X_r < \hat{X} < \bar{X}} \ C(\hat{\mathbf{X}}) = k \right\} \qquad (9)$$

where $\bar{\mathbf{X}} = [X_1, \ldots, X_{r-1}, \bar{X}, X_{r+1}, \ldots, X_N]$, and $\hat{\mathbf{X}} = [X_1, \ldots, X_{r-1}, \hat{X}, X_{r+1}, \ldots, X_N]$. Confidence intervals measure maximal deviation from the value X_r that do not change the most probable classification of the vector $\mathbf{X}$, assuming that all other feature values are unchanged. If the vector $\mathbf{X}$ lies near the class border the confidence intervals are narrow, while for vectors that are typical for their class confidence intervals should be wide.

Probabilistic intervals of confidence (PIC) should guarantee that *the winning* class k is considerably more probable than the most probable alternative class:

$$X_{min}^{r,\varrho} = \min_{\bar{X}} \left\{ C(\bar{\mathbf{X}}) = k \ \wedge \ \forall_{X_r > \hat{X} > \bar{X}} \ C(\hat{\mathbf{X}}) = k \ \wedge \ \frac{p(C^k | \bar{\mathbf{X}})}{\max_{i \neq k} p(C^i | \bar{\mathbf{X}})} > \varrho \right\}$$

$$X_{max}^{r,\varrho} = \max_{\bar{X}} \left\{ C(\bar{\mathbf{X}}) = k \ \wedge \ \forall_{X_r < \hat{X} < \bar{X}} \ C(\hat{\mathbf{X}}) = k \ \wedge \ \frac{p(C^k | \bar{\mathbf{X}})}{\max_{i \neq k} p(C^i | \bar{\mathbf{X}})} > \varrho \right\}$$

The ϱ factor determines the confidence level. Observation of changes in confidence intervals for different levels of ϱ may be quite informative. Comparison of probabilistic intervals for the winning class and alternative classes helps to estimate the likelihood of a winning class. Such method escapes the danger of relaying only on the decision borders of logical rules. Assuming that other features are held constant for a given case $\mathbf{X}$ three probabilities for each feature X_r are displayed in Fig. 3, 4. The solid curve is the probability of the winning class defined by $p(C(\mathbf{X}) | \bar{\mathbf{X}}; M)$. The class may change for different values of $\bar{\mathbf{X}}$. The dotted curve is the probability $p(C^{k_2} | \bar{\mathbf{X}})$ of the most probable alternative class $k_2 = \arg\max_i \{p(C^i | \mathbf{X}; M), \ C^i \neq C(\mathbf{X})\}$. The k_2 class is determined for the point $\mathbf{X}$ only. The dashed line presents the probability $p(C^{k_M} | \bar{\mathbf{X}})$ of the most probable alternative class at $\bar{\mathbf{X}}$. The class index $k_M = \arg\max_i \{p(C^i | \bar{\mathbf{X}}), \ C^i \neq C(\mathbf{X})\}$ may change, while k_2 does not change. These three probabilities carry all information about the case given for analysis, showing the stability of classification against perturbation of each feature and the importance of alternative classes in the neighborhood of the input $\mathbf{X}$.

4 Real-life example

Using the theoretical ideas described here we have developed a rule-based expert system to support psychological diagnoses. The description of psychometric data and the test used has already been given in [9] and [10].

Here we will focus on interpretation of the results only. 14 coefficients are calculated from analysis of answers to the psychometric test, giving after normalization "psychological scales", often displayed in a histogram (called "a psychogram"). The first four coefficients are used for control, measuring consistency of answers or the number of "don't know" answers, allowing to find malingerers. The next 10 coefficients form clinical scales, developed to measure tendencies towards hypochondria, depression, hysteria, psychopathy, paranoia, schizophrenia, etc. For example values between 70 and 80 in the hypochondria scale may be interpreted as "very strong worries about own health, leading to psychosomatic reactions".

We have worked with two datasets, one for women, with 1027 cases belonging to 27 classes (normal, neurotic, drug addicts, schizophrenic, psychopaths, organic problems, malingerers, persons with criminal tendencies etc.) determined by expert psychologists, and the second for men, with 1167 cases and 28 classes. Rules were generated using C4.5 classification tree [11], a very good classification system which may generate logical rules, and the Feature Space Mapping (FSM) neural network [12,13] since these two systems were the easiest to use on such complex data. These results are for the reclassification accuracy only using generated sets of rules. Statistical estimation of generalization by 10-fold crossvalidation gave 82-85% correct answers with FSM (crisp unoptimized rules) and 79-84% correct answers with C4.5. Fuzzification improves FSM crossvalidation results to 90-92%. A summary of results is given in Table 1. Accuracy refers there to the overall reclassification accuracy. Results from IncNet, a neural network model used in our group [7], obtained 93-95% accuracy in crossvalidation tests, comparing with 99.2% for reclassification.

Table 1. Comparison of results on psychometric data. Fuzzy accuracy refers to results with optimal uncertainty (C4.5, FSM) or results with bicentral functions obtained with IncNet.

Dataset	System	Crisp Rules	Accuracy	Fuzzy accuracy
women	C4.5	55	93.0	93.7
women	FSM	69	95.4	97.6
women	IncNet	–	–	99.2
men	C4.5	61	92.5	93.1
men	FSM	98	95.9	96.9
men	IncNet	–	–	99.2

These rules are most accurate on the available data if about 1% of the uncertainty of measurement in each of the scales is assumed, corresponding to a Gaussian dispersion centered around measured values. Larger uncertainties,

8

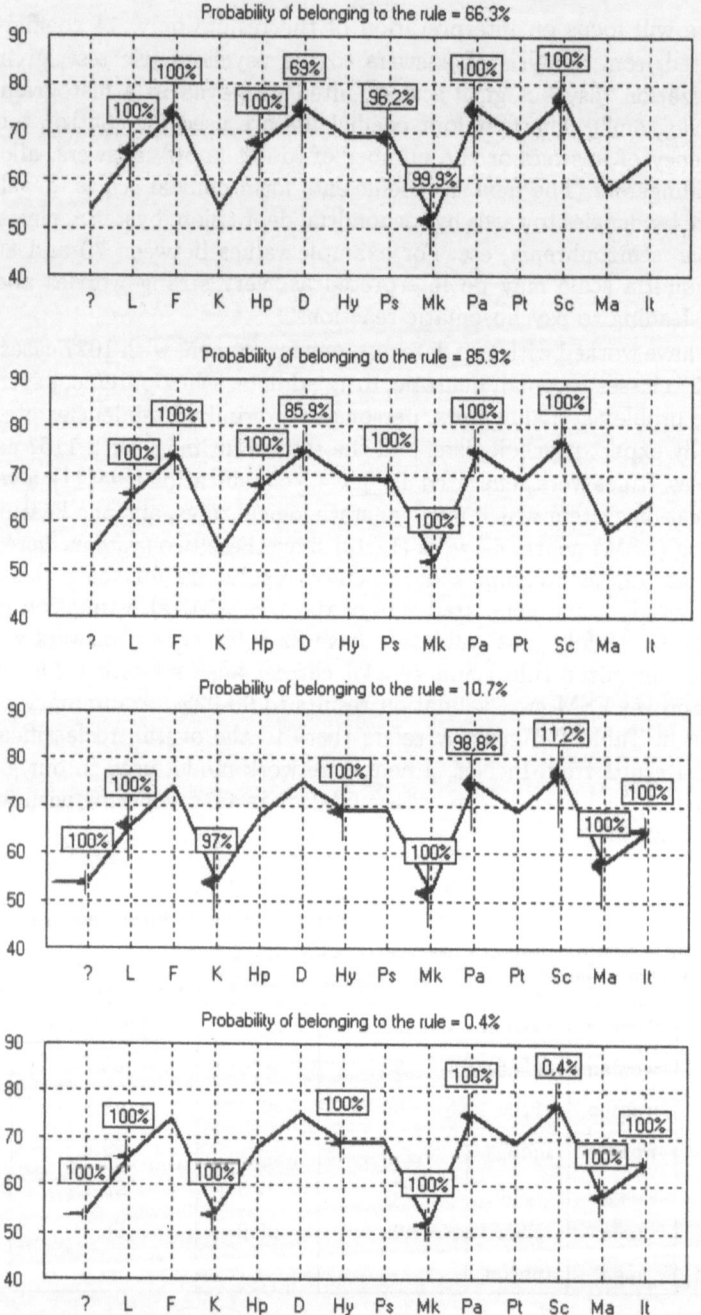

Fig. 1. Two rules applied to a case with small and large uncertainties.

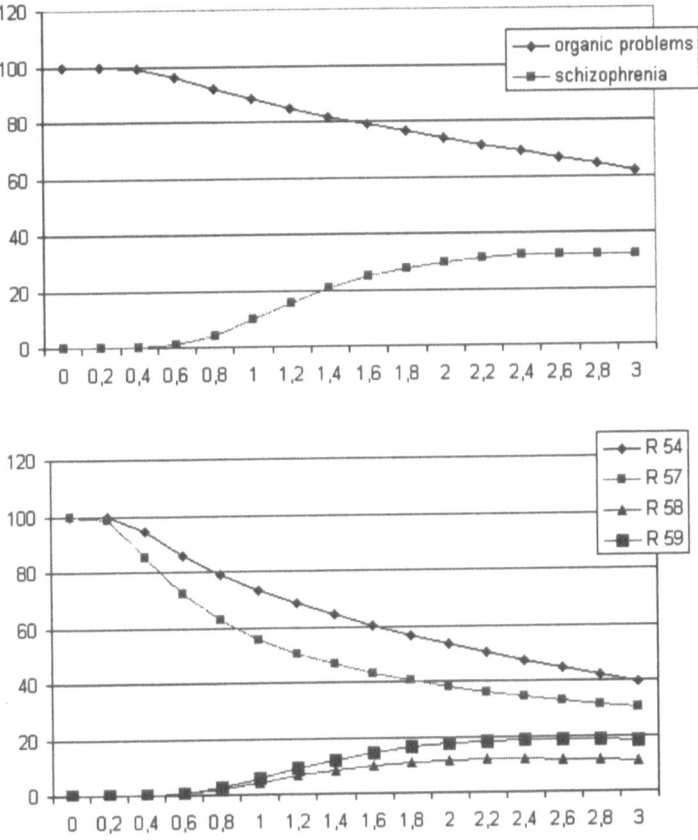

Fig. 2. Probabilities of classes and rules (in percents) for different vlaues of assumed uncertainties s_i, in percentage of the total range of the feature values.

on the order of 5%, lead to about the same number of classification errors as the original crisp rules, but provide softer evaluation of possible diagnoses, assigning non-zero probabilities to classes that were not covered by slightly fuzzified rules. Taking the input vector (66 74 54 68 75 69 69 52 75 69 77 58 65) for one of the cases difficult to diagnose, in Fig. 1 the influence of growing uncertainties has been presented. The top two plots show the profile and gaussian curves for each of the attributes occurring in rule No. 54 classifying the "organic problems" cases. In the first of these standard deviation of all attributes is equal to 1.3 times the range of possible values, while in the second standard deviation is equal to 3 times the range. The boxes above each feature value present the probability of belonging to a single premise of the rule. The bottom two plots show analogical properties for rule No. 59 which classifies to the "schizophrenia" class. Figure 2 shows how the probabilities in this example depend on the assumptions about the data uncertainty.

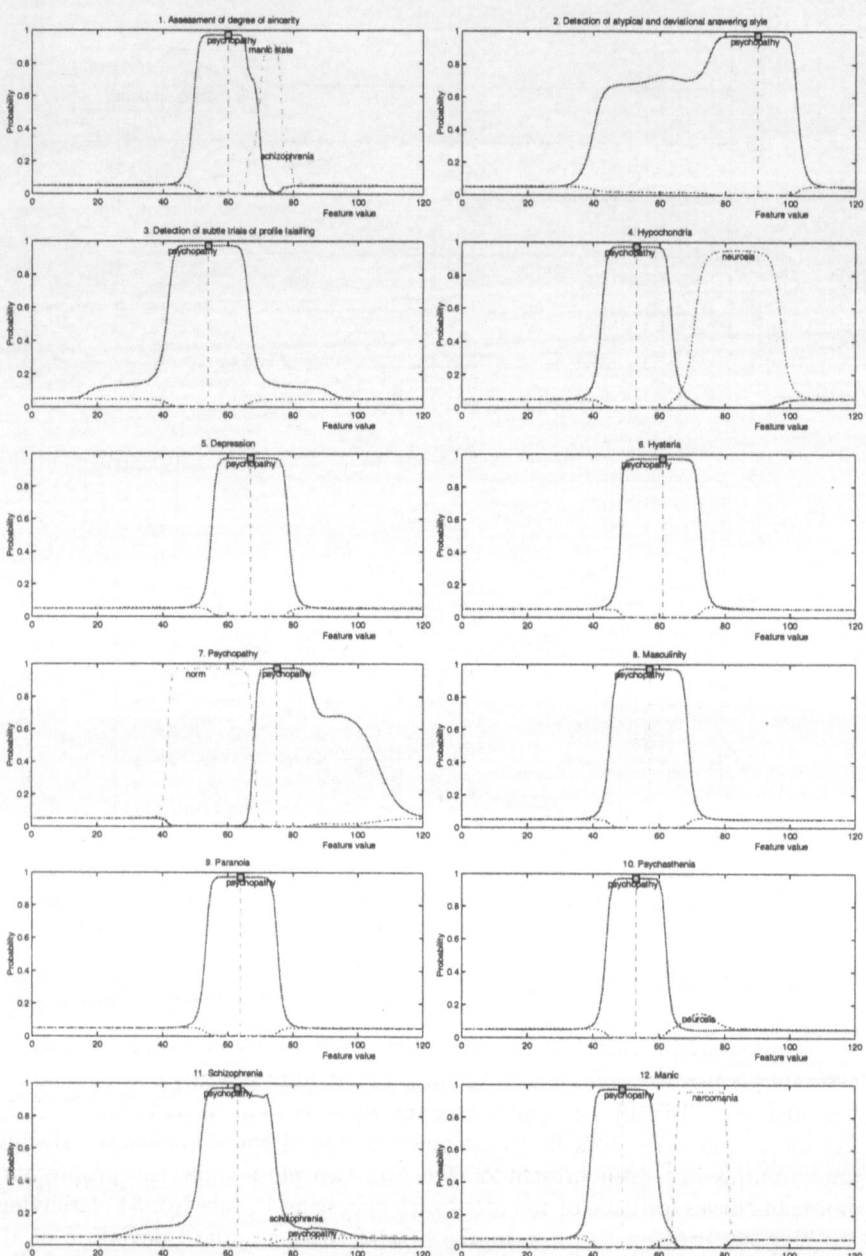

Fig. 3. Class: Psychopathy (prob. 0.97); alternative class: neurosis (prob. 0.002).

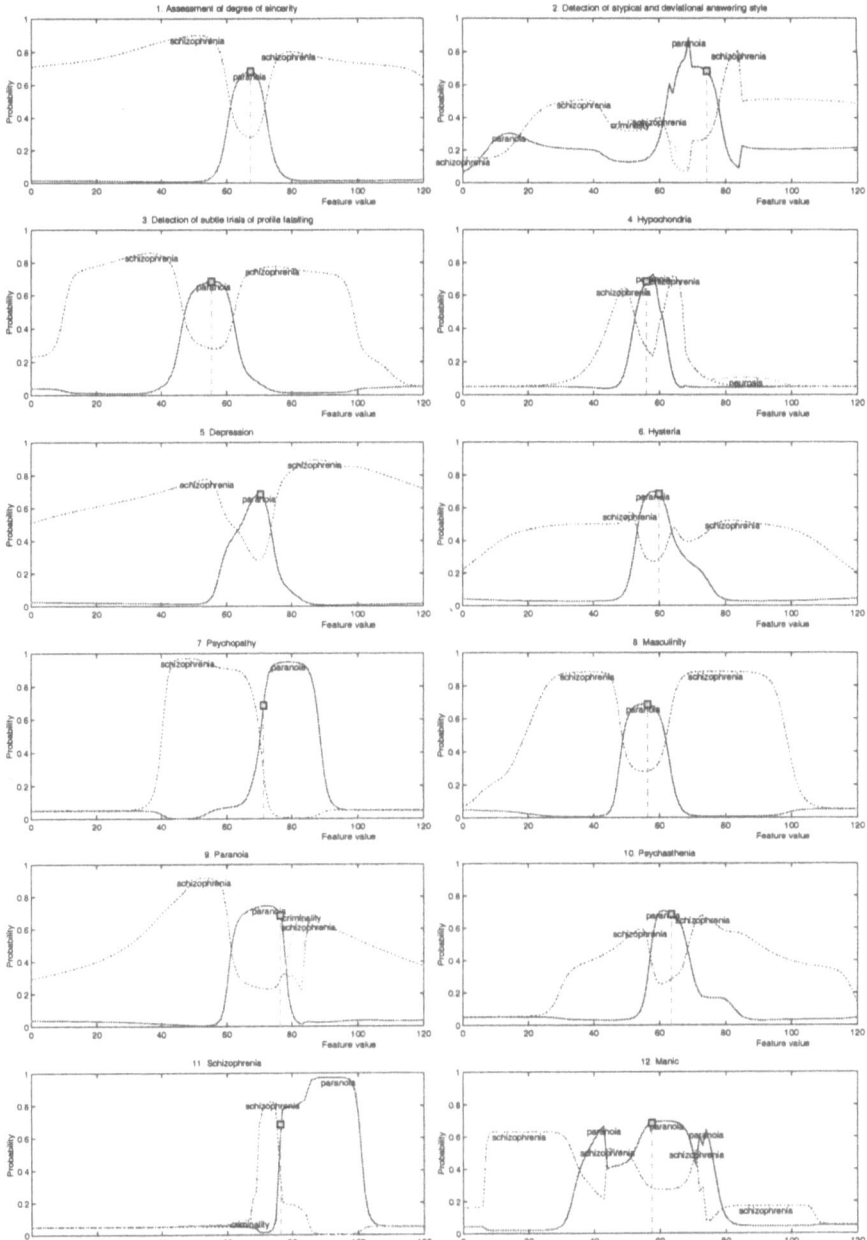

Fig. 4. Class: Paranoia (prob. 0.68); alternative class: schizophrenia (prob. 0.28).

If the change of the input uncertainty has strong influence on the probability of the winning class a more detailed analysis may be useful. In contrast to rule-based classifiers we will focus here on a single case, using all features and estimation of conditional probabilities from IncNet classifier [7]. Figures 3 and 4 show probabilistic intervals of confidence for two quite different patients (the first and the last scale has been omitted, therefore only 12 features are displayed). The little squares show the probability of the winning class corresponding to the measured input values of the psychometric scales. Figure 3 presents an easy case: the psychopathy has a large probability 0.97 and the case is quite far from any other alternative classes. The whole range of values, 0-120, is shown and an alternative class appears only for features 4, 7 and 12, but the confidence intervals are quite broad. Classification does not depend on the precise values of some features r (for example features 2, 3, 5, 6, etc) since there are no alternative classes in the whole range of values $\bar{\mathbf{X}}$ may take. The second set of plots, Fig. 4, is not so simple. The winner class, paranoia, has probability 0.68 while the alternative class, schizophrenia has probability 0.28. The analysis of plots shows that the values for scales 7 and 11 are close to the border and therefore both diagnoses are probable.

5 Discussion

Machine Learning community has focused on artificial cases where a few symbolic attributes are defined (for example, the three Monk's problems). In real data mining problems many continuous-valued attributes may be presented and large sets of rules may be needed. Rule-based classifiers are useful only if rules are reliable, accurate, stable and sufficiently simple to be understood. Most classifiers are unstable [5] and lead to rules that are significantly different if the training set is slightly changed. Such rules contain little useful information and in fact may be rather misleading. Even if stable and robust rules are found [1] the user should be warned about potential misclassifications, other probable classification possibilities and influence of each feature on the classification probability.

In this paper optimization and interpretation of sets of rules have been described. The method is equivalent to a specific fuzzification of crisp membership functions, equivalent to an assumption of uncertainties in the inputs. Analysis of the change of probabilities of classification in response to the change in uncertainties allows to estimate confidence in the performance of a rule-based system. If the confidence is low a more detailed analysis of the influence of each feature on classification probability is started. Probabilistic confidence intervals may be applied to any classificator estimating $p(C_k|\mathbf{X})$, enabling detailed interpretation of cases. In practical applications users are interested in relevant features and may rarely be satisfied with answers to questions "why" based on quotation of complex sets of logical rules. Similarity to prototypes, or case-based interpretation, is an alternative to rule-based systems. Therefore one should not exaggerate the importance of logical description as the only understandable alternative to other classification methods.

Support by the KBN, grant 8 T11F 014 14, is gratefully acknowledged.

References

1. Duch, W., Adamczak, R., Grąbczewski, K. (in print) Methodology of extraction, optimization and application of crisp and fuzzy logical rules. IEEE Transactions on Neural Networks.
2. Duch, W., Adamczak, R., Grąbczewski, K. (1999) Methodology of extraction, optimization and application of logical rules. Intelligent Information Systems VIII, Ustroń, Poland, 14-18.06.1999, pp. 22-31
3. Duch, W., Adamczak, R., Grąbczewski, K. (1998) Extraction of logical rules from backpropagation networks. Neural Processing Letters **7**, 1-9
4. Duch, W., Adamczak, R., Grąbczewski, K. (1999) *Neural optimization of linguistic variables and membership functions*. Int. Conference on Neural Information Processing (ICONIP'99), Perth, Australia, Nov. 1999, Vol. II, pp. 616-621
5. Breiman L. (1998) Bias-Variance, regularization, instability and stabilization. In: C. Bishop (ed.) Neural Networks and Machine Learning. Springer Verlag
6. Duch, W., Jankowski, N. (1999) *New neural transfer functions*. Neural Computing Surveys **2**, 639-658
7. Jankowski, N., Kadirkamanathan, V. (1997) Statistical control of RBF-like networks for classification. 7th Int. Conf. on Artificial Neural Networks, Lausanne, Switzerland 1997, pp 385-390, Springer Verlag.
8. Jankowski, N., (1999) Ontogenic neural networks and their applications to classification of medical data. PhD thesis (in Polish), Department of Computer Methods, Nicholas Copernicus University, Toruń, Poland
9. Duch W., Adamczak R., Grąbczewski K. (1999) Neural methods for analysis of psychometric data. Proc. of Enginnering Applications of Neural Networks (Duch W, ed.), Warsaw, Poland, Sept. 1999, pp. 45-50
10. Duch, W., Kucharski, T., Gomuła, J., Adamczak, R., (1999) Metody uczenia maszynowego w analizie danych psychometrycznych. Zastosowanie do wielowymiarowego kwestionariusza osobowości MMPI-WISKAD. Toruń, March 1999; 650 pp, ISBN 83-231-0986-9
11. Quinlan J.R. (1993) C4.5: Programs for machine learning. San Mateo, Morgan Kaufman
12. Duch, W., Diercksen, G.H.F. (1995) *Feature Space Mapping as a universal adaptive system*, Computer Physics Communication **87**, 341–371
13. Duch, W., Adamczak, R., Jankowski, N. (1997) New developments in the Feature Space Mapping model. 3rd Conf. on Neural Networks, Kule, Poland, Oct. 1997, pp. 65-70

Comparative Analysis of Selected Association Rules Types

Marcin Gajek

Institute of Computer Science, Warsaw University of Technology,
Nowowiejska 15/19, 00-665 Warsaw, Poland
e-mail: gajek@ii.pw.edu.pl

Abstract. Discovery of association rules from large databases of item sets is an important data mining problem. In this paper selected association rules types are compared in respect to various properties of these sets of rules. Hierarchical, representative rules and interesting rules based on neighbourhood or using hierarchy of items are considered. The algorithms generating the foregoing types of association rules were implemented and tested in the *miner* system [3].

Keywords: knowledge discovery, data mining, association rules

1   Introduction

The problem of mining association rules was introduced for sales transaction database [1]. Let us consider the transactional database presented in Table 1, where each transaction is a set of items.

Table 1. Example of sales transaction database

TId (transaction identifier)	items
1.	{suit, hiking boots}
2.	{T-shirt, jacket, low shoes}
3.	{jacket}
4.	{T-shirt, jacket}

An example of association rule discovered in Table 1 is: "50 % of transactions that contain *T-shirt* and *jacket* also contain *low shoes*; 25 % of all transactions contain both these items". Here 50 % is called the *confidence* of the rule and 25 % the *support* of the rule. The basic problem is to find all association rules that satisfy user specified minimum support and minimum confidence constraints. Applications for association rules range from decision support to telecomunication alarms diagnosis and prediction.

One of the essential problems concerning data mining is development of suitable measures, which are to determine, how far the generated rules are interesting. Having this information provided, user would be able to analyse only the most interesting rules instead of the great number of all rules.

In this paper several methods of selection of the most valuable rules from the set of association rules will be presented and compared. An approach proposed in [4] is not based on any statistical measure, but on a *cover operator* concept, used to derive the set of association rules from a given rule, without accessing a database. Another method, concerning the hierarchical association rules, applies information from item hierarchy to determine, whether the rule is interesting or not [6]. The third approach is based on neighbourhood of rule concept. The fact, the rule is interesting or not, depends thus not only on support and confidence of any given rule, but on support and confidence of rules in its neighbourhood [2].

The foregoing methods were implemented and investigated in data mining system *miner* [3]. The experiments were performed to measure number and length of mined association rules of different types depending on the support, the confidence and additional statistical parameters.

2 Problem Statement

Let $\mathcal{I} = \{i_1, i_2, ..., i_m\}$ be a set of m distinct literals called items. $\mathcal{D}$ is a set of transactions over $\mathcal{I}$. Each transaction contains a set of items $i_1, i_2, ..., i_k \subseteq \mathcal{I}$. An *association rule* is an expression of the form $X \Rightarrow Y$, where $X, Y \subseteq I$ and $X \cap Y = \emptyset$.

Two parameters: support and confidence were introduced in order to filter less interesting associations between items. The support is the joint probability to find all X and Y expressions in one group of items. The support is a measure of statistical significance. The rule confidence is the conditional probability to find in the group of items Y, having found X. The confidence is a measure of strength of rule. It is denoted by $conf(X \Rightarrow Y)$ and defined as the ratio $sup(X \cup Y)/sup(X)$.

The problem of mining association rules is to generate all rules that have support and confidence not less than user specified minimum support and minimum confidence thresholds, respectively.

3 Representative Rules

In [4] a concept of representative rules was introduced. It was shown there how to derive the set of association rules from a given rule by means of a *cover operator* without accessing a database. A least set of association rules that allows to deduce all other rules satisfying user specified constraints was called a set of representative association rules. A user may be provided with the set of representative rules instead of the whole set of association rules. The association rules, which are not representative ones, may be generated on demand by transformations of representative rules.

The *cover C* of the rule $X \Rightarrow Y, Y \neq \emptyset$, is defined as follows:

$$C(X \Rightarrow Y) = \{X \cup Z \Rightarrow V \mid Z, V \subseteq Y \text{ and } Z \cap V = \emptyset \text{ and } V \neq \emptyset\}$$

Each rule in $C(X \Rightarrow Y)$ consists of a subset of items occuring in the rule $X \Rightarrow Y$. The antecedent of any rule r covered by $X \Rightarrow Y$ contains X and perhaps some items from Y, whereas r's consequent is a non-empty subset of the remaining items in Y. For example, for the dataset in Table 1 the rule

$\{T\text{-}shirt\} \Rightarrow \{jacket, low shoes\}$ $support = 0.25, confidence = 0.5$

covers following rules:

$\{T\text{-}shirt\} \Rightarrow \{jacket\}$ $support = 0.25, confidence = 1$
$\{T\text{-}shirt\} \Rightarrow \{low shoes\}$ $support = 0.25, confidence = 0.5$
$\{T\text{-}shirt, jacket\} \Rightarrow \{low shoes\}$ $support = 0.25, confidence = 0.5$
$\{T\text{-}shirt, low shoes\} \Rightarrow \{jacket\}$ $support = 0.25, confidence = 1$

It was proved in [4] that if r is an association rule satisfying support s and confidence c then each rule r' belonging in the cover $C(r)$ is an association rule whose support is not less than s and confidence is not less than c. Hence, if r belongs to the set of association rules satisfying support and confidence, then every rule r' in $C(r)$ also belongs to this set.

4 Hierarchical Association Rules

One of the extentions of association rules are hierarchical rules that can be obtained by using a taxonomy [6]. The taxonomy may be presented by means of a tree, where each node is associated with a class of items and its descendants are subclasses. The leaves represent items in the database. An example of a taxonomy is shown in Fig. 1.

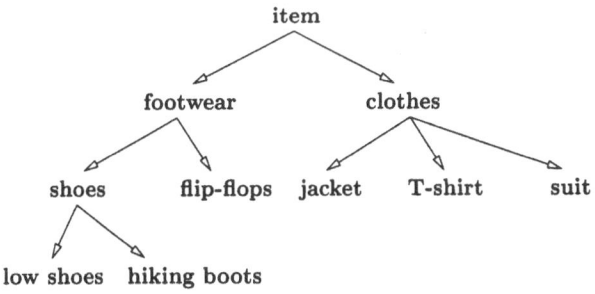

Fig. 1. Example of a taxonomy

This taxonomy says that *low shoes* and *hiking boots is-a shoes, shoes is-a footwear* etc. Users are interested in generating rules that span different levels of taxonomy. For example, we may infer that *clothes* and *hiking boots* are often bought together. However, the support for the rule {*clothes*} ⇒ {*hiking boots*} may not be the sum of the supports for the rules: {*suit*} ⇒ {*hiking boots*}, {*jacket*} ⇒ {*hiking boots*} and {*T-shirt*} ⇒ {*hiking boots*} in case of *suit, jacket, T-shirt* and *hiking boots* are bought in one transaction. Also {*shoes*} ⇒ {*clothes*} may be a strong rule, while {*hiking boots*} ⇒ {*clothes*} and {*footwear*} ⇒ {*clothes*} may not. The former may not have minimum support, and the latter may not have minimum confidence.

Finding rules across different levels of the taxonomy is valuable since taxonomies can be used to filter uninteresting and redundant rules.

Let $\mathcal{T}$ be a directed acyclic graph on the literals $i \in \mathcal{I}$. An edge in $\mathcal{T}$ represents an *is-a* relationship, and $\mathcal{T}$ represents a set of taxonomies. The items in transaction T are leaves in taxonomy $\mathcal{T}$. Transaction T supports an item $x \in \mathcal{I}$ if x is in T or x is an ancestor of some item in T.

A *hierarchical association rule* is an expression of the form $X \Rightarrow Y$, where $X, Y \subset \mathcal{I}$, $X \cap Y = \emptyset$ and no item in Y should be an ancestor of any item in X. The support and the confidence of the hierarchical rule is defined in the same way as for association rules.

5   Hierarchical Interesting Rules

In this subsection an approach to interestingness measure is presented that uses information included in hierarchy of items [6]. For example, consider the rule {*shoes*} ⇒ {*T-shirt*} (s=0.08, c=0.70). If *shoes* is a parent of *low shoes* and about a quarter of sales of *shoes* are *low shoes*, we would expect the rule {*low shoes*} ⇒ {*T-shirt*} to have support of 0.02 and confidence of 0.70. If the actual support and confidence for foregoing rule are around 0.02 and 0.70 respectively, the rule can be considered redundant since does not convey any additional information and is less general than the first rule.

Let $\mathcal{T}$ be a directed acyclic graph on the literals $i \in \mathcal{I}$ and the items in transaction T are leaves in taxonomy $\mathcal{T}$. We call $\hat{Z}$ an ancestor of Z (where Z, $\hat{Z}$ are sets of items such that $Z, \hat{Z} \subseteq \mathcal{I}$) if we can get $\hat{Z}$ from Z by replacing one or more items in Z with their ancestors and Z and $\hat{Z}$ have the same number of items.

We call the rules $\hat{X} \Rightarrow \hat{Y}$, $X \Rightarrow \hat{Y}$ or $\hat{X} \Rightarrow Y$ ancestors of the rule $X \Rightarrow Y$. Given a set of rules, we call $\hat{X} \Rightarrow \hat{Y}$ a close ancestor of $X \Rightarrow Y$ if there is no rule $X' \Rightarrow Y'$ such that $X' \Rightarrow Y'$ is an ancestor of $X \Rightarrow Y$ and $\hat{X} \Rightarrow \hat{Y}$ is an ancestor of $X' \Rightarrow Y'$. Similar definitions apply for $\hat{X} \Rightarrow Y$ and $X \Rightarrow \hat{Y}$.

Consider a rule $X \Rightarrow Y$, and let $Z = X \cup Y$. The support of Z will be the same as the support of the rule $X \Rightarrow Y$. Let $E_{\hat{Z}}(sup(Z))$ denote the expected support of Z given the support of $\hat{Z}$, where $\hat{Z}$ is an ancestor of Z. Let $Z = \{z_1, \ldots, z_n\}$ and $\hat{Z} = \{\hat{z}_1, \ldots, \hat{z}_j, z_{j+1}, \ldots, z_n\}$, $1 \leq j \leq n$, where $\hat{z}_i$ is an ancestor of z_i. Then expected support of Z is defined as follows:

$$E_{\hat{Z}}(sup(Z)) = sup(\hat{Z}) \times \frac{sup(Z_1)}{sup(\hat{Z}_1)} \times \ldots \times \frac{sup(Z_j)}{sup(\hat{Z}_j)}$$

Similarly, let $E_{\hat{X} \Rightarrow \hat{Y}}(conf(X \Rightarrow Y))$ denote the expected confidence of the rule $X \Rightarrow Y$ given the rule $X' \Rightarrow Y'$. Let $Y = \{y_1, \ldots, y_n\}$ and $\hat{Y} = \{\hat{y}_1, \ldots, \hat{y}_j, y_{j+1}, \ldots, y_n\}$, $1 \leq j \leq n$, where $\hat{y}_i$ is an ancestor of y_i. Then expected confidence of $X \Rightarrow Y$ is defined as follows:

$$E_{\hat{X} \Rightarrow \hat{Y}}(conf(X \Rightarrow Y)) = conf(\hat{X} \Rightarrow \hat{Y}) \times \frac{sup(Y_1)}{sup(\hat{Y}_1)} \times \ldots \times \frac{sup(Y_j)}{sup(\hat{Y}_j)}$$

A rule $X \Rightarrow Y$ is R-interesting w.r.t an ancestor $\hat{X} \Rightarrow \hat{Y}$ if the support of the rule $X \Rightarrow Y$ is R times the expected support based on $\hat{X} \Rightarrow \hat{Y}$, or the confidence is R times the expected confidence based on $\hat{X} \Rightarrow \hat{Y}$.

Given a set of rules and a minimum interest R, a rule $X \Rightarrow Y$ is *interesting* if it has no ancestors or it is R-interesting with respect to its close ancestors.

6 Interesting Rules Based on Neighbourhood

In [2] several measures of interestingness of association rules based on some parameters of neighbourhood of rules were introduced. In one approach it is used information about distribution of confidence in neighbourhood of given rule. In the another a measure of density of rules in neighbourhood is applied.

Using mountains as an analogy, normally one would not say that all peaks of the Himalayas Range of height > 4000 meters are more interesting than the highest mountain in North America and Japan, although these peaks are higher than the highest mountain in North America and Japan. Indeed, the interestingness of a moutain depends on its hight as well as on its position in its neighbourhood. Mount Fuji of Japan is famous because there are no comparable peaks in its neighbourhood. In the terminology of association rules, the interestingness of a rule should depend on its confidence as well as on the degree of the confidence fluctuation in its neighbourhood and the density of mined rules.

6.1 Distance and Neighbourhood Definitions

In order to specify neighbourhood of rule definition of distance function between rules is needed. On the basis of the distance concept we can specify if the rule is situated in neighbourhood of other rules and inversely. One of the propositions of distance definition was presented in [2].

This distance function is defined in such a way that one can give different scales of importance to differences for different parts of rules. Item set differences are divided into three parts: (i) the symmetric difference of all items in the two rules, (ii) the symmetric difference on the left sides of the two rules, (iii) the symmetric difference on the right sides.

The symmetric difference between two itemsets X and Y is calculated as follows:

$$X \ominus Y = (X - Y) \cup (Y - X)$$

Distance between two rules $R_1\colon X_1 \Rightarrow Y_1$ and $R_2\colon X_2 \Rightarrow Y_2$ is defined as follows:

$$Dist(R_1, R_2) = \delta_1 * |(X_1 \cup Y_1) \ominus (X_2 \cup Y_2)| + \delta_2 * |X_1 \ominus X_2| + \delta_3 * |Y_1 \ominus Y_2|$$

The parameters δ_1, δ_2 and δ_3 are non negative real numbers specifying the importance of individual parts. Such defined distance has all properties of a metric distance.

Different choice of values for δ_1, δ_2 i δ_3 can be used to reflect users preferences. One of the proposals presented in [2] are values: $\delta_1 = 1$, $\delta_2 = \frac{n-1}{n^2}$ and $\delta_3 = \frac{1}{n^2}$, where $n = |I|$. Having $\delta_1 > \delta_2 > \delta_3$ reflects our belief that the three kinds of itemset differences should contribute differently to the distance: the whole difference $(X_1 \cup Y_1) \ominus (X_2 \cup Y_2)$ is more important that the left-hand side difference $X_1 \ominus X_2$, which in turn is more important than the right-hand side difference $Y_1 \ominus Y_2$.

In [2] was introduced the notion of neighbourhood of rule. On the basis of the parameters of rules belonging to neighbourhood of given rule we may specify interestingness of rule. The notion of *r-neighbourhood* of rule R_0 (where $r > 0$) is defined as follows:

$$N(R_0, r) = \{R : Dist(R, R_0) \leq r\}$$

where R is a potential association rule, that is any rule, which can be created from items belonging to the set $\mathcal{I}$.

Characteristic type of neighbourhood is the 1-neighbourhood denoted as $N(R_0, 1)$. It has the property that all rules in 1-neighbourhood have the same frequent itemset and consequently they all have the same support. It follows from the assumption that $\delta_1 = 1$ and $\delta_1 > \delta_2 > \delta_3$. As a result all rules with the same itemset have the same neighbourhood.

6.2 Interesting Rules with Unexpected Confidence

To capture rules with unexpected confidence there were introduced two measures of the fluctuation of the confidences of mined rules in a neighbourhood: *average confidence* and *standard deviation* of confidence [2].

Suppose M is a set of the mined rules for given minimum support and confidence thresholds, R_0 is a mined rule, $r > 0$.

- The *average confidence* of the r-neighbourhood of R_0 is defined as the average of the confidences of rules in the set $M \cap N(R_0, r) - \{R_0\}$; there is used $avg\_conf(R_0, r)$ to denote this value.
- The *standard deviation* of the r-neighbourhood of R_0 is defined as the standard deviation of the confidences of rules in the set $M \cap N(R_0, r) - \{R_0\}$; there is used $std\_conf(R_0, r)$ to denote this value.

When the set $M \cap N(R_0, r) - \{R_0\}$ is empty, these two values are set for 0.

A rule R_0 is the *interesting* in its r-neighbourhood if $std\_conf(R_0, r)$ is much less than $|conf(R_0) - avg\_conf(R_0, r)|$.

7   Experiments

The experiments were carried out to compare sizes and other properties of discovered sets of rules: hierarchical, representative and interesting.

All experiments were performed on a PC Pentium 100 MHz with 32Mbytes of main memory running *Linux RedHat 5.2*. The data resided in a database *Oracle 8.0.5*.

Three different datasets were used to properties comparison of selected association rules types:

- *D10KT15I8*; synthetic dataset modeling sales transaction database. There are 10000 transactions with the average size of transaction amounted 15 items.
- *D10KT5I2h*; synthetic dataset with parameters: the number of transactions – 10000, the average size of transaction – 5 items. Additionally, the dataset is completed by plain hierarchy of items with 1000 items grouped in 10 classes of the first level and 2 classes of the second level.
- *nursery*; real-life dataset containing 12960 tuples and 9 attributes. All values of attributes are nominal without occuring missing values.

7.1   Investigation of Representative Rules Properties

There is a large disproportion in the number of mined rules depending on dataset used in research, as the performed experiments showed (Fig. 2).

For the *D10K15I8* set there is rather simple relation between the number of generated representative rules and the value of minimum confidence; where the gradual decrease in the number of representative rules in line with the minimum confidence increase can be seen. Within the investigated range of the confidence, the proportion of all rules number to the number of representative rules is well preserved. The representative rules constitute 20–30 % of all rules. Generally, one can say, that the difference rises with the increase in length of frequent itemsets. However, in the case of the *nursery* set there are some irregularities as to the number of obtained rules. The representative rules set is more or less constant within the range of minimum confidence not exceeding the value of 0.1 and even slightly growing then. Here, one of the properties of representative rules sets can be seen, namely, that the certain rules can become the representative ones, if the rule, representative for them so far, will cease to satisfy to the minimum confidence threshold. This is a sort of the "multiplying" of representative rules.

Figure 3 shows the number of all association rules and representative rules of given length. As one can observe, the number of generated rules of given length is not necessarily lower for the higher value of the minimum confidence. It is valid only for 2-rules and is caused mainly by the general decrease in the number of all rules and, in consequence, of representative rules (the number of representative rules cannot exceed the number of all rules). For example,

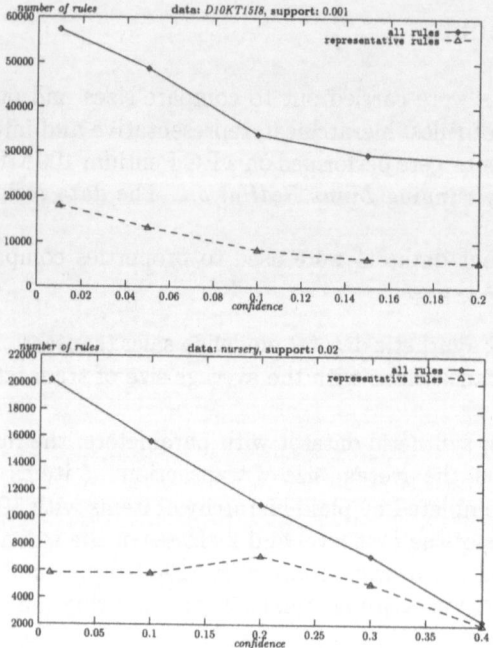

Fig. 2. Number of all association rules and representative rules

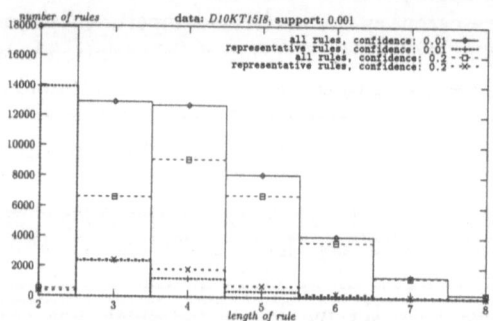

Fig. 3. Number of all association rules and representatives rules of given length

in the case of the minimum confidence of 0.01 there are 8 representative rules of 8-item length. They have only one item in the antecedent of rule. For the minimum confidence value of 0.2, there are as many as 28 representative rules of 8-item length but all of them contain two items in the antecedent of rule. The previously discussed rules are representative for them.

For the large values of the minimum confidence, the majority of all rules is also the representative rules and the sizes of both rule sets are comparable then (Fig. 2).

7.2 Investigation of Hierarchical Interesting Rules Properties

The tests were performed to measure the obtained number of hierarchical interesting rules depending on the minimum confidence and the R parameter.

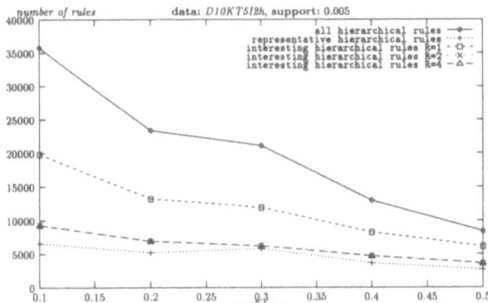

Fig. 4. Number of all hierarchical rules and interesting rules for $R = 1, 2, 4$

Figure 4 shows the number of mined rules for various values of R in the minimum support function. The size of generated interesting rules set is, on average, proportionally constant as regards the size of all hierarchical rules set. For $R = 4$ the proportion of the number of rules from both sets is about 30 %. It can be observed that further increase of R results in only small decrease of rules set. Some sort of saturation appears, caused mainly by lack of any ancestor in all selected interesting rules. Presumably, the rules set was limited only to the most general rules, that meet conditions of the minimum support and the minimum confidence.

Figure 5 presents the comparison of size of hierarchical interesting rules sets of given length. One can see the regularity in limitation of rules set in line with the R increase for all given rule length.

7.3 Investigation of Interesting Neighbourhood Based Rules Properties

During the experiments, the measurements of the number of all interesting rules and rules of given length were performed. Figure 6 presents the number of interesting rules generated for various values of T depending on the minimum confidence.

In the case of the synthetic *D10KT15I8* dataset, the set of mined rules decreases more or less proportionally with the increasing of the T threshold, regardless of the minimum confidence value. The limitation of rule number, on average to approx. 80 % for $T=0.5$, 60 % for $T=1.0$ and 40 % for $T=1.5$, was obtained. The measurements performed for *nursery* showed that the relationship between the interesting rules number and the minimum confidence

24

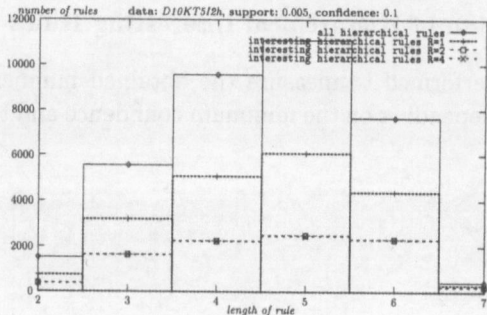

Fig. 5. Number of all hierarchical rules and interesting rules of given length for $R = 1, 2, 4$

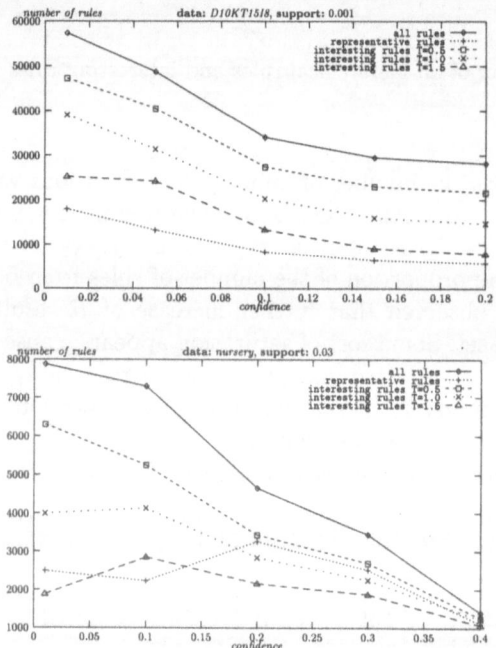

Fig. 6. Number of all rules, representative rules and interesting rules for $T = 0.5, 1.0, 1.5$

is not monotonic. The decrease of the obtained set of interesting rules is not always connected with the increase of the minimum confidence value. For example, if there are only two rules of similar confidence in the certain neighbourhood, none of them will be interesting as to unexpected confidence. However, if the rule with a lower confidence will be filtered out, the only one rule remaining in the neighbourhood automatically will become interesting.

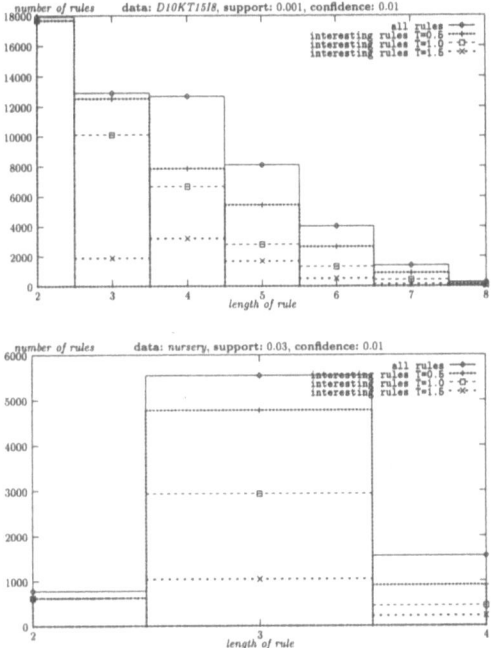

Fig. 7. Number of all rules and interesting rules of given length for $T = 0.5, 1.0, 1.5$

Figure 7 presents the number of interesting rules of given length for the specific values of the minimum support and the minimum confidence. As one can see, for virtually all the sizes of rule, the rule set decreases regularly with the increase of the T threshold, with the exception of rule size equal to 2, when the number of interesting rules is steady for all T. It is caused by fact that both 2-rules in the 1-neighbourhood are automatically filtered if they have the same confidence (in this case, the difference of confidence of a given rule and the average confidence equals to 0). If their confidence values are different, then, because of their standard deviations equal to 0, each becomes interesting, regardless of the T threshold value.

8 Conclusions

The selection of the most interesting rules from the generated rules set is highly desirable. In the paper three distinct approaches to the problem were presented. The survey showed, that representative rules are only 30 % of all rules. The all rules set can be easily obtained, given only representative rules, what is their advantage.

The other approach to the most interesting rules mining deals with rules based on the hierarchy of items. Input data supplemented by the taxonomy of items give more complete and general information of associations in database. The finding of the most general rules in order to replace the number of too detailed ones is essential. Implementation of the mentioned algorithm resulted in limitation to 30 % of all hierarchical association rules set.

The third approach deals with interesting rules based on neighbourhood concept. The algorithm generating mentioned rules was implemented; as a criterion of how much a given rule is interesting was used the unexpected confidence in the neighbourhood. The tests showed that the method is suitable for the limitation of all rules set to the size desired only by the selection of the T threshold value, e.g. 80 % for $T=0.5$, 60 % for $T=1.0$ and 40 % for $T=1.5$. Additionally, this approach enables selection not only of global interesting rules but even rules that are distinctive in the near neighbourhood.

References

1. Agrawal R., Imielinski T., Swami A. (1993) Mining Association Rules between Sets of Items in Large Databases. Proceedings of the 1993 ACM SIGMOD International Conference on Management of Data, Washington D.C., May 1993, 207–216
2. Dong G., Li J. (1998) Interestingness of Discovered Association Rules in Terms of Neighborhood-Based Unexpectedness. in LNAI 1510, Principles of Data Mining and Knowledge Discovery, Proceedings of Second European Symposium, PKDD'98, Nantes, France, September 1998, Springer-Verlag 1998, 72–86
3. Gajek M., (1999) Discovery of Generalized Association Rules. M.Sc. Thesis, Warsaw University of Technology, Institute of Computer Science, Warsaw, Poland
4. Kryszkiewicz M. (1998) Representative Association Rules. in LNAI 1394, Research and Development in Knowledge Discovery and Data Mining, Proceedings of Second Pacific-Asia Conference, PAKDD'98, Melbourne, Australia, April 1998, Springer 1998, 198–209
5. Kryszkiewicz M. (1998) Fast Discovery of Representative Association Rules. in LNAI 1424, Rough Sets and Current Trends in Computing, Proceedings of First International Conference, RSCTC'98, Warsaw, Poland, June 1998, Springer 1998, 214–221
6. Srikant R., Agrawal R. (1995) Mining Generalized Association Rules. Proceedings of the 21st International Conference on Very Large Data Bases, Zurich, Swizerland, September 1995, 407–419

Data Mining Experiments with a Melanoma Data Set

Jerzy W. Grzymala-Busse[1] and Zdzislaw S. Hippe[2]

[1] Department of Electrical Engineering and Computer Science, University of Kansas, Lawrence, KS 66045, U.S.A.
[2] Department of Computer Chemistry, Rzeszow University of Technology, 35-041 Rzeszow, Poland

Abstract: A data set describing melanoma was prepared by the Outpatient Advice Center for Dermatology in Rzeszow, Poland. Our objective was to study the importance of the TDS index, one of the attributes of the data set, broadly used in the initial classification of melanoma tumor diagnosis. Our experiments show that the same accuracy of diagnosis may be accomplished by a data set containing TDS as an attribute and another data set with fewer but more sophisticated attributes without TDS.

Key words: Nevi pigmentosi, TDS index, classification rules, LERS system, LEM2 algorithm.

1 Introduction

A data set describing cases of skin cancer amongst a population from the southeast part of Poland has been compiled for several years by the Outpatient Advice Center for Dermatology in Rzeszow, Poland [1]. The data set, called NEVI_DCC, carefully verified (inter alia, by extended histological investigations), contains personal information (*Age*, *Gender*), information about the apparent origin of the disease (*Nevus_origin*, *Family_inheritance*, *Exposure_to_sun*, *Sunburn_in_childhood*), and a description of melanoid marks on the skin (*Number_of_changes*, *Location*, *Diameter*, *Elevation*, *Roughness*, *Symmetry*, *Border*, *Structure*, *Color*, and *TDS*). Each of the cases was diagnosed as belonging to one of four classes: *benign nevus*, *blue nevus*, *suspicious nevus*, or *melanoma malignant* of the decision *Nevi Pigmentosi*.

The main data set NEVI_DCC, critically reviewed in [8], was prepared, in a format required by a program deriving decision trees [6], at the Department of Computer Chemistry (Rzeszow University of Technology). Currently the data set NEVI_DCC contains 250 cases, with almost equal distribution of all four classes of *Nevi Pigmentosi*.

The data set NEVI_DCC contains four attributes that are necessary to compute the TDS index. However, these four NEVI_DCC attributes are simplified and it would be impossible to compute the TDS index from them.

Another data set, called NEVI_NDE, is a modified version of the NEVI_DCC data set. First, NEVI_NDE does not contain the TDS index. Secondly, four attributes from NEVI_DCC were selected and transformed into a set of 13 attributes in the data set NEVI_NDE. The information contained in these 13 attributes from NEVI_NDE is more detailed than information contained in the original four attributes from NEVI_DCC. For example, the attribute *Color* from NEVI_DCC is replaced by the following six binary attributes in NEVI_NDE: *Color_white*, *Color_blue*, *Color_black*, *Color_red*, *Color_light_brown* and *Color_dark_brown*, with values *yes* or *no*. A case may be described by the value *yes* for more than one of these six attributes associated with color. The corresponding attribute *Color* in NEVI_DCC has only one of the four possible values (*blue*, *black*, *light_brown*, and *dark_brown*). Similarly, the attribute *Structure* from NEVI_DCC is replaced by five binary attributes in NEVI_NDE, and any of these five new attributes may have value *yes*, while the corresponding attribute, NEVI_DCC, has only four values. Yet another attribute, *Border*, was ternary in NEVI_DCC. This attribute is more accurate in NEVI_NDE because it is numerical, with nine values. The fourth attribute, *Symmetry*, is identical in both data sets: NEVI_DCC and NEVI_NDE.

The data set NEVI_NDE contains improper information to compute the TDS index. The value of any of the four attributes that are needed for the TDS formula must be unique; for example, the value of *Color* is, say, *red*. In NEVI_NDE the corresponding attributes may have more than one value; for example, both *Color_black* and *Color_red* may have values *yes*.

An additional data set, NEVI_DCC_NO-TDS was created to study the importance of the TDS index. This data set is identical with NEVI_DCC except one attribute, TDS, was deleted from NEVI_DCC, with all of its values, to create NEVI_DCC_NO-TDS.

The TDS index mentioned here (TDS stands for Total Dermatoscopic Score), according to [3], may be conveniently used as a measure for non-invasive diagnosing of *melanocytic nevi* and *melanoma malignant*. The numerical value of this index is computed using ABCD-rules, where A stands for asymmetry (asymmetry is called *Symmetry* in our data sets), B for *Border*, C for *Color*, and D for diversity of the structural changes on the skin (this attribute is called *Structure* in our data sets):

$$TDS = 1.3 * Asymmetry + 0.1 * Border + 0.5 * Color + 0.5 * Diversity\_of\_structure$$

Braun-Falco [3] assigned the following values of the TDS index to previously mentioned classes of *Nevi Pigmentosi*:

$$Nevi\_pigmentosi = benign\_nevus \text{ or } blue\_nevus \text{ if } 1.0 < TDS < 4.75,$$

$$Nevi\_pigmentosi = suspicious\_nevus \text{ if } 4.75 \leq TDS < 5.45,$$

$$Nevi\_pigmentosi = melanoma\_malignant \text{ if } 5.45 \leq TDS.$$

However, a detailed inspection of literature data revealed that the designation of the TDS-values to a given class of *Nevi Pigmentosi* was executed using traditional statistical analysis. Moreover, the selection of features (symptoms) for diagnosing of the disease was based on a limited population of cases (about 175 registered cases altogether). The entire data set (according to [3]), used for finding statistical regularities, contained in fact only about half of the 175 cases because the basic set was split evenly into a training set and a testing set. Results of our preliminary examination [5] forced us to start an extended research, aimed at developing a new measure of endangerment by melanoma. Also, we would like to search for statistically strong dependencies between causes and consequences, allowing an early and non-invasive identification of tumor. The following problems arise:

(i) how the hierarchy of coefficient importance of in the ABCD-rules should be changed for more reliable classification of skin marks?

(ii) would the assignment of other values to these coefficients improve diagnosing of melanoma endangerment?

(iii) would other symptoms of melanoma permit an increase in tumor identification certainty?

Some experiments along these lines, using decision tree generating program [6] and the rule induction system LERS [7] were performed. Initial results are presented and discussed further in this paper.

2 Initial results: the problem of the TDS index

Results of our initial experiments on searching for hidden regularities in the database NEVI_DCC were obtained with the use of a developing decision tree tool [6]. Briefly speaking, it may be stated that analysis of various decision trees obtained lead to an important conclusion about location of selected attributes in particular nodes of a tree. Namely, in almost all data sets we experimented with, the attribute *Color* was placed in the root of each tree. Moreover, estimation of the location (within the decision tree) of other attributes used for calculation of the TDS index, allowed us to appraise the hierarchy of importance of successive attributes (symptoms) applied for classification of *Nevi Pigmentosi*.

Referring to our preliminary experiments it may be assumed that the most relevant attribute to classify melanoid marks on the skin seems to be *Color*. Two other attributes, commonly used in calculation of the TDS index, namely *Symmetry* and *Border* have smaller diagnostic power. They also display similar importance in the classification of the investigated cases. On the other hand, the attribute *Structure*, scored by Braun-Falco [3] with coefficient on the level of 0.5, according to our observation has negligible influence on the classification process. These findings pointed out that the coefficients currently accepted for calculation of the TDS index from ABCD-rules have been erroneously selected. It may be expected that assignment of other numerical values carefully elucidated (e.g. trying to preserve the discovered hierarchy of attributes) to these coefficients, would cause more effective discrimination of the investigated cases, hence, more reliable diagnosing of melanoma tumor. This conclusion was confirmed directly or indirectly in further steps of our research, especially by the development of various sets of decision rules.

3 Discretization

All three data sets, NEVI_DCC, NEVI_DCC_NO-TDS, and NEVI_NDE, contain symbolic and numerical attributes. In our experiments we performed discretization by using an option of LERS based on hierarchical cluster analysis [3]. The main idea is to find , recursively, two closest cases, using only numerical attributes, and create a new cluster, containing these two cases.

The discretization intervals for NEVI_DCC are the following:

Scheme for *Age* : 2 new values: [4, 28) with 134 hits and [28, 78] with 116 hits,

Scheme for *Number_of_changes* : 2 new values: [1, 15) with 149 hits and [15, 100] with 101 hits,

Scheme for *Diameter* : 2 new values: [0.2, 9.0) with 247 hits and [9.0, 14.0] with 3 hits,

Scheme for *Elevation* : 1 new value: [0, 2.5] with 250 hits,

Scheme for *TDS* : 2 new values: [1.0, 4.8) with 111 hits and [4.8, 8.0] with 139 hits.

Thus, the attribute *Elevation* was evaluated as useless by LERS [6]. Remaining attributes became binary. The threshold for TDS, 4.8 is amazingly closed to the threshold used by experts (4.75). Similarly, the discretization scheme for NEVI_DCC_NO-TDS also eliminated attribute *Elevation*:

Scheme for *Age* : 2 new values: [4, 28) with 134 hits and [28, 78] with 116 hits,

Scheme for *Number_of_changes* : 2 new values: [1, 10) with 109 hits and [10, 100] with 141 hits,

Scheme for *Diameter* : 2 new values: [0.2, 0.6) with 36 hits and [0.6, 14.0] with 214 hits,

Scheme for *Elevation* : 1 new value: [0, 2.5] with 250 hits,

In the data set NEVI_NDE, the only numerical attribute became ternary:

Scheme for *Border* : 3 new values: [0, 0.2) with 127 hits, [0.2, 0.6) with 78 hits, and [0.6, 0.8] with 45 hits.

After discretization, all three data sets: NEVI_DCC, NEVI_DCC_NO-TDS, and NEVI_NDE were consistent. Notice that LERS uses different notation for intervals. For example, in the *Age* intervals, the LERS notation, is 4..28 instead of [4, 28) and 28..78 instead of [28, 78].

4 Rule Induction, Classification, and Validation

Rule sets were induced by the data mining system LERS [7]. The system LERS is ready for rule induction from inconsistent data sets (LERS stands for Learning from Examples based on Rough Sets), computing typical for rough set theory lower and upper approximations for every concept. However, in our data sets this feature was not used, since all three of our data sets were consistent. On the other hand, LEM2 is especially designed to work with consistent data sets, results of preprocessing by other module of LERS. In general, LERS has four options for rule induction [7]; only one, called LEM2 was used for our experiments.

Procedure LEM2
(**input:** a set B;
output: a single local covering **T** of set B);
begin
  $G := B$;
  T$:= \emptyset$;
  while $G \neq \emptyset$ **do**
     begin
     $T := \emptyset$;
     $T(G) := \{t \mid [t] \cap G \neq \emptyset\}$;
     while $T = \emptyset$ **or** (**not** $[T] \subseteq B$) **do**
       begin
           select a pair $t \in T(G)$ with the highest attribute priority, if a tie occurs, select a pair $t \in T(G)$ such that $|[t] \cap G|$ is maximum; if another tie occurs, select a pair $t \in T(G)$ with the smallest cardinality of $[t]$; if a further tie occurs, select first pair;
           $T := T \cup \{t\}$;
           $G := [t] \cap G$;
           $T(G) := \{t \mid [t] \cap G \neq \emptyset\}$;
           $T(G) := T(G) - T$;
        end; {while}
     for each t in T **do**
        if $[T - \{t\}] \subseteq B$ **then** $T := T - \{t\}$;
     T $:= $ **T** $\cup \{T\}$;
     $G := B - \bigcup_{T \in \mathbf{T}}[T]$;
  end {while};
  for each $T \in$ **T** **do**
     if $\bigcup_{S \in \mathbf{T}-\{T\}} [S] = B$ **then** **T** $:= $ **T** $- \{T\}$;
end {procedure}.

The process of classification used in LERS has four factors: *Strength*, *Specificity*, *Matching_factor*, and *Support*. The original approach is known under the name *bucket brigade algorithm* [2, 9]. In this approach, the classification of a case is based on three factors: strength, specificity, and support. The additional factor, used for partial matching, was added to LERS. In the bucket brigade algorithm partial matching is not used at all. These four factors are defined as following:

Strength is a measure of how well the rule performed during training. It is the number of cases correctly classified by the rule in training data. The bigger strength is, the better.

Specificity is a measure of completeness of a rule. It is the number of conditions (attribute-value pairs) of a rule. It means a rule with a bigger number of attribute-value pairs is more specific. Specificity may or may not be used to classify cases.

For a specific case, if complete matching (where all attribute-value pairs of at least one rule match all attribute-value pairs of a case) is impossible, LERS tries partial matching. During partial matching all rules with at least one match between the attribute-value pairs of a rule and the attribute-value pairs of a case are identified. *Matching_factor* is a measure of matching of a case and a rule. Matching_factor is defined as the ratio of the number of matched attribute-value pairs of a rule with a case to the total number of attribute-value pairs of the rule.

Support is related to a class C. It is the sum of scores of all matching rules from C. The class C for which the support, defined as follows:

$$\sum_{partially\_matching\_rules\_R\_describing\_concept\_C} \text{Matching\_factor}(R) * \text{Strength}(R) * \text{Specificity}(R).$$

is the largest is a winner and the case is classified as being a member of C.

For example, the rule set induced from the discretized version of NEVI_DCC contained 37 rules with 145 conditions. Strong rules (with the strength greater than or equal to 20), induced from the discretized version of NEVI_DCC, are the following:

23

(TDS, 1..4.8) & (Gender, woman) & (Structure, 2) -> (Nevi_pigmentosi, benign_nevus)

26

(TDS, 1..4.8) & (Color, light_brown) -> (Nevi_pigmentosi, benign_nevus)

20

(Color, dark_brown) & (TDS, 1..4.8) -> (Nevi_pigmentosi, benign_nevus)

64

(Color, blue) -> (Nevi_pigmentosi, blue_nevus)

24

(TDS, 4.8..8) & (Nevus_origin, acquired) & (Number_of_changes, 1..15) & (Roughness, yes) & (Structure, 3) -> (Nevi_pigmentosi, melanoma_malignant)

22

(Nevus_origin, acquires) & (Symmetry, 2) -> (Nevi_pigmentosi, melanoma_malignant)

Every rule is preceded by its strength. Note, that the rule

(Color, blue) -> (Nevi_pigmentosi, blue_nevus)

has strength equal to 64, i.e., this simple rule describes all 64 cases of *blue nevus*.

All three data sets were validated by the ten-fold cross validation. The results are presented in Table 1.

Table 1.

Discretized version of the data set	NEVI_DCC	NEVI_DCC_NO-TDS	NEVI_NDE
Error rate	11.6%	16.8%	11.6%

5 Conclusions

Two data sets, discretized NEVI_DCC and NEVI_NDE, are of the same quality—both yield the same error rate of 11.6%. The discretized NEVI_DCC contains simplified attributes and the index TDS. Thus, the discretized version of NEVI_NDE, with the more sophisticated 13 attributes, without TDS, is equivalent to the discretized data set NEVI_DCC, 16 simpler attributes, including the important attribute TDS. However, if we exclude from NEVI_DCC the attribute TDS, then, even though the new set, NEVI_DCC_NO-TDS, is still consistent, the error rate increases.

Currently, the database NEVI_DCC is stepwise extended by adding new cases, belonging mainly to the class *benign nevus* or *suspicious nevus*. The influence of values of coefficients (used in ABCD-rules for the calculation of the TDS index) on reliability of non-invasive diagnosing of *Nevi Pigmentosi* is now being extensively tested. These investigation, although still in an early stage, suggests a complete change of the general concept of evaluating *Color* per the ABCD-rules. Namely, it may be concluded that the global symptom *Color* should be split into six more sophisticated attributes, representing all real colors met in *Nevi Pigmentosi*, and, additionally, having assigned different coefficients. In the future we plan on performing more experiments, testing different formulas for TDS.

34

References

1. Bajcar, S., Grzegorczyk, L. *et al.* (1997) Endangerment by skin cancer among population of south-east part of Poland. Hospital #1, Res. Report, Rzeszow.
2. Booker, L. B., Goldberg, D. E., and Holland, J. F. (1990) Classifier systems and genetic algorithms. In *Machine Learning. Paradigms and Methods*. Carbonell, J. G. (Ed.), The MIT Press, 235–282.
3. Braun-Falco, O., Stolz, W., Bilek, P., Merkle, T., and Landthaler M. (1990) *Das Dermatoskop. Eine Vereinfachung der Auflichtmikroskopie von pigmentierten HautverŠnderungen*. Hautartzt 40: 131–135.
4. Chmielewski, M. R. and Grzymala-Busse, J.W. (1996) Global discretization of continuous attributes as preprocessing for machine learning. *Int. Journal of Approximate Reasoning* 15: 319–331.
5. Krzyz, P. and Ryzner G. (1999) Diploma Thesis. Department of Computer Chemistry, University of Technology, Rzeszow.
6. Hapgood, W. (1989) 1stClass, Programs in Motions, Inc., Wayland (MA).
7. Grzymala-Busse, J. W. (1992) LERS—A system for learning from examples based on rough sets. In *Intelligent Decision Support. Handbook of Applications and Advances of the Rough Sets Theory*. Slowinski, R. (ed.), Kluwer Academic Publishers, 3–18.
8. Hippe, Z. S. (1999) Data Mining in Medical Diagnosis. In *Computers in Medicine*. Kacki E. (Ed.), Polish Society of Medical Informatics, Lodz vol. 1, 25–34.
9. Holland, J. H., Holyoak K. J., and Nisbett, R. E. (1986) *Induction. Processes of Inference, Learning, and Discovery*. The MIT Press, 1986.

Description of the Machine Operation in Varying Conditions with the Use of Dynamic Scene Idea

Anna Timofiejczuk

Silesian Technical University of Technology, PL 44-100 Gliwice, Poland

Abstract. The diagnostic investigations of rotating machinery in varying conditions of its operation make it possible to observe machine responses on different excitations. The vibration signals are effects of phenomena related or not related to the variability of the machine operation conditions. The time-frequency methods of analysis of vibration signals enable us to detect signal components and their variability in the time. The time-frequency characteristics allow visual estimation of signal components, which are connected and not connected with the changes of machine operation. Most of these components are symptoms of some phenomena occurring during object action. These phenomena might be related to the changes of machine properties (eg. resonance properties) as well as they may be related to the environmental or operation conditions of the machine. It should be stressed that these characteristics are very often out of use in automatic diagnostic systems. In this case identified symptoms should be separated and first of all they must be described in proper manner. It can be solved by many ways. The paper deals with the description of the machine operation in the varying conditions with the use of dynamic scene idea.

Keywords: varying conditions of machine operation, separation of diagnostic symptoms, dynamic scene

1 Introduction

Investigations of rotating machinery may be carried out in fixed or varying conditions of its operation. The fixed conditions mean constant values of same parameters, for example, a rotating speed, a sub-assembly temperature, a oil temperature and so on. The varying states can be characterised by variability of them. The diagnostic investigations in varying conditions are more interesting due to this kind of investigations makes it possible to observe a machine responses to different (often nonstationary) excitations. The main goal of these investigations is, in particular, variability identification of resonance properties of the machine. The resonance properties changes might be caused by a fatigue crack of a shaft, a presence of excessive backslash, a variability of bearings operation or a crack in machine foundation. One of the ways of diagnostic investigations of the rotating machinery in varying conditions is research during run-up or run-down conditions. In this case, the role of a vibration exciter is played by the machine itself, especially by residual unbalances which are always present. The generated vibrations in these conditions are the results of different phenomena (the resonance phenomena, phenomena, which take place in the neighbourhood of the machine, phenomena related to rotation of machine elements, as well as friction or impact). On the other hand, the vibration signals recorded during varying conditions of machine operation are effects of different phenomena: connected or not connected with the variability of the machine operation conditions. It must be stressed that because of relation to the time these signals are always nonstationary.

The estimation of vibration signals generated by the machine observed during run-up or run-down is difficult. The detection capability of the above mentioned phenomena requires a method, which enables us to obtain time-frequency results. The time-frequency representation allows the detection of signal components and, particularly their variability in time. At present, the analysis of these signals is mainly based on the Short Time Fourier Transform (STFT) [1] [5] [7] [8]. This method consists in signal estimation in small time periods, which width is constant. Shortcomings of this method are known very well, and they are described in [3] [4]. There is a lot of different time-frequency, or generally, two-dimensional methods of nonstationary signal analysis. The most interesting are methods not requiring compromise between length of a time segment and frequency resolution. The wavelet transform (WT) is an example of such analysis of this sort [3]. The essence of this method is the fact, that it offers two very important features. The first one consists in the frequency localisation, which is logarithmic and indirectly proportional to the frequency level. As a consequence, time localisation is better in the highest frequencies. It makes this method more useful for nonstationary signal analysis, in particular, for identification components, which are effects of phenomena characterised by different time duration. The second feature consists in choice of a basis function named wavelet. It will be described in the next section.

The results of time-frequency methods of analysis of vibration signals may be presented as the run-up or run-down characteristics. These diagrams allow, on the base of identified diagnostic symptoms, the description of the technical state of the object and its resonance properties, particularly their variability. The way of determination of these characteristics is strictly connected with signal analysis techniques used. It should be stressed that the way of signal analysis has the great influence on the capability of identification of symptoms of phenomena taking place during machine action and the run-up or run-down characteristics contain information on the different phenomena occurring during machine action. For these reasons, the choice of the method of signal analysis is the most important aspect of diagnostic investigations of technical objects in varying conditions of their operation. Observation of identified symptoms, as described above, lets us to state that there are results of phenomena related to the changes of operation conditions and symptoms not related to them. The first group of symptoms is independent from the properties of the machine. Properties of the machine are reflected in the second group of symptoms. The time-frequency characteristics allow visual identification of both of them. This kind of presentation of results of vibration signal analysis is almost completely out of using in automatic diagnostic systems. In this case symptoms of occurring different phenomena should be separated. The partitioning of symptoms on the base of time-frequency characteristics can be performed in visual way only. The separation of symptoms may be solved in many ways. An example can be the spectral estimation of signals and order tracking analysis, which can make it possible to determine signal components related to the changes of operation conditions. However, both of them do not enable us to separate symptoms into groups. It has been solved by the application of the RLS analysis, which allows partitioning symptoms. This special way of viewing of time-frequency characteristics allows us to divide the analysed signal components into two independent parts: resonance and representative ones. The paper also deals with the dynamic scene idea. An application of this idea makes it possible to group symptoms identified during vibration signal analysis into some sets and to treat them as a first plane features and others as a second plane ones. These sets are reflection of the changes of the observed machine properties and its environment. Additional advantage of this idea is capability of its application in automatic diagnostic systems.

2. The time-frequency analysis of signals

Signals recorded during investigations carried out in varying operation conditions of machine are always nonstationary. Their structure is characteristic and they contain wide band components and narrow band components, which are effect of different phenomena. These components identification with special respect to capability of determination of their variability in time requires the analysis carried out in two-dimensional representation. The analysis of these signals may be based on the Short Time Fourier Transform (STFT) or the Wavelet Transform (WT).

Theoretical backgrounds of time-frequency signal, analysis based on the Fourier transform, are described [3] [4] [8]. This kind of signal estimation consists in linear decomposition of signal to sum of basis function (in this case only pure harmonic function). It can be written as formula (1).

$$S(t,f) = \int_{-\infty}^{\infty} x(t)w(\tau - t)e^{-jft} d\tau \qquad (1)$$

where $x(t)$ is the signal realisation in time domain, $w(\tau-t)$ means the time window and τ is a shift in the time domain. The result of signal analysis is spectrum row, which corresponds to the successive time moments. This method has a lot of shortcomings, e. g. a capability of application as basis function harmonic function only and fixed resolution in both, time and frequency domains.

38

There is a lot of different two-dimensional methods of signal analysis. An example of a method giving very good results in nonstationary signal estimation is the analysis using the Wavelet Transform (WT) [8]

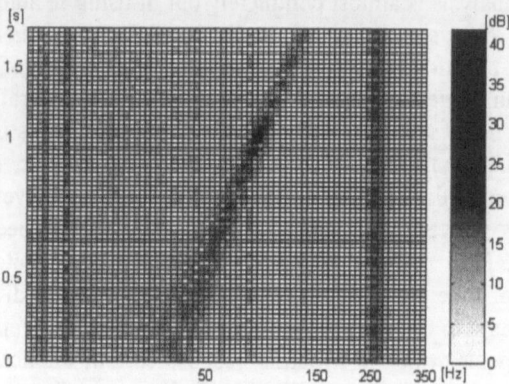

Fig. 1. Time frequency characteristic [8]

There are results of an application of the wavelet analysis of the signal containing constant frequency component and varying frequency component in Fig.1. The wavelet analysis, as in the previous case, consists in linear decomposition of signal to sum of basis functions named wavelets. Effect of its application is matrix of wavelet coefficients (graphically presented in Fig.1) which are measure of fitting of corresponding basis function to the subrealisation of signal. The characteristic feature of the wavelet analysis is its varying resolution during analysis process in the frequency and in the time domains. It is effect of relation of basis function to two parameters: the shift in the time domain and the scale parameter. General formula of wavelet transform can be written as:

$$S(a, \tau) = \frac{1}{\sqrt{a}} \int_{-\infty}^{\infty} \psi\left(\frac{t - \tau}{a}\right) x(t) dt \qquad (2)$$

where $x(t)$ means the realisation of signal in the time domain, ψ (..) means the basis function of the wavelet transform, τ is the shift in the time domain, and a is the scale parameter.

In the described investigations, the wavelet analysis application was connected with the necessity of solving of additional tasks, which consist in fitting of analysis parameters to the known signal structure [6]. The first step was to look for an optimal basis function. The second step was to determine the scale parameter that was solved by synchronisation of values of scale parameter and values of rotating speed. The fitting of analysis parameters makes it possible to apply the RLS method of partitioning of signal components (symptoms of different phenomena). The name of this method derives from names of three independent spectra.

It has been proved that the WT analysis gives better results than the STFT analysis [7] [8], so, in this paper, results of time-frequency signal analysis were limited to the results of the WT analysis only.

3. The symptom partitioning

The time-frequency run-up or run-down characteristics can be viewed as functions of absolute values of frequency (resonance signal components) and as relative values of frequency, with respect to the rotating speed (representative signal components). This way of separation makes it possible to identify a group of symptoms, which are effect of periodic excitations and group of symptoms connected with the resonance excitations. This is the main assumption of the RLS method. Additionally, it is assumed that the presented method will be applied in diagnostics of machinery during its operation in varying conditions. In this case it is possible to determine characteristic excitation frequencies. The application of the RLS analysis is also related to the assumption of the model of substitutional signal source. The power spectrum W of signal can be viewed as the sum of three independent spectra [1] [2].

$$\underline{W} = \underline{S} + \underline{R} + \underline{L} \quad [\text{dB}] \tag{3}$$

where S is the spectrum of representative signal, R is the spectrum of resonance signal and L is the spectrum of pink noise. A schematic way of examination of time-frequency characteristic is shown in Fig.2.

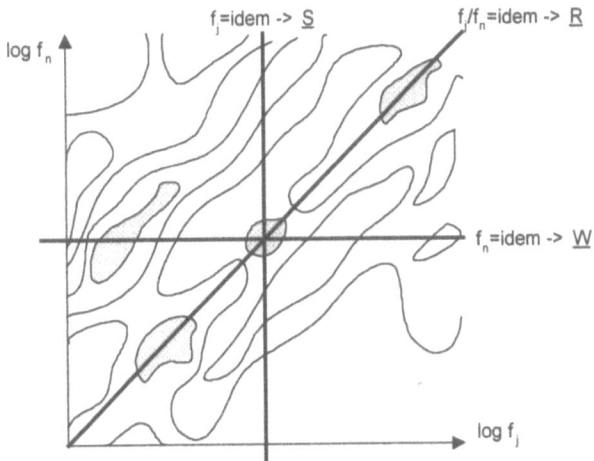

Fig.2. Schema of run-up characteristic [2]

The spectrum of the representative signal can be written by series of the constant relative frequency scale:

$$\underline{S} = \{s(k), k = k_p, \ldots, k_k\} \tag{4}$$

where $s(k)=s_k(k+m)$. The spectrum of resonance signal R consists of features which carries information on the changes of resonance properties of the object:

$$\underline{R} = \left\{ r(j), j = j_p, \dots, j_k \right\} \tag{5}$$

Application of the RLS method requires at least two spectra obtained for signals acquired while the machine was operating with the successive characteristic frequencies f_m and f_{m+1}. It makes it possible to write the following system of equations.

$$W_m = S_m + R + L_m$$
$$W_{m+1} = S_{m+1} + R + L_{m+1} \tag{6}$$

where unknowns are S_m, S_{m+1}, R, L_m, L_{m+1}. The system of equations (6) has infinite number of solutions. The invariants of solutions family are named differential spectra, representative and resonance ones, respectively. They are represented in following forms:

$$\Delta S = \left\{ \Delta s(k); k = j_p - m, \dots, j_k - m - 1 \right\} \tag{7}$$

$$\Delta R = \left\{ \Delta r(j); j = j_p + 1, \dots, j_k - 1 \right\} \tag{8}$$

The schematic description of the RLS analysis of signal was presented in Fig.3.

The described way of viewing of time-frequency characteristics was applied at the first time for the results of the STFT analysis. These results are levels of signal power so in this case there is no necessity of their transformation. The RLS analysis can be also applied for results of application of the WT analysis. The general concept of symptom separation is the same. A very important difference between them is the way of consideration of the rows signed by W. In the wavelet case they cannot be viewed as levels of signal power but as a rows of wavelet coefficients. As mentioned above, these coefficients are a measure of similarity of signal to the basis function. The set of wavelet coefficients can be written as the formula [8]:

$$\underline{WF} = \underline{SF} \cdot \underline{RF} \cdot \underline{LF} \tag{9}$$

where WF is a set of wavelet coefficients for constant scale variable, SF means representative part of signal, RF is resonance part of signal and LF is pink noise.

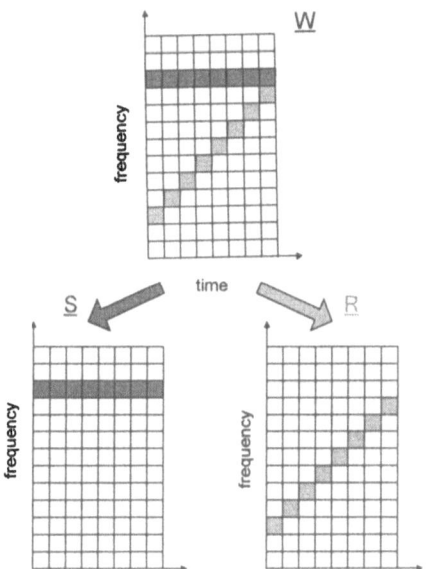

Fig.3. Schematic description of the RLS analysis [8]

Two-sided logarithmisation leads to the formula:

$$\log(WF) = \log(SF) + \log(RF) + \log(LF) \qquad (10)$$

The equations (6), correct for spectra, could be applied for the results of application of the wavelet analysis as (10). In this case wavelet coefficients can be viewed as power levels. The results of the application of the RLS analysis were presented in Fig.4 [8].

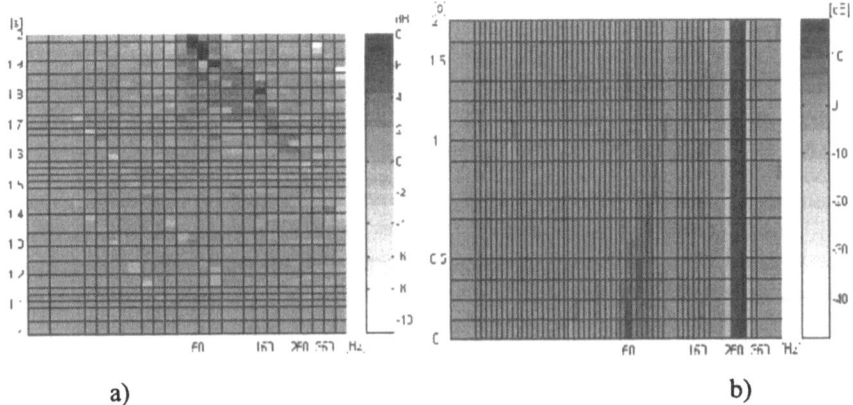

a) b)

Fig.4. Representative (a) and resonance (b) parts of signal [8]

4. Idea of dynamic scene

The idea of a dynamic scene can be based on the scene in the common mining. In this sense, the scene can be understood as a part of operation of the observed machinery. This object action may be characterised by changes of conditions of machine operation and changes taking place in its environment. The scene term is connected with the additional terminology, which can be treated as an analogy from the scene term in common mining.

The scene S is defined as the set of features describing the machine operation, particularly its operation conditions, its environment, reactions taking place in object and reactions of object and environment. There might be determined three subsets in the scene set: the first one it is the set describing machine operation A, the second one it is the set, which contains information on environment Se and third set consists of information on plan of machine action Sc. Each of mentioned sets contains elements, which are ordered pairs {name of feature, value of feature}. Elements of Sc set describe machine action. There also should be determined set of controlling features Ct, set of information on operation conditions C (eg. rotating speed) and set of properties of the investigated object (eg. resonance frequency). The Se set contains a subset named B, which is the set of features that carry no information on technical state of machinery. This set is the analogy of a background of the scene and may contain features such as noise, signed by N or features, which are effects of reaction of object and environment, signed by R.

The set signed by A, among others contains, all features which carry information on technical state of machine. These features are the most important results in diagnostic investigations of machinery in varying conditions of its operations, and are named diagnostic symptoms. The diagnostics symptoms can be partitioned into two groups. The first one it is a group of symptoms, which are effects of reaction taking place in the object. The second group contains reactions between object and environment. These reactions can be connected or not connected to the changes of operation conditions of the object. In the first case they belong to the Ct set, and in the second case they belong to the C set.

Examples of elements of A set can be vibration signal components connected to the rotation of the shaft (components related to the operation conditions of the object) as well as resonance symptoms, impacts (components not related to the operation conditions of the object). Elements of this set can be also components, which are results of changes of machine foundation. There are mentioned above sets in Fig.5.

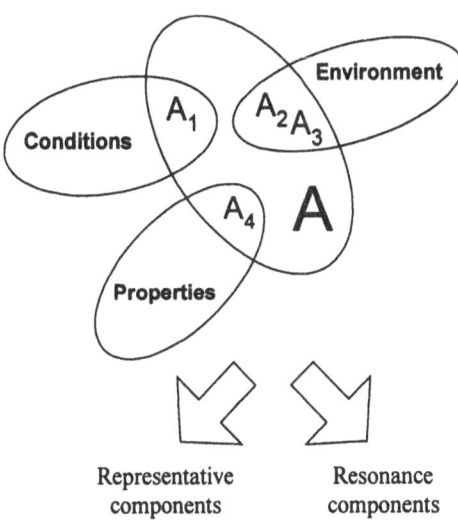

Figure 5. Main subsets of the scene

Taking into account changes of features describing machine operation, the description of technical object action may be named a dynamic scene. An example of the dynamic scene is the set of spectra collected in the time domain (time-frequency characteristic). The single spectrum of this characteristic can be treated as the single scene. The analysis of these sets can be the source of very interesting information. The most interesting in this case is the identification of *A* set, and particularly its symptom subset. The identification of diagnostic symptoms is the basis of the determination of technical state and its changes. Changes of technical state are usually connected with the changes of resonance properties of the object. The consequence of this can be the capability of identification of the technical state by partitioning of symptoms into two groups (symptoms connected and not connected to the changes of operation conditions of machine). There should be established that the same groups of symptoms will be treated as first plane features and rest of features will be playing the second role. This way of viewing of the symptoms makes it possible to partitioning the set of features connected to the operation conditions and features of object.

The initial partitioning of symptoms identified in the run-up or run-down characteristics can be realised by the application of the RLS analysis. This kind of signal analysis makes it possible to view symptoms as the subset playing first and second role. The results of the RLS analysis are two sets containing respectively resonance and representative vibration signal components.

5. Conclusions

The results of the dynamic scene idea and the RLS analysis can be used in automatic recognition of machine state. The first problem in this case is coding of the time-frequency characteristics, which are effects of application of the time-frequency analysis and the RLS analysis. The second problem is connected with features choice with taking into account the typical states of machinery. The next problem consists in the find the choice of weighting function of selected features. The most important problem is method of learning and identification of particular states of machinery. Each of above mentioned problems is very complex and important. The works having in view to solve these problems are in progress.

6. References

[1] Cholewa W.: Estimation of acoustic noise for constructional investigations of gear trains. PhD thesis, Gliwice 1974.

[2] Cholewa W.: Differential representative spectrum of substitutional source of signal investigations of machinery. Archiwum akustyki 1976, nr 3, 275-289.

[3] Daubechies I.: Ten lectures on wavelets. Society for industrial and applied mathematics, Philadelphia, Pennsylvania 1992.

[4] Gade S., Gram-Hansen K.: Non-stationary Signal Analysis using Wavelet Transform, Short-time Fourier Transform and Wigner-Ville Distribution. Technicale Review No. 2 - 1996 Bruel & Kjaer.

[5] Moczulski W.: The method of vibroacoustical investigations of rotating machinery in run-up or run-down. PhD thesis, Gliwice 1984.

[6] Timofiejczuk A.: The basis function of wavelet transform for signals recorded during varying conditions of machine operation. Conference „Metody i systemy komputerowe w badaniach naukowych i projektowaniu inżynierskim", Kraków 25-26.11.1997

[7] Timofiejczuk A.: Method of separation of failure symptoms identified during run-up or run-down of machine operation. 9th IMECO TC-10 Conference on: Integration in Technical Diagnostics, Wrocław 22-24.09.1999

[8] Timofiejczuk A.: Method of investigations of rotating machinery in run up or run down conditions. PhD thesis. Gliwice 1999.

Application of Decision Trees to Wavelet-based Classification of Musical Instrument Sounds

Alicja A. Wieczorkowska

Polish – Japanese Institute of InformationTechnologies

ul. Koszykowa 86, 02-008 Warsaw, Poland

alicja@pjwstk.waw.pl or awieczor@uncc.edu

Abstract: In this paper, an application of decision trees for automatic classification of musical instrument sounds is presented. The sounds are described using feature vector, based on wavelet analysis. Decision trees are used for assessment of parameters applied to the sound, and the structure of the generated trees allows evaluation of the role of particular parameters in the decision process. The experiments concerning audio signal classification using decision trees are presented in the paper, and the results are also discussed.

Keywords: decision tree, sound parameterization, sound classification

1 Introduction

Motivation to this work comes from musical sound recognition and database searching. If information about the musical instrument performing a piece of music is not attached to the file, then there is no possibility to classify instruments inside files automatically. The possibility of the automatic recognition of musical instrument sounds can be useful for the users of any musical files.

Since digital recordings contain a large amount of data, the first step to automatic classification of sound consists in parameterization, i.e. reduction of the data describing sounds. Unfortunately, musical instrument sounds depend on many factors: musical articulation, the instrument itself, reverberation, arrangement of microphones, etc. Moreover, timbre of the sound of same instrument can vary within the musical scale (and articulation as well), whereas sounds of different instruments can be very similar. If one wants to perform automatic classification of musical instrument sound independently on the pitch, the parameterization has to be done quite carefully. In the described research, wavelet analysis has been used as a basis for parameterization of musical sound [1], [3], [4], [5].

There are many systems for automatic classification of data, such as decision trees, neural networks, rough set based systems and so on [6], [9], [10], [11], [13]. Since decision tree algorithms are fast and clearly illustrate the role of particular parameters in the process of recognition, the described research is based on decision trees, using C4.5 algorithm [9].

2 Wavelet-based parameterization of musical instrument sounds

Wavelet analysis of any function is a multiresolution analysis, based on a theory proposed by Gabor [2]. In the presented research, octave-based analysis has been performed. In this case, the wavelet transform of the function f is performed as a decomposition of f using a mother wavelet ψ and a scaling function φ in the following way:

$$f = \sum_{j,k} \langle f, \psi_{j,k} \rangle \psi_{j,k},$$

where: $\diamond$ - inner product,
$\quad\quad j$ – resolution level,
$\quad\quad k$ – time instant,

$$\{\psi_{jk}(t) = 2^{j/2}\psi(2^j t - k)\}, \ \psi(t) = \sqrt{2}\sum_k g_k \varphi(2t - k),$$

$$\{\varphi_{jk}(t) = 2^{j/2}\varphi(2^j t - k)\}, \ \varphi(t) = \sqrt{2}\sum_k h_k \varphi(2t - k).$$

In the described analyses, mother wavelets and the scaling functions proposed by Daubechies and Coifman have been used. These functions are depicted in Fig. 1.

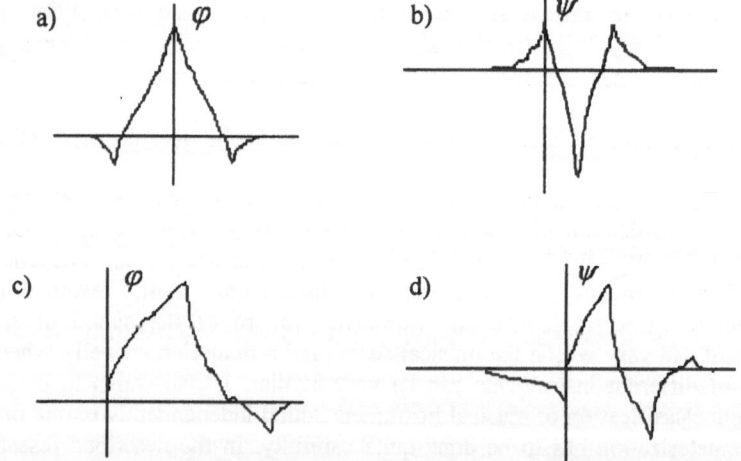

Fig. 1. Scaling functions φ and mother wavelets ψ (of order 2) proposed by Coifman (a, b) and Daubechies (c, d) [4]

The result of such an analysis is usually presented in the form of a spectrogram: the darker the area in the figure, the greater the magnitude. As one can observe, frequency bands are divided into octaves. For the purpose of parameterization, a part of the diagram containing the coefficient of the greatest energy has been chosen. Exemplary result of wavelet analysis of a sound, where the area chosen for parameterization has been marked, is presented in Fig. 2.

Analyses in the described experiments have been performed using a frame containing 4096 samples, for sampling frequency 44.1kHz. On the basis of these analyses, the following parameters have been calculated [11], [12]:

- W_1, ..., W_{38} – energy of the parameterized spectrum bands for the Daubechies wavelet of order 2, in the middle of the starting transient; $W_i=E_i/E$, where:

  E – overall energy of the parameterized part of the frame;

  E_i – partial energy:

  i=23,...,38 – spectral components in the frequency band 11.025-22.05kHz,

  i=15,...,22 – spectral components in the frequency band 5.5125-11.025kHz,

  i=11,...,14 – spectral components in the frequency band 5.5125-11.025kHz,

  i=9,10 – spectral components in the frequency band 2.75626-5.5125kHz,

  i=1,...,8 – spectral components for lower frequency bands;

- W_{39}, ..., W_{76} – energy for Daubechies wavelet of order 2, in the middle of the steady state;

- W_{77} - position of the middle of the starting transient, $W_{77} \in (0, 1)$;

- W_{78} - position of the middle of the steady state, $W_{78} \in (0, 1)$;

- W_{79}, ..., W_{115} – energy of the parameterized spectrum bands for the Coifman wavelet of order 2, in the middle of the starting transient; $W_i=E_i/E$, where:

  i=100,...,115 – spectral components in the frequency band 11.025-22.05kHz,

  i=92,...,99 – spectral components in the frequency band 5.5125-11.025kHz,

  i=88,...,91 – spectral components in the frequency band 5.5125-11.025kHz,

  i=86,87 – spectral components in the frequency band 2.75626-5.5125kHz,

  i=79,...,85 – spectral component in lower frequency bands;

- W_{116}, ..., W_{152} – energy for Coifman wavelet of order 2, in the middle of the steady state.

Wavelet based parameterization is more convenient than traditional Fourier based one, because it does not require calculation of the pitch. As one can observe, the proposed parameterization involves 2 stages of the sound – both starting transient and steady state, using 2 mother wavelet functions. The feature vector corresponds to a singular sound of one instrument. This feature vector may be redundant for automatic classification of musical instrument sounds, but decision tree algorithms can help us find the most useful attributes. The investigated data represent musical instruments commonly used in contemporary orchestras The following instruments have been investigated during the described research:

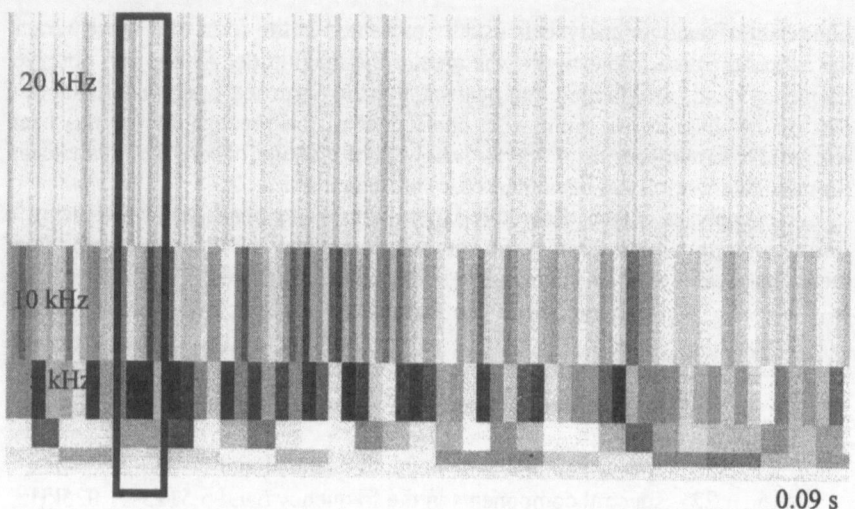

Fig. 2. Wavelet analysis (Daubechies φ and ψ) of the clarinet sound – a^3, 1760 Hz, sampling frequency 44.1 kHz, analyzing frame 4096 Sa

- bowed string instruments: violin, viola, cello and double bass,
- woodwinds: flute, oboe and clarinet,
- brass: trumpet, trombone, French horn and tuba.

The sounds used in experiments were played using various techniques, called articulation: bowed vibrato technique, pizzicato (then strings are plucked with fingers), with and without muting. The source of sounds is a collection of audio CDs MUMS by McGill University [8], recorded with sampling frequency 44.1 kHz as 16-bit stereo sound files. These CDs include consequent sounds in the musical scale of instruments, and the data used in the experiments have been arranged in the same way.

3 Decision trees

Decision trees very clearly represent classification of data. The accuracy of classification for decision trees is usually high and comparable with the accuracy for neural networks, but the training process is incomparably faster, and most important parameters describing data can be easily found. In the decision tree, nodes are labeled with condition attributes (parameters) and edges with values of these attributes. Leaves of the tree are labeled by classes' names. In the described research, decision tree based classifier C4.5 has been applied [9], using the maximal gain ratio criterion to find attributes labeling the nodes:

$$Gr = \frac{I(a \rightarrow d)}{H(a)} , \qquad \text{where:}$$

$I(a \rightarrow d) = H(d) - H(d \mid a)$ - information gain for the attribute a and the decision d,

$$H(d) = -\sum_{i=1}^{k} p(d_i) \cdot \log p(d_i) \text{ - entropy of the decision } d,$$

$$H(d \mid a) = -\sum_{j=1}^{l} p(a_i) \cdot \sum_{i=1}^{k} p(d_i \mid a_j) \cdot \log p(d_i \mid a_j) \quad \text{- conditional entropy}$$

for d and a,

$p(v)$ – probability of the value v.

The described program builds a binary tree, performing binary quantization of real value data, where optimal cut points are found on the basis on the entropy criterion. Exemplary decision tree describing the investigated data (a part only) is presented in Fig. 3.

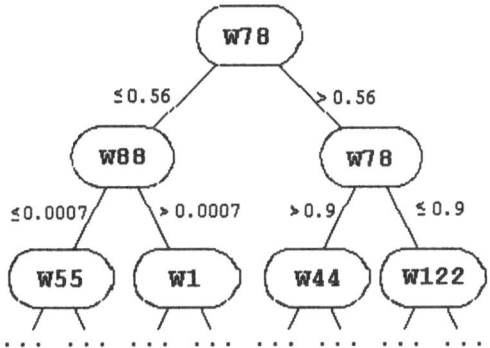

Fig. 3. A part of an exemplary decision tree for the investigated data

After finishing the construction of the classifier, the tree is pruned so as to avoid overfitting the data and remove attributes that are not necessary for the recognition process. Additionally, classification rules may also be extracted on the basis of the tree.

4 Experiments and results

The investigated data have been divided basically into 18 classes, describing sounds of one instrument, performed with the same articulation. The classes are as follows:

1. B flat clarinet,
2. double bass, vibrato,
3. double bass, pizzicato,
4. cello, pizzicato,
5. cello, vibrato,
6. C trumpet,
7. C trumpet, muted,
8. flute, vibrato,
9. French horn,

10. French horn, muted,
11. oboe, vibrato,
12. tenor trombone,
13. tenor trombone, muted,
14. tuba,
15. viola, pizzicato,
16. viola, vibrato,
17. violin, pizzicato,
18. violin, vibrato.

Exemplary rules of classification for these data are presented in Tab. 1. As one can observe, some rules are very short (for example, the presented rule for the trumpet muted consist of one condition only), whereas some of them are quite long (the double bass vibrato, for instance). The accuracy of classification has been tested using 90/10 random partition of data into training and test set. The achieved result is 65.9% of correct classifications.

Tab. 1. Exemplary rules of classification, extracted from the tree, for the investigated data

Conditions	Class
$W_6 \leq 0.77$, $W_9 > 0.0006$, $W_{78} > 0.9$, $W_{120} > 0.06$	clarinet
$W_3 > 0.0001$, $W_6 \leq 0.75$, $W_7 \leq 0.08$, $W_{70} > 0.0001$, $W_{77} > 0.04$, $W_{78} > 0.56$, $W_{116} \leq 0.03$, $W_{119} > 0.002$, $W_{122} \leq 0.37$, $W_{148} \leq 0.0001$	double bass vibrato
$W_5 > 0$, $W_{77} > 0.01$, $W_{78} \leq 0.56$, $W_{82} > 0$, $W_{84} \leq 0.02$, $W_{88} \leq 0.0007$, $W_{128} \leq 0.0005$	double bass pizzicato
$W_1 \leq 0.002$, $W_5 > 0.08$, $W_{78} \leq 0.56$, $W_{88} > 0.0007$	cello pizz.
$W_{55} > 0.001$, $W_{78} \leq 0.56$, $W_{88} \leq 0.0007$	cello vibrato
$W_{46} > 0.76$, $W_{78} > 0.9$	trumpet
$W_{76} > 0.0009$	trumpet muted
$W_{77} > 0.18$, $W_{122} > 0.37$	flute
$W_{15} \leq 0.00002$, $W_{38} \leq 0.0001$, $0.56 < W_{78} \leq 0.91$, $W_{121} > 0.26$, $W_{122} > 0.37$	French horn
$W_1 \leq 0.002$, $W_{46} > 0.04$, $0.56 < W_{78} \leq 0.91$, $W_{121} \leq 0.59$, $W_{122} \leq 0.37$	French horn muted
$W_{70} > 0.0002$, $W_{77} \leq 0.03$, $0.56 < W_{78} \leq 0.91$, $W_{122} > 0.37$	oboe
$W_{71} \leq 0.0002$, $0.56 < W_{78} \leq 0.91$, $W_{121} > 0.59$, $W_{127} > 0.04$	trombone
$W_{32} \leq 0.0001$, $W_{36} \leq 0.0001$, $W_{59} > 0.0004$, $0.56 < W_{78} \leq 0.91$, $W_{104} \leq 0.0001$, $W_{121} > 0.59$, $W_{127} \leq 0.04$	trombone muted
$W_{44} > 0.9$, $W_{78} > 0.9$	tuba
$W_{43} \leq 0.002$, $W_{78} \leq 0.56$, $W_{88} \leq 0.0007$	viola pizz.
$W_{26} > 0.00001$, $W_{32} > 0.0001$, $W_{71} \leq 0.0002$, $W_{77} > 0.06$, $W_{122} \leq 0.37$, $W_{127} \leq 0.04$	viola vibrato
$W_1 \leq 0.002$, $W_2 \leq 0.001$, $W_{77} \leq 0.08$, $W_{78} \leq 0.56$, $W_{83} \leq 0.11$, $W_{88} > 0.0007$	violin pizzicato
$W_{17} > 0.05$, $W_{76} \leq 0.0009$, $W_{78} \leq 0.91$, $W_{122} \leq 0.37$	violin vib.

This result is comparable to correctness obtained by other researchers for similar data [7], i.e. to 70% without discerning between sounds performed with various articulation techniques.

On the basis of the decision tree, one can find the most important attributes of the sound for wavelet based parameterization. In the calculated tree, the root has been labeled with the attribute W_{78} (as shown in Fig. 3), another important attributes are W_{77}, W_{88}, W_{121} and W_{122}. Altogether, 62 attributes have been used in the tree; these attributes describe both the attack and the steady state of the sound, using both Daubechies and Coifman wavelet. On the basis of the tree, 33 classification rules have been extracted.

Apart from the experiments described above, the other ways of division of the data into groups have also been investigated. The classes represent:
- instruments, disregarding articulation (11 classes):
  violin, viola, cello, double bass, flute, oboe, clarinet, trumpet, trombone, French horn, tuba,
- families of instruments, disregarding articulation (3 classes):
  strings, woodwinds, brass;
- families of instruments – sounds in each class represent the same articulation (5 classes):
  strings vibrato, strings pizzicato, woodwinds, brass with muting, brass without muting,
- articulation (3 classes):
  vibrato (strings, flute, oboe), without vibrato (clarinet, brass), pizzicato (strings),
- articulation, with muting singled out (4 classes):
  vibrato (strings, flute, oboe), pizzicato (strings), muting (trumpet, French horn, trombone), without vibrato or muting (clarinet, brass).

For such methods of grouping, the accuracy of classification has been even higher: from about 60% for instruments for standard settings of C4.5 and about 65% for non-standard settings, up to 80% for divisions into 3-5 classes, and has reached 82.3% of correctness for the classification of the articulation, for non-standard settings of C4.5. The improvement of results in these cases is quite obvious, since number of classed was significantly diminished.

Other research concerning automatic classification of musical instrument sounds, both conducted by the author and other researchers, is based on analyses different from wavelet based one; Fourier analysis is the most popular. The used parameters have to be planned very carefully and they usually require complicated calculations.

5 Conclusions

The main goal of the research was to investigate the possibility of application of decision trees to the classification of musical instrument sounds. As a preprocessing, wavelet based parameterization has been applied to the sounds. The correct classification of instrument independently on the pitch is a difficult task even for an expert, therefore the proposed parameterization describes the sound in detail, and the obtained feature vector is redundant. However, decision trees not only allow classification of data, but also make the evaluation of parameters possible. Additional virtue of decision tree algorithms is their fast performance, especially as far as the training phase is concerned.

The obtained results of classification, presented in this paper, are comparable to those obtained by other researchers for similar data. These results exceed 65% for recognition of the instrument and the articulation, and exceed 80% for groups of instruments. The produced tree was also used to generate classification rules, and 33 rules describing 18 classed were obtained. The structure of the tree shows that parameters describing time domain of the sound, i.e. W_{77} and W_{78}, are important for the classification of musical instrument sounds.

The presented paper confirms usefulness of wavelet based parameterization in the process of classification of musical instrument sounds, and also gives classification rules for the investigated data.

Acknowledgements

The research has been performed at the Sound Engineering Department, Faculty of Electronics, Telecommunications and Informatics at the Technical University of Gdańsk.

References

1. Arfib D., Analysis, Transformation, and Resynthesis of Musical Sounds with the Help of a Time-Frequency Representation, in: De Poli G., Piccialli A., Roads C. (ed.), *Representations of Musical Signals*, MIT Press, Cambridge, Massachusetts, 1991.
2. Gabor D., Theory of Communication, J. IEE (London), 1946, Vol. 93, Part III, No. 26, Internet (abstract): http://tyche.mat.univie.ac.at/gabor/archive/abstracts/1946/gab1_46.html.
3. Keele (Don) D. B. Jr., Time-Frequency Display of Electro-Acoustic Data Using Cycle-Octave Wavelet Transforms, 99th Audio Eng. Conv., New York 1995, preprint 4136.
4. Wolfram Research, Mathematica, Wavelet Explorer, Champaign, Illinois, 1996.
5. Kronland-Martinet R., Grossmann A., Application of Time-Frequency and Time-Scale Methods (Wavelet Transforms) to the Analysis, Synthesis, and Transformation of Natural Sounds, in: De Poli G., Piccialli A., Roads C. (ed.), *Representations of Musical Signals*, MIT Press, Cambridge, Massachusetts, 1991, pp. 45-85.
6. Kubat M., Bratko I., Michalski R. S., A Review of Machine Learning Methods, in: Michalski R., Bratko I., Kubat M. (ed.), *Machine Learning and Data Mining: Methods and Applications*, John Wiley & Sons Ltd., Chichester 1998.

7. Martin K. D., Kim Y. E., 2pMU9. Musical instrument identification: A pattern-recognition approach, presented at the 136th meeting of the Acoustical Society of America, October 13, 1998. Internet: ftp://sound.media.mit.edu/pub/Papers/kdm-asa98.pdf.

8. Opolko F., Wapnick J., MUMS – McGill University Master Samples, compact discs, McGill University, Montreal, Canada, 1987.

9. Quinlan J. R., C4.5: Programs for Machine Learning, Morgan Kaufmann Publishers, San Mateo, California, 1993.

10. Reduct Systems, Datalogic/R, 1995 Reduct Systems Inc., Regina, Saskatchewan, Canada.

11. Wieczorkowska A., The recognition efficiency of musical instrument sounds depending on parameterization and type of a classifier (in Polish), Ph.D. Dissertation, Politechnika Gdańska, Gdańsk, 1999.

12. Wieczorkowska A., Wavelet Based Analysis and Parameterization of Musical Instrument Sounds, VIII Int. Symposium on Sound Engineering and Mastering, Gdańsk 1999.

13. Żurada J., Barski M., Jędruch W., Artificial neural networks (in Polish), Wydawnictwo Naukowe PWN, Warszawa 1996.

Mining for Action-Rules in Large Decision Tables Classifying Customers

Zbigniew W. Ras<*><**> and Alicja Wieczorkowska<***><*>

<*> UNC-Charlotte, Computer Science Dept., Charlotte, NC 28223, USA

<**> Polish Academy of Sciences, Inst. of Comp. Science, Warsaw, Poland

<***> Polish-Japanese Institute of Information Tech., 02-018 Warsaw, Poland

e-mail: ras@uncc.edu   or   awieczor@uncc.edu

Abstract: Large decision tables classifying customers into groups of different profitability are used for mining rules classifying customers. Attributes are divided into two groups: stable and flexible. By stable attributes we mean attributes which values can not be changed by a bank (age, marital status, number of children are the examples). On the other hand attributes (like percentage rate or loan approval to buy a house in certain area) which values can be changed or influenced by a bank are called flexible. Rules are extracted from a decision table given preference to flexible attributes. This new class of rules forms a special repository of rules from which new rules called action-rules are constructed. They show what actions should be taken to improve the profitability of customers.

Keywords: knowledge discovery, large databases, profitability of customers, action-rules, flexible attributes, stable attributes.

1 Introduction

Data mining became successful because knowledge extracted from data provides competitive advantage in support of decision making. In the banking industry, the most widespread use of data mining is in the area of customer and market modeling, risk optimization and fraud detection. In the long run, however, knowledge discovered from data will support decision-making throughout the entire business process.

In financial services, data mining is used in performing so called trend analysis, in analyzing profitability, helping in marketing campaigns, and in evaluating risk. There are many software applications on the market that use data mining for stock prediction.

In the area of marketing, data mining is used to answer questions like:
1.   What types of customers are buying specific products?
2.   What are the latest product trends?
3.   What types of products can be sold together?
4.   What determines the best product mix to sell?

Data mining helps in predictive modeling of markets and customers, in support of marketing. It can identify the traits of profitable customers and reveal the "hidden" traits. It helps to search for the sites that are most convenient for customers as well as trends in customer usage of products and services. Examples of specific questions include:
1.   What are micromarkets for specific products?
2.   What is the likelihood that a given customer will accept an offer?
3.   What actions improve the profitability of customers?
4.   What customers switch to other services?

Credit issuers are very concerned about the ability to raise alarm when a credit card transaction is fraudulent. There are systems today that can check credit transactions and provide a hint of whether to allow a credit charge or not. Beginning last year, credit fraud detection is in place to monitor more than 160 milion payment card accounts. While fraud is decreasing, applications for payment card accounts are raising as much as 50% a year.
Many other forms of fraud are possible. Often the fraud can be treated as a deviation from a pattern. In those cases the detection of patterns in customer behavior is a necessary precondition.

Even if it is very tempting to use limited tools and seek quick answers to very specific questions, it is important to keep a broad perspective on knowledge. For instance, while the direct data make a particular offer look profitable, a more thorough analysis may reveal cannibalization of other offers and the overall decrease in profit.

Specific questions about profitability must be answered from a broader perspective of customer and market understanding. For instance, customer loyalty can be often as important as profitability. In addition to short term profitability the decision makers must also keep eye on the lifetime value of a customer. Also, a broad and detailed understanding of customers is needed to send the right offers to the right customers at the most appropriate time. Knowledge about customers can lead to ideas about future offers which will meet their needs.

2 Information Systems and Decision Tables

An information system is used for representing knowledge. Its definition, presented here, is due to Pawlak [2] .

By an information system we mean a pair $S = (U,A)$, where:

1. U is a nonempty, finite set called the universe,
2. A is a nonempty, finite set of attributes i.e. $a:U \rightarrow V_a$ for $a \in A$, where V_a is called the domain of a.

Elements of U are called objects. In our paper objects are interpreted as customers. Attributes are interpreted as features, offers made by a bank, characteristic conditions etc.

In this paper we consider a special case of information systems called decision tables [2]. In any decision table together with the set of attributes a partition of that set into conditions and decisions is given. Additionally, we assume that the set of conditions is partitioned into stable conditions and flexible conditions. We consider decision tables with only one decision attribute to be seen as "profit ranking" with values being integers. This attribute classifies objects (customers) with respect to the profit for a bank. Date of Birth is an example of a stable attribute. Interest rate on any customer account is an example of a flexible attribute (dependable on bank). We adopt the following definition of a decision table:

A decision table is any information system of the form $S = (U, A_1 \cup A_2 \cup \{d\})$, where $d \notin A_1 \cup A_2$ is a distinguished attribute called decision. The elements of A_1 are called stable conditions, whereas the elements of A_2 are called flexible conditions.

The cardinality of the image $d(U) = \{ k: d(x)=k \text{ for some } x \in U\}$ is called the rank of d and is denoted by $r(d)$.

Let us observe that the decision d determines the partition $CLASS_S(d) = \{X_1,X_2,...,X_{r(d)}\}$ of the universe U, where $X_k = d^{-1}(\{k\})$ for $1 \leq k \leq r(d)$. $CLASS_S(d)$ is called the classification of objects in S determined by the decision d.

In this paper, as we mentioned before, objects correspond to customers. Also, we assume that customers in $d^{-1}(\{k1\})$ are more profitable for a bank than customers in $d^{-1}(\{k2\})$ for any $k2 \leq k1$. The set $d^{-1}(\{r(d)\})$ represents the most profitable customers for a bank. Clearly the goal of any bank is to increase its profit. It can be achieved by shifting some customers from the group $d^{-1}(\{k2\})$ to $d^{-1}(\{k1\})$, for any $k2 \leq k1$. Namely, through special offers made by a bank, values of flexible attributes of some customers can be changed and the same all these customers can be moved from a group of a lower profit ranking to a group of a higher profit ranking.

3 Action Rules

In this section we describe a method to construct so called action rules from a decision table containing both stable and flexible attributes.

Before we introduce several new definitions, assume that for any two collections of sets X, Y, we write, $X \subseteq Y$ if $(\forall x \in X)(\exists y \in Y)[\,x \subseteq y\,]$. Let $S = (U, A_1 \cup A_2 \cup \{d\})$ be a decision table and $B \subseteq A_1 \cup A_2$. We say that attribute d depends on B if $CLASS_S(B) \subseteq CLASS_S(d)$, where $CLASS_S(B)$ is a partition of U generated by B (see [2]). Assume now that attribute d depends on B where $B \subseteq A_1 \cup A_2$. The set B is called d-reduct in S if there is no proper subset C of B such that d depends on C. The concept of d-reduct in S was introduced to induce rules from S describing values of the attribute d depending on minimal subsets of $A_1 \cup A_2$. In order to induce rules in which the THEN part consists of the decision attribute d and the IF part consists of attributes belonging to $A_1 \cup A_2$, subtables $(U, B \cup \{d\})$ of S where B is a d-reduct in S should be used for rules extraction. By Dom(r) we mean all attributes listed in the IF part of a rule r. For example, if r = [(a1,3)*(a2,4) → (d,3)] is a rule then Dom(r) = {a1,a2}. By d(r) we denote the decision value of a rule. In our example d(r) = 3.

If r1, r2 are rules and $B \subseteq A_1 \cup A_2$ is a set of attributes, then r1/B = r2/B means that the conditional parts of rules r1, r2 restricted to attributes B are the same. For example if r1 = [(a1,3) → (d,3)], then r1/{a1} = r/{a1}.

Example 1. Assume that S = ({x1,x2,x3,x4,x5,x6,x7,x8}, {a,c} {b} {d}) be a decision table represented by Figure 1. The set {a,c} lists stable attributes, in {b} we have flexible attributes and d is a decision attribute. Also, we assume that H denotes customers of a high profit ranking and L denotes customers of a low profit ranking.

	a	b	c	d
x1	0	S	0	L
x2	0	R	1	L
x3	0	S	0	L
x4	0	R	1	L
x5	2	P	2	L
x6	2	P	2	L
x7	2	S	2	H
x8	2	S	2	H

Figure 1

In our example r(d)=2, r(c)=3, r(a)=2,

$CLASS_S(d)=\{\{x1,x2,x3,x4,x5,x6\},\{x7,x8\}\}$,

$CLASS_S(\{b\})=\{\{x1,x3,x7,x8\},\{x2,x4\},\{x5,x6\}\}$,

$CLASS(\{a,b\})=\{\{x1,x3\},\{x2,x4\},\{x5,x6\},\{x7,x8\}\}$,

$CLASS_S(\{a\})=\{\{x1,x2,x3,x4\},\{x5,x6,x7,x8\}\}$,

$CLASS_S(\{c\})=\{\{x1,x3\},\{x2,x4\},\{x5,x6,x7,x8\}\}$,

$CLASS(\{b,c\})=\{\{x1,x3\},\{x2,x4\},\{x5,x6\},\{x7,x8\}\}$.

So, $CLASS(\{a,b\}) \subseteq CLASS_S(d)$ and $CLASS(\{b,c\}) \subseteq CLASS_S(d)$. It can be easily checked that both {b,c} and {a,b} are d-reducts in S.

Rules can be directly derived from d-reducts and the information system S. In our example, we get the following rules:

$$(a,0)\wedge(b,S) \rightarrow (d,L), \qquad (b,S)\wedge(c,0) \rightarrow (d,L),$$

$$(a,0)\wedge(b,R) \rightarrow (d,L), \qquad (b,R)\wedge(c,1) \rightarrow (d,L),$$

$$(a,2)\wedge(b,P) \rightarrow (d,L), \qquad (b,P)\wedge(c,2) \rightarrow (d,L),$$

$$(a,2)\wedge(b,S) \rightarrow (d,H), \qquad (b,S)\wedge(c,2) \rightarrow (d,H).$$

We use information system S to simplify them. We get :

$$(a,0) \rightarrow (d,L), \qquad\qquad (c,0) \rightarrow (d,L),$$

$$(b,R) \rightarrow (d,L), \qquad\qquad (c,1) \rightarrow (d,L),$$

$$(b,P) \rightarrow (d,L), \quad (a,2)\wedge(b,S) \rightarrow (d,H), \qquad (b,S)\wedge(c,2) \rightarrow (d,H).$$

Now, let us assume that $(a, v \rightarrow w)$ denotes the fact that the value of attribute a has been changed from v to w. Similarly, the term $(a, v \rightarrow w)(x)$ means that $a(x)=v$ has been changed to $a(x)=w$. Saying another words, the property (a,v) of a customer x has been changed to property (a,w).

Assume now that $S = (U, A_1 \cup A_2 \cup \{d\})$ is a decision table, where A_1 is the set of stable attributes and A_2 is the set of flexible attributes. Assume that rules $r1, r2$ have been extracted from S and $r1/A_1 = r2/A_1$, $d(r1)=k1$, $d(r2)=k2$ and $k1 < k2$. Also, assume that $(b1, b2,..., bp)$ is a list of all attributes in $Dom(r1) \cap Dom(r2) \cap A_2$ on which $r1, r2$ differ and $r1(b1)= v1, r1(b2)= v2,..., r1(bp)= vp, r2(b1)= w1, r2(b2)= w2,..., r2(bp)= wp$.

By $(r1,r2)$-action rule on $x \in U$ we mean a statement:

$[(b1, v1 \rightarrow w1) \wedge (b2, v2 \rightarrow w2) \wedge...\wedge (bp, vp \rightarrow wp)](x) \Rightarrow [(d,k1) \rightarrow (d,k2)](x).$

If the value of the rule on x is true then the rule is valid. Otherwise it is false.

Let us denote by $U^{<r1>}$ the set of all customers in U supporting the rule $r1$. If $(r1,r2)$-action rule is valid on $x \in U^{<r1>}$ then we say that the action rule supports the new profit ranking $k2$ for x.

Example 2. Assume that $S = (U, A_1 \cup A_2 \cup \{d\})$ is a decision table from the Example 1, $A_2=\{b\}$, $A_1 =\{a,c\}$. It can be checked that rules $r1=[(b,P) \rightarrow (d,L)]$, $r2=[(a,2)\wedge(b,S) \rightarrow (d,H)]$, $r3=[(b,S)\wedge(c,2) \rightarrow (d,H)]$ can be extracted from S. Clearly $x5, x6 \in U^{<r1>}$. Now, we can construct $(r1,r2)$-action rule executed on x:

$[(b, P \rightarrow S)](x) \Rightarrow [(d,L) \rightarrow (d,H)](x).$

It can be checked that this action rule supports the new profit ranking H for $x5$ and $x6$.

Example 3. Assume that $S = (U, A_1 \cup A_2 \cup \{d\})$ is a decision table represented by Figure 2. Assume that $A_1 = \{c, b\}$, $A_2 = \{a\}$.

	c	a	B	d
x1	2	1	1	L
x2	1	2	2	L
x3	2	2	1	H
x4	1	1	1	L

Figure 2

Clearly $r1 = [(a,1) \wedge (b,1) \rightarrow (d,L)]$, $r2 = [(c,2) \wedge (a,2) \rightarrow (d,H)]$ are optimal rules which can be extracted from S. Also, $U^{<r1>} = \{x1, x4\}$. If we construct (r1,r2)-action rule:

$$[(a, 1 \rightarrow 2)](x) \Rightarrow [(d,L) \rightarrow (d,H)](x).$$

then it will certainly support the new profit ranking H for x1 but only possibly for x4.

Algorithm to Construct Action Rules

Input: Decision table $S = (U, A_1 \cup A_2 \cup \{d\})$,

               A_1 – stable attributes, A_2 – flexible attributes,

               $\lambda 1, \lambda 2$ – weights.

Output: R – set of action rules.

Step 0. $R := \varnothing$.

Step 1. Find all d-reducts $\{D_1, D_2, ..., D_m\}$ in S which satisfy the property

            $card[D_i \cap A_1]/card[A_1 \cup A_2] \leq \lambda 1$

(reducts with a relatively small number of stable attributes)

Step 2.   FOR EACH pair (D_i, D_j) of d-reducts (found in step 1) satisfying the property $card(D_i \cap D_j)/card(D_i \cup D_j) \le \lambda 2$ DO
find set R_i of optimal rules in S using d-reduct D_i ,
find set R_j of optimal rules in S using d-reduct D_j .

Step 3.   FOR EACH pair of rules $(r1, r2)$ in $R_i \times R_j$ having different THEN parts DO
if $r1/A_1 = r2/A_1$, $d(r1)=k1$, $d(r2)=k2$ and $k1< k2$, then
   if $(b1, b2,..., bp)$ is a list of all attributes in $Dom(r1) \cap Dom(r2) \cap A_2$ on which $r1, r2$ differ and
   $r1(b1)= v1, r1(b2)= v2,..., r1(bp)= vp,$
   $r2(b1)= w1, r2(b2)= w2,..., r2(bp)= wp$
      then the following $(r1,r2)$-action rule add to R:
         if   [(b1, v1 → w1) ∧ (b2, v2 → w2) ∧...∧ (bp, vp → wp)](x) then [(d, k1) → (d,k2)](x)

The resulting $(r1,r2)$-action rule says that if the change of values of attributes of a customer x will match the term

   [(b1, v1→w1) ∧ (b2, v2 →w2) ∧...∧ (bp, vp →wp)](x)

then the ranking profit of customer x will change from *k1* to *k2*.

This algorithm was initially tested on a sampling containing 20,000 tuples extracted randomly from a large banking database containing more than 10 milion customers. We used DataLogicR$^+$ for rule extraction. Both "roughness" and "rule precision threshold" has been set up to 0.85. We found many pairs of rules $(r1,r2)$ meeting the conditions required by the above algorithm for generating $(r1,r2)$-action rules. For instance, we extracted the following three rules:

   $[A79 > 610.70] \wedge [A75 > 640.50] \wedge [A73 > 444.00] \rightarrow [\ PROFIT = 1\ ],$
   $[A79 \le 610.70] \wedge [A75 > 640.50] \wedge [A78 \le 394.50] \rightarrow [\ PROFIT = 1\ ],$
   $[A75 \le 640.50] \rightarrow [\ PROFIT = 3\ ].$

Attributes A73, A75, A78, A79 are all flexible.

The following action rule can be generated:

   if $[A75, (A75 > 640.50) \rightarrow (A75 \le 640.50)](x)$

      then $[(PROFIT = 1) \rightarrow (PROFIT = 3)].$

4 Conclusion

Proposed algorithm identifies the customers which might be moved to a group of higher profit ranking if values of some flexible attributes describing them are changed. Also, the algorithm shows what attribute values should be changed and what their new values should be (what offers should be sent by a bank to all these customers).

We will continue testing this algorithm on large banking data.

References

1. Chmielewski M. R., Grzymala-Busse J. W., Peterson N. W., Than S., "The Rule Induction System LERS - a Version for Personal Computers", in *Foundations of Computing and Decision Sciences*, Vol. 18, No. 3-4, 1993, Institute of Computing Science, Technical University of Poznan, Poland, 181-212.

2. Pawlak Z., "Rough Sets and Decision Tables", in *Lecture Notes in Computer Science* **208,** Springer-Verlag, 1985, 186-196.

3. Skowron A., Grzymala-Busse J., "From the Rough Set Theory to the Evidence Theory", *in ICS Research Reports* 8/91, Warsaw University of Technology, October, 1991

Generation of Exhaustive Rule Sets Using a Reduct Generating Algorithm

Robert Susmaga

Institute of Computing Science, Poznan University of Technology,
Piotrowo 3a, 60-965 Poznan, Poland,
E-mail: robert.susmaga@cs.put.poznan.pl

Abstract *The paper addresses the problem of computing exhaustive sets of decision rules in information/decision tables. Rule sets, including exhaustive ones, may have useful applications in descriptive and prescriptive analyses of the data sets, but the problem of searching for interesting rules is, in general, very time consuming. This is a direct consequence of the fact that the computational complexity of the exhaustive rule set generation problem is non-polynomial. Practical experiments demonstrate, however, that decision rules may be successfully computed for many real life data sets using some advanced algorithms. This paper introduces and experimentally evaluates an algorithm that is based on the notion of the discernibility list and that may be used for generating decision rules as well as attribute reducts. All the results of the experiments reported in this paper have been obtained for real-life data sets.*

Keywords *information/decision tables, decision rules, rule set covers, reducts of attributes, binarization*

1 Introduction

Generation of decision rules in information/decision tables is an important element of their analysis. Rules express regularities that occur in data and may be used both for descriptive and prescriptive purposes. Algorithms for rule generation have been the subject of numerous papers in the fields of Rough Sets and Machine Learning, e. g. [1, 3, 5, 6, 9, 10, 13, 17, 18].

This paper focuses on exact rules, as introduced in [5]. Exact rules are probably rules of the simplest form, but experience in generating them may prove very beneficial, also in algorithms generating other form of rules. Another important aspect of the analysis is the characteristics of the rule set to be generated. In this paper we are interested in generating exhaustive set of rules. From the computational point of view it is the most difficult problem, as the computing time may grow exponentially with the number of attributes and the cardinality of their domains. Additionally, it must be stressed that generating exhaustive set of decision rules need not be the best possible solution. Often only a subsets of rules, especially one generated by a heuristic algorithm, proves satisfactory. Satisfactory sets of decision rules may also be defined by applying some constraints to the basic characteristics of the rules, e.g. their length [13]. Again, however, the experience gained in effective generation of exhaustive rule sets may turn out very useful when constructing other rule generating algorithms. In particular, the presented algorithm can be easily made to search for rules of length limited by a pre-defined threshold.

The rest of the paper is organized as follows. After the Introduction, Section 2 presents the formal definition of exact decision rules and exhaustive rule sets. Section 3 presents in detail the algorithm for generating exhaustive sets of exact decision rules. Section 4 presents the experimental evaluation of the algorithm results and Section 5 concludes the paper.

2 Formal Definition of Exact Rules

The main data set to be analysed is a *decision table* [9], which is a special case of an *information table*. Formally, the decision table is defined as a 4-tuple $DT=\langle U,Q,V,\delta \rangle$, where:

- U is a non-empty, finite set of objects under consideration,
- Q is a non-empty, finite set of condition (C) and decision (D) attributes such that $C \cup D = Q$ and $C \cap D = \varnothing$,
- V is a non-empty, finite set of attribute values,
- δ is an information function, $\delta: U \times Q \rightarrow V$.

We additionally assume that the domains of all the attributes are either originally discrete or have to undergo a discretization process [2, 4, 8].

The idea of an exact decision rule in DT is that all objects matched by the rule belong to the same decision class, i.e. they are characterized by the same value of the decision attribute [5, 13]. More formally, it may be defined as follows. Let $c_j \in C$, V_j be a finite domain of c_j and let $v_j \in V_j$. Expression $(c_j=v_j)$ is called a simple condition on c_j. By $[(c_j=v_j)]$ we denote the set of objects satisfying the condition:

$$[(c_j=v_j)] = \{x \in U: \delta(x,c_j)=v_j\}.$$

Any conjunction of simple conditions is called a selector:

$$Sel = (c_1 = v_1) \ \& \ (c_2 = v_2) \ \& \ ... \ (c_p = v_p).$$

Analogously, by $[Sel]$ we denote the set of objects that satisfy all the simple conditions in the selector.

Expression of the type:

$$IF \ Sel \ THEN \ (d = v),$$

where $d \in D$, $v \in V$ and V is the domain of the attribute d, is called discriminant if $[Sel] \subseteq [(d=v)]$. This expression is called minimal with regard to inclusion if a removal of any simple condition from the selector Sel renders the expression non-discriminant. An expression which is both discriminant and minimal with regard to inclusion is called an exact rule in DT.

It is important that discriminance and minimality are the two features of exact rules that are also specific to the notion of attribute reduct [1, 9, 10, 12, 14]. This suggests using a reduct generating algorithm to the problem of generating exhaustive rule sets.

3   The Discernibility List–Based Algorithm for Generating Exhaustive Sets of Exact Decision Rules

Despite some common characteristics, there are two important differences between the problem of generating reducts and that of generating exact rules. First, the reduct contains a minimal subset of attributes while the rule contains a minimal subset of simple conditions. The second difference is the nature of the discriminating conditions – a reduct has to discern any two objects that belong to lower approximations of two different classes and that are discerned by the set of all attributes. An exact rule, on the other hand, must match only objects belonging to a single class – in this sense the rule discerns these objects from objects belonging to other classes. Finally, generating reducts requires taking into account the relation between all the objects at once, while the process of generating rules considers combinations of values of the binarized attributes, one at a time.

The rule generating algorithm presented in this paper is a straightforward modification of the Reduct Generating Algorithm [14]. The main difficulty in adapting this algorithm to the problem of generating rules is forcing the algorithm to search for discriminating subsets of simple conditions instead of just the discriminating subsets of attributes. Luckily, this may be easily accomplished by employing binarization [8, 18], i.e. by substituting all condition attributes with multiple binary attributes. During binarization a discrete attribute q, whose domain is $V_q = \{v_1, v_2, ..., v_L\}$, is replaced with L attributes: $q_1 \ q_2, ..., q_L$, such that for every object u : $\delta(u,q_i)=1$ iff $\delta(u,q)=v_i$, otherwise $\delta(u,q_i)=0$. In the binarized information table every binary attribute q_i corresponds univocally to the following simple condition ($q=v_i$) from the original table.

When generating rules the algorithm takes the binarized information table as its input. The discernibility list [11, 15] used by this algorithm is defined using atoms [9], i.e. unique combinations of values of the condition attributes. Additionally, the algorithm considers only atoms that are not ambiguous. An atom is ambiguous if there exist at least two objects that have the same combination of values of the binarized attributes as the atom but different values of the decision attribute.

Given the set of objects U, $|U|=N$, the set of binarized attributes B, and an unambiguous reference atom a_k, the elements of the list (C_{ik}) are calculated using other unambiguous atoms a_i as:

$$C_{ik}=\{q\in B:\ \delta(a_k,q)\neq\delta(a_i,q)\ \text{and}\ \delta(a_k,d)\neq\delta(a_i,d)\},\ \text{for}\ i=1..N,\ i\neq k.$$

The elements of the discernibility list retain the necessary differences between those atoms that must remain discernible. This obviously preserves differences also between the necessary objects. The main idea of generating minimal discriminant sets of simple conditions, i.e. exact rules, is that if a set of simple conditions is to remain discriminant, its corresponding subset of binarized attributes must have a non-empty intersection with each non-empty element of the discernibility list. As a result, the set of all exact rules may be viewed as a family of all minimal subsets of binarized attributes having non-empty intersections with all the non-empty elements of the discernibility list.

The main strength of the method is a proper handling of the discernibility list, which may be considerably reduced in size by applying the law of absorption. During absorption all the empty, repeated and non-minimal (with regard to inclusion) elements are discarded from the list. Additionally, the list is sorted in the ascending order of the cardinality of its elements [14]. As a result, the subsequent search for minimal subsets of binarized attributes is done using the sorted, absorbed discernibility list (*SADL*) and may become very effective even with non-trivial data sets.

To generate all possible exact rules the algorithm is run for each unambiguous atom a_k in turn. The result of such a run is $Rul(a_k)$ – the set of all exact rules matching the atom a_k. Because the sets of rules generated for different atoms may have non-empty intersections, which means that the same rules may be generated in different runs, the final task of each run is to eliminate the redundant rules from the final solution. This may be effectively done using an absorbed redundancy list, *ARL*, the elements of which are defined as follows:

$$C_{ik}=\{q\in B:\ \delta(a_k,q)\neq\delta(a_i,q)\ \text{and}\ \delta(a_k,d)=\delta(a_i,d)\},\ \text{for each}\ i<k.$$

The elements of the redundancy list retain the necessary differences between the current reference atom a_k and atoms a_i for which the rules have already been created. Like the *ADL*, the redundancy list is also absorbed in order to accelerate all subsequent computations. An important difference, however, between the two lists is that atoms a_k and a_i, which are used to create the redundancy list, belong to the same class.

The main idea of identifying non-redundant rules, i.e. rules that have not been created in previous runs of the algorithms, is that their corresponding subsets of binarized attributes must have a non-empty intersections with each element of the absorbed redundancy list.

Summarizing, the algorithm generating exhaustive subsets of exact rules consists of three main phases. The first phase creates, absorbs and sorts the discernibility list. The second one performs a breadth-first search for minimal subsets of binarized attributes. Finally, the third phase removes redundant rules from the solution. To generate the exhaustive set of all exact rules the three phases of the algorithm are run for each unambiguous atom a_k in turn.

The pseudo-code version of the algorithm is presented in Figure 1.

Figure 1. The discernibility list–based algorithm for generating exhaustive sets of exact decision rules

Input: A set of objects U ($|U|=N$) described by binarized attributes.
An unambiguous reference atom a_k.

Output: The set K of all non-redundant exact rules matching a_k.

PHASE I – Creation of the Sorted Absorbed Discernibility List (SADL)

Step 1

Create the discernibility list DL as (C_{ik}), where:

$C_{ik} = \{q \in B: \delta(a_k,q) \neq \delta(a_i,q) \text{ and } \delta(a_k,d) \neq \delta(a_i,d)\}$, for $i=1..N$, $i \neq k$.

Step 2

Absorb the discernibility list DL by discarding its

empty and non-minimal elements (create ADL)

Step 3

Sort the ADL in the ascending order of the

cardinality of its elements (create SADL).

PHASE II A breadth-first search for minimal subset of attributes

Step 1

$Rul_0 := \{\emptyset\}$.

Step 2

For every $C_i \in SADL$, $i=1..d$, compute:

$$S_i := \{R \in Rul_{i-1} : R \cap C_i \neq \emptyset\}.$$

$$T_i := \bigcup_{q \in C_i} \bigcup_{R \in R_{i-1}: R \cap C_i = \emptyset} \{R \cup \{q\}\}.$$

$$MIN_i := \{R \in T_i : Min(R) = true\}.$$

$$Rul_i := S_i \cup MIN_i.$$

PHASE III – Creation of the Absorbed Redundancy List (ARL)

Step 1

Create the redundancy list RL as (C_{ik}), where:

$C_{ik} = \{q \in B: \delta(a_k, q) \neq \delta(a_i, q)$ and $\delta(a_k, d) = \delta(a_i, d)\}$, for each $i < k$.

Step 2

Absorb the discernibility list RL by discarding its

empty and non-minimal elements (create ARL)

Step 3

Move to K all those elements of Rul_d that have

non-empty intersections with all elements of ARL

A very important part of the algorithm is the function *Min*. This function tests if its argument *R*, which is a subset of attributes, is minimal with regard to inclusion. This test may be, in its simplest form, defined as:

$$Min(R, SADL, i) \equiv \begin{cases} true, & \forall_{q \in R} \; \exists_{Cj \in SADL_{1..i}} \; R \cap Cj = \{q\}, \\ false, & \text{otherwise.} \end{cases}$$

where $SADL_{1..i}$ is a list of i initial elements of $SADL$: $SADL_{1..i} = (C_1, C_2, ..., C_i)$, and i is the current iteration of the breadth-first search loop. Practical evaluations of various implementations of this tests are described in detail in [16].

A very important characteristics of the presented algorithm is its flexibility. Because the generation of the minimal subsets of simple conditions is implemented as a breadth-first search, it is extremely easy to make the algorithm search not for all exact rules but e.g. for shortest exact rules or for rules that are not longer than a pre-specified threshold. The modification to this algorithm follow closely those required to make the original Reduct Generating Algorithm to search for shortest reducts or for reducts that are not longer than a pre-specified threshold. Details of these modifications are presented in [15].

4 Experimental Evaluation of the Algorithm

The information tables used in experiments are all real-life data sets of miscellaneous origin. Their short characteristics are presented in Table 1. All these data sets were created for scientific purposes and used in different experiments and analyses, which were, however, not necessarily related to rule generation [7].

It is important to stress that the foremost criterion for selecting these particular data sets was the non-triviality of the experiment, rather than the usefulness of the results. The chosen data sets are not trivial in the sense that each of them contains at least half a million of exact rules (with one exception of the Iono4 set, which contains exactly 224100 rules). This is because the experiments with the above data sets were designed and conducted with the main purpose of demonstrating the strictly computational characteristics of the algorithm. The very important issues related to the problems of generating and interpreting the exact rules are far beyond the scope of the paper and are not discussed here.

Table 2 presents results of two basic experiments. In the first of them, exhaustive sets of exact rules were generated. The numbers of all exact rules and the computing times are presented in columns 2 and 3 of this table. In the second experiment, only those exact rules that contain no more than two simple conditions were generated. The numbers of such rules and the appropriate computing times are presented in columns 4 and 5 of Table 2.

It is clear that in case of the presented data sets the usefulness of the exhaustive sets of rules is extremely low due to the sheer size of these sets. As a result, the analyst may be interested in generating some additionally constrained subsets of rules, e.g. sets of rules that contain a limited number of simple conditions. This not only truncates dramatically the size of the generated rule sets, but also allows to find the most interesting regularities in the data set, because short rules tend to be matched by many objects. If so, the experiment confirms excellent behaviour of

72

the presented algorithm, as the times needed to generate the most important rules in the selected, non-trivial data set were fairly satisfactory (it never exceeded half a minute).

Table 1. Basic characteristics of the data sets used in the experiments

Data Set	#Cond. Attr.	#Objects	#Classes
Elc444	30	444	2
Iono4	33	351	2
Lsd265	35	265	15
Mushroom	21	8124	2
Urod2	33	343	2
Urology1	33	500	2
Urology2	33	500	3
Urology3	33	500	6

Table 2. The results of the experiments

Data Set	#All Rules	Time [s]	#Rules≤2	Time [s]
Elc444	632300	392	3316	18.1
Iono4	504936	366	1456	8.1
Lsd265	224100	95	335	4.1
Urod2	541881	323	693	6.7
Urology1	889785	594	655	13.5
Urology2	915920	552	647	14.4
Urology3	1768145	882	496	17.1

The computing platform in all the experiments was a SUN SPARCstation 5 running at 110 MHz.

5 Conclusions

The main purpose of the research reported in this paper has been the introduction and practical verification of an effective algorithm for generating exhaustive sets of exact rules. The main idea of the presented algorithm is the use of the discernibility list, which has been shown to be very effective with real-life applications. The new algorithm employs a breadth-first type of search to generate minimal subsets of binarized attributes, which are used to create a rule. This approach allows achieving considerable computational speeds, which reach thousands of rules per second.

Future research concerning the same domain will be directed towards designing further effective algorithms for rule generation, e.g. by employing parallel or incremental approaches.

References

1. Bazan J.: 'A Comparison of Dynamic and non-Dynamic Rough Set Methods for Extracting Laws from Decision Tables', In: Skowron A., Polkowski L., (eds), *Rough Sets in Data Mining and Knowledge Discovery*, Springer-Verlag, Berlin (1998).

2. Chmielewski M., Grzymala Busse J.: 'Global Discretization of Continuous Attributes as Preprocessing for Machine Learning', In: Lin T.Y., Wildberger A.M., (eds), *Soft Computing*, Society for Computer Simulation, San Diego (1995), 294–301.

3. Clark P., Niblett T.: 'The CN2 induction algorithm', Machine Learning, **3**, No. 4 (1989), 261–283.

4. Dougherty J. Kohavi R., Sahami M., 'Supervised and Unsupervised Discretizations of Continuous Features', In: *Proceedings of the 12th International Conference on Machine Learning*, Morgan Kaufmann, San Mateo, Ca, (1995), 194–202.

5. Grzymala-Busse J.: 'LERS – a system learning from examples based on rough sets', In: Slowinski R. (ed.) *Intelligent Decision Support*, Kluwer Academic Publishers, (1992), 3–18.

6. Michalski R.: 'A Theory and Methodology of Inductive Learning', In: Michalski R., Mitchell T., Carbonell J. (eds) *Machine Learning: An Artificial Intelligence Approach*, Vol. 1, Morgan Kaufmann, San Mateo, Ca, (1983), 83–134.

7. Murphy P.M., Aha D.W.: 'UCI Repository of Machine Learning Databases', University of California, Department of Information and Computer Science, Irvine, CA (1992), WWW page: http://www.ics.uci.edu/~mlearn, e-mail: ml-repository@ics.uci.edu.

8. Nguyen S.H., Skowron A.: 'Quantization of Real Value Attributes: Rough Set and Boolean Reasoning Approach', In: *Proceedings of the Second Joint Annual Conference on Information Sciences*, Wrightsville Beach, North Carolina, (1995), 34–37

9. Pawlak Z. *Rough Sets. Theoretical Aspects of Reasoning About Data*, Kluwer Academic Publishers, Dordrecht, 1991.

10. Skowron A., Polkowski L.: 'Decision Algorithms: A Survey of Rough Set–Theoretic Methods', *Fundamenta Informaticae*, **30**, No. 3–4 (1997), 345–358.

74

11. Skowron A., Rauszer C.: 'The Discernibility Functions Matrices and Functions in Information Systems', In: Slowinski R., (ed.), *Intelligent Decision Support. Handbook of Applications and Advances of the Rough Set Theory*, Kluwer Academic Publishers, Dordrecht (1992), 331–362.

12. Slowinski R., Stefanowski J.: 'Rough-Set Reasoning about Uncertain Data', *Fundamenta Informaticae*, **27**, No. 2–3 (1996), 229–244.

13. Stefanowski J.: 'Handling continuous attributes in discovery of strong decision rules', *Lecture Notes in Artificial Inteligence*, Vol. 1424, Springer-Verlag (1998), 394-401

14. Susmaga R.: 'Experiments in Incremental Computation of Reducts', In: Skowron A., Polkowski L., (eds), *Rough Sets in Data Mining and Knowledge Discovery*, Springer-Verlag, Berlin (1998a).

15. Susmaga R.: 'Computation of Shortest Reducts', *Foundations of Computing and Decision Sciences*, Vol. 23, No. 2, Poznan, Poland (1998b), 119–137.

16. Susmaga R.: 'Effective Tests for Minimality in Reduct Generation', *Foundations of Computing and Decision Sciences*, Vol. 23, No. 4, Poznan, Poland (1998c), 219–240.

17. Ziarko W., Shan N. 'Data-Based Acquisition and Incremental Modification of Classification Rules', *Computational Intelligence*, **11**, No. 2 (1995a), 357–370.

18. Ziarko W., Shan N., 'KDD-R: A Comprehensive System for Knowledge Discovery in Databases Using Rough Sets', In: Lin T.Y., Wildberger A.M., (eds), *Soft Computing*, Society for Computer Simulation, San Diego (1995b), 298–301.

Optimal Decision Making with Data-Acquired Decision Tables

Wojciech Ziarko

University of Regina Regina, Saskatchewan, S4S 0A2, Canada

Abstract. The paper deals with predictive decision models acquired from data called probabilistic decision tables. The methodology of probabilistic decision tables presented in this article is derived from the theory of rough sets. In this methodology, the probabilistic extension of the original rough set theory, called variable precision model of rough sets, is used. The theory of rough sets is applicable to identification and characterization of dependencies occurring in data. Each identified dependency is represented in the form of a decision table which subsequently is analyzed and optimized using rough sets-based methods. The original model of rough sets is restricted to the analysis of functional, or partial functional dependencies. The variable precision model of rough sets extends the capabilities of the rough set model to identify probabilistic dependencies, probabilistic reducts and cores allowing for construction of probabilistic predictive models. The paper reviews the variable precision model of rough sets with the main focus on setting the parameters of the model and on decision strategies to maximize the expected gain from the decisions.

1   Introduction

Decision tables are tabular models of the functional dependencies between input conditions and decisions or actions taken in response to the occurrence of some combinations of conditions. They have been used in software engineering, circuit design and other application areas for years [6]. The dependency is encoded by the table designer in the form of a set a disjoint decision rules covering all possible input situations. However, in many problems related to decision making with uncertainty, machine learning, pattern recognition and data mining, the condition-decision dependency is typically unknown and almost always non-deterministic. Often, it is hidden in empirical data. A number of analytical methodologies have been developed in recent years to approximate this kind of the dependency for the purpose of prediction or better understanding of the nature of the relationship, for example, by using decision trees, neural networks or rough sets (see, for instance, [3,5, 9-12]).

In this paper, we will focus on using decision tables extracted from data for that purpose. The research into decision tables acquisition from data was initiated by Pawlak in the context of rough sets theory[1,2]. His original works were concerned with the acquisition of deterministic, or partially deterministic tables. We demonstrate how an extended approach, called variable precision rough sets model (VPRS), can be applied to acquistion of non-deterministic decision tables with probabilistic characterization of their decision accuracy [8]. In what follows, the review of the methods of rough sets for the above mentioned data-based modeling problem is presented and illustrated with simple examples. A comprehensive discussion of the optimal decision making strategies and parameter setting for the model is also included. Generally, the objective is not to construct a predictive system which would guarantee always correct predictions (which is typically impossible) , but to have a system which would support decisions with sufficient success rate in the longer run, or sufficient expected gain or profit from the decision making.

The paper is organized as follows. We first discuss the basics of the formal model of decision tables acquired from data. Then, the main definitions of the variable precision model of rough sets are introduced. In the next sections, they are used to define extended notions of the dependency between attributes, of the extended reduct and core attributes. A separate section is devoted to the discussion of the optimal decision making with the probabilistic decision tables. The final version of the paper will include the results of the experimental evaluation of the presented approach which were not yet available at the time of writing of this article.

2   Decision Tables Acquired from Data

Generally, the decision table is defined here as a tabular representation of a relation discovered in data. The relation is identified through a classification process in which data objects having the same values of selected attributes, or having the same values of properly selected functions of the attributes (for example, using some attribute value discretization technique), are considered to be identical. It should be noted, however, that this kind of the decision table does not necessarily represent functional relationship as it is the case with "classical" decision tables known in software engineering and other areas. More precisely, the data-extracted decision table is defined as follows:

Let U be the universe of objects $e \in U$ and $a \in A$ be the attributes of the objects, that is functions $a : e \rightarrow a(e)$ assigning some features (attribute values) to objects. We assume that every attribute maps into a finite set of values, $v_a \in range(a)$. The attributes are divided into two categories, condition attributes $C = \{a_1, a_2, ..., a_m\}$ and the decision attributes D. Typically, the condition attributes represent measurable properties of objects whereas decision attributes are the "predictive" attributes (variables) whose values are normally predicted based on known values of condition attributes. We will assume here, without loss of generality, that there is only one binary-valued decision attribute $d \in D$ and one value v_d^i ($i = 0$ or 1) of this attribute has been selected as a prediction or modeling "target". With all these assumptions, the decision table can be expressed as a quadruple $< U, C, d, v_d^i >$.

CLASS	S	H	E	C	$P(T = 1 \| E_i)$	$P(T = 0 \| E_i)$
E_1	0	0	1	0	0.10	0.90
E_2	1	0	2	1	0.85	0.15
E_3	1	1	1	0	0.01	0.99
E_4	0	2	1	1	1.00	0.00
E_5	1	2	1	0	0.82	0.18
E_6	1	0	1	0	0.12	0.88
E_7	1	2	2	1	0.92	0.08
E_8	0	0	2	1	0.91	0.09

Table 1. Classification by condition attributes only

Each of the two values v_d^0, v_d^1 of the decision attribute d corresponds to a set of objects matching that particular value. We will denote these sets as X^0 and X^1 respectively. Clearly, $X^0 = \neg X^1$ and $X^0 \cup X^1 = U$. Our objective in the construction and analysis of the decision tables is to develop a simple predictive model for the target set which would enable us to predict, with an acceptable confidence, whether an object matching a combination of attribute values occurring in the decision table belongs to the target set, or to its complement.

3 VPRS Model of Rough Sets

In data mining and predictive modeling applications the variable precision model of rough sets (VPRS) was used for analysis of decision tables extracted from data. The VPRS model extends the capabilities of the original model of rough sets to handle probabilistic information. The main aspects of the VPRS model are presented below.

Let R be an equivalence relation (called the indiscernibility relation) and let R^* be the set of equivalence classes of R. Typically, the relation R represents the partitioning of the universe U in terms of the values of condition attributes as defined in Section 2. Also, let $E \in R^*$ be an equivalence class (elementary set) of the relation R. With each class E we can associate the estimate of the conditional probability $P(X|E)$ by the formula: $P(X|E) = card(X \cap E)/card(E)$ assuming that sets X and E are finite. This situation is illustrated in Table 1 which represents the classification of raw data in terms of condition attributes S,H,E,C, with each class E_i being assigned probabilities $P(T = 1|E_i)$ and $P(T = 0|E_i)$.

Let $0 \leq l < u \leq 1$ be real-valued approximation *precision control* parameters called lower and upper limits respectively. For any subset $X \subseteq U$ we define the *u-positive* region of X, $POS_u(X)$ as a union of those elementary sets whose conditional probability $P(X|E)$ is not lower than the upper limit , that is

$$POS_u(X) = \bigcup \{E \in R^* : P(X|E) \geq u\}$$

CLASS	S	H	E	C	E_i REGION
E_1	0	0	1	0	NEG
E_2	1	0	2	1	POS
E_3	1	1	1	0	NEG
E_4	0	2	1	1	POS
E_5	1	2	1	0	POS
E_6	1	0	1	0	NEG
E_7	1	2	2	1	POS
E_8	0	0	2	1	POS

Table 2. The probabilistic decision table with $u = 0.8$ and $l = 0.2$

The *u-positive* region of X represents an area in the universe which contains objects with relatively high probability of belonging to the set X.

The *(l,u)-boundary* region $BNR_{\ell,u}(X)$ of the set X with respect to the lower and upper limits ℓ and u is a union of those elementary sets E for which the conditional probability $P(X|E)$ is higher than the lower limit ℓ and lower than the upper limit u. Formally,

$$BNR_{\ell,u}(X) = \bigcup \{E \in R^* : \ell < P(X|E) < u\}$$

The boundary area represents objects which cannot be classified with sufficiently high confidence (represented by u) into set X and which also cannot be excluded from X with the sufficiently high confidence (represented by $1 - l$).

The *l-negative* region $NEG_l(X)$ of the subset X, is a collection of objects which can be excluded from X with the confidence not lower than $1 - l$, that is,

$$NEG_l(X) = \bigcup \{E \in R^* : P(U - X|E) \geq 1 - l\}$$

The *l-negative* region represents objects of the universe for which it is known that it is relatively unlikely that they would belong to X.

In the Table 2, each of the classes E_i of Table 1 is assigned to one of the *rough approximation regions*, according to the above definitions, with $u = 0.8$ and $l = 0.2$. The decision table in which each combination of condition attributes is assigned its approximation region with respect to the target value of the decision attribute (in this example, $T = 1$) is called *probabilistic decision table* [8]. The probabilistic decision table can be used to predict the target value of the decision attribute, or its complement, with probabilities not lower than u and $1 - l$, respectively.

4 (l, u)-Dependency in Decision Tables

The analysis of decision tables extracted from data involves inter-attribute dependency analysis, identification, elimination of redundant condition attributes and attribute significance analysis [2]. The original rough sets model-based analysis involves detection of functional, or partial functional dependencies and subsequent dependency-preserving reduction of condition attributes. In this paper, we extend this idea by using *(l, u)-probabilistic dependency* as a reference rather than functional or partial functional dependency. To define (l, u)-probabilistic dependency we will assume that the relation R corresponds to the partitioning of the universe U in terms of values of condition attributes C in the decision table $< U, C, d, v_d^i >$, $(i = 0$ or $1)$. In other words, we assume that objects having identical values of the attributes are considered to be equivalent.

The *(l, u)-probabilistic dependency* $\gamma_{l,u}(C, d, i)$ between condition attributes C and the decision attribute d in the decision table $< U, C, d, v_d^i >$ is defined as the total relative size of (l, u)-approximation regions of the subset $X^i \subseteq U$ corresponding to target value of the decision attribute . In other words, we have

$$\gamma_{l,u}(C, d, i) = (card(POS_u(X^i)) + card(NEG_l(X^i)))/card(U)$$

The dependency degree can be interpreted as a measure of the probability that a randomly occurring object will be represented by such a combination of condition attribute values that the prediction of the corresponding value of the decision attribute could be done with the acceptable confidence, as represented by (l, u) pair of parameters.

To illustrate the notion of *(l, u)-dependency* let us consider the classification given in Table 1 again. When $u = 0.80$ and $l = 0.15$ the dependency equals to 1.0. This means that every object e from the universe U can be classified either as the member of the target set with the probability not less than 0.8, or the member of the complement of the target set, with the probability not less than 0.85. The lower and upper limits define acceptable probability bounds for predicting whether an object is, or is not the member of the target set.

If (l, u)−dependency is less than one it means that the information contained in the table is not sufficient to make either positive, or negative prediction in some cases. For instance, if we take $u = 0.83$ and $l = 0.11$ then the probabilistic decision table will appear as shown in Table 3. As we see, when objects are classified into boundary classes, neither positive nor negative prediction with acceptable confidence is possible. This situation is reflected in the $(0.11, 0.83)$−dependency being 0.75 (assuming even distribution of atomic classes $E_1, E_2, ..., E_8$ in the universe U).

5 (l, u)-Reduct and (l, u)-Core of Attributes

One of the important aspects in the analysis of decision tables extracted from data is the elimination of redundant condition attributes and identification of the most important attributes. In line with the definition given in [2], by redundant condition attributes we mean any attributes which could be elim-

CLASS	S	H	E	C	E_i REGION
E_1	0	0	1	0	NEG
E_2	1	0	2	1	POS
E_3	1	1	1	0	NEG
E_4	0	2	1	1	POS
E_5	1	2	1	0	BND
E_6	1	0	1	0	BND
E_7	1	2	2	1	POS
E_8	0	0	2	1	POS

Table 3. The probabilistic decision table with $u = 0.83$ and $l = 0.11$

inated without affecting the dependency degree between remaining condition attributes and the decision attribute. The minimum subset of condition attributes preserving the dependency degree is termed *reduct* [2]. In the context of the VPRS model of rough sets we adapt the original notion of reduct to accommodate the (l, u)-probabilistic dependency among attributes as well by defining (l, u)-reduct $RED_{l,u}(C, d, i) \subseteq C$ as follows:

- $\gamma_{l,u}(RED_{l,u}(C, d, i), d, i) = \gamma_{l,u}(C, d, i)$, that is, the dependency preservation condition is imposed;
- For every $a \in RED_{l,u}(C, d, i)$ we have $\gamma_{l,u}(RED_{l,u}(C, d, i), d, i) > \gamma_{l,u}(RED_{l,u}(C, d, i) - \{a\}, d, i)$, that is, the elimination of an attribute from the reduct can only result in the drop of the dependency degree.

For example, one (l, u)-reduct of attributes in Table 3 contains attributes S,H and E. The decision table projected on these three attributes and the attribute REGION will have the same predictive accuracy as the original Table 2. Many possible (l, u)- reducts can be computed, in general leading to alternative minimal representations of the relationship between conditions and the decision attributes.

The (l, u)-significance $SIG_{l,u}(a)$ of an attribute $a \in C$ within reduct can be obtained by calculating the relative degree of dependency drop due to elimination of the attribute from the reduct:

$SIG_{l,u}(a) = (\gamma_{l,u}(RED_{l,u}(C, d, i), d, i) - \gamma_{l,u}(RED_{l,u}(C, d, i) - \{a\}, d, i)) / \gamma_{l,u}(RED_{l,u}(C, d, i), d, i)$

For instance, the (l, u)-significance of attributes S, H, E, C of Table 3 is respectively $0.25, 0.375, 0.0$ and 0.0. This indicates that the attribute H is the most significant one whereas some of the attributes E and C could potentially be eliminated.

The set of most important attributes, these which would be included in every reduct is called core set of attributes [2]. It can be shown that the (l, u)-*core* set of attributes $CORE_{l,u}$, the intersection of all reducts, is given by:

$$CORE_{l,u}(C, d, i) = \{a \in C : \gamma_{l,u}(C - \{a\}, d, i) > 0\}$$

For example, the core attributes of the decision table given in Table 3 are S and H . These attributes will be included in all reducts of the Table 3 which means that they are essential for preservation of the prediction accuracy.

6   Optimization of Precision Control Parameters

An interesting question, inspired by practical applications of the variable precision rough set model, is how to set the values of the precision control parameters l and u to achieve desired quality of prediction. It is, in fact, an optimization problem, strongly connected to the external knowledge of possible gains and losses associated with correct, or incorrect predictions, respectively. It also depends on the quality of the information encoded in data used to create the probabilistic decision table. In general, setting lower values of l and higher values of u results in increasing the size of the boundary area on the expense of positive and negative regions. In practical terms, this means that we my not be always able to make decisions with the confidence level we would like it to be. If nothing is known about the potential gains or losses associated with the decisions, the reasonable goal is to increase the likelihood of positive correct prediction about the target value of the decision attribute, i.e. above random guess probability of success (by positive correct prediction we mean correctly predicting that the selected value will occur). Similarly, we are interested in increasing the probability of negative correct prediction, i.e. predicting correctly that a particular target value will not occur. We would like this probability to be above random guess probability of success as well. That is, given the distribution of the target value of the decision attribute to be $(p, 1 - p)$, where p is the probability that an object has the target value of the decision attribute, and $1 - p$ is the probability that it does not, the reasonable settings of the parameters are $0 \leq l < p$ and $1 \geq u > p$. With the settings falling into these limits, in the negative region the prediction that object does not belong to the target set would be made with the confidence higher than random guess, i.e. with the probability not less than $1 - l > 1 - p$ and, in the positive region, the prediction that an object belongs to the target set would be made with the probability not less than u,

Clearly, other factors can affect the selection of the precision control parameters. In particular, an interesting question is how to set those parameters in a game playing situation, where each decision making act is carrying a cost (*bet cost* $b > 0$) and incorrect decision results in a *loss* whereas correct decision results in a *win*. Because there are two possible outcomes of the decision, and one can pick any of these outcomes, there are two kinds of losses and two kinds of wins:

- positive win, when positive outcome is bet (that is, that the target value will occur) and that outcome really occurred; the win is denoted here as $q^{++} > 0$ and the cost of this betting is denoted as b^+;

- positive loss, when positive outcome is bet but that outcome did not occur; the loss is denoted here as $q^{+-} < 0$;
- negative win, when the negative outcome is bet (that is, that the target value will not occur) and that outcome really occurred; the win is denoted here as $q^{--} > 0$ and the cost of this betting is denoted as b^-;
- negative loss, when the negative outcome is bet but that outcome did not occur; the loss is denoted here as $q^{-+} < 0$;

In addition to the assumptions listed above we will assume that both positive and negative wins are not smaller than the cost of betting, that is $q^{--} \geq b^- > 0$ and $q^{++} \geq b^+ > 0$, and that the absolute values of both negative and positive losses are not smaller than the bet, that is $|q^{-+}| \geq b^-$ and $|q^{+-}| \geq b^+$.

Also, with each approximation region we will associate an *expected gain* function, which is the weighted average of wins and losses in the respective region. Our decision making strategy assumes that in the positive region the positive outcome is bet, and that in the negative region, the negative outcome is bet. The bet in the boundary region will depend on the value of the expected gain function, and we will assume that the bet which maximizes the gain function is selected. The gain functions $Q(approximation\ region)$ are defined as follows:

- $Q(POS) = p(+|POS) * q^{++} + p(-|POS) * q^{+-}$ where $p(+|POS)$ and $p(-|POS)$ are conditional probabilities of positive and negative outcomes respectively within the positive region;
- $Q(NEG) = p(+|NEG) * q^{-+} + p(-|NEG) * q^{--}$ where $p(+|NEG)$ and $p(-|NEG)$ are conditional probabilities of positive and negative outcomes respectively within the negative region;
- $Q(BND) = p(+|BND) * q^{++} + p(-|BND) * q^{+-}$ or $Q(BND) = p(+|BND) * q^{-+} + p(-|BND) * q^{--}$, depending on the bet, whichever value is higher with the positive, or negative bet, where $p(+|BND)$ and $p(-|BND)$ are conditional probabilities of positive and negative outcomes respectively within the boundary region.

Let us note that:

1. $Q(POS) \geq u * q^{++} + (1 - u) * q^{+-}$ and
2. $Q(NEG) \geq l * q^{-+} + (1 - l) * q^{--}$.

The uncertain decision is considered advantageous and justified if the expected gain is not lower than the cost of the bet, i.e. if $Q(POS) \geq b$ and $Q(NEG) \geq b$, assuming that positive outcome is bet in the positive region and negative outcome is bet in the negative region. By focusing on these two regions we can determine from (1) and (2) the bounds for parameters l and u to maximize the size of positive and negative regions while guaranting that $Q(POS) \geq b$ and $Q(NEG) \geq b$. From conditions $u * q^{++} + (1 - u) * q^{+-} \geq b$

and $l * q^{-+} + (1 - l) * q^{--} \geq b$ we get the following bounds for the precision control parameters:

$$1 \geq u \geq \frac{b^+ - q^{+-}}{q^{++} - q^{+-}} \quad \text{and} \quad 0 \leq l \leq \frac{b^- - q^{--}}{q^{-+} - q^{--}} \cdot$$

To maximize the sizes of both positive and negative areas the upper limit should assume the minimal range value and the lower limit should assume the maximal range value, that is:

$$u = \frac{b^+ - q^{+-}}{q^{++} - q^{+-}} \quad \text{and} \quad l = \frac{b^- - q^{--}}{q^{-+} - q^{--}} \cdot$$

To illustrate the above result with an example, let us assume that $p = 0.1$, $q^{++} = 20$, $b^+ = 3$, $q^{+-} = -3$, $b^- = 9$, $q^{--} = 10$, $q^{-+} = -9$. It is assumed that positive and negative loss means loosing the bet. It can be easily checked that with the target probability $p = 0.1$ the expected gain when betting either positive, or negative outcome is always less than the cost of the bet. This means that this is a loosing game for the "player", in the longer run. However, after putting the assumed values of bets, wins and losses in the above formula we get $u = 0.026$ and $l = 0.052$. This means, that after identifying positive and negative regions of the decision table with these parameters, predictions made in cases falling within these regions will produce a a positive gain for the decision maker, in the longer run.

We should be aware, however that bounds l and u set only the requirements how the rough approximation regions should be defined in order to obtain desired *expected* results of decision making processes. The actual data set may not support these bounds in the sense that the positive, negative or both regions may be empty in which case there would be no benefit. In general, it can be demonstrated that in the boundary area, regardless whether positive or negative bet is made, the expected gain is always less than the respective bet, that is $Q(BND) < b^+$, if the positive bet is taken, and $Q(BND) < b^-$, if the negative bet is taken. Consequently, if the decision has to be made in the boundary area, one should take the one which maximizes $Q(BND)$, but in the longer run the "player" is in the loosing position anyway in the boundary area. The expected gain G from making decisions based on the whole decision table, according with the assumptions and decision strategy described above, is given by:

$$G = p(POS) * Q(POS) + p(NEG) * Q(NEG) + p(BND) * Q(BND)$$

where $p(POS)$, $p(NEG)$ and $p(BND)$ are the probabilities of respective approximation regions (the probabilities mentioned here can be approximated based on frequency distribution of data records belonging to the respective regions). Only if the overall expected gain G is higher than the expected cost of betting the "player" is winning in the longer run.

7 Summary and Conclusions

The main distinguishing feature of the presented approach is that it is primarily concerned with the acquisition of decision tables from data and with their analysis and simplification using notions of attribute dependency, reduct, core and attribute significance. The decision tables represent "discovered" inter-data dependencies which implies that, in general, a number of decision tables can be extracted from a given data collection. An important issue in the whole process of decision table acquisition from data is a choice of the mapping from original attributes, in which raw data are expressed, to finite-valued attributes used in the decision table. This is an application domain-specific task, often requiring deep knowledge of the domain. One popular technique is discretization of continous attributes. The decision making with probabilistic decision tables is typically uncertain. The decision strategy involves making positive prediction in the positive region, negative prediction in the negative region, and positive or negative prediction in the boundary region, depending on the value of the gain function. The techniques described in this article are aimed at constructing probabilistic decision tables which would support uncertain decision making leading to long range gains rather than to correct decisions in each case. They seem to be applicable to practical problems involving making guesses based on past data, such as some forms of gambling, stock market price movements prediction or market research.

8   Acknowledgment

The research reported in this article was partially supported by a research grant awarded by Natural Sciences and Engineering Research Council of Canada.

References

1. Pawlak, Z. Grzymała-Busse, J. Słowiński, R. and Ziarko, W. (1995). Rough sets. *Communications of the ACM*, 38, 88–95.
2. Pawlak, Z. (1991). *Rough Sets - Theoretical Aspects of Reasoning about Data*. Kluwer Academic.
3. Ziarko, W. (ed.) (1994). *Rough Sets, Fuzzy Sets and Knowledge Discovery*. Springer Verlag.
4. Ziarko, W. (1993). Variable precision rough sets model. *Journal of Computer and Systems Sciences*, vol. 46, no. 1, 39-59.
5. Polkowski, L., Skowron, A. (eds.) (1998). *Rough Sets in Knowledge Discovery*. Physica Verlag, vol. 1-2.
6. Hurley, R. (1983). *Decision Tables in Software Engineering*. Van Nostrand Reinhold.
7. Son, N. (1997). Rule induction from continuous data. In: Wang, P.(ed.), *Joint Conference of Information Sciences*. Duke University, Vol. 3, 81–84.
8. Ziarko, W. (1998). Approximation region-based decision tables. In: Polkowski, L., Skowron, A. (eds.). *Rough Sets and Current Trends in Computing*. Lecture Notes in AI 1424, Springer Verlag, 178-185.

9. Zhong, N., Dang, J., Ohsuga, S. (1998). Soft techniques to data mining. In: Polkowski, L., Skowron, A. (eds.). *Rough Sets and Current Trends in Computing.* Lecture Notes in AI 1424, Springer Verlag, 231-238.

10. Munakata, T. (1998). *Fundamentals of the New Artificial Intelligence.* Springer Verlag.

11. Lenarcik, A., Piasta, Z. (1998). Rough classifiers sensitive to costs varying from object to object. In: Polkowski, L., Skowron, A. (eds.). *Rough Sets and Current Trends in Computing.* Lecture Notes in AI 1424, Springer Verlag, 221-230.

12. Tsumoto, S. (1998). Formalization and induction of medical expert system rules based on rough set theory. In: Polkowski, L., Skowron, A. (eds.) (1998). *Rough Sets in Knowledge Discovery.* Physica Verlag, vol. 2,.307-323.

Applying Data Mining Methods for Cellular Radio Network Planning

Piotr Gawrysiak, Michał Okoniewski

{gawrysia, okoniews}@ii.pw.edu.pl

Institute of Computer Science, Warsaw University of Technology

ul. Nowowiejska 15/19, 00-665

Warsaw, Poland

Abstract: This paper contains description of a knowledge discovery experiment performed in radio planning department of one of Polish celular telecom providers. The results of using various data mining methods for GSM cell traffic prediction are presented. The methods used include both standard and well established approaches such as decision trees and k-means clustering, and new methods invented for this experiment, such as regressional clustering. Remarks on importance of discretization methods for quantitative data mining are presented, together with general discussion on data mining of technical (i.e. mostly numeric and automatically generated) data.

Keywords: data mining, automatic knowledge discovery, cellular networks, clustering, multiple regression, discretization

1. Introduction

Data mining team, which was formed in the Institute of Computer Science at the Warsaw University of Technology, has been asked to investigate the possibility of applying data mining techniques for one of Polish cellular telecommunication companies. Because the idea of this project came out from technological departments of this company, the mining team started its research in this area. The problems that have been identified in the department, as good candidates for data mining, were not the typical applications of KDD (knowledge discovery in databases) in telecommunications such as described in [1] and [5]. Of course typical problems, such as churn analysis or customer segmentation are also very important in telecom companies, but as they are obviously related to marketing, we have not been yet investigating them. Moreover, the purely technological problems that were analyzed with data mining methodologies proved to be much more interesting, since the classical knowledge discovery methods could not be applied here.

This paper describes a first one in longer series of knowledge discovery experiments. Our team started with data mining in the sub-department of radio network planning division. The project consists of much more experiments, some of which are still ongoing, and may be described in more detail in further papers.

2. Problem definition

One of the most important areas for a young cellular telecom provider is network expansion. This creates a need for traffic prediction i.e. we would like to estimate the number of calls made during a certain time span, on an area where we want to build a new base station. Such information is crucial for station equipment design - there must be enough transceivers to ensure that every subscriber in the GSM cell created by this station is able to place or receive call. On the other hand, there should not be too much available - and unused - radio channels, because this would mean unnecessary costs.

Traffic prediction is a complex task, as the number of subscribers present on a certain area may vary. After all GSM is an abbreviation of name Global System for Mobile Telecommunications, and GSM subscribers travel between cells, for example moving into city centers at day, and going to suburbs (where their homes are) in the evening. Similar effect can be observed also for longer time periods. So called vacation traffic analysis shows that in the summer average traffic generally increases in popular resort areas - like mountains, seashore etc.

Fortunately our analysis showed that these variations are periodic and predictable, at least for regions with well developed GSM coverage. We can therefore try to predict traffic for a certain characteristic time period - say, for vacation time - using measurements of existing network elements, and than interpolate obtained values.

In this particular experiment we were able to extract two types of information from GSM network monitoring system. First was the traffic information: for each cell we obtained average of weekly traffic measured at busy hour (usually around midday). Other type of information has been extracted from company's geographical information system (GIS): for each cell, the types of terrain occupied have been established. The GIS database contained information about nine terrain types (landuses) that may occur in particular cell. These were:

1={Fields}, 2={Forests}, 3={Water}, 4={Rocks, seashores, swamps}, 5={Roads, concrete, parks}, 6={Suburbs} 7={Urban area}, 8={Dense urban area}, 9={Industrial area}

For each cell the amount of ground pixels occupied by every landuse have been measured, where one ground pixel width and length is approximately 5 arc seconds of parallel or meridian respectively.

Our initial data about existing network have been collected and recorded in a table with following attributes:

- cell identification number

- landuse type (a number {1..9} corresponding to above landuse types list)

- number of pixels occupied by this landuse

- area number that allows to determine region in which the cell is situated

- average weekly traffic value in Erlangs for this cell

In the latest experiments additional data about the population and average wealth on every cell area was added. These experiments are still in progress, so they are not fully described in this paper. Data preprocessing included converting above representation into table that contains percentages of landuses for each cell. Both relative and non-relative distributions of landuses were supposed to be meaningful.

3. Statistical foundations of the solution

In an inception phase of research, a multiple regression have been proposed as a problem solution (see [3] and [5]) . Indeed, if we treat the ground pixels as entities generating traffic for a cell than we can represent traffic value as a linear combination of landuse distribution values :

$$t(cellnr)=l_1(cellnr) \cdot d_1 + ... + l_9(cellnr) \cdot l_9 \qquad (1)$$

where t represents traffic generated by this pixel, l_n represents the amount of pixels of n-th landuse type in cellnr GSM cell, and d_n traffic density for this landuse type

Above equation can be also written in matrix representation:

$$T = L \cdot D \qquad (2)$$

where T is a traffic vector, L is a matrix of landuses for each cell and D is a vector of density coefficients $[d_1...d_9]$.

In this particular problem, the vector D has as many rows as landuses. This fact is caused by problem definition, that does not specify any constant addend in equation (1). Of course, landuses are not only factors that may be taken into consideration when estimating traffic. Other factors may be population density, wealth of a region or number of landline telephones installed, so the traffic equation may be formulated in a more complex way. In fact our further experiments involve working with such parameters, but the ovrerall estimation method remains the same.

Using multiple regression we were able to calculate all density coefficient values. In the case presented above, the multiple regression hyperplane which is best approximation in least square sense, may be calculated with the estimator:

$$G = (L^T L)^{-1} L^T T \tag{3}$$

that is a vector of approximated traffic density coefficients in particular landuses. The quality of approximation may be assessed here with estimators

$$\hat{R} = \sqrt{1 - \frac{\sum_{i=1}^{n}(t-\hat{t})^2}{\sum_{i=1}^{n}(t-\bar{t})^2}} \tag{4}$$

$$\hat{R} = \sqrt{1 - \frac{T^T T - G^T L^T T}{T^T T - \frac{1}{n}(1^T T)^2}} \tag{5}$$

R^2 is an estimator of correlation coefficient, that has value range between 0 and 1. $R^2=0$ means total lack of correlation - variable T is not correlated with $l_1, l_2, ..., l_k$. On the other hand $R^2=1$ means perfect fit - each point from the population belongs to regression hyperplane.

Above estimators is a good measures for comparison of regression approximation quality in different samples of traffic results, since such comparison is necessary to operate on data collected on various time periods.

4. Initial problems and requirements

The problem that arisen was the unacceptably high regression error rate. This is not surprising as analyzed cells had various sizes and characteristics, and therefore the same amount of landuse pixels can have different impact on total traffic in different cells. Consider for example such three cells:

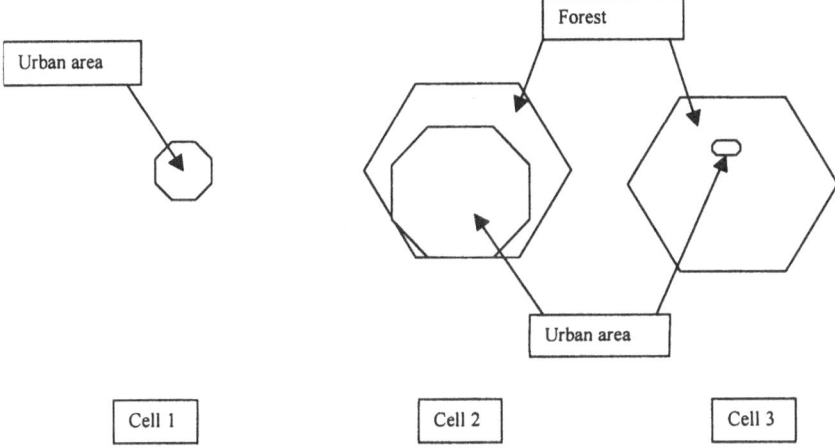

Fig. 1. Cells example

Cell 1 is a very small cell, probably an inter-urban one. This means that the urban area within is densely populated, and therefore generates lots of traffic. Urban characteristics is probably similar in Cell 2, albeit here total traffic will be sum of traffics generated by urban area, and forest area (which probably will have minor contribution to total value). The situation is very different in Cell 3. The urban area is very small here and completely surrounded by forest area (it could be for example a forester's house). This means that the number of people residing in this area will be smaller than number of subscribers located in the same type and size area in Cells 2 and 3. That suggests the need to categorize all cells into several groups, in which such differences as depicted above will be minor. If we had more information about the cells (such as map of landuse distribution etc.), and less cells to classify, it could possibly be done manually. As such data were not available and the number of cells in the whole network is several thousand, the use of automatic knowledge discovery methods here is fully justified.

Another controversy between network engineers and data mining team at the beginning of research was the interpretation of negative density coefficients. The cellular network experts claimed that each pixel should generate certain amount of traffic within its cell. Nonetheless, the coefficients obtained with regression method often happened to be negative, especially for landuses 1-4 (fields, forests, water, swamp and rocks). The results partially convinced them to change their interpretation : some landuses may deter subscribers from using a cellular phone and generate 'negative traffic'(for example forest area in Cell 3 from above figure could possibly have such coefficent). Of course it is possible to approximate the traffic function with hyperplane that has only positive coefficients, but the regression error (4) would grow in such case.

5. Data mining solutions

The preprocessed data, with traffic and percentages of landuses, were then discretized using quartiles and chi-square discretization techniques. Generally dividing both landuse percentages and traffic into four levels, as in quartile approach, proved to be best for retrieval and visualization of qualitative knowledge about groups of cells. The fastest available data mining approach was the use of existing software tools for the classification of cells. For this purpose such tools as IBM Intelligent Miner for Data and SGI Mine Set were used. The main idea was to find first a classification of cells, and then calculate multiple regression function for each group. Algorithms used in this experiment were classic k-means clustering and C4.5 decision trees.

5.1 Decision trees

The decision tree based on discretized traffic as a decisive attribute, after pruning, has brought about a result of 12 decision groups (leaves). The number of cells in leaves varied from 12 to 700 cells. The only problem was the purity of classification that was only 61%. For each group of cells multiple regression function was calculated. Most important tests were based on the value of the landuse 5, 6 and 9.

5.2 K-means clustering

Classic clustering did not seem much promising as a method of obtaining a meaningful classification. We anticipated that the euclidean distance measure is not very relevant to desired classification that should follow regressional hyperplane. Anyway, the results were more valuable for the experts than it was expected at the beginning. The population of cells was distributed among variuos number of clusters: from 2 clusters up to 10 clusters. For each cluster of cells multiple regression function was calculated. Using Intelligent Miner visualization tools we presented results to cellular network experts. They interpreted clusters as 'rural', 'urban', 'suburban'or 'industrialized'and agreed that traffic density coefficients in regression function calculated for discovered clusters are meaningful and differences between clusters are significant.

5.3 Regression results for clusters and decision groups.

The regression calculated for groups obtained from decision tree and clustering differs significantly from the regression calculated for the whole population. Below we present few examples, d1,...,d9 are density coefficients in erlangs per pixel:

Table 1. Density coeficients

	d9	d7	d6	d5	d4	d3	d2	d1
All cells	0.04542	0.25430	0.02261	0.02650	-0.0027	2.9E-05	-9.0E-05	-0.0001
Warsaw	0.14418	1.2673	0.35689	0.01579	0.18514	0.00615	-0.0214	-0.0039
Cluster1	-0.0153	0.47448	0.01167	0.01767	-0.0720	0.00059	-0.0003	2.6E-05
Cluster2	0.08538	0.42911	0.26581	0.06834	Not present	Not present	-0.0350	-0.0686
Leaf 1	0.04888	1.37615	0.01465	0.00650	-0.0009	2.6E-05	7.5E-05	4.7E-05
Leaf 2	0.00764	0.03676	0.01468	0.01133	-0.0069	0.00027	0.00018	6.7E-05
Leaf 3	0.02747	0.08926	0.00795	0.01766	-0.0005	0.00014	8.3E-05	1.7E-05
Leaf 4	-0.0143	0.79967	0.01260	0.04572	-0.1584	0.00302	0.00099	3.1E-05
Leaf 10	0.00849	2.63297	-1.4994	1.92417	-0.4569	-0.0618	0.09407	-0.2049
Leaf 12	0.06138	0.42556	0.08418	0.03659	Not present	0.03045	-0.0029	-0.0018

where:

Cluster 1 = { l4,l7,l9=medium;l1=huge}

Cluster 2 = { l5,l6=huge;l1,l3,l4=small}

Leaf 1 ={ l5=medium and small;l6=small;T=small}

Leaf 2 ={ l6=medium and big;l5=medium}

Leaf 3 = { l6=medium and big;l5=small}

Leaf 4 = { l5=medium and small;l6=huge}

Leaf 10 = { l5=big;l6=big;l9=huge}

Leaf 12 = { l5=huge;l6=big}

5.4 Clustering with regressional distance measures

As classic clustering does not seem to optimize the value of estimator R for clusters, there was a need for a new clustering algorithm that will solve the main problem of this project. According to initial assumptions this clustering algorithm has to use estimators of regression quality to assess the quality of clusters. The problem is that in this approach there is no obvious variable that may be used as a measure of quality for a single cluster. The only way to classify cells in this way is to move cells between two clusters and compare the estimator R before and after the operation. The decision whether to leave the moved cell in the cluster or move it back to the previous place should be taken according to changes in the R estimator for both clusters:

R11, R21, - the values of R before moving a cell record

R12, R22, - the values of R after moving a cell record between clusters.

If R12> R11 and R21> R22 - the records should definitely be moved between clusters

If R12 +R22> R11 +R21 - the cells should be moved

If R12 +R22< R11 +R21 - the cells should not be moved

If R12> R11 and R21> R22 - the records definitely should not be moved between clusters

The general form of such algorithm may look like this:

```
1 regess_clustering(clusters_set cl[k],BOOL strict)
2 {
3  cluster a,b;
4  records ra,rb;
5  double R11,R12,R21,R22;
6
7  add_records_to_clusters(cl);
8  while (calculate_general_regression_results(cl)< MAXRESULT)
9  {
10   choose_clusters(a,b,clusters[k]);
11   choose_records_to_move(a,b,ra,rb);
12   R11 = correlation(a);
13   R21 = correlation(b);
14   move_records(a,b,ra,rb);
15   R12 = correlation(a);
16   R22 = correlation(b);
17   if (R12>R11 && R21>R22)
18    reverse_move(a,b,ra,rb);
19   else
20   if (R12+R22>R11+R21 && strict==TRUE)
21    reverse_move(a,b,ra,rb);
22  }
23  calculate_regression_coefficients_in_clusters (cl);
24 }
```

The function correlation(cluster) is used to calculate the quality of regression. It may use estimator formulas (4) - other ways to estimate the regression quality are also possible. The main loop (line 8) is trying to check if the overall clustering is good enough. If it is not, two clusters are chosen (line 10). In each cluster algorithm has to find two records - possibly having negative impact on regression quality (line 11). Then records are moved between clusters, and the correlation function is evaluated before and after this operation (lines 12-16). Results are compared, and if they do not fulfill normal or strict condition, records are moved back to native clusters. This algorithm creates requested number of clusters with requested quantity of records in every cluster. The final quantities are the same as created by function add_records_to_clusters(cl). If necessary it is easy to rewrite above algorithm into one that creates clusters with variable quantity of records, by moving only one record between clusters instead of exchanging records.

These algorithms have been experimentally implemented, but further research is still necessary to find better and more efficient forms of sub-algorithms calculate_general_regression_results(), choose_clusters(), choose_record_to_move(), than those used by us. Although above algorithms are not the typical versions of clustering, they are the right and exact answer to network planners needs. The problem of efficiency is not critical here, because of the fact that cellular network planning is done only once - before the new cell starts to operate.

Another approach that we plan to implement for deriving clusters maximizing regression quality for within-cluster records is genetic algorithm. We can build population entities chromosomes in such a way, that each entity represents certain distribution of cells among predefined number of clusters. The sum of regression quality estimators for each cluster defines a fit function. Having such definitions a classic genetic algorithm procedures, as defined inand , may be used. This approach should generate better results than above heuristic method, but the performance maybe worse.

5.5 Association rules

The application of association rules did not show in this case much more than facts revealed by decision trees and clustering. As discretization used by us generated relatively few (three to six) qualitative values, and there were 8, 9 or 10 attributes, the experts of cellular network planning suggested that only rules with support over 10% and confidence over 50% are meaningful. Such rules either confirmed the knowledge previously obtained by C4.5 tree or clustering or were similar to the experts' engineering intuition. For example association rules confirmed that cells that have large area usually have little traffic, and small cells have relatively more traffic - because they are typically within cities.

5.6 Neural networks approach

Members of the data mining team applied also some artificial intelligence tools to solve the problem. One of them was simple 3 layer non-linear neural network, built with 50 neurons. Network inputs were percentages of landuses, and output was the traffic level. After training the network, the mean square error of predicted traffic values was about 2 erlangs, while average traffic in a cell is equal or a little over 3 erlangs. However the experiments with the network proved the importance of the population data. Adding the population as an input to the network reduced the error rate by 10-15 %.

6. Conclusions

Although the amount of time for the experiment described in this paper was very limited, and the experiment is still running (as for December 1999), it has brought about some interesting outcome. Main results were in this case all the obtained clusters and decision trees with the calculations of multiple regression coefficients and error estimators. All this knowledge is ready to use by the network planning engineers for the purpose of planning new base stations and splitting existing cells. Even more immediate and spectacular results were changes in landuse classification that were made soon after the results of clustering and regression trees were presented by us to the planning engineers. The most important attribute in decision tree appeared to be landuses 5 (roads, concrete, parks) and 6 (suburbs). Experts were surprised finding out that landuse 5 has so decisive role in distribution of traffic. It turned out that the definition of this landuse is too general, and in future planning it will have to be split into two or more subclasses.

Another outcome of the experiment was noticing the importance of discretization methods for such data mining tasks. First applied discretization method was simple use of quartiles. Other preliminary methods used by us distributed records into sets of the same quantity for every attribute. The difficulty with such discretization is that it was useless for some attributes (those having mostly zero values). Because of this, another step was discretization for only these values that are not zero, and appending zero as additional class - in this way quartiles discretization results in five discretized values. Attributes that were equal zero proved to be very important in decision tree tests. For example cell that had no landuse type 6 pixels was mostly classified as 'rural'and therefore with below-average traffic.

Another discretization tool that was used in this experiment was based on research results from Warsaw University [6]. We tested mostly chi-square method that for some, but not all of the attributes, seemed to be much better than quartiles - the purity of a decision tree was better by 10%. This example proves that it is still need for new methods in mining numeric databases. To obtain rules or trees the attributes have to be discretized, and this still means some loss of information. It would be good to find methods of knowledge discovery for quantitative data, that does not need discretization - and it is another topic for future deeper research that is pointed out by this experiment.

The experiment also proved data mining reputation as an area where multi-methodology approach is common and advantageous. Many different techniques coexisted and were mutually supporting - no matter if they were from machine learning field, statistics or artificial intelligence area. For best support for planning traffic in designed cells all obtained models will be used. Four proposed by our team models are : decision tree with multiple regression, k-means clustering with multiple regression, regressional clustering (see 5.4), neural networks. Combining above models should help cellular network engineers to predict with traffic maximal accuracy.

This experiment also proved, that automatic knowledge discovery is a very promising tool also in purely technical applications. As we already mentioned, data mining is still perceived as mostly marketing and business decision tool, yet we think that experiments with applying data mining methodology to technical problems such as process control, systems planning etc. can be very advantageous, and represent an interesting and challenging research opportunity.

Acknowledgments : We would like to thank our scientific supervisors - prof. Mieczysław Muraszkiewicz and prof. Henryk Rybinski - and also other members of Data Mining Team for support and valuable discussions.

References

[1] Mattison, R. (1997): Data Warehousing and Data Mining for Telecommunications. Artech House Computer Science Library

[2] Keim, D. (1999): Clustering Methods for Large Databases: From the Past to the Future. SIGMOD'99 Conference Tutorial

[3] Statsoft Inc. (1999): Electronic Statistics Textbook. Tulsa

[4] Lindgren, Bernard W. (1976): Statistical Methods. McMillan Publishing

[5] Berry M. J. A., Linoff G.(1997): Data Mining Techniques : For Marketing, Sales, and Customer Support. John Wiley & Sons

[6] Skowron A., Nguyen S. H. (1995): Quantization of Real Value Attributes.Scientific Report. Warsaw University of Technology

[7] Goldberg D.E. (1989): Genetic Algorithms in Search, Optimization and MachineLearning. Addison-Wesley

[8] Michalewicz Z. (1992): Genetic Algorithms + Data Structures = Evolution Programs. Springer Verlag, Berlin Heidelberg New York

SBL-PM: A Simple Algorithm for Selection of Reference Instances in Similarity Based Methods

Karol Grudziński and Włodzisław Duch

Department of Computer Methods, Nicholas Copernicus University,
Grudziądzka 5, 87-100 Toruń, Poland.
E-mail: kagru,duch@phys.uni.torun.pl

Abstract. SBL-PM is a simple algorithm for selection of reference instances, a first step towards building a partial memory learner. A batch and on-line version of the algorithm is presented, allowing to find a compromise between the number of reference cases retained and the accuracy of the system. Preliminary experiments on real and artificial datasets illustrate these relations.

1 Introduction

The **SBL** system (Similarity Based Learner) is a set of computer programs encompassing many methods which are based on evaluation of similarity between the case under evaluation and reference cases constructed from the training library. A unified framework for similarity based methods (SBM) has been presented recently [1,2]. Methods belonging to this framework include the k–Nearest Neighbor (k–NN) algorithm and it's extensions, methods originating from pattern recognition and machine learning (instance based learning, memory based learning), as well as some neural network methods, such as the multi–layer perceptron networks (MLP) or networks based on radial–basis functions (RBF). All these methods may be viewed as examples of similarity based methods based on specific parameterization of the $p(C_i|\mathbf{X}; M)$ posterior classification probability, where the model M involves all procedures and parameters that are optimized in a given method.

Within the SBM framework we have implemented many variants of the k–NN algorithm with optimization of the number of neighbors k, various functions for weighting of their influence, various parameterizations of the similarity (distance) functions, several methods that automatically assign weights to input attributes (based on minimization of the cost function or on searching in the weight space) and methods for selection of the most important attributes [3]. Currently our research is focused on neural network-like implementations of the SBM methods [4] and on various algorithms aiming at speeding up the calculations.

Selection of the reference cases is an important issue in all similarity-based methods. Reducing the size of the training set leads to minimization of the memory requirements and faster classification, usually at slight expense of prediction accuracy on test cases. Eliminating redundant cases and leaving only the most interesting prototypes allows to understand why an unseen case was classified to a particular class by analyzing the prototypes that were selected in the SBM method. Such analysis may sometimes replace the need for logical analysis of the data, providing an alternative to the rule-based classifiers. SBL-PM, the algorithm proposed in this paper, is a new addition to the set of SBM framework programs. The algorithm is described in the next section. In the third section preliminary empirical tests to evaluate its performance and measure it's ability to reduce the size of a reference set are presented, and the last section concludes this paper.

2 Selection of the Reference Instances

In the simplest case the SBM classification algorithm may include all training cases as reference vectors. For several reasons it is not a good solution:

1. If the training set is very large most of the cases have no influence on classification; including them decreases only the computing performance of the algorithm.
2. If there is noise in data or the training set contains wrongly classified instances decreasing the number of reference vectors may increase the prediction ability of the system on unseen cases.
3. Large number of reference instances do not allow to identify interesting prototypes, making it difficult to understand the structure of the data.
4. If the number of the training instances is quite small it may be worthwhile to include virtual reference cases or to optimize the existing reference cases.

The first group of methods, which should work well for large datasets, is based on clusterization techniques. One has to select a relatively small reference set from the training cases laying near the centers of clusters. Such methods have been implemented in the Feature Space Mapping (FSM) network to select the initial prototypes [5,6] that are further optimized. FSM also belongs to the similarity-based method framework, but its algorithm is aimed at modeling the probability density functions and is more complex than most of the SBL algorithms.

The SBL-PM algorithm proposed here in principle can be used with any classification system, but because of the performance reasons it has been used so far only with the classical k–Nearest–Neighbor method. The algorithm is summarized below:

1. Set the partial memory of the system (reference set) to the entire training set, $\mathcal{R}=\mathcal{T}=\{\mathbf{R}_i\}, i = 1..N$.

2. Set the target accuracy Δ to Δ_1 obtained from the leave-one-out test on $\mathcal{T}$.

3. Set the lowest accuracy Δ_m that should be considered.

4. Define the δ parameter determining steps in which the target accuracy Δ is lowered, for example $\delta = 0.05$.

    (a) Until $\Delta < \Delta_m$

        i. For i=1 to N

        ii. Select one vector $\mathbf{R}_i$ from $\mathcal{R}$ and set the temporary reference set to $\mathcal{R}'=\mathcal{R}-\mathbf{R}_i$.

        iii. Using the leave-one-out test and the current reference set $\mathcal{R}'$ calculate the prediction accuracy A_c on the whole training set $\mathcal{T}$.

        iv. If $A_c \geq \Delta$ set $\mathcal{R}=\mathcal{R}'$.

    (b) Set $A_e(\Delta) = A_c$ to record the accuracy at the end of this step.

    (c) Set $\mathcal{R}(\Delta)=\mathcal{R}$ to remember reference vectors at this stage.

    (d) Change $\Delta \leftarrow \Delta - \delta$.

5. Select the references obtained for the highest $A_e(\Delta)$.

Vectors are sequentially eliminated from the reference set unless the classification accuracy drops below the target accuracy Δ. Since Δ is set to the leave-one-out accuracy Δ_1 on the entire training set $\mathcal{T}$ this algorithm should not degrade the results of the k-NN classifier – in the worst case it will leave all training vectors as references. The threshold value Δ is lowered in several steps δ, allowing for some degradation of the performance as a penalty for reduction of the reference set. Displaying the function $A_e(\Delta)$ allows to select the optimal value of Δ, depending on our goal. The final reference set should be significantly smaller than the original training set with minimal degradation of the prediction accuracy.

The Δ parameter controls the number of reference cases that remain in the partial memory. We have used cumulative accuracy estimation here. Since the accuracy is decreased in small steps δ important references that may significantly decrease the accuracy, are not removed from the reference set. If the δ steps are not sufficiently small an additional parameter specifying the allowed threshold of A_c decrease due to the removal of a single reference may be specified.

SBL-PM procedure is repeated for several values of Δ to find a good compromise between classification accuracy and the number of reference vectors. If our goal is to maximize performance, estimation of the predicted accuracy $A_e(\Delta)$ should combine results $A_t(\Delta)$ obtained for the rejected vectors, i.e those in the $\mathcal{T}-\mathcal{R}$ set, and results $A_r(\Delta)$ for the reference vectors $\mathcal{R}$. Accuracy $A_r(\Delta)$ for the reference vectors may only be estimated using the leave-one-out test. The goal of the reference selection algorithm is to obtain a small number of non-redundand reference cases. However, if all N_r references are non-redundant the accuracy $A_r(\Delta)$ may be quite low. Thus for sufficiently small Δ that corresponds to a small number of references, $A_t(\Delta)$ estimation should be used, while for $\Delta \approx \Delta_1$ the $A_r(\Delta)$ estimation is also important.

In the k-NN method selection of the number of neighbors k has strong influence on the final number of reference vectors and therefore k should be set before the selection procedure. Additional parameters (such as the selection and weighting of features or parameterization of the similarity function) may be optimized on the training set after the references are fixed. The order of optimization may be important for performance of the final system. Finding an optimal order of various optimizations in the SBM systems is still an open research issue.

The off-line SBL-PM procedure described above requires an access to all vectors in the training set T in the batch mode. In the on-line version of the method the system has to decide whether a new training case $\mathbf{X}_k$, coming from the input stream, should be added to the reference set (partial memory of past cases). An obvious approach, used for example in the IB2 procedure [7], is to check whether the new instance $\mathbf{X}_k$ is correctly classified using the reference set $\mathcal{R}$ created so far, and add $\mathbf{X}_k$ to $\mathcal{R}$ only if it is not handled correctly. To make this algorithm resistant to noise one may introduce a "candidate reference" vectors, that are included in $\mathcal{R}$ only on the preliminary basis. Candidate reference vectors $\mathbf{R}_c$ are then checked in the batch selection step described above, repeated after a specified number of references is created. In this approach the number of reference vectors is initially growing and when it becomes too large it is reduced. Partial memory of the system tries to match the complexity of the classification model to the complexity of the incoming data. The on-line SBL-PM algorithm looks as follows:

1. Set the maximum number of reference vectors N_{max}^r and the maximum number of training vectors N_{max}^t.
2. Take the first incoming vector $\mathbf{X}_1$ as the first reference $\mathcal{R}= \{\mathbf{X}_1\}$ and as the first training vector $T= \{\mathbf{X}_1\}$.
3. Repeat for all incoming vectors $\mathbf{X}_k$:
   (a) Add the incoming vector $\mathbf{X}_k$ to the training set T created so far.
   (b) Determine the class $C(\mathbf{X}_k)$ of this vector using the reference set $\mathcal{R}$ created so far.
   (c) If $C(\mathbf{X}_k)$ is not correct add $\mathbf{X}_k$ to the current $\mathcal{R}$.
   (d) If $N_r \geq N_{max}^r$ or $N_t \geq N_{max}^t$, where N_r (N_t) is the number of vectors in $\mathcal{R}$ (T), then
      i. Perform the batch step reducing $\mathcal{R}$.
      ii. Empty the training set T.

The SBL-PM algorithm in the on-line version builds a partial memory system, forgetting the references that did not appear for a longer time. The N_{max}^r and N_{max}^t values should be sufficiently large to avoid forgetting important reference cases. N_{max}^t is called the length of the growing epoch – it sets the upper limit for the number of incoming vectors that are evaluated between two batch reductions. For large N_{max}^t this algorithm may become computationally expensive (due to the batch reduction costs), therefore another approach is recommended, allowing for smaller N_{max}^r and N_{max}^t values.

References that survive several batch reductions are given an extra importance and should not be removed for a longer period. In the Feature Space Mapping neural network [5,6] a "mass" index is used for each prototype, counting how many vectors are correctly classified thanks to the contribution of this prototype. The same approach may also be used in the on-line SBL-PM algorithm to keep important references.

The advantage of the SBL-PM approach is its simplicity, therefore it may be used as a reference against more sophisticated methods (cf. the GIGA algorithm in which genetic algorithm is used for selection of reference set [8]). The high computational costs is a disadvantage: in the batch version classification of all N training samples T has to be repeated about N times to get the final reference set, while in the on-line version only N_r times. One way to speed up the batch algorithm is to remove groups of vectors rather than single ones. Reduced reference set leads to a lower computational cost during further optimization of the parameters of the SBL system and during actual classification, saving time and memory.

3 Experimental Results

The performance of the batch SBL-PM algorithm for the k-NN method is illustrated first on the Iris example. This classic benchmark data has been taken from the UCI repository [9] and contains 3 classes (Iris Setosa, Virginica and Versicolor flowers), 4 attributes (measurements of leaf and petal widths and length), 50 cases per class. The entire Iris dataset has been shown here (Fig. 1) in two dimensions, x_3 and x_4, which are much more informative the other two (cf. [10]). In Fig 2. the reference set obtained by taking the value of Δ from the leave-one-out test on the entire data and running the SBL-PM procedure for $k = 1$ is displayed. Only 6 reference vectors remained.

For $k = 1$ in the 10-fold stratified cross-validation test repeated 10 times on the Iris dataset the classical k-NN classifier gave 95.8% accuracy, with 0.3% variance. In the same test SBL-PM with $k = 1$ gave 95.3% accuracy (an insignificant decrease), with variance 1.7%. On average 6.7 reference vectors were used, which is only about 4% of the size of the training base (in 10-fold cross-validation the number of training cases is 135). A single Iris Setosa prototype is sufficient to perfectly account for this class.

For $k = 10$ in the same crossvalidation tests standard k-NN gives 97.0% accuracy, with 0.9% variance, while SBL-PM gives 95.3% $\pm$ 1.4% using on average 22.7 cases (about 17% of the training set). For larger k the minimum number of prototype vectors is equal k divided by the number of classes – in this case at least 4 vectors are necessary to have a majority of neighbors from one class. Since our goal is to illustrate the reference selection algorithm rather than obtain the best results we do not present detailed comparisons for the Iris dataset with results obtained by other classification systems. Due to

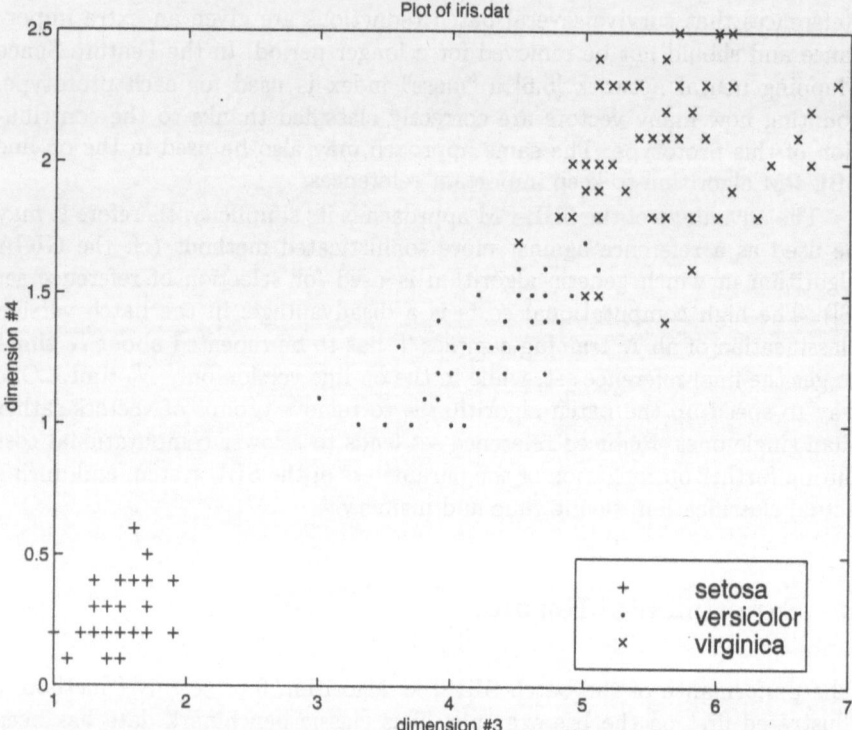

Fig. 1. Original 150 Iris data vectors displayed using the last two features.

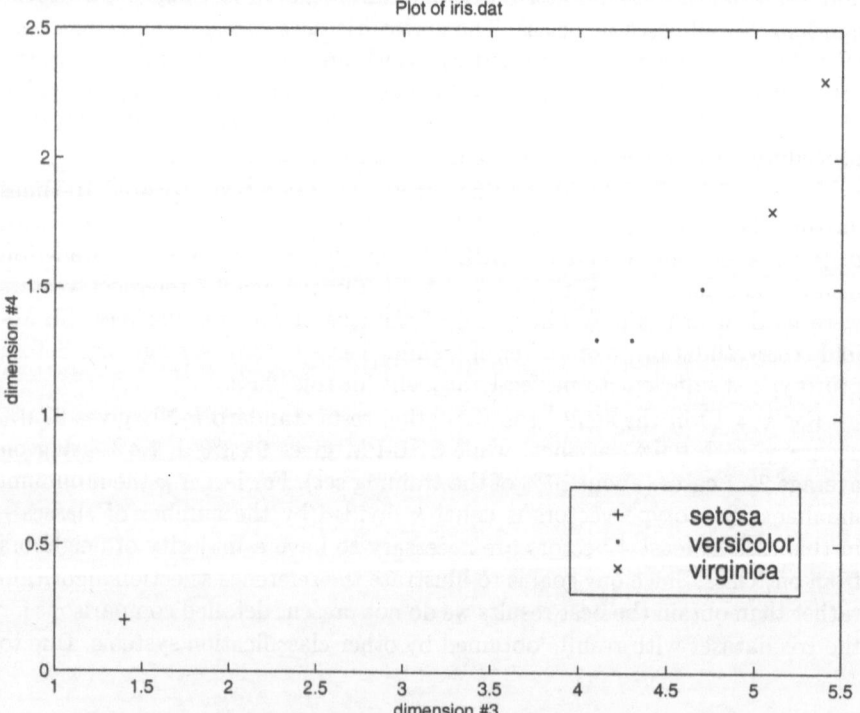

Fig. 2. 6 reference vectors left after the SBL-PM batch procedure.

the noisy character of the data the limit in the leave-one-out or crossvalidation tests is about 98% [10].

Another set of experiments was done on the 3 Monk datasets [11]. On this artificial data SBM gives good results (100% of correct answers on the first problem, 85% on problem 2, and over 97% on problem 3) only if feature selection and/or weighting is included [3]. We do not perform feature selection here, illustrating only the effect of selection of references on the performance. The Monk problems are more suitable for rule-based classification systems than for SBM systems that on real, noisy data work frequently better than any other systems (cf. [12]).

For $k = 1$ on Monk1 (2 classes, 124 training cases, 432 in test set) standard k-NN gives 85.9% while SBL-PM for the same value of k gives 70.6%, a significant decrease in prediction ability on unseen cases. The reference set contains only 10 cases, which constitutes only 2.3% of the entire training set. For Monk2 dataset (2 classes, 169 training cases, 432 in test set) standard k-NN for $k = 1$ gives 76.6% on the test set while SBL-PM gives 64.6% with only 18 reference cases (11% of the training set). Also in this case the decrease of prediction ability is significant. For Monk3 dataset (2 classes, 122 training, 432 testing cases) standard k-NN gives 90.1% on test set while SBL-PM gives 85.0% on test using only 11 instances (2.5% of the training set).

Poor results of the above experiments are due to the poor leave-one-out results on the training partition. Increasing the value of Δ above the value taken from the leave-one-out procedure improves the results significantly but the algorithm uses more cases in partial memory. Setting the value of Δ to 90% instead of 85.9% SBL-PM on Monk1 dataset gives 80.3% on test set using 36 cases (29%) of the size of training set) and for $\Delta = 95\%$ we obtained 83.1% on test set using 52 cases (42% of the size of the training set). For Monk2 for $\Delta = 80\%$ SBL-PM gave 70.4% on test set using 50 cases (approximately 30% of the size of the training set). For Monk3 for $\Delta = 90\%$ SBL-PM gave 88.4% on test set using 20 cases (16.4% of the size of the training set).

4   Conclusions

A preliminary implementation of the SBL-PM algorithm creating the reference set of cases (partial memory) in similarity-based methods (SBM) has been described. The procedure may be used in the batch or on-line mode, allowing to find a compromise between the number of reference cases retained and the accuracy achieved. It can be combined with other procedures (such as the feature weighting and selection procedures) and parameter optimizations (such as the distance-related parameters) to create SBM system with partial memory. Our goal is to implement mechanisms of different type – optimization of the distance functions, weighting functions, scaling and selection of features, and many other procedures, in one program. This will enable us to search, in space of available models, for the most appropriate model for a given data. The SBM framework is quite rich, containing many possibilities that have not been explored so far. Interaction of different optimization and selection procedures has not been addressed yet. For example, selection of the reference set may be done before, after or simultaneously with selection of the best k, selection of features or weighting of features.

The limited empirical evidence presented in previous section indicates that for real data with continuos attributes the number of references may be significantly reduced without loss of accuracy (Iris data), while for artificial data (symbolic Monk problems) the loss of accuracy may be significant. Tests to find out if the combination of the selection of references and attributes will allow to preserve high accuracy are being conducted. Generalization abilities and the degree of the memory resources reduction offered by the SML-PM algorithm should be compared to other partial memory systems like IB2 [7] or AQ-PM [13]. Strategies to determine representative examples from the input stream may follow the IB2 procedure [7] or an on-line variant of clusterization methods used for initialization of neural methods [6]. Optimization of individual vectors in the spirit of LVQ (Learning Vector Quantization) methods is an obvious next step that should be considered. A lot of theoretical and experimental work remains to be done before we will understand in details the optimal way of selection of the reference cases in the SBM framework.

Acknowledgments: Support by the KBN, grant 8 T11F 014 14, is gratefully acknowledged.

References

1. Duch W. (1998) A framework for similarity-based classification methods, Intelligent Information Systems VII, Malbork, Poland, June 1998, pp. 288-291
2. Duch W., Grudziński K. (1999) Search and global minimization in similarity-based methods, Int. Joint Conf. on Neural Networks, Washington, July 1999, paper no. 742
3. Duch W., Grudziński K. (1999) Weighting and selection of features. Intelligent Information Systems VII, Ustroń, Poland, 14-18 June 1999, pp. 32-36
4. Duch W., Grudziński K. The weighted k-NN method with selection of features and its neural realization, 4th Conf. on Neural Networks and Their Applications, Zakopane, May 1999, pp. 191-196
5. Duch, W., Diercksen, G.H.F. (1995) *Feature Space Mapping as a universal adaptive system*, Computer Physics Communication **87**, 341-371
6. Duch W., Adamczak R., Jankowski, N. (1997) Initialization of adaptive parameters in density networks, 3rd Conf. on Neural Networks, Kule, Oct. 1997, pp. 99-104
7. Aha D., Kibler D., Albert M. (1991) Instance-based learning algorithms, Machine Learning **6**: 37-66
8. Fuchs M. (1996) Optimized nearest-neighbor classifiers using generated instances. LSA-96-02E Technical Report, Learning Systems & Applications Group, Univeristy of Kaiserslautern, Germany
9. Mertz C.J., Murphy. P.M. (1999) UCI repository of machine learning databases, http://www.ics.uci.edu/pub/machine-learning-data-bases.

10. Duch, W., Adamczak, R., Grąbczewski, K. (in print) Methodology of extraction, optimization and application of crisp and fuzzy logical rules. IEEE Transactions on Neural Networks.

11. Thrun S.B. *et al.* (1991) The MONK's problems: a performance comparison of different learning algorithms. Carnegie Mellon University, CMU-CS-91-197

12. Duch, W., Adamczak, R., Grąbczewski, K., Żal G., Hayashi, Y. (1999) Fuzzy and crisp logical rule extraction methods in application to medical data. Computational Intelligence and Applications – Springer Studies in Fuzziness and Soft Computing, Vol. 41, ed. P.S. Szczepaniak, pp. 593-616

13. Michalski R. (1999) AQ-PM: A System for Partial Memory Learning. Intelligent Information Systems VII, Ustroń, Poland, June 1999, pp. 70-79

Geometrical Approach to a Coherent Set of Operational Definitions

Andrzej Ossowski[1] and Jan M. Żytkow[2,3]

[1] IPPT, Warsaw
[2] Computer Science Department, UNC Charlotte, Charlotte, N.C. 28223
[3] Institute of Computer Science, Polish Academy of Sciences
aossow@ippt.gov.pl ; zytkow@uncc.edu

Keywords: operational definition, measurement procedure, real-world algorithm, differential geometry, map, atlas, homeomorphism, equivalent definitions, scientific law.

Abstract. Knowledge representation which is internal to computer lacks empirical meaning so it is insufficient for the investigation of the external world. Operational definitions are necessary to provide empirical meaning of concepts, but they were largely ignored by the research on automation of discovery and in AI. Operational definitions can be viewed as algorithms that operate in the real world. Each provides a mapping from objects to numbers. Such mappings prompt an analogy with geometry of differential manifolds. We discuss philosophical foundations of the analogy between geometry and object descriptions by many operationally defined concepts. Many operational definitions that are needed for one concept are analogous to many local maps in an atlas on a differentiable manifold. Conceptual framework of differential manifolds can be used to define the notion of procedure equivalence, as well as the requirement that all operational definitions of the same concept must form a coherent set. No set of operational definitions is complete so that expansion of operational definitions is one of the key tasks. Among many possible expansions, only a very special few lead to a satisfactory growth of scientific knowledge. The selection criteria can be represented in the framework of differential manifolds.

1 Sets of operational definitions correspond to maps over differentiable manifolds

Sophisticated knowledge is required in order to develop measurement methods in advanced empirical sciences. It is particularly important to the growth of scientific knowledge to study new situations for which no known method can measure a particular quantity. For instance, we may wish to measure temperatures lower than the capabilities of all existing instruments. Or we want to measure temperature change inside a living cell, as the cell undergoes a specific process.

When no known measurement method applies, new methods must be discovered and linked to the known methods so that they expand the empirical meaning of existing concepts. For instance, a new thermometer must produce measurements on a publicly shared scale of temperature. The actual verification in empirical science is limited to empirical facts. Operational definitions determine all scientific facts; thus they determine the scope of scientific verification. Each independent variable requires a manipulation mechanism which sets a given object or situation to a specified value, while a response value of a dependent variable is obtained by a measurement mechanism. In this paper we focus on measurement procedures.

Earlier (Zytkow, 1999) we argued that research in AI has neglected operational definitions and that formal semantics are insufficient to provide empirical meaning. In the wake of robotic discovery systems, operational semantics must, at the minimum, provide realistic methods to acquire data. We also argued that many operational definitions are needed for each concept and that such procedures must form a coherent set, such that each pair of procedures is linked by a chain of overlapping procedures, which are equivalent in the areas of overlap.

Representation of many measurement methods, which we also call operational definitions, is the central problem in this paper. We adapt the formalism of differential manifolds (Massey, 1967; Wallace, 1968) which uses overlapping maps to express geometry in coordinate systems. In this formalism we represent individual procedures, verify new methods and justify choices among competing methods. We also introduce geometrical interpretation of many procedures and of their areas of overlap. The formalism of numerical homeomorphisms helps to express relations between concepts and laws used in expanding empirical meaning of concepts through new procedures.

In this paper we limit our attention to numerical properties of objects, states and events. The numbers that result from measurements, for instance temperature or distance from the origin of a coordinate system, we call *values* of empirical concepts.

We focus on many procedures for a single concept, and we also consider how procedures link many concepts through the use of scientific laws.

2 Operational definition: a real world algorithm

A very simple example of an operational definition is an algorithm:

```
Soluble(x)
  Put x in water!
  Does x dissolve?
```

As an algorithm, operational definition consists of instructions that prescribe manipulations, measurements and computations on the results of measurements. Iteration can enforce the requirements such as temperature stability at a desired value, which can be a precondition for measurements. Iteration can be also used in making measurements. A loop exit condition such as the equilibrium of the balance, or coincidence of a mark on a measuring rod with a given object, triggers the completion of a step in the measurement process.

It happens that one or another instruction within procedure ψ does not work in a specific situation. In those cases ψ cannot be used. Each procedure may fail for many reasons. Some of these reasons may be systematic. For instance, a given thermometer cannot measure temperatures below -40C because the thermometric liquid freezes, or above certain temperature, when it boils. Let us name the range of physical situations to which ψ applies by R_ψ.

Often, a property is measured indirectly. Consider distance measurement by sonar or laser. The time interval is measured between the emitted and the returned signal. Then the distance is calculated as a product of time and velocity. Let $C(o)$ be the quantity measured by procedure ψ for object o. When ψ terminates, the returned value of C is $f(x_1, ..., x_m)$, where $x_1, ..., x_m$ are the values of different quantities of o and of empirical situation around o, measured or generated by instructions within ψ. f is a computable function on those values.

Our main purpose it to express the knowledge about operational definitions in terms of differential geometry and to show that from the perspective of differential geometry many conditions on the set of operational procedures are "natural".

Consider the class M of all empirically admissible physical objects. Each existing object that is empirically available is represented by a specific element in M, but some elements in M correspond to objects that may exist sometime. Any measurement procedure (operational definition), applies only to a subclass $U \in M$. This corresponds to the locality (limited range) of maps in differential geometry.

Suppose that the collection of quantities $\mathbf{x} = (x_1, ..., x_k)$ describes each object in M. The practical range R_ψ of any procedure ψ, that measures one of x_i in $\mathbf{x}$, should be an open region in R^k, as differential geometry requires topologically open regions. We can agree that ranges of procedures are open, as (1) there are no concrete values which form the boundaries within the range of each procedure, and (2) the values measured close to the boundaries carry larger error and are less trustworthy.

Any collection of operational definitions, one for each quantity (attribute) in $\mathbf{x}$, applicable to each object in $U \in M$, determines a map $\phi : U \to R^k$ which can be interpreted as a local coordinate system on the space M.

Since maps ϕ must be mutually unique (1-1) functions, the space M can be viewed as a space of (1) abstraction classes of objects identical with respect to the set of attributes $\mathbf{x}$. But a theoretically more adequate interpretation of M to goes beyond (1) and considers a larger space (2) of all possible classes of objects, each class mapped on one possible combination of values $\mathbf{x}$.

3   Set of procedures as atlas of local maps

In everyday situations distance can be measured by a yard-stick or a tape. But a triangulation method may be needed for objects divided by a river. Triangulation can be also applied to measurement of distance from the Earth to the Sun and the Moon. Then, after we have measured the diameter of the Earth orbit around the Sun, we can use triangulation to measure distances to many stars.

But there are stars for which the difference between the angle measured at the opposite sides of Earth's orbit are non-measurably small, so another method of distance measurement is needed. Cefeids are some of the stars within the range of distance measured by triangulation. They pulsate and their maximum absolute brightness varies according to the logarithm of periodicity. Another law, determined on Earth and applied to stars claims that the perceived brightness of a constant light source diminishes with distance d as $1/d^2$. This law jointly with the law for cefeids allows us to determine the distance to cefeids beyond the range of triangulation. This way we can also measure the distance to galaxies in which individual cefeids are visible.

For such galaxies the Hubble Law was empirically discovered. It claims proportionality between the distance and red shift in the lines of hydrogen spectrum. The Hubble Law is used to determine the distance of the galaxies so distant that cefeids cannot be distinguished. Red shift is measured and then the distance is determined by the use of Hubble Law.

Similarly, while a gas thermometer applies to a large range of states, in very low temperatures any gas freezes or gas pressure becomes non-measurably small. Another thermometer, applied in those situations measures magnetic susceptibility of paramagnetic salts and uses Curie-Weiss Law to compute temperature. Gas thermometer has other limitations, too. There are high temperatures in which no vessel can hold a gas, or states in which the inertia of gas thermometer has unacceptable influence on the measured temperature. Measurements of thermal radiation can be used in the former case while electrical resistance in the latter.

Our examples of distance and temperature demonstrate that measurements of each quantity (more generally, each concept) require a set of operational definitions. That applies to any measured quantity in $\mathbf{x}$. Consider an object o in M and a set of operational definitions Ψ suitable for measurements of all quantities in $\mathbf{x}$. Those definitions apply to a set of objects R_Ψ that includes o. Since it is typical that many procedures apply to the same object, they yield many overlapping maps. Since many measurement procedures for one quantity in $\mathbf{x}$ are needed to cover the entire M, a collection (atlas) of local maps (coordinate systems) are needed to cover as much of the space M as possible. The atlas can vary in one more dimension: different measurement scales for each single quantity. But in this paper we do not consider different measurement scales.

We can hypothesize that, in the limit, all objects belonging to M can be described by an atlas of maps that cover the whole space M. In such a case a natural topology can be induced on the space M by using standard topological procedures. The natural topology on M is the weakest topology for which all maps ϕ are homeomorphisms. In practice, only a part of the global atlas is available. Still, the same topological procedure allows us to describe the topology of that part of M covered by the available maps.

4 Methods are linked by equivalence

Consider two operational definitions ψ_1 and ψ_2 that measure the same quantity C. When applied to the same objects, their results should be empirically equivalent within the accuracy of measurement. If ψ_1 and ψ_2 provide different results on a class of objects, one or both must be adjusted until their empirical equivalence is regained.

From the antiquity it has been known that triangulation provides the same measurement results, within the limits of measurement error, as a direct use of measuring rod or tape. But in addition to the empirical study of equivalence, procedures can be compared with the use of empirical theories and equality of their results may be proven.

Triangulation uses two angles in a triangle and the side adjacent to both angles. The length of that side is known, perhaps measured by yardstick. A basic theorem of Euclidean geometry justifies theoretically the consistency of two methods: by the use of yard-stick and by triangulation. To the extent in which Euclidean geometry is valid in the physical world, whenever we make two measurements of the same distance, one using a tape while the other using triangulation, the results are consistent.

Let us consider any two maps ϕ_i, ϕ_j on M such that their domains U_i, U_j overlap. As we discussed it earlier, each map is made by application of many operational procedures, one per quantity in $\mathbf{x}$. The maps belonging to one atlas should be empirically equivalent i.e. they should uniquely describe the space M within the intersection of regions $U_i \vee U_j$. This condition requires that the composition map $\phi_i * (\phi_j)^{-1}$ as a function from R_{U_j} onto R_{U_i} is a homeomorphism and the number k of independent coordinates determined by various maps on M should be the same. If all maps of the atlas on M satisfy the above conditions the space of objects M becomes a topological manifold of dimension k over R^k. In practical applications it is convenient to assume differentiability of all maps. Then the space of objects becomes a differentiable manifold over R^k.

In summary, the correct description of a class of objects M by a set of local attributes is equivalent to the existence of the corresponding topological/differentiable manifold structure on the space of objects M.

5 A coherent set of procedures and a connected topological space

We have considered several procedures that measure distance. But distance can be measured in many other ways. Even the same method, when applied in different laboratories, varies in details. How can we determine that different measurement procedures define the same physical concept? Procedures can be coordinated by the requirements of empirical and theoretical equivalence in the areas of common application. However, we must also require that each two methods are connected by a chain of overlapping methods.

Definition: A set $\Psi = \{\psi_1, ..., \psi_n\}$ of operational definitions is coherent **iff** for each i, j = 1,...,n

(1) ψ_i is empirically equivalent with ψ_j. Notice that this condition is trivially satisfied when the ranges of both operational definitions do not overlap;

(2) there is a sequence of definitions $\psi_{i_1}, ..., \psi_{i_k}$, such that $\psi_{i_1} = \psi_i$, $\psi_{i_k} = \psi_j$, and for each $m = 1, ..., k-1$ the ranges of ψ_{i_m} and $\psi_{i_{m+1}}$ intersect.

The measurements of distance in our examples form such a coherent set. Rod measurements overlap with measurements by triangulation. Different versions of triangulation overlap with one another. The triangulation applied to stars overlaps with the method that uses cefeids, which in turn overlaps with the method that uses Hubble Law.

Similarly, the measurements with gas thermometer are used to calibrate the alcohol and mercury thermometers in their areas of joint application. For high temperatures, measurements based on the Planck Law of black body radiation overlap with the measurements based on gas thermometers. For very low temperatures, the measurements based on magnetic susceptibility of paramagnetic salts overlap with measurements with the use of gas thermometer.

The requirement of coherence can be interpreted in terms of differential geometry on the manifold M. Any atlas on M, by definition, is a collection of coherent maps ϕ_i, $i \in I$. The coordinate changes $\phi_i * \phi_j^{-1}$ are homeomorphisms or dipheomorphisms.)

Within the framework of differential geometry a concept applicable to the class of objects M can be identified with continuous/differentiable real functions on the manifold M. In fact, if C is a differentiable function on the manifold M, then local representation of the function in a map ϕ_i takes the form

$$\psi_i(\mathbf{x}_i) = C * \phi_i^{-1}(\mathbf{x}_i),$$

where $\mathbf{x}_i = (x_1, x_2, ..., x_k)_i$ is a set of local independent attributes. The map $\psi_i(\mathbf{x})$ is nothing but a local (operational) definition that enables to compute values of the concept C locally on M within the domain of the map. It is easy to see that the set of operational definitions $\psi_i(\mathbf{x}_i), i \in I$ is coherent.

Indeed, empirical equivalence of definitions ψ_i, ψ_j with the intersecting ranges is obvious because

$$\psi_i(\mathbf{x}_i) = C * \phi_i^{-1}(\mathbf{x}_i) = C * \phi_i^1 * \phi_i * \phi_j^{-1}(\mathbf{x}_i) = \psi_j(\mathbf{x}_j).$$

Similarly, the existence of the corresponding chain of coherent operational definitions between any two (not intersecting) definitions ψ_i, ψ_j can be deduced directly from the fact that the set of maps $\phi_i, i \in I$ is an atlas on the manifold M and the natural assumption that M is a simply connected topological space. In case when the manifold M is a sum of simply connected components $M_1, M_2, ...$, then each of the components can be interpreted as the space of independent class of objects.

In summary, (1) global concepts that describe properties of all objects are continuous/differentiable real functions on the corresponding manifold M; this applies to each quantity in $\mathbf{x}$; (2) operational definitions are local representations (in local maps on the manifold M) of each global concept C; (3) differential manifolds representing independent classes of real objects are simply connected topological spaces.

6 Laws of science used in operational definitions as geometry constraints

Operational definitions can expand each concept in several obvious directions, towards smaller values, larger values, and values that are more precise. But the directions are far more numerous. Within the range of "room" temperatures, consider the temperature inside a cell, temperature of a state that is fast varying and must be measured every second, or temperature on the surface of Mars. Each of these cases requires different methods. Similarly the concept of distance may be expanded in many directions, for example towards greater accuracy. A scientist may examine the shift of tectonic plates by comparing the distances on the order of tens of kilometers over the time period of a year, when the accuracy is below a millimeter.

Whenever we consider expansion of operational definitions for an empirical concept C to a new range R, the situation is similar:

(1) we can observe objects in R for which C cannot be measured with the needed accuracy;

(2) some other attributes $x_1, ..., x_n$ of objects in R can be measured, or else those objects would not be empirically available;

(3) some of $x_1, ..., x_n$ are linked to C by empirical laws or theories. We can use one or more of those laws in a new method: measure some of $x_1, ..., x_n$ and then use laws to compute the value of C.

Consider the task: determine distance D from Earth to each in a set R of galaxies, given some of the measured properties of R: $x_1, x_2, ..., x_n$. Operational definitions for $x_1, ..., x_n$ are available in the range R. For instance, let x_2 measure the redshift of hydrogen spectrum. Let $D = h(x_2)$ be Hubble Law. The new method is:

```
For a galaxy g, when no individual cefeids can be distinguished:
  Measure the redshift x2 of the light coming from g
  Compute the distance D(Earth, g) as h(x2(g))
```

The same schema can yield other operational definitions that determine distance by properties measurable in a new range, such as yearly parallax, perceived brightness or electromagnetic spectrum.

Some laws cannot be used even though they apply to galaxies. Consider $D = a/\sqrt{B}$ (B is brightness). It applies even to the most remote sources of light. But B used in the law is the absolute brightness at the source, not the brightness perceived by an observer. Only when we could determine the absolute brightness, we could determine the distance to galaxies by $D = a/\sqrt{B}$.

In terms of manifolds, each law that applies to quantities in **x** is a constraint on geometry in R^k. Hubble Law defines a geometrical constraint in the range where both distance and red shift can be measured independently. Expansion of concept C to a new range R can be viewed as a mapping from the set of distinguishable classes of equivalence with respect to C for objects in R to a set of possible new values of C, for instance, the values larger than those that have been observed with the use of the previous methods. But possible expansions are unlimited. The use of an existing law narrows down the scope of possible concept expansions to the number of laws for which the above algorithm succeeds. But the use of an existing law does not merely reduce the choices, it also justifies them. Which of the many values that can be assigned to a given state corresponds to its temperature? If laws reveal the real properties of physical objects, then the new values which fit a law indicate concept expansion which has a potential for the right choice. In terms of differential geometry we can express the same principle as the principle for preservation of geometrical constraints. If we apply Hubble Law as a definition of distance, we expand the geometrical constraint to a new area of the most remote galaxies. If that definition of distance is sometime confirmed by other measurements, it means that the geometrical constraint is not merely conventional but has empirical contents.

The practical process of expanding the description (measurements) of a given class of objects M with the use of new measurement methods (operational definitions) corresponds to expanding the set of maps on the space M that are consistent with the previous maps in their area of overlap. The necessary condition of finiteness of cognition is the existence of a finite atlas on the manifold M. This condition imposes specific constraints on the manifold. In particular, if the manifold M is compact, then there always exists a finite atlas on M.

Two atlases on the manifold M are said to be equivalent if the union of their sets of maps is also an atlas on M. An atlas on M is said to be complete if no more local maps can be added without loss of the manifold structure on M (the loss of map equivalence). It is interesting that many nonequivalent atlases may exist on a given manifold. Practically this means that there are possible nonequivalent and complete descriptions of the real world.

The geometric interpretation of laws used to form operational definitions is simple. The possibility of expressing one set of attributes by another set of attributes is equivalent to the possibility of coordinate changes locally on the manifold M. The dimensionality of M is less than the dimensionality of the vector of $\mathbf{x}$ of k quantities that apply to objects in M. Empirical numerical equations are simply local representations of certain laws of nature describing the class of objects in M. The question is how can natural laws can be interpreted globally, that means coordinate-free or without local representations? For challenging and detailed answers consider Giles (1964) and Field (1980). In the framework presented in this paper, natural laws describing a given class of real objects determine the topological and differentiable structure of the corresponding manifold M.

References

Field, H. 1980. *Science Without Numbers*, Princeton Univ. Press.

Giles, R. 1964. *Mathematical Foundations of Thermodynamics*, Pergamon, Oxford.

Massey, W.S. 1967. *Algebraic Topology: An Introduction*, Harcourt, Brace & World Inc., New York.

Wallace, A.H. 1968. *Differential Geometry*, W.A.Benjamin, Inc., New York, Amsterdam.

Zytkow, J.M. 1999. Discovery of concept expansions, in *Intelligent Information Systems VIII, Proceedings of the Workshop held in Ustron, Poland, 14-18 June*.

Generating Optimal Repertoire of Antibody Strings in an Artificial Immune System[(ℵ)]

Sławomir T. Wierzchoń

Institute of Computer Science, Polish Academy of Sciences, Warsaw, Poland

Dep. of Computer Science, Białystok University of Technology, Białystok, Poland

e-mail: stw@ipipan.waw.pl

Abstract: In this paper an idea of the artificial immune system (or AIS for brevity) is explained. Restricting to so-called binary AIS, methods for generating a repertoire of lymphocytes of minimal size are reviewed and new algorithm of low space complexity is discussed. Besides, recipes for counting so-called holes, as well as counting the total number of unrecognizable strings are given.

Keywords: Artificial Immune Systems, Anomaly Detection, Receptors Generation

1. Introduction

Careful analysis of biological processes and phenomena has led to many interesting computer applications. Reflecting on fundamental principles of animal behaviour, Norbert Wiener proposed cybernetics - a general framework for studying different aspects of communication and control in living organisms. Imprecise nature of human reasoning and perception gave an impulse to fuzzy sets theory initiated by Lotfi Zadeh. The works by Warren Mc Culloch focused on mathematical formalism describing the behaviour of a single neurone resulted in Rosenblat's perceptron and next, in highly elaborated neural networks. John Holland's genetic algorithms are a resemblance of the basic idea of evolution formulated by Darwin and Lamarck. Molecular computing, initiated by Leonard Adleman, transfers evolutionary concepts into their roots: DNA strands compete in artificially prepared environment and solve complex problems.

Immunology is another branch of biological sciences. Starting from early 70's it becomes a subject of growing interest of mathematicians, physicists and computer scientists. Perelson and Weisbuch in [18] provide an exhaustive review of different models of natural immune system (NIS) as well as a historical perspective of the researches in this field, while edited by Dasgupta volume [6] is

---

[(ℵ)] This work was partly supported by the Technical Univ. of Białystok grant no. S/II/1/98

120

devoted to computer-science oriented applications. The main problem the NIS cope with is that of distinguishing between *self* and *non-self* (called pathogens or *antigens*) proteins. From a computer science perspective the NIS is a complex, self organizing and highly distributed system that has no centralized control and uses learning and memory when solving particular, complex, tasks. The learning process does not require negative examples and the acquired knowledge is represented in explicit form. Such a system has the advantages of classifier systems, [7], neural networks and case-based retrieval, 13]. One should take into account, however, that the field of Artificial Immune Systems (or, AIS) is not a well established discipline. It is too young, and even there is a lack of definite models and theories of the NIS. Nevertheless, it affords interesting metaphor according to which a problem to be solved is treated as an *antigen* and a solution to the problem as an *antibody* (i.e. a protein that detects and destroys the antigen). This metaphor, has found interesting implementations, like: computer virus detection [8], monitoring UNIX processes [9], anomaly detection in time series [5], fault analysis [16], process diagnosis [17], numerical optimization [1], recognizing promoters in DNA sequences [14] or mortgage fraud detection [15].

In this paper we focus on the problem of generating a repertoire of nonredundant antibodies (termed here *receptors*) that can be used in detecting anomalies in a given data set. Here both self and non-self proteins are represented as binary strings of fixed length. This binary representation is commonly used in the literature, cf. [7], [8]. After introducing the method of receptors activation (Sect. 2.1) and defining building blocks for receptors generation (Section 2.2) various methods of constructing the repertoire are discussed (Section 2.3). Section 3 introduces a new algorithm generating complete repertoire of receptors. In Sect. 3.1 a graphical representation of the receptors is proposed. Using this representation, in Sect. 3.2, a simpler method to count so-called holes is given and its generalization to counting the number of all unrecognizable strings from a given strings universe is presented. By the way we obtain a startling result: the set of self strings blocks some templates making impossible to construct some additional (apart of holes) receptors. This means that (at least in small immune systems) we cannot make the probability of detecting an intrusion arbitrarily small (an assumption commonly used in the literature). Section 3.2 is of great practical importance: the algorithms presented here allow to find *in advance* the number of receptors and to determine their quality expressed in the number of unrecognizable strings. Finally, an effective (of low space complexity) algorithm for generating nonredundant receptors repository is presented in Section 3.3.

2. Anomaly detection

The idea of using immunological principles in anomaly detection was proposed in [10]. It can be expressed as the problem of distinguishing *self* from *nonself*, where by *self* we understand all typical ("normal") patterns of activity of a system (or process) or a collection that we wish to protect or monitor and *nonself* is all irregular (or unacceptable) patterns. To solve this problem Forrest and her co-workers developed in [10] a negative-selection algorithm imitating the behaviour of T-lymphocytes in the NIS. It consists of four main steps:

1. Define S as a collection of self patterns.
2. Generate a set of receptors R, such that each $r \in R$ doesn't recognize any self pattern, $s \in S$.
3. Apply R to monitoring data set D.
4. If at least one receptor activates when analyzing information $d \in D$, it means that d manifests anomaly.

The algorithm has a number of features which distinguish it from most other methods (cf. [3] for details): it doesn't require any prior knowledge of anomalies, it uses incomplete but tunable (by varying the threshold τ) detection, and the detection scheme is inherently distributable, i.e. small sections of the protected system can be checked separately by independently created receptor sets. To implement the algorithm we should define: (a) patterns and receptors representation, (b) the method of their activation, (c) the method of receptors generation, and possibly, (d) algorithm efficiency.

In the sequel we will focus on the simplified binary representation of the patterns introduced by Farmer, Packard and Perelson in [7]. That is we will assume that U is the set of all binary strings of length λ; obviously it has $|U| = 2^{\lambda}$ different strings. Both S and R are subsets of U, and the elements of $U - S$ represent antigens. Having defined receptor representation we can discuss the problems of their activation and generation. This is the subject of succeeding subsections.

2.1 Receptors activation

In the NIS lymphocytes, treated here as receptors, detect pathogens by binding to them. Receptors can only be activated by a pathogen, a member of $U - S$, if the receptors similarity (affinity in biological nomenclature) for the pathogen exceeds a certain affinity threshold. Affinity is computed in a way reminiscent from the classical *lock and key* metaphor: two molecules bind if they have complementary shapes. In our framework, the process of a receptor's activation can be defined as follows. Suppose that r and x are two strings such that the former represents receptor and the later represents a protein. We introduce a Boolean function match(r,x) such that match(r,x) = FALSE if $x \in S$ (i.e. s is a self string) and match(r,x) = TRUE if x is an antigen.

There is no unique definition of the match(r,x) function. In the simplest case it can be the Hamming distance between both strings, but here we will use τ-contiguous-bits rule proposed in [11]: match(r,x) = TRUE only if r and x are identical on at least τ contiguous positions, where τ is a given threshold value. If, for instance, $\lambda = 6$, $\tau = 3$ and the strings r (receptor) and x_1, x_2 are of the form $r = 000110$, $x_1= 001100$ and $x_2= 000100$, then match(r,x_1) = FALSE while match(r,x_2) = TRUE, so x_1 is a self pattern and x_2 is an antigen. Other matching rules are discussed in [7] and [14].

2.2 Templates

The idea of a template was introduced in [11]. Roughly speaking, templates are building blocks from which the receptors are constructed.

Let w be a binary string of length τ (τ is the threshold value mentioned in Sect. 2.1). We will consider strings of length λ over the alphabet $\{0,1,*\}$ where $*$ stands for "irrelevant"[1]. By a template $t_{i,w}$ of order τ, we understand a string (of length λ), whose substring of length τ taken from position i equals w, and all the remaining positions of the template are filled by the $*$ symbol. In genetic algorithms terminology (consult e.g. [12]) a template of order τ is a schema of order[2] τ in which all the significant bits are contiguous. For instance, when $\lambda = 6$, $\tau = 3$, $w = 010$ then $t_{1,w} = 010***$, $t_{2,w} = *010**$, $t_{3,w} = **010*$, and $t_{4,w} = ***010$.

The set of all possible templates, denoted T, contains $(\lambda - \tau +1)\cdot2^\tau$ different elements. We split T into two disjoint subsets: T_S consisting of all the templates contained in at least one self string and the set of remaining templates, T_R, used to construct receptor strings. Typically T_S is a relative small fraction of T. Following [2] we will naively[3] represent the set T as the matrix T with 2^τ rows and $(\lambda - \tau +1)$ columns: $T[w,i] = 0$ if $t_{i,w} \in T_S$ and $T[w,i] = 1$ if $t_{i,w} \in T_R$.

Example 1: Let $\lambda = 10$, $\tau = 4$. Given the set of twelve self strings shown in the leftmost column of Table 1, the sets T_S (of self templates) and T_R (of non-self templates) are represented by the table T consisting of 16 rows and 7 columns shown below.

2.3 Existing algorithms for receptors generation

Working with a binary AIS we face the next problem: Having the set S of self strings, generate the set R containing as small as possible receptors which recognize all the antibodies from $U - S$.

---

[1] It is possible to consider strings over an alphabet Σ of m symbols, however we restrict our analysis to the binary systems.

[2] The order of a schema is defined as the number of relevant positions in this schema. For instance if $x_1 = 0000****$ and $x_2 = 00000***$ then $order(x_1) = 4$ and $order(x_2)=5$.

[3] Linked lists or sparse arrays are more efficient representations. We use the matrix representation for its illustrative power only.

S	no	w	T[w,1]	T[w,2]	T[w,3]	T[w,4]	T[w,5]	T[w,6]	T[w,7]
0011000000	0	0000	0	0	1	1	0	0	0
0011010000	1	0001	0	1	0	1	1	1	1
0011110000	2	0010	1	0	1	0	1	1	1
0000010000	3	0011	0	0	1	1	1	1	1
0001010000	4	0100	1	1	0	1	0	1	1
0001000000	5	0101	1	1	0	1	1	1	1
0001110000	6	0110	1	0	1	1	1	1	1
1000010000	7	0111	1	0	0	1	1	1	1
1100010000	8	1000	0	0	1	0	0	0	1
1101000000	9	1001	1	1	1	1	1	1	1
1111000000	10	1010	1	0	1	0	1	1	1
0011100000	11	1011	1	1	1	1	1	1	1
	12	1100	0	1	0	0	0	1	1
	13	1101	0	1	0	1	1	1	1
	14	1110	1	0	0	0	1	1	1
	15	1111	0	1	0	1	1	1	1

Table 1. Matrix T representing the set T_S (of self) and T_R (of nonself) templates

A naive solution of this problem is to generate randomly candidate receptors and then test (*censor*) them to see if they match any self string. If a match is found, the candidate is rejected. This process is repeated until the desired number of receptors is generated. This algorithm resembles the way in which T-cells are recruited in the thymus. It is ineffective, however, because the receptors grow exponentially with the size of self. Denoting P_m the probability that two random strings match at least τ contiguous positions and P_f - the probability that the set of receptors fail to detect an antigen, the time complexity of this algorithm is $O(-\ln(P_f) \cdot |S| / (P_m \cdot (1-P_m)^{|S|})$ and the space complexity is $O(\lambda \cdot |S|)$, cf. [4] for details.

Helman and Forrest proposed in [11] a more efficient algorithm which runs in linear time with the size of self (and receptors). It consists of two stages. First, the set of templates from which receptors can be constructed is identified, and numbering of the templates is established. Next, this numbering is used to construct randomly the receptors. Unfortunately, this way we obtain many redundant receptors. In [2] a greedy algorithm based on the same principles was proposed; it generates better coverage of the string space by placing detectors as far apart as possible. However, its space complexity is of order $O((\lambda - \tau)^2 \cdot 2^\tau$.

3. New algorithm for generating receptors

3.1 Graphical representation of the receptors

Suppose that T_R consists of n templates $t_{1,w}$ ($n=9$ in Example 1). In [19] it was observed that we can construct n binary trees, whose roots are just these templates. A template $t_{i+1,v}$ is a child of $t_{i,w}$, $1 \leq i \leq (\lambda - \tau + 1)$, only if both the templates are identical on the positions $i+1,..,i+\tau-1$. Having such a binary tree we read off subsequent receptors by: (a) fixing a path from the root to a leaf, (b) copying the substring w from the template $t_{1,w}$ to first τ positions of the receptor, and finally, copying on $(\tau+i-1)$-th position, $1 \leq i \leq (\lambda - \tau + 1)$, the last significant bit from the templates $t_{i+1,w}$. To be more concrete consider the next example studied in [2].

Example 2: Suppose that S consists of ten strings: 001100, 001101, 001111, 010001, 010101, 011100, 011111, 100001, 110001, 110100, that is $\lambda = 6$ and $\tau = 3$. The sets T_S and T_R are shown in Table 2 (given later) and Figure 1 shows the binary trees that represent seven receptors: $r_1 = 000110$, $r_2 = 101000$, $r_3 = 101010$, $r_4 = 101011$, $r_5 = 111000$, $r_6 = 111010$, $r_7 = 111011$.

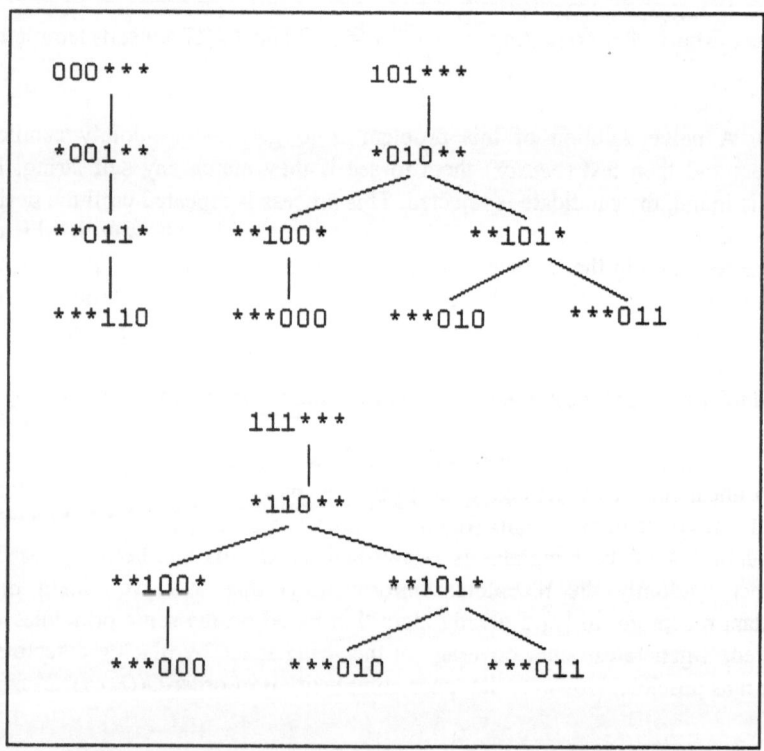

Fig. 1 Binary trees representing receptors from Example 2

Fig. 2 shows a simple procedure allowing generating complete repertoire of the receptors. Here we use the next terms: partial receptor is a string of length $l < \lambda$ obtained by concatenating templates $t_{1,w}, \ldots, t_{i,v}$ where $i = l-\tau+1$. If p is a partial receptor of length l its left child is the template $t_{i+1,z}$ where the last character in z is 0 and its right child is the template $t_{i+1,z'}$ where the last character in z' is 1.

Procedure `IdentifyReceptors`
begin
   Identify all the templates $t_{1,s} \notin T_S$ and write them on a file, say `file1`. Call a member of `file1` a partial receptor (initially its length is just τ).
   while (length of partial receptor p is less than λ) **do**
   begin
      while not (end of `file1`) **do**
         Read a partial receptor, p, and check if the left and right child exists. If the left child exists write on `file2` the string $p+$'0'; if the right child exists write on `file2` the string $p+$'1'.
      end {of **while**}
      Rename `file2` as `file1`.
   end {of **while**}
end

Fig. 2 A pseudocode of the procedure generating full set of receptors

This procedure is ineffective because of two main reasons: (a) there exist partial receptors having no children, and (b) the number of *efficient* receptors is actually smaller than that computed by `IdentifyReceptors`. To explain the last drawback, let us examine Fig. 1. The templates $t_{2,010}$ and $t_{2,110}$ belonging to different trees have common children or more precisely, common subtrees: one rooted at $t_{3,100}$ and the second at $t_{3,101}$. Hence the trees from Fig. 1 can be represented more compactly by the structures shown in Fig. 3.

     Receptors r_3, r_4, r_6 and r_7 contain the template $t_{3,101}$. It is easy to note that the strings containing the template $t_{1,101}$ are recognized by the receptors r_3 and r_4, while the string containing the template $t_{1,111}$ are recognized by r_6 and r_7. Similarly, the receptors containing the template $t_{4,010}$ are recognized by r_3 and r_6, and receptors containing the template $t_{4,011}$ - by r_4 and r_7. Analyzing the "neighbourhood" of the template $t_{3,101}$ we state that the strings that agree with the schema $1*10**$ are detected by the receptors r_3, r_4 if the second position equals 0 or r_6, r_7 if the second position equals 1. Similarly, the strings containing $***01*$ are recognized by the receptors r_3, r_6 if the sixth position equals 0 or r_4, r_7 if the sixth position equals 1. This shows that constructing an effective set of receptors, we must choose (in common subtrees) path ending on different leaves. In our case the effective set of receptors is of the form $\{r_1, r_2, r_3, r_7\}$ or $\{r_1, r_2, r_4, r_6\}$ or $\{r_1, r_3, r_5, r_7\}$ or $\{r_1, r_4, r_5, r_6\}$.

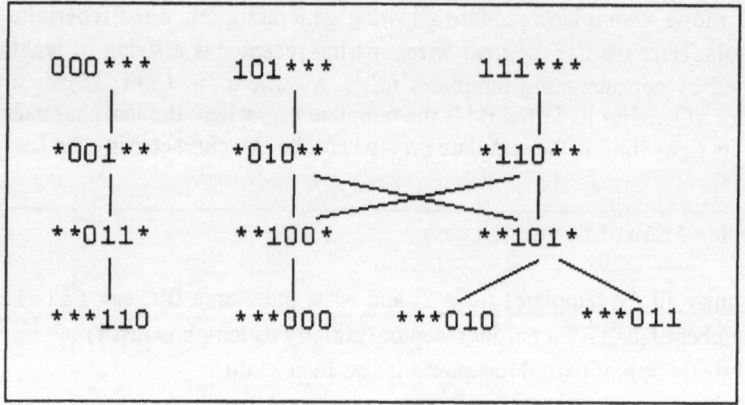

Fig. 3 Compact representation of the receptors from Fig. 1

In the real problems situation slightly complicates. Fig. 4 presents a typical situation: in the original tree (cf. Example 1 with $\lambda=10$, $\tau=4$) common nodes for different paths have been identified. An interested reader can verify that in this situation the minimal set of receptors is obtained by identifying 12 paths starting from the root $0010******$ and ending in the leaves[4]. Theorem 1, proved in [20] summarizes these observations and gives a hint how to create the set of nonredundant receptors.

Theorem 1. Let j be a fixed integer such that $1 \leq j < \lambda-\tau+1$. Let p_1 and p_2 be two partial receptors of length $\tau+j-1$ with identical $\tau-1$ last characters. Denote these characters as tmp. If $tmp+$'0' and $tmp+$'1' are valid templates, then the set of full length receptors obtained from the four receptors p_1+'0', p_1+'1', p_2+'0' and p_2+'1' has the same discriminative power as the set of receptors obtained from the partial receptors $\{p_1+$'0', p_2+'1'$\}$ or $\{ p_1+$'1', p_2+'0'$\}$.

Concerning the first drawback, consider the set T_R from Example 1 and assume we want to create receptors starting from the template $t_{1,0111}$. Its children are $t_{2,1110}$ (left child) and $t_{2,1111}$ (right child). Since $t_{2,1110} \in T_S$, we can search for the children of $t_{2,1111}$ only. But both the children of $t_{2,1111}$ are members of T_S, what means that the templates $t_{1,0111}$ and $t_{2,1111}$ should be excluded from T_R. The problem of how to reduce the original set T_R is discussed in the next section.

---

[4] To simplify the picture, the star symbols are omitted. One should remember that the template on i-th level has $(i-1)$ leading stars and $(\lambda-\tau-i+1)$ stars after the last significant position.

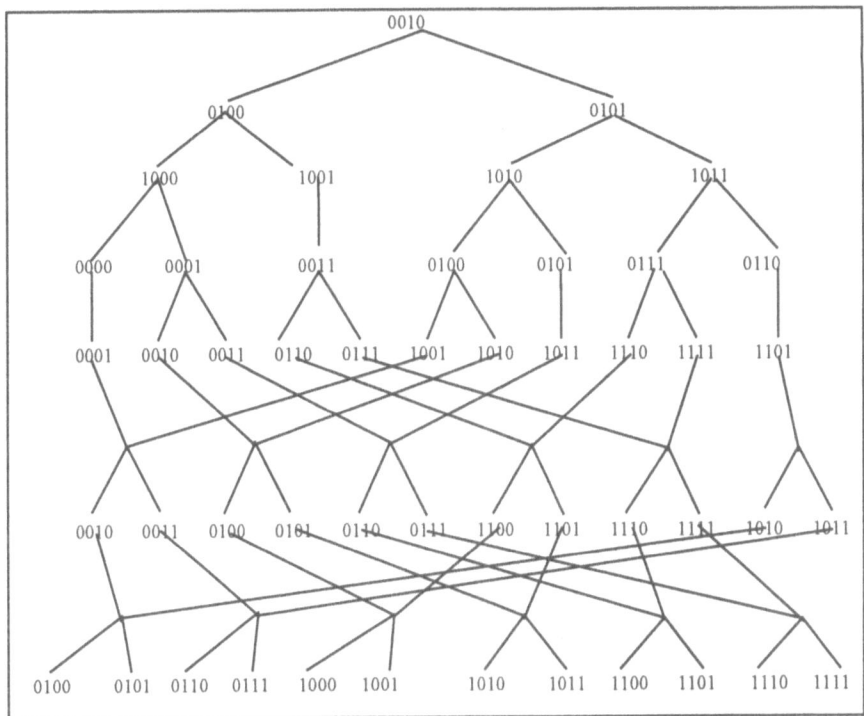

Fig. 4 More realistic representation of the set of detectors

3.2 Counting the set of nondetectable strings

D'haeseleer noted in [2] that the set of all possible receptors is not capable of recognizing all non-self strings. Particularly, if S contains two strings s_1 and s_2 that match each other over $(\tau-1)$ contiguous bits, they may induce two other strings h_1 and h_2 that cannot be detected because any candidate detector would also match either s_1 or s_2; h_1 and h_2 are said to be *holes*. This can be proved using the arguments similar to these exploited in previous subsection.

More precisely, suppose that S contains two strings $s_1 = w_1 w_2 w_3$, $s_2 = w_4 w_2 w_5$, where the length of substring w_2, denoted λ_2, is $(\tau-1) \leq \lambda_2 \leq (\lambda-2)$, substrings w_1 and w_4 are of length $1 \leq \lambda_1 \leq (\lambda-r)$, and substrings w_3 and w_5 are of length $1 \leq \lambda_3 \leq (\lambda-\tau)$, and $\lambda_1 + \lambda_2 + \lambda_3 = \lambda$. Then the strings $h_1 = w_4 w_2 w_3$, $h_2 = w_1 w_2 w_5$, belong to the set $U - S$, but cannot be detected by any of the receptors. To illustrate this phenomena, consider the set of self strings from Example 2, i.e. $\lambda = 6$ and let $\tau = 3$. Let us choose two strings $s_1 = 001101$, $s_2 = 011100$. We observe that the substring w_2 has the form 11. Hence the holes are: $h_1 = 011101$, $h_2 = 001100$. The string h_1 contains the next schemas: $\{011***, *111**, **110*, ***101\}$. The first three schemas are also present in the self string s_2, whereas the last schema is present in the string s_1. This means that each schema used to detect h_1 is contained in the string s_1 or s_2.

To determine the number of holes we can use again the reasoning from previous section. That is we construct a graphical structure, but this time we focus on the templates from the set T_S. Figure 5 presents such a structure for the set S defined above.

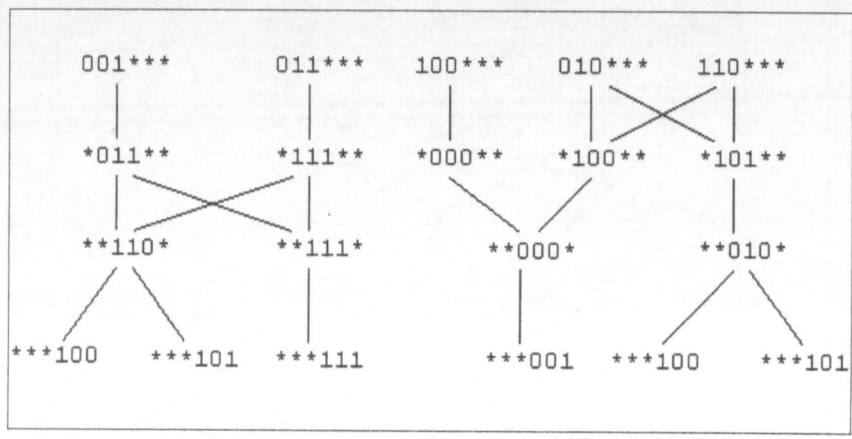

Fig. 5 Graphical representation of the set of holes generated by the set S from Example 2.

To generate the holes we can use the procedure `GenerateReceptors` with minor modification: this time we use only the templates from the set T_S. Since we search for a maximal number of paths from the roots to the leaves, hence we can apply the method proposed in [11]. First we define the table H with entries $H[w,i]$ = 1 - $T[w,i]$[5]. Now if $H[w,i] \neq 0$ (i.e. the template $t_{i,w} \in T_S$) we modify its value according to the equation

$$H[w,i] = H[LeftParent(w),i-1 + H[RightParent(w),i-1]$$

for $i = 2,...,\lambda-\tau+1$. For instance if $w = 101$ then $LeftParent(w) = 010$ and $RightParent(w) = 110$. Table 4 shows the result of using this procedure. Summing up the values from the last column we find that the number of holes equals 13. Note however that, according to Fig. 4, this number includes self strings. Hence the number of strict holes induced by strings from S is 13 - 10 (the cardinality of S) = 3.

---

[5] This method is more effective than that proposed in [2]. Particularly, when the algorithm is implemented with linked lists, its space complexity is $O(|S| \cdot (\lambda-\tau+1)$ where $|S|$ stands for the cardinality of S.

The existence of holes is not quite negative phenomena. They can be treated as manifestation of an "almost" normal behaviour. Besides, it was proved in [3] that all practical matching rules with a constant matching probability (i.e. each detector matches equally many strings and vice vers) can exhibit holes.

$t_{1,w}$	$H[w,1]$	$t_{2,w}$	$H[w,2]$	$t_{3,w}$	$H[w,3]$	$t_{4,w}$	$H[w,4]$
000***	0	*000**	1	**000*	3	***000	0
001***	1	*001**	0	**001*	0	***001	3
010***	1	*010**	0	**010*	2	***010	0
011***	1	*011**	1	**011*	0	***011	0
100***	1	*100**	2	**100*	0	***100	4
101***	0	*101**	2	**101*	0	***101	4
110***	1	*110**	0	**110*	2	***110	0
111***	0	*111**	1	**111*	2	***111	2

Table 2. Counting the number of holes

It appears that the number of unrecognizable strings is in general greater than that computed by the procedure described above. The reason is such that T_R contains inefficient templates. A template $t_{i,w} \in T_R$ is inefficient if either its children or parents belong to T_S. D'haeseleer in [2] proposed a solution to this problem manipulating on the set T_R. Here we propose another solution using only the set T_S which is much smaller than T_R. The procedure FindIneffective shown in Fig. 6 solves this problem. Its effect on the initial set T_R given in Example 1 is shown in Table 3 (new members of T_S are in bold).

Since the set T_R consists now of the effective templates only, counting holes generated by the enriched set T_S we are able to find total number of unrecognizable strings in U given the set S of self strings. In our case the number of unrecognizable strings equals actually 96.

3.3 Generating effective receptors

To identify a subset of relevant receptors in the set of all receptors we must extend the main while-loop of the procedure from Fig. 2. Suppose we have constructed a partial receptor (its length is smaller than λ) and by means of while-step we must merge it with its left and/or right child. If it has only one child, we precede as before. Otherwise, we make use of Theorem 1, that is we must check if current j-th template belongs to more that one tree. To do so we store current templates on a linked list *redundant*. If a current template belong to the list it means that this is the case and we should choose only one path in each tree. The full idea is explained on Fig. 7.

```
Procedure FindIneffective;
begin
    for i:=2 to (λ-τ+1) do
    for all t_{i,w} ∈ T_S do
    begin {remove parents whose children belong to T_S }
        identify parents of the child t_{i,w}; if all the children of the parents belong to T_S,
        move the parents to T_S.
    end;
    for i:=1 to (λ-τ) do
    for all t_{i,w} ∈ T_S do
    begin {remove children whose parents belong to T_S }
        find the children of t_{i,w} and check if the second parent also belongs to T_S ; if
        so, mark both the children as members of T_S..
    end;
    for i:=(λ-τ+1) downto 2 do
    for all t_{i,w} ∈ T_S do
    begin
        identify parents of the child t_{i,w}; if all the children of the parents belong to T_S,
        move the parents to T_S.
    end;
end; {FindIneffective}
```

Fig. 6 Pseudocode for finding efficient set T_R

S	no	w	T[w,1]	T[w,2]	T[w,3]	T[w,4]	T[w,5]	T[w,6]	T[w,7]
0011000000	0	0000	0	0	**0**	1	0	0	0
0011010000	1	0001	0	**0**	0	1	1	**0**	**0**
0011110000	2	0010	1	0	1	0	1	1	**0**
0000010000	3	0011	0	0	1	1	1	1	**0**
0001010000	4	0100	1	1	0	1	0	1	1
0001000000	5	0101	1	1	0	1	**0**	1	1
0001110000	6	0110	1	0	1	1	1	1	1
1000010000	7	0111	**0**	0	0	1	1	1	1
1100010000	8	1000	0	0	1	0	0	0	1
1101000000	9	1001	**0**	1	1	**0**	1	**0**	1
1111000000	10	1010	1	0	1	0	1	1	1
0011100000	11	1011	**0**	1	1	**0**	1	1	1
	12	1100	0	1	0	0	0	1	1
	13	1101	0	1	0	1	1	1	1
	14	1110	1	0	0	0	1	1	1
	15	1111	0	**0**	0	**0**	1	1	1

Table 3. The effect of the procedure FindIneffective applied to the data
from Table 3 (new ineffective templates are in bold)

To illustrate the effectiveness of the algorithm two dataset were taken: one consisting of 12 self strings of length 10 (given in Example 1) and the second consisting of 20 random strings of length 12. Table 4 shows the result of the algorithm given in Fig. 2 and its modified version from figure 7. We observe that an increase of 1 in τ changes the number of receptors almost two times. This follows from the fact that a single receptor recognizes $2^{\lambda-\tau-1} \cdot (\lambda-\tau+2)$ different strings[6], [20]. Hence the number of receptors grows approximately as $2 \cdot (\lambda-\tau+2)/(\lambda-\tau+1)$

Interestingly, we can use the procedure FindIneffective to study the effectiveness of the set of receptors. Namely, we construct the set T_S by adding to it the templates that are not present in any receptor. Then, for instance we can count fast and easily the number of unrecognized strings by any subset of the set of receptors. Table 4 shows results of this procedure - cf. columns c,d,g, and h.

Procedure IdentifyNonredundantReceptors
begin
    Identify all the templates $t_{1,s} \notin T_S$ and write them on a file, say file1. Call a member of file1 a partial receptor (initially the length of the partial receptor is just τ).
    for j = 2 **to** $\lambda-\tau+1$ **do**
    begin
    redundant $\leftarrow$ **nil**
    while not (end of file1) **do**
        Read a partial receptor, *p*. If it has only left child write on file2 the string *p*+'0'; if it has only right child write on file2 the string *p*+'1'. If it has left and right child, create the substring *tmp* = Copy(*p*+'1',*j*,τ) and check if *tmp* $\in$ *redundant*. If *tmp* $\notin$ *redundant* then add *tmp* to the list and write on file2 the strings *p*+'0' and *p*+'1'. Otherwise remove from file2 all partial receptors containing *tmp* and write on file2 the string *p*+'1' only.
    end of while.
    Rename file2 as file1.
    end of for
end

Fig. 7 Pseudocode of the modified procedure from Fig. 2

---

[6] This is true if $\tau \geq \lambda/2$; when $\tau < \lambda/2$ this value must be reduced by the number of overlapping schemas induced by the templates constituting single receptor.

132

τ	λ=10				λ=12			
	a	b	c	d	e	f	g	h
4	208	12	96	2	14	5	1231	461
5	442	28	24	0	285	18	484	5
6	672	59	5	0	1238	50	61	35
7	860	118	16	0	2471	109	23	12
8	946	245	7	0	3200	236	4	4
9	990	500	2	0	3708	492	0	0
10	1012	1012	0	0	3936	1004	0	0
11					4036	2028	0	0
12					4076	4076	0	0

Table 4. Number of rules generated by the algorithms from Fig. 2 (columns **a** and **c**) and the algorithm from Fig. 7 (column **b** and **f**). Columns **c** and **g** show the number of unrecognized strings and columns **d** and **h** - the number of holes.

4. Conclusions

In this paper we studied some ideas of generating the repertoire of receptors of minimal size. The algorithm presented in Sect. 3.3 generates receptors, each of which contains maximal number different templates. The results supported by simulations seem to be quite promising. Particularly for the set S consisting of 200 different strings of length λ =20, and representing a normal behaviour of a real process, the algorithm generated 42 receptors with threshold $\tau = 6$ ($P_f = 0.0334$) and 122 receptors with threshold $\tau = 7$ ($P_f = 0.0012$).

Bibliography

1. H. Bersini, F.J. Varela. Hints for adaptative problem solving gleaned from immune networks. In, LNCS 496, pp. 343-354, Springer-Verlag: 1990.

2. P. D'haeseleer. Further efficient algorithm for generating antibody strings, Tech. Rep. CS-95-03, The Univ. of New Mexico, Albuquerque, NM, 1995

3. P. D'haeseleer An immunological approach to change detection: Theoretical results. *IEEE Computer Security Foundations Workshop*, 1996

4. P. D'haeseleer, S. Forrest, and P. Helman. An immunological approach to change detection: algorithms, analysis, and implications. In *Proc. of IEEE Symposium on Research in Security and Privacy*, Oakland, CA, 1996.

5. D. Dasgupta, and S. Forrest. Novelty detection in time series using ideas from immunology. In: [6], pp. 262-276

6. D. Dasgupta (ed.), *Artificial Immune Systems and Their Applications*, Springer-Verlag, Berlin Heidelberg: 1998

7. J.D. Farmer, N.H. Packard, and A.S. Perelson. The immune system, adaptation and machine-learning. *Physica D*, **22**: 187-204, 1986

8. S. Forrest, B. Javornik, R.E. Smith, and A.S. Perelson. Using genetic algorithms to explore pattern recognition in the immune system. *Evolutionary Computation* 1(3): 191-211, 1993

9. S. Forrest, S.A. Hofmeyr, A. Somayaji, and T.A. Longstaff. A sense of self for UNIX processes. In: *Proc. of the 1996 IEEE Symposium on Research in Security and Privacy*, Oakland, CA.

10. S. Forrest, A.S. Perelson, L. Allen, and R. Cherukuri. Self-nonself discrimination in a computer. In *Proc. of IEEE Symposium on Research in Security and Privacy, Oakland*, CA, May 16-18, 1994, pp. 202-212

11. P. Helman, and S. Forrest. An efficient algorithm for generating random anti-body strings. Tech. Rep. CS-94-07, The Univ. of New Mexico, Albuquerque, NM, 1994

12. J.H. Holland. *Adaptation in Natural and Artificial Systems*. University of Michigan Press: Ann Arbour, 1975

13. E. Hunt, D.E. Cooke, and H. Holstein. Case memory and retrieval based on the immune system. In: M. Weloso and A. Aamodt (eds.) *Case-Based Reasoning Research and Development*, LNAI 1010, Springer: 1995, pp. 205-216

14. J. Hunt, and D.E. Cooke. Learning using an artificial immune system. *J. of Network and Computer Applications* **19**(1996): 189-212

15. J. Hunt, *et. al.* Jisys: The development of an artificial immune system for real world applications. In [6], pp. 157-186.

16. Y. Ishida, F. Mizessyn. Learning algorithms on an immune network model: Application to sensor diagnosis. In: *Proc. Internat. Joint Conference on Neural Networks*, vol. 1, pp. 33-38, China, November 3-6, 1992.

17. Ishiguru, Y. Watanabe, and Y. Uchikawa. Fault diagnosis of plant system using immune networks. In: *Proc. 1994 IEEE Internat. Conf. on Multisensor Fusion and Integration for Intelligent Systems* (MFI'94), pp. 34-42.

18. A.S. Perelson, G. Weisbuch. Immunology for physicists, *Reviews of Modern Physics*, **69**:1219-1265, 1997

19. S.T. Wierzchoń. Computer immunology: models and applications (in Polish). In: Proc. of 6-th Workshop of Polish Simulation Society, Białystok-Białowieża, 26-27 August 1999, pp. 85-87

20. S.T. Wierzchoń. Generating antibody strings in an artificial immune system. ICS Pas Report No. 892, Institute of Computer Science, Polish Academy of Sciences, Warszawa 1999

Modeling Agent Organizations

Stanislaw Ambroszkiewicz[1], Krzysztof Cetnarowicz[2], Jaroslaw Kozlak[2], Tomasz Nowak[1], and Wojciech Penczek[1]

[1] Institute of Computer Science, Polish Academy of Sciences, al. Ordona 21, 01-237 Warsaw, Poland, email: sambrosz, penczek@ipipan.waw.pl, http://www.ipipan.waw.pl/mas/
[2] Institute of Computer Science, University of Mining and Metallurgy, al. Mickiewicza 30, 30-059 Krakow, Poland, cetnar, kozlak@uci.agh.edu.pl

Abstract. We present a formal specification of an environment created by our mobile platform Pegaz [17]. Since all existing mobile agent platform create more or less the same infrastructure on a computer network, this formal specification may be seen as a formal representation of the cyberspace Then, we present a concept of agent organizations in a model of production environment. It is argued that such organizations can be applied in the cyberspace. Agents are supposed to form enterprises producing the commodity specified by the system designer, and then sell the commodity at the market. The goal of the designer is to create efficient enterprises producing the desired commodity. The market is modeled as the price oligopoly. The price oligopoly serves to eliminate enterprises that are not efficient.

1 Introduction

Computer networks [15] offer new application scenarios that cannot be realized on a single workstation. Resources and services may be distributed because of e.g. political, organizational reasons which make centralization impossible. The parallelism gained through the simultaneous processing of sub-tasks at distributed sites may lead to a better system throughput.

However, for large computer networks like the cyberspace (the open world created by the global information infrastructure and facilitated by the Internet and the Web), the classical programming paradigm in not sufficient. It is hard to imagine and even harder to realize the control, synchronization and cooperation for hundreds of processes each of them running on a different workstation. It is at least inefficient, if not unrealistic, to program, run and control each application on each workstation separately. Hence, the Network Programming paradigm should go beyond the classical paradigm of distributed computing where each process is run separately and the communication between the processes is already given.

The basic middleware that assures interoperability for heterogeneous workstations (for example, CORBA [8]) seems to be not sufficient.

Agents are programs that can act autonomously. Autonomous, adaptive and cooperative software agents (see [16,12]) are well suited for domains that require constant adaptation to changing distributed environment or changing

136

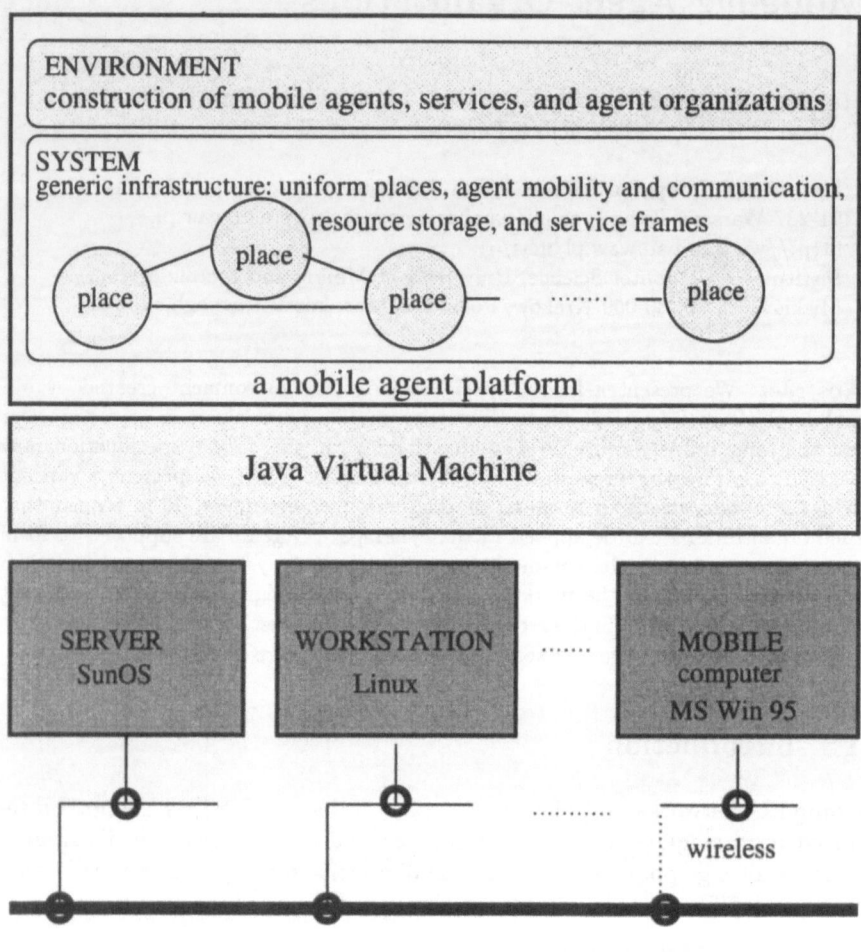

ENVIRONMENT
construction of mobile agents, services, and agent organizations

SYSTEM
generic infrastructure: uniform places, agent mobility and communication,
resource storage, and service frames

place

place

place

....

place

a mobile agent platform

Java Virtual Machine

SERVER
SunOS

WORKSTATION
Linux

....

MOBILE
computer
MS Win 95

wireless

Internet / Intranet / WAN / LAN (TCP,UDP)

Fig. 1. Functioning of a mobile agent platform, e.g. Pegaz

demands. Especially the idea of mobile software agents [6] inhabiting the cyberspace seems to be a good solution here. A mobile agent is an executing program that can migrate from host to host across a heterogeneous network under its own control and interact with other agents. However, it is clear that a single agent alone can not perform efficiently its tasks (like information gathering, looking for resources, marketing, and making e-commerce) in a large world without cooperation with other agents.

For large open worlds with a lot of agents simple cooperation mechanisms based on bilateral communication are not enough, especially if the agents' goals are interrelated in a way that fulfilling the goal of a single agent must involve a cooperation of a large number of agents. So that sophisticated interaction mechanisms and services are needed. During interactions the agents are supposed to communicate, negotiate, and form organization structures.

In order to realize the concept of mobile agents together with agent interaction and service infrastructure, a special middleware (called "mobile agent platform") is needed.

There are several platforms available over the Internet, for example Concordia [7], Grasshopper, Mole, Odyssey, Voyager to mention only some of them. These platforms are systems for creating infrastructure on computer networks, so that details of network functioning are hidden from the users as well as for the agents, see Fig. 1. This makes programming more easy. A programmer need not manually construct agent communication, or agent transportation with its data. This may be viewed as high level abstraction from network communication protocols, operation systems (due to Java) working on particular servers, data structures, and so on. Only the generic frame of infrastructure is visible for the programmer who uses a platform. In order to solve a problem the programmer constructs an infrastructure on the available computer network, then the programmer implements agent interaction mechanisms and services, and introduces agents into the running system. Any agent is given a goal to fulfill. So that the problem to be solved by the programmer is realized by fulfilling the individual goals by autonomous agents.

Most of the existing mobile agent platform create similar infrastructures. It seems that a formal specification of the generic infrastructure can be abstracted from them. The generic infrastructure is needed to define principles of the standard architecture of the cyberspace. The standard architecture may serve as a common ontology needed for the agents (coming maybe from different platforms) in communication to understand each other.

On the basis of such common ontology, the meaning of agent communication language could be constructed. The language is necessary for defining agent negotiation protocols, joint plans, intentions, and so on.

As far as we know, this is one of the first attempts towards defining formal generic representation of the cyberspace in the literature. Another effort, taken by FIPA [11]], is not completed yet.

The research presented in the paper is based on our experiences gained during realization of Pegaz - our mobile agent platform [17].

2   Overview of Pegaz

Pegaz is a mobile agent platform. Initially, the platform was designed as a tool for modeling agent virtual organizations as sophisticated agent interaction mechanisms (AVO, see www.ipipan.waw.pl/mas/). The platform makes it possible to run real network applications, and to simulate large computer networks on one or several servers.

On the platform there is implemented the concept of "mobile software agent", that is, a software agent that can move from one server to another together with its data. There can be also realized services for (mobile) agents to interact and cooperate.

The main goal of Pegaz is the creation of a common environment (infrastructure) for network programming and agent-based programming. The platform assures basic services for the agents like mobility and communication, and supports dynamic constructions of new services. There is an interface for users to create dynamically (mobile) agents without worrying about low level problems like registration in the network or management of the communication protocol.

Pegaz is composed of *System* and *Environment*. *System* consists of programs: Node, Starter, and Monitor. Node is the basic program of Pegaz. In order to joint a computer to the infrastructure created by Pegaz, the program Node must be executed on that computer and connected to another running Nodes in the network. Running system consists of a network of running Nodes. Starter is for introducing new agents into the running system. The program Monitor is for monitoring the behavior of agents. *Environment* consists of Java interfaces and classes needed by the user for agent and service construction. A service is located on a Node. Agents can migrate (together with their data) from one Node to another one and use the available services.

The platform is implemented in Java under JDK 1.1.7B. Hence, Pegaz can be ran on the majority of operation systems like MS Windows 95/NT, SunOS, DEC UNIX, Linux.

The idea of Pegaz architecture goes along the same lines as the architecture of Concordia [7], however there are some basic differences. One of them is that Concordia has one central Administration Manager for providing remote administration of the whole system, whereas Pegaz is completely distributed so that two or more Pegaz systems running independently can be composed into one just by making at least one connection between a Node of one system and a Node of the other system. This may be seen as an advantage, however several problems with naming and communication must be solved. There is one central component of Pegaz system; it is Monitor. However, it collects the data sent by the agents and displays them on one window, so that it is a tool only for monitoring the agents' behavior. Pegaz is still under development although several applications have been already implemented on it.

It is important to notice here that the world that can be created by Pegaz is open in the sense that it can be extended (in the runtime) to include new places and new agents from another Pegaz infrastructure created by a different programmer on a different computer network.

3 Towards formal specification of the environment created by Pegaz

The aim of this section is to describe, as formal as possible at this stage, the generic infrastructure frame. In the case of Pegaz, the main components of the infrastructure are Nodes (called also places), services located at the places, and agents that can move from place to place, use the services, communicate, and exchange data and resources with other agents. A service is defined as an operation that produces some resources from another resources. The types of the resources are fixed for that operation. Agents can collect, store, exchange, and transport the resources. Any service is managed by one agent. Producing something by a service is an action performed by one agent associated with an operation.

Hence, in our formal description the primitives are: places, services, agents, actions, resources.

Places are composed into a graph. The graph nodes represent places whereas an edge between two nodes in the graph expresses the fact that there is an immediate connection between the corresponding places.

Resources are primitives grouped into types, analogously as types of data, and objects in programming languages.

Services are represented as operations on resources and are of the form: $Op : A \to B$, producing object of type B from object of type A.

Agent's local state (denoted by l) is composed of mental state m (representing its knowledge), and contents s of its own storage. Let M denote the set of all possible agent's mental states; for details and formal definitions see the companion paper [1]. Let S denote the set of possible contents of agent's storage. Additionally any agent has goal g to fulfill and current intentions int to realize this goal. The goal is represented by a subset of the set of all possible agent's local states $L \stackrel{df}{=} M \times S$, so that $g \subset L$. The intention is a protocol chosen, from a library of available protocols denoted by $Prot$, to realize agent's goal. Protocol is of the form $prot : L \to 2^A$, where A is the set of agent's actions whereas 2^{A_i} is the set of all subsets of A_i. The meaning of $prot(l) = A'$ is as follows. In local state l execute one action from the set A'.

Agent's intention is defined as its commitment to realize a particular protocol from its library. Agent's decision mechanism is of the form:

$$Dec : L \times G \times Prot \to Prot$$

We are not going to specify or to characterize the decision mechanism in this paper. This definition is to show how the introduced notions are used in the agent decision making.

Suppose that the current agent's mental state is m, goal is g, and intention int is its commitment to follow the protocol $prot$. Then $Dec(m, g, int) = int$ means that the agent keeps on the current intention int.

If, however, $Dec(m, g, int) = prot'$, then it means that the agent gives up the current intention int and commits to realize another protocol $prot'$; this makes new intention int'.

Contents of agent's storage is determined by the resources the agent has got.

Agent's mental state is represented by contents of simple relational database. The database is of the same type for all the agents; any record stands for a common notions of all the agents in the system. Agent's mental state is updated and revised by agent's perception and communication; for details see [1]. This constitutes the principles of agent architecture.

In our working example we have introduce one special type of resources, called energy or money. During its "life" any agent needs energy so that it must spend money. The money is stored in agent's personal account. It is assumed that for any kind of actions there is a fixed fee to be paid for performing an action of this kind. Once the action is performed, the appropriate fee is subtracted from agent's personal account. If agent's account is equal zero, the agent is obliged to finish its activity and go to the 'sleeping state'. Any agent is supposed to act in a way that results in increasing the agent's personal account as much as possible. This constitutes the general goal of a self interested agent. This may be viewed as a distributed control mechanism over the agent population.

3.1 Actions

We can distinguish the following primitive actions in our formal framework: Action of **meeting** of two agents. This is a joint action of two agents. Action of **moving** to another place. It is an individual action not always allowed because some agents have no permission to enter some places. Action of **production** of a resource by an operation. This is individual action of the agent associated to that operation. The action is allowed if the agent has got all resources needed for production. Action of **getting a resource** from other agent. Action of **giving a resource** to other agent. Action of **committing to a protocol.** Action of **giving up the current commitment. Communication** actions that are defined in [1]. Action of **finishing activity** and go to the 'sleeping state'.

4 Modeling cooperation mechanisms

It seems that there is a critical level of complexity of multi-agent system where a single agent is inefficient or even unable to realize its goal. This very critical level can be clearly seen for environments where fulfilling single agent's goal needs a complex workflow to be performed and the workflow involves a large number of self interested agent to cooperate with each other. Undoubtedly, cyberspace and manufacturing enterprise are environments of such kind. For such environments agent organizations seem to be a panacea to manage the necessary cooperative work. The concepts of organization formation as advanced cooperation mechanisms, although regarded as important, were not so far a subject of extensive research, modeling and application in in the field of multi-agent systems, an exception is [9,13] and recently [10,2–4].

Perhaps it is surprising that the general environment frame presented in the previous section resembles a production environment. However the emergence of electronic commerce proves that the resemblance is not accidental.

Hence, agent organizations in cyberspace can be modeled and tested in a production environment. For this very purpose we have simulated a production environment. Preliminary concepts of agent virtual enterprises can be found in [3,4].

5 Simulating production environment

The initial specification of the production environment to be simulated is the same as the specification of cyberspace.

We have introduced money for the very purpose of controlling agent population and make agents more efficient (due to limited amount of money) in realizing their goals.

In what follows we introduce three control factors of the simulated production system. These factors are controlled by the designer of the system for achieving desired system behavior. Usually the desired behavior means that, for specified final commodities, the system is able to form enterprises that produce them efficiently.

The first control factor is the initial money accounts of the agents, that is, how much money the agents have at the start of the system.

The second control factor consists in determining the fees for performing particular kind of actions. Staying at a place for some unit of time is also the subject of paying a fixed fee.

The third control factor is money distribution among the agents. For defining this factor the demand for final commodities must be specified first. Once the type of final commodity is determined, a mechanism is needed for buying the final commodity from the already formed enterprises that are able to produce that commodity. As the mechanism we choose price oligopoly, see [19,5]. The enterprises compete with prices of the final commodity. Depending of the proposed price each enterprise is given the amount of commodity to produce that is bought at the price proposed by this enterprise. It is a subject to a particular enterprise how to distribute its profit among its members.

5.1 Price oligopoly

Our model of oligopoly is an extension of the duopoly models presented by Keser [14] and Sorger [18]. In the classical oligopoly model, the agent who sets the lowest price captures the entire market. In our model agent gains or looses a part of the market depending on the difference between the average price (of the prices set by all the agents participating in the market) and its price. That is, if its price is greater than the average price, the agent looses a part of the market. Otherwise it captures a part.

To be more formal, price oligopoly is a n-person, T-period, dynamic game. It is assumed that there are n agents. Each of them is the manager of an enterprise producing commodity in the market. The agents are enumerated by the set $N = \{1, 2, \dots n\}$. Each agent is equipped with an initial account K_1^i at period 1. Its production cost of a unit of the commodity is c_i.

Consumers, that are supposed to buy the commodity produced by the agent i at time t, are represented by its potential demand D_t^i. So that D_1^i is the initial potential demand of agent i.

For each agent i, (K_t^i, D_t^i) constitutes agent i local state at the beginning of period t (or at the end of period $t - 1$).

At the beginning of the period t, each agent i, $i \in N$, must choose its price p_t^i such that $c_i \le p_t^i \le D_t^i$.

Then, for this price the agent sells the amount of the commodity x_t^i given by $x_t^i \stackrel{df}{=} D_t^i - p_t^i$
So that in t-th period the agent i's gain is $z_t^i = (p_t^i - c_i)x_t^i$.
At the end of the t-th period its account is equal

$$K_t^i \stackrel{df}{=} K_{t-1}^i + (p_t^i - c_i)x_t^i - \pi_i \tag{1}$$

where π_i is the fee to be paid by agent i. This fee refers to the cost of maintenance of the enterprise structure managed by the agent i.

The potential demand for agent i is changed to

$$D_t^i \stackrel{df}{=} D_{t-1}^i + \hat{p}_t - p_t^i, \quad \text{where} \quad \hat{p}_t = \tfrac{1}{n} \sum_{j \in N} p_t^j, \tag{2}$$

Hence, agent i's local state at the end of period t and at the beginning of the period $t + 1$ is (K_{t+1}^i, D_{t+1}^i).

If in a period t, K_t^i becomes less than 0 or $\bar{D}_t^i < p_t^i$ then agent i is eliminated from the game. Its potential demand $\bar{D}_t^i$ is either given to a new agent entering the game or divided proportionally between the other active agents. This means, that global potential demand remains constant during all periods.

In the paper [5], four classes of strategies have been defined and characterized, namely greedy, myopic, stationary, and separated from the production cost strategies. The greedy strategy characterizes the agent maximizing its potential demand in the next period whereas the myopic strategy characterizes the agent maximizing its account in the next period. Stationary, and separated from the production cost strategies are more sophisticated strategies for optimization in some longer horizon.

These four classes of strategies are examples of agent protocols defined in Section 3. In our experiments the agents use only these four classes of strategies.

5.2 Management agents and production agents

We distinguish two kinds of agents in the system: production agents and management agents. A production agent is associated to an operation, say $O : A \rightarrow B$, and is responsible for production of resource B from A. A management agent is responsible for forming and management of an enterprise producing final commodity specified in the system demand. It is supposed that any management agent have restricted range, that is, can not enter some places, so that, in order to form complete supply chain and then to manage the production process the agent must cooperate with other management agents. The mechanism of enterprise formation built into management agent architecture is based on on the idea of teams [2]. The limit of space does not allow us to present the mechanism in detail.

The model of production environment described above is implemented in C++ on MS Windows NT. The experiments are being carried out on environments of rather small size, i.e. with simple technologies (trees of depth up to 5) of the final commodity, and a small number of management agents (up to 20). The preliminary results prove that it is the subject of the agents' initial accounts how fast the optimal solutions are reached. The optimal solutions mean here formations of the most efficient enterprises producing the desired final commodity. The oligopoly model is constructed in the way that in a long run only the most efficient enterprises survive. However, if agents' initial accounts are to large, then the process of capturing the whole market by the most efficient enterprise may take a long time. On the other hand, if the initial accounts are too small, then the agents can not afford to seek better solutions. That is, in order to survive they must produce and sell instead of spending money on enterprise reconfiguration.

So far our experiments have been carried out for small environments. In order to have more comprehensive results, experiments with large environments are needed.

6 Acknowledgments

The work was supported by the State Committee for Scientific Research under the grant No. 8 T11C 008 12, and by ESPRIT project No. 20288 CRIT-2.

References

1. S. Ambroszkiewicz, W. Penczek, and T. Nowak. (2000) "Towards Formal Specification and Verifications of Generic Cyberspace Infrastructure for Mobile

Agents." In Proc. The first Goddard Workshop on Formal Approaches to Agent-Based Systems, 6th-7th April 2000, NASA Goddard Space Flight Center, Greenbelt, MD, USA

2. S. Ambroszkiewicz, O. Matyja, and W. Penczek. (1998) "Team Formation by Self-Interested Mobile Agents." In Proc. 4-th Australian DAI-Workshop, Brisbane, Australia, July 13, 1998. Published in Springer LNAI 1544. http://www.ipipan.waw.pl/mas/

3. S. Ambroszkiewicz, K. Cetnarowicz, O. Matyja, and B. Radko. (1998) "Modeling Virtual Enterprise: agent-based approach." In Proc. Multi Agent Systems Models Architecture and Applications. F. J. Garijo, and Ch. Lemaitre (Eds.), II Iberoamerican Workshop on D.A.I and M.A.S., October 1-2 1998 Toledo, Spain.

4. S. Ambroszkiewicz. (1999) "Agent Virtual Organizations within the Framework of Network Computing: a case study." In Proc. CEEMAS'99, The First International Workshop of Central and Eastern Europe on Multi-agent Systems, May 30, June 2, 1999, St. Petersburg, Russia.

5. S. Bylka, S. Ambroszkiewicz, and J. Komar. Discrete Time Dynamic Game Model for Price Competition in an Oligopoly. To appear in Annals of Operation Research 1999.

6. D. Chess. C. Harrison, A. Kershenbaum. (1997) Mobile Agents: Are They a Good Idea? In J. Vitek and Ch. Tschudin (Eds.) Mobile Object Systems. Springer LNCS 1222.

7. CONCORDIA http://www.meitca.com/HSL/Projects/Concordia/

8. The Object Management Group's Common Object Request Broker Architecture (OMG/CORBA) http://www.acl.lanl.gov/CORBA/

9. Y. Demazeau and A.C. R. Costa "Populations and Organisations in Open Multi-Agent Systems", 1st Symposium on Parallel and Distributed AI, Hyderabad, India, July 1996.

10. J. Ferber and O. Gutknecht. A meta-model for the analysis and design of organizations in multi-agent systems. In Proc. ICMAS-98.

11. The Foundation for Intelligent Physical Agents (FIPA) http://www.fipa.org/

12. Software Agents in Communications Network Management: An Overview. Knowledge Engineering Review 1999.

13. T. Ishida, M. Yokoo, and L. Gasser. (1990) An organizational Approach to Adaptive Production Systems. In *Proc. of 8th National Conf. on Artificial Intelligence,* Boston, USA.

14. Claudia Keser. (1991) *Experimental duopoly markets with demand inertia,* Bonn, PhD thesis under supervision of Richard Selten.

15. E. Kuhn and G. Nozicka. (1996) Post Client / Server Coordination Tools. In W. Cohen, G. Neumann (Eds.) Coordination Technologies for Collaborative Applications. LNCS 1364. pp.231-253.

16. J. P. Mueller. (1998) Architectures and Applications of Intelligent Agents: A Survey. Knowledge Engineering Review.

17. Pegaz - a mobile agent platform implemented at the Instutute of Computer Science PAS (WWW: http://www.ipipan.waw.pl/mas/).

18. G. Sorger. (1995) Time Dynamic Game Models for Advertising Competition in a Duopoly. *Optimal Control and Application and Methods.* Vol. 16, 175–188.

19. J. Tirole. (1994) *The Theory of Industrial Organizations.* The MIT Press, London.

Expressiveness of $-Calculus: What Matters?

Eugene Eberbach *

Jodrey School of Computer Science, Acadia University, Wolfville, NS B0P 1X0, Canada, eugene.eberbach@acadiau.ca

Abstract. $-calculus is a higher-order polyadic process algebra for resource bounded computation. It has been designed to handle autonomous agents, evolutionary computing, neural nets, expert systems, machine learning, and distributed interactive AI systems, in general. $-calculus has built-in cost-optimization mechanism allowing to deal with nondeterminism, incomplete and uncertain information. In this paper, we investigate expressiveness of $-calculus. We show that due to infinitary means, it allows to express models having richer behavior than Turing machine, including cellular automata, interaction machines, neural networks, and random automata networks. We also investigate the importance of synchronization, representation of continuity, and higher-order.
Keywords: resource bounded computation, interactive distributed intelligent systems, process algebras, interaction machines, expressiveness, multiagent systems.

1 Introduction

The *$-calculus* (read: cost calculus) [5–7] is a higher-order polyadic *process algebra* with a quantitative aspect (cost) which naturally expresses adaptability (optimization) and self-modification for interactive distributed systems. Agents interact and infer by send, receive and mutation primitives. It differs from other models by including cost (time, resources, etc.) as a basic component expressing the optimization behavior typical of many AI systems, and in particular, resource bounded computation. Resource bounded computation attempts to find the best answer possible given operational constraints. The approach is known under a variety of names, including flexible computation [14], anytime algorithms [3], imprecise-computation [16], or design-to-time scheduling [11]. Anytime algorithms together with closely related decision-theoretic metareasoning are two new promising techniques and their application to general decision-making architectures has not yet been investigated in any depth [22]. $-calculus attempts to formalize resource bounded computation using process algebras.

To avoid combinatorial explosion, on-line optimization often considers a restricted subset of agents, and only a few steps of execution. In $-calculus, self-modification (meta-control) and cost-optimization are the driving force for problem solving, control and automatic program synthesis. The approach aims at developing a general model for distributed systems with intelligence

* research partially supported by a grant from NSERC No. OGP0046501

working under bounded resources. It has been designed to specify, investigate, and implement systems exhibiting meta-computation (e.g., self-modification) and optimization, including expert systems, neural networks, evolutionary computation, artificial life, adaptive autonomous agents, plan generation, fault-tolerant systems, computer viruses, machine learning, and evolvable hardware.

The work is related to other general models for sequential and parallel computation, including λ-calculus [2] and π-calculus [18–20]. The $-calculus leads to a new programming paradigm: cost languages, and a new class of computer architectures: cost-driven machines [4].

In this paper, we concentrate on the problem of expressiveness of $-calculus. We demonstrate that $-calculus can express formalisms which have richer behavior than Turing machines: including cellular automata [1], interaction machines [24–26], neural networks, and random automata networks [12]. We believe that such expressive power is needed to tackle with construction universality, self-reproduction, and evolution problems. We present basic $-calculus constructs needed to support these claims. Other details of the $-calculus: like predefined crisp, probabilistic, and fuzzy cost functions, optimization problems for strong and weak bisimilarity are not discussed in this paper.

2 Cost Expressions: Syntax and Description

Throughout the paper we will use a prefix notation, i.e., we will write data T, functions F, and modifications (higher-order functions) M uniformly as $(f\ x)$, where f is a function (data, modification) name (label) and $x = (x_1, x_2, ...)$ is a vector of its parameters (possibly countably infinite). Sometimes if it is clear from the context, we will omit parameters, and we will write simply f. Also if it clear we will call data, functions, and modifications, all simply functions.

Let $a, b, c, ...$ be *names* over sets T, F and M, and each with an arity - an integer ≥ 0 (representing number of parameters) for each terminal, function and modification. Let $\circ, \|, \uplus, \sqcup, \$, \neg, \rightarrow, \leftarrow, \mapsto, :=$ be predefined (reserved) names. We will assume also that basic arithmetic and relational operators are predefined and available to be used, e.g. $(+\ 1\ 2)$, $(<\ x\ 4)$ etc.

Let P, Q, R, ... range over the $-expressions $\mathcal{P}$ (read: cost expressions, also can be called agents, programs, processes, objects) and let X, Y, Z, ... be process variables. We will distinguish simple (or atomic) $-expressions, executed (evaluated, reduced) in one indivisible step, or considered to be indivisible because it is more convenient from the point of a user (like atomic transactions in databases). $-expressions return other cost expressions as the result of their evaluation (in particular, they may return nothing after successful execution, or they may block after a failure in execution).

Then the syntax of $-expressions is the smallest set $\mathcal{P}$, which includes the following kinds of cost expressions (assuming that P, Q, P_i are arbitrary cost expressions):

$$P, Q, P_i ::= (\circ_{i \in I} P_i) \quad \text{sequential composition}$$
$$| \quad (\|_{i \in I} P_i) \quad \text{parallel composition}$$
$$| \quad (\uplus_{i \in I} P_i) \quad \text{cost choice}$$
$$| \quad (\sqcup_{i \in I} (\circ\ \alpha_i\ P_i)) \text{ general choice}$$
$$| \quad (f\ Q) \quad \text{call of (user) defined $-expression (application)}$$
$$| \quad (:= (f\ X)\ P) \quad \text{recursive definition (abstraction)}$$

Simple $-expressions (considered to be executed in one atomic indivisible step):

$$\alpha ::= (\$\ P) \quad \text{cost}$$
$$| \quad (\to (a\ Q)) \text{ send}$$
$$| \quad (\leftarrow (a\ X)) \text{ receive}$$
$$| \quad (\mapsto (a\ Q)) \text{ mutation}$$
$$| \quad (a\ Q) \quad \text{call of (user) defined simple $-expression}$$
$$| \quad (\neg a\ Q) \quad \text{negation of (user) defined simple $-expression}$$

Cost, negation, choices, compositions, send, receive, mutation, primitive arithmetic, logic and relational functions are examples of built-in functions. Other functions and data structures can be specified using definition. Send, receive, and mutation perform message passing. In $-calculus everything is a cost expression: agents, environment, communication/interaction links, inference engines, modified structures, data, code, and meta-code. Here I is a possibly countably infinite indexing set; in the case $I = \emptyset$ we will write the empty parallel composition, general and cost choices as $\perp$, and the empty sequential composition as ε.

In the above syntax $(f\ Q)$ represents a call of user defined cost expressions and $(a\ Q)$ a call of user-defined simple cost expressions. Syntax is the same - they use only different names for functions. "Simple" $-expressions can be quite complex, and it is a matter of choice what to consider as elementary steps in execution. Simple cost expressions can be also defined using definition, but dissimilar to other cost expressions, their execution will be assumed to be done in one indivisible step (independently how many steps requires their evaluation), i.e. a body of their definition will be assumed to be evaluated in one atomic step.

Note that general choice is different from cost choice: in the former selection is based on satisfiability of guards, whereas in cost choice decision is based on the values of cost functions. Additionally, wrong choices (because of incomplete information on cost values) can be corrected in cost choices, but not in general choice (in cost choices context after choice is preserved, but not in a general choice).

The operators $\leftarrow$ and $:=$ are **X**-*binders*, i.e. in the processes ($\circ$ ($\leftarrow$ (a **X**)) P) and ($:=$ (f **X**) P) the occurrences of **X** in P are considered bounded, with the usual rules for scoping. The *free variables* of P, i.e. those variables which do not occur in the scope of any binder, are denoted by $fv(P)$, and bounded variables by $bv(P)$. The *alpha-conversion* of bounded variables is defined as usual, and the renaming (or substitution) $P\{Y/X\}$, where $|Y| = |X|$ is defined as the result of replacing all occurrences of $X_1, X_2, ..., X_n$ in P by $Y_1, Y_2, ..., Y_n$, possibly applying alpha-conversion to avoid capture.

The operational semantics of $-expressions has been defined using a Labeled Transition System (LTS), which leads to the notion of a *derivation tree* recording the successive transitions or actions which may be performed by given process.

In this paper, the definition of cost functions, meta-system controling resource-bounded optimization will not be presented. We will concentrate on the problem which definition features are important for expressiveness of the model for distributed interactive systems and $-calculus, in particular.

3 Expressiveness of $-calculus: What Matters?

3.1 Infinite versus Finite

Currently, it appears that π-calculus [18–20], interaction machines [24–28,13] or random automata networks [12] could be considered to be the closest to a formal model for interactive distributed systems to describe their theoretical limits. Both last two models go beyond conventional Turing machine model and are based on infinitary concepts - an infinite input tape or an infinite number of finite state machines connected by an arbitrary interconnection topology. As many others pointed out before, unbounded input tape, workspace, time, precision, power oracles, etc. greatly increase the expressiveness of almost any formalism, thus the results confirm such a need for good models of interactive distributed systems. Such models are important to realize what the limits of the agent approach are; to reason about agent systems scalability and complexity, although in practice, the number of existing agents in implementation is always finite.

We will start with illustrating examples trying to achieve a more moderate goal, i.e. showing that in $-calculus we can encode λ-calculus and π-calculus. Next we will show that $-calculus can express formalisms which have richer behavior than Turing machines: including cellular automata [1], interaction machines [24,25,27,28,13], neural networks, and automata networks [12], exactly due to allowing infinite (but enumerable) application of the parallel composition operator.

EXAMPLE 31 *Encoding of the λ-calculus*
Because $-calculus is higher-order, encoding of λ-calculus is straightforward:

λ-calculus	\$-calculus encoding
x - variable	x - variable name
MN - application	$(f\ N)$ - function call
$\lambda x.M$ - abstraction	$(:=\ (f\ x)\ M)$ - function definition

Operational semantics:

$(\lambda x.M)\ N \to M[N/x]$ $(f\ N) \to M[N/x]$, where $(:=\ (f\ x)\ M)$
function application
(β-reduction)

We can claim that λ-calculus is a subcalculus of the \$-calculus, because of the one-to-one correspondence between reductions in λ-terms and in their corresponding \$-calculus terms.

EXAMPLE 32 Encoding of the π-calculus

π-calculus (πC)	\$-calculus ($\$C$) encoding
0 - inert process	$\bot$ - zero (blocking)
$x(y).P$ - input prefix	$(\sqcup\ (\circ\ (\leftarrow\ x\ y)\ P)$ - receive
	$(\circ\ (in\ x\ y)\ P))$
$\bar{x}y.P$ - output prefix	$(\sqcup\ (\circ\ (\to\ x\ y)\ P)$ -send
	$(\circ\ (out\ x\ y)\ P))$
$P + Q$ - sum	$(\sqcup\ (\circ\ \varepsilon\ P)\ (\circ\ \varepsilon\ Q)$ - general choice
$P\ |\ Q$ - parallel composition	$(\ \|\ P\ Q)$ - parallel composition
$(\nu\ x)\ P$ - restriction	$(block\_in\_out\ x\ P)$
$!\ P$ - replication	$(:=\ (!\ P)\ (\ \|\ P\ (!\ P)))$

Simulation requires introduction of (user defined) operators: *in*, *out* and *block_in_out*, but \$-calculus allows to do it. Then the input prefix is simulated by general choice either to do \$-calculus receive (requiring synchronization with corresponding send) or by a new operator $(in : x : y)$ working like receive, but not requiring synchronization neither with send nor out. In a similar way, the output prefix is simulated by general choice of send (it does not matter whether we will use mutation or send, because in first-order π-calculus only names/values are allowed to be transmitted) and a new operator out. Restriction operator is simulated by a new operator *block_in_out* blocking/synchronizing execution of *in* and *out* operators for a given fresh channel x (and this is a general idea of π-calculus restriction operator). If we want to use a handshaking communication, the pairs: send/receive or mutation/receive could be used instead. The presence of ε in simulation of sum +, guarantees that there will be no blocking, i.e., choice without checking of guards, because ε executes silently without blocking. Simulation of replication operator by recursive definition is straightforward.

If to not be too picky about the necessity to use new (user) defined operators in, out, and block, then π-calculus could be claimed to be a subcalculus of the \$-calculus, because each operator of π-calculus is simulated by a corresponding operator(s) from \$-calculus. We have the choice to encode numerals, true, false boolean values, if-then-else operator either as in λ-calculus or as in π-calculus, but we prefer the third way: $\perp$ is used to denote *false* (similar to the implementation of negation by failure in Prolog, where exactly one of α or $\neg\alpha$ will be blocked (will fail, i.e. return $\perp$), and if-then-else we can express easily by general choice with positive and negated guards.

Because of the higher-order features, we could also encode higher-order π-calculus (HOπ) in \$-calculus. We assume that in a function definition, a function name can be either a constant or a variable. Sangiorgi [23,19] has proved that higher-order π-calculus is not more expressive than (first-order) π-calculus. Thus such simulation becomes superfluous.

From the above and Milner in [19] showed has to simulate λ-calculus by π-calculus, we obtain

THEOREM 33 *Every process realizable on Turing machine (by λ-calculus) can be implemented by some π-calculus process, which in turn can be implemented by some \$-calculus process, i.e.*

$$TM \subseteq \pi C \subseteq \$C \tag{1}$$

In [26] it is claimed that Turing Machines are too weak to express interaction of object-oriented and distributed systems, and Interaction Machines (IMs) are proposed as a stronger model that better captures computational behavior for finite interactive computing agents. Interaction Machines consist of Sequential Interaction Machines (SIMs) and Multi-Stream Interaction Machines (MIMs).

Interaction Machines (IM) correspond to Turing machines with infinite tapes. Whereas the number of inputs of a Turing machine are countable, the number of potential streams of an interaction machine is nonenumerable. Interaction machines extend the Turing machine model by adding input and output actions (read and write statements). Whereas Turing machines require all inputs to appear on the tape prior to the computation and shut out the world during the process of computation, interaction machines allow inputs to be dynamically generated and require inputs to be represented by a potentially infinite stream, since any finite stream can be dynamically extended by adversaries. Interactive systems interact with an external environment they cannot control. Adversaries have the last word and can always extend any finite sequence. The behavior of adversaries is better modeled by infinite processes that express the cardinality of the real numbers (Cantor diagonalization) than by enumerable sequences.

SIMs are stream processing machines that model sequential interaction by I/O streams. *Sequential Interaction Machines (SIMs)* are state-transition machines $M = (S, I, m)$, where S is an enumerable set of states, I is an enumerable set of dynamically bound inputs, and the transition mapping $m : S \times I \rightarrow S \times O$ maps state-action pairs into new states and outputs. Each computation step $(s, i) \rightarrow (s', o)$ of a SIM can be viewed as a complete TM computation, where i is dynamically supplied input token (string), the output

o may affect subsequent inputs, and s' is the next state of the SIM. Elements of both S and I are finite at any given time but their size is unbounded.

Multi-stream Interaction Machines (MIMs) are finite agents that interact with multiple autonomous streams: for example, distributed databases or ATM systems that provide services to multiple autonomous clients. MIM behavior is not expressible by SIMs in the sense that MIMs can make a richer class of observational distinctions (perform a larger class of tasks) than SIMs. TMs express the behavior of a single agent, SIMs express the interaction of 2 agents, while MIMs express the interaction of n agents for $n > 2$. MIMs provide a formal framework for distributed systems. A system (computing agent) is distributed iff its interaction can be described by a MIM but not by a SIM.

Wegner [26] states that π-calculus, because of the restriction to interleaving and not true concurrency, has an expressive power of serializable interaction machines, i.e.

THEOREM 34

$$\pi C \subseteq SIM \subset MIM \tag{2}$$

In other words, interaction machines realize more powerful interaction than π-calculus.

In $-calculus we can simulate both sequential interaction and multi-agent interaction by send/mutation (out) and receive (in) primitives, and although each send is matched with a single receive, many such pairs can be active and synchronize simultaneously (true parallelism). If we restrict interaction to at most one pair of send and receive at the time we will obtain the SIM type of interaction. Each step $(s, i) \rightarrow (s', o)$ from interaction machines can be simulated in two $-calculus steps: assuming that $s = (\circ\ (\leftarrow c\ x)\ (\mapsto c\ x)\ s')$, the agent will receive i in the first step leading to $(\circ\ (\mapsto c\ i)\ s')$, and in the second step it will transmit o (by mutating i to o) through channel c arriving at a new state s'. The interaction will be with another agent or environment, which is responsible for transmitting i and receiving o and arriving in its new state p. Together their behavior is captured by the following $-expression: $(\ \|\ (\circ\ (\rightarrow c\ i)(\leftarrow c\ y)\ p)\ (\circ\ (\leftarrow c\ x)\ (\mapsto c\ x)\ s'))$. For MIMs many such interactions can be active simultaneously, the same is true for $-calculus. In fact, the size of cost expressions can be unbounded (e.g., an enumerable number of parallel or sequential compositions, choices). The same applies to the number of send/receive pairs involved in communication. Thus we can conclude that $MIM \subseteq \$C$. The above conjecture cannot be proved at this moment, because the formalization of MIMs is subject of current research [27,28,13]. Intuitively, it seems be probable, because $-calculus allows for simultaneous interactions, transmission can be either synchronous or asynchronous, and channels because of polyadic features of $-calculus can be either broadcasting/multicasting (not a single, but a vector of expressions can be transmitted/received through the broadcasting channel simultaneously) or unicasting.

Together with the previous results it gives

CONJECTURE 35

$$TM \subseteq \pi C \subseteq SIM \subset MIM \subseteq \$C \qquad (3)$$

Now, we will compare expressiveness of $-calculus with other models for parallel interaction, i.e. cellular automata, neural nets, and random automata networks.

In Cellular Automata (CA), a copy of a common finite state machine M occupies each vertex of a regular graph (cellular space, possibly infinite) which is then called a cell. Synchronously, each copy of M looks up its input in the states $x_1, ..., x_d$ of its neighboring cells and its own state x_0, and then changes its state according to its local dynamics δ. The cellular automaton performs its calculation by repeating these atomic local rules for all sites resulting in emergent behavior (global dynamics) of the whole system.

Neural Networks (NN) differ from cellular automata that the underlying (possibly infinite) network is no longer homogeneous but an arbitrary digraph; and the transition functions compute weighted sums of inputs from neighboring cells. Neural networks can be discrete or continuous (operating on real numbers).

Automata (Random) Networks (AN) operate also on an arbitrary (potentially infinite) digraph where in each node an arbitrary finite state machine is located.

It is known that cellular automata are more expressive than Turing machines, and that an arbitrary cellular automaton can be simulated by discrete neural networks, and discrete neural networks can be simulated by random automata networks [12].

THEOREM 36 *Every self-map $T : C \to C$ realizable on a cellular automaton can be implemented by some neural network, and every discrete neural network by some random automata network, i.e.,*

$$CA \subseteq NN \subseteq AN \qquad (4)$$

Turing machines can be simulated by 1D cellular automata but there exist problems solvable by CA, but not by TM (for example, 1D CA taking as an input a real number, represented as an infinite binary expansion, and stabilizing iff it is an integer. A TM cannot solve this problem since the real number can be given as 0.999..., and hence TM will not even finish reading its input in finite time).

THEOREM 37

$$TM \subset CA \qquad (5)$$

Formally, an automata network [12] is a pair $(D, \{M_i\})$ consisting of a cellular space $(D, \{Q_i\})$ (countably infinite, locally-finite directed graph D with states Q_i assigned to i-th node) and an associated family of finite-state machines M_i (only finitely many of which are distinct) with input alphabet $\Sigma_i = Q_{i_1} \times ... \times Q_{id_i}$ and local transition functions

$$\delta_i : Q_i \times \Sigma_i \to Q_i$$

The global evolution (dynamics) of an automata network is best viewed as a discrete dynamical system (self-map) $T : C \times C$, where $C = \Pi_i Q_i$ is a set of configurations (total states)

$$T(x)_i = \delta_i(x_i, x_{i_1}, ..., x_{i_{d_i}})$$

An automata network operates locally as follows. A copy of a finite-state machine M_i occupies each vertex (cell) i of D. Synchronously, each copy M_i looks up its input in the states $x_{i_1}, ..., x_{id_i}$ of its neighbor cells and its own state x_i, and then changes its state according to a local dynamics δ_i. Next the atomic move is repeated any (possibly very large) number of times.

In $-calculus we simulate an automata network as follows. We define a finite-state machine M_i with free variables $x_i, x_{i_1}, ..., x_{id_i}$

$$(:= M_i (\| (\mapsto (a_i (\delta_i x_i x_{i_1} ... x_{i_{d_i}}))) (\circ (\leftarrow (a_i x_i)) M_i)))$$

and AN as $(\|_i M_i)$. M_i calculates a new value of x_i by mutating/evaluating $(\delta_i x_i x_{i_1} ... x_{i_{d_i}})$ and passes it by mutation and receive pair to a new call of M_i. If the cost function is defined in such a way that parallel actions are cheaper than sequential ones, then the parallel composition will execute all transitions for all M_i simultaneously. This means than $-calculus can simulate an arbitrary automata network. In fact, our simulation is stronger - it allows for asynchronous work of M_i's because mutation and receive pairs will take care about synchronization requirements. Alternatively, we can encode an automata network by defining firstly all transition functions $(:= (\delta_i x_i x_{i_1} ... x_{i_{d_i}}) ...)$ defining for all input parameter instances the return value, and all network connections $(:= x_{j_k} (\delta_i x_i x_{i_1} ... x_{i_{d_i}})), ...$ and calling an automata network by $(\|_i (\delta_i x_i x_{i_1} ... x_{i_{d_i}}))$.

Summarizing, from the last result and from (4),(5) we obtain the following hierarchy of expressiveness of the models.

THEOREM 38
$$TM \subset CA \subseteq NN \subseteq AN \subseteq \$C \qquad (6)$$

If to allow infinitary concepts in π-calculus (probably, the most important - an infinite unbounded parallel composition and true concurrency), then π-calculus could also express interaction machines, cellular automata, discrete neural networks, and automata networks. Replication and definition from

π-calculus do not suffice to model an arbitrary automata network, having pattern of nodes which cannot be described by recursive constructs.

To confirm that infinity really matters, in [12] the solution of the halting problem for Turing machine, using an infinite discrete neural network, has been presented. However, neural networks (what could be expected) cannot solve their own NN halting problem.

3.2 Higher-Order versus First-Order

We prefer to have in our calculus higher-order features, for a simple reason. $-calculus is deemed to model interactive distributed systems, and although theoretically, every call by value (passing processes) can be replaced by call by name (passing process names), and vice versa, in distributed processing (remote procedure calls, TCP/IP protocols), the implementation of call by names is very difficult (if not impossible), i.e. passing pointers to objects in disjoint address spaces leads to tremendous implementation difficulties. For these reasons, stub procedures replace names by values in remote procedure calls. Thus although processes can be replaced by call to them [23,19], reducing higher-order to first-order makes sense if the access is really transferable.

Additionally, it is difficult to specify the behavior of self-modifying systems (and this is one of the main objectives of the $-calculus) without higher-order.

3.3 Asynchrony versus Synchrony

Of course, it matters whether we use synchronous or asynchronous send or receive. However, everything depends how asynchrony and synchrony are defined. In ("synchronous") π-calculus both synchronous and asynchronous input and output prefixes are permitted (thus I would hesitate to call it synchronous - it is equally synchronous as asynchronous), in asynchronous π-calculus only the pair: asynchronous output prefix and synchronous input prefixes are permitted, thus asynchronous π-calculus becomes a subset of "synchronous" π-calculus. Then, for instance, the leader election problem can be solved in synchronous π-calculus, but not in an asynchronous one [21]. However, to see how much everything depends on the definition, in [10] the leader election problem has been solved using asynchronous CSP (ACSP).

Thus it is not safe to claim that synchronous is more expressive than asynchronous unless we precisely define both notions. Do we consider only synchronous and asynchronous send and receive, or also synchronous and asynchronous start and termination of parallel execution (i.e., parbegin/parend versus fork/join constructs)? For example, Wegner [26] states that "asynchronous is more expressive than synchronous interaction, because the behavior of asynchronous distributed systems with no global notion of time clearly includes synchronous systems with global time as a special case".

3.4 Continuous versus Discrete

With continuity inherently is associated the notion of infinity, even more - the infinity is then nonenumerable. Thus we can expect that continuous systems are more expressive than discrete systems. Due to inherent hidden infinity, continuous (i.e. real number domain) neural networks are very expressive. One such neuron can simulate an arbitrary push-down automaton, two neurons - an arbitrary Turing machine [15]. Similar results have been reported for hybrid automata (state machines with real value variables) and analog computers. As it often happens, these theoretical results are blurred by an implementation problem - to implement them an arbitrary precision is required.

It is an open problem, whether we gain any expressive power by adding more than two (but finite) number of neurons. Obviously, an infinite number of continuous neurons is more expressive than two neurons, but how much? Is the expressiveness of infinite discrete neural networks the same as of infinite continuous neural networks?

4 Conclusions

We can conclude that regarding expressiveness infinity definitely matters, i.e. systems with infinitary means are more expressive than those without; higher-order theoretically does not matter, but practically may simplify implementation; synchrony matters, but you should be careful whether asynchronous behaviors are defined as subsets of synchronous behaviors or vice versa; and continuity matters, but it is unknown how much.

$-calculus allows for infinity, synchrony and asynchrony, continuity, and higher-order. Self-replication, universal computation and universal construction can be studied in the context of $-calculus (self-modifiable algorithms) with a slight difference. The notion of universal computation and universal construction should be upgraded, because $-calculus allows to express models having richer behavior than Turing machine. So far, there are no such equivalents in other process algebras.

There are several open problems. Formal semantics of $-calculus is given in a traditional form for process algebras, i.e., in the form of the Labeled Transition System. In [27], it has been suggested that interactive systems, i.e., process coalgebras, require models based on non-well-founded sets, coinduction and greatest fixed points. The axiomatization of utility-cost functions requires thorough studies. The same applies to optimization problems, i.e., emerging global optimization through local optimization, and integration of deliberative and reactive approaches in real-time.

$-calculus although being a new approach has found already several applications. It has been applied to the Office of Naval Research SAMON Project for coordination of multiple heterogeneous Autonomous Undersea Vehicles (AUVs) [8,9]. The Generic Behavior Message-Passing Language (GBML) has been derived from $-calculus for communication and script design of multiple cooperating mobile robots. $-calculus is also used for empirical cost profiling in Reactive Sensor Networks DARPA project at ARL Penn State. Potentially it could be used for design of cost languages, cellular evolvable cost-driven hardware, DNA-based computing and molecular biology, electronic commerce, and quantum computing. The project on $-calculus aims at investigation, design and implementation of a wide class of adaptive real-time complex systems exhibiting meta-computation and optimization. This includes robotics, software agents, neural nets, and evolutionary computation.

Acknowledgements. I would like to thank Dina Goldin, Richard Brooks, Max Garzon and Catuscia Palamidessi for discussion and comments.

References

1. Burks A. (1970) Essays on Cellular Automata, Univ. of Illinois Press.
2. Church A. (1941) The Calculi of Lambda Conversion, Princeton, N.J., Princeton University Press.
3. Dean T., Boddy M. (1988) An Analysis of Time-Dependent Planning, in Proc. Seventh National Conf. on Artificial Intelligence, Minneapolis, Minnesota, 49-54.
4. Eberbach E. (1994) SEMAL: A Cost Language Based on the Calculus of Self-modifiable Algorithms, Intern. Journal of Software Engineering and Knowledge Engineering, vol.4, no.3, 391-408.
5. Eberbach E. (1997) A Generic Tool for Distributed AI with Matching as Message Passing, Proc. of the Ninth IEEE Intern. Conf. on Tools with Artificial Intelligence TAI'97, Newport Beach, California, 11-18.
6. Eberbach E. (1997) Enhancing Genetic Programming by $-calculus, Proc. of the Second Annual Genetic Programming Conference GP-97, Morgan Kaufmann, Stanford University, 1997, 88 (a complete version in Proc. of the Tenth Australian Joint Conf. on Artificial Intelligence AI'97, The ACS National Committee on AI and ES, Perth, Australia, 1997, 77-83).
7. Eberbach E., Brooks R. (1999) $-Calculus: Flexible Optimization and Adaptation under Bounded Resources in Real-Time Complex Systems, Applied Research Laboratory, The Pennsylvania State University.
8. Eberbach E., Brooks R., Phoha. S. (1999) Flexible Optimization and Evolution of Underwater Autonomous Agents, in: New Directions in Rough Sets, Data Mining, and Granular-Soft Computing, Proc. of the 7th Intern. Workshop on Rough Sets, Fuzzy Sets, Data Mining and Granular-Soft Computing RSFDGrC'99, Yamaguchi, Japan, LNAI 1711, Springer-Verlag, 519-527.
9. Eberbach E., Phoha S. (1999) SAMON: Communication, Cooperation and Learning of Mobile Autonomous Robotic Agents, Proc. of the 11th IEEE Intern. Conf. on Tools with Artificial Intelligence ICTAI'99, Chicago, IL, 229-236.
10. Francez N., Stomp F.A. (1993) A Proof System for Asynchronously Communicating Sequential Processes, Dept. of Computer Science, Technion - Israel Institute of Technology, Tech. Rep. #772.

11. Garvey A., Lesser V. (1993) Design-to-Time Real-Time Scheduling, IEEE Transactions on Systems, Man, and Cybernetics, 23(6), 1491-1502.
12. Garzon M. (1995) "Models of Massive Parallelism: Analysis of Cellular Automata and Neural Networks", Springer-Verlag.
13. Goldin D. (2000) Persistent Turing Machines as a Model of Interactive Computation, FoIKS'00, Cottbus, Germany (also http://www.cs.umb.edu/~dqg).
14. Horvitz E. (1987) Reasoning about Beliefs and Actions under Computational Resources Constraints, in Proc. of the 1987 Workshop on Uncertainty in Artificial Intelligence, Seattle, Washington.
15. Koiran P., Cosnard M., Garzon M. (1994) Computability With Low-Dimensional Dynamical Systems, Theoretical Computer Science, 132, 113-128.
16. Liu J.W.S., Lin K.J., Shih W.K., Yu A.C., Chung J.Y., Zhao W. (1991) Algorithms for Scheduling Imprecise Computations, IEEE Computer, 24, 58-68.
17. Milner R. (1980) A Calculus of Communicating Systems, Lect. Notes in Computer Science vol.94, Springer-Verlag.
18. Milner R., Parrow J., Walker D. (1992) A Calculus of Mobile Processes, I & II, Information and Computation 100, 1-77.
19. Milner R. (1992) The Polyadic π-Calculus: A Tutorial, in F.L.Bauer,W.Brauer (eds.) Logic and Algebra of Specification, Springer-Verlag, 203-246.
20. Milner R. (1993) Elements of Interaction, CACM, vol.36, no.1, 78-89.
21. Palamidessi C. (1997) Comparing the Expressive Power of the Synchronous and the Asynchronous π-calculus, Proc. of the 24th ACM Symp. on Principles of Programming Languages (POPL), ACM, 256-265.
22. Russell S., Norvig P. (1995) Artificial Intelligence: A Modern Approach, Prentice-Hall.
23. Sangiorgi D. (1992) Expressing Mobility in Process Algebras: First-Order and Higher-Order Paradigms, Ph.D.Thesis, Dept. of Computer Science, Univ. of Edinburgh.
24. Wegner P. (1997) Why Interaction is More Powerful Than Algorithms, CACM, vol.40, no.5, 81-91.
25. Wegner P. (1997) Interactive Software Technology, in: The Computer Science and Engineering Handbook (ed. A.B. Tucker Jr.), CRC Press, 2440-2463.
26. Wegner P. (1997) Interactive Foundations of Computing, Theoretical Computer Science (also http://www.cs.brown.edu/people/pw).
27. Wegner P., Goldin D. (1999) Coinductive Models of Finite Computing Agents, Electronic Notes in Theoretical Computer Science, vol.19 (also http://www.cs.umb.edu/~dqg).
28. Wegner P., Goldin D. (1999) Interaction, Computability, and Church's Thesis, Accepted to the British Computer Journal (also http://www.cs.umb.edu/~dqg).

Distributed Artificial Intelligence: A Case Study of Implementations of a Parallel Algorithm Computing All Homomorphisms of Finite Automata

Boleslaw Mikolajczak

Computer and Information Science Department

University of Massachusetts Dartmouth

Dartmouth, MA 02747

bmikolajczak@umassd.edu

Abstract

This paper is composed of two main parts: a description of a parallel algorithm computing the set of all state homomorphisms between two finite deterministic complete automata; experimental results of algorithm's performance evaluation in several programming environments including transputer-based reconfigurable multicomputer architectures and distributed shared memory environment of Linda. We deal with two parallelization paradigms: data parallelism and process parallelism. The parallel algorithm computing all state homomorphisms of deterministic complete finite automata is composed of the following steps: selection of autonomous factors, computation of connected components, computation of graph-theoretic characteristics of connected components (set of generators, cycles, lengths of cycles, tails, and distances between vertices), and computation of the shapes of connected components (cycles, trees, and quasi-trees). Computations of connected components, graph-theoretic characteristics of connected components, and shapes of connected components are performed in parallel for both automata. Several necessary conditions are checked to reduce the exponential explosion in the number of candidate mappings. These conditions are: the cycle length divisibility condition, the vertex level condition, the vertex distance condition, and the function condition.

Keywords

Finite automata, automata homomorphisms, parallel algorithm, distributed implementation, performance evaluation of parallel algorithms, speedup, efficiency

160

Introduction and remarks on sequential state homomorphism algorithm for finite complete automata

Finite automata are fundamental in computer science as mathematical models describing behavior of finite state systems. Finite automata are used in analysis of semantics of programming languages, formal specification of communication protocols, design of object-oriented software, and in knowledge representation. Homomorphisms of finite automata are used to represent larger finite state system by smaller one, with preservation of system transitions [9]. This application is of special significance for systems which behavior exhibits exponential growth in the number of states. Homomorphisms are important since there exists one-to-one relationship between a homomorphism and the SP-partition (right congruence) for deterministic complete finite automata. This property holds both for state as well as generalized homomorphisms [8]. This implies application of homomorphisms to decomposition of finite state systems. The decision problem of whether a homomorphism exists between two automata is also interesting because this is an NP-complete problem. NP-completeness of the automata homomorphism problem follows from considerations presented in Mikolajczak [8]. The proof of polynomial reducibility is derived from *GRAPH K-COLORABILITY*. Sequential algorithms for NP-complete problems run in exponential time and therefore parallel algorithms for these problems have exponential cost in processor count. For such problems three general approaches are in place: sequential approximation algorithm, good probabilistic algorithm, and sequential/parallel heuristic algorithms.

Let A= (S, Σ, δ) be a deterministic complete automaton with finite nonempty set of states, finite nonempty set of input symbols and *transition function (next state function)* δ: SxΣ → S, where δ(s,σ) = s'. We shall extend a transition function δ such that it will point to the next state not only for single letters of alphabet Σ, but also for words from Σ^*, so that δ : S x Σ^* → S. For any s in S we define:

δ(s,λ) = s, where λ is the empty word,

(For every x in Σ^*)(For every σ in Σ) [(s,x) in Dom(δ) & δ((s,x),σ) in Dom(δ)

→ δ(s,xσ) = δ(δ(s,x),σ)]

Notice, that the domain of an *extended transition function* has been defined recursively. Now for every state s in S we define the set of input-valid words:

Dom_s (δ) = { x in Σ^* : (s,x) in Dom (δ) } .

A *function preserving operation* or a *homomorphism* of automata A and B is a mapping of A into B such that the 'behavior' of the transition function of A is preserved in operations of B. If both, the set of states and the set of inputs are mapped between both automata, then we call this mapping as a *state-*

input homomorphism; if the set of states is mapped only then the mapping is called a *state homomorphism*.

Let $A = (S_A, \Sigma_A, \delta_A)$ and $B = (S_B, \Sigma_B, \delta_B)$ be two deterministic complete automata. A pair of functions (h_S, h_Σ) is a *generalized homomorphism* of automaton A into automaton B if:

$$h_S : S_A \to S_B \text{ and } h_\Sigma : \Sigma_A^* \to \Sigma_B^*$$

and

$$(\text{For every } s \text{ in } S_A)(\text{For every } x \text{ in } \Sigma_A^* [h_S (\delta_A (s,x)) = \delta_B (h_S (s), h_\Sigma (x))]$$

If function h_Σ is an identity then generalized homomorphism is said to be a *state homomorphism*. The set of state homomorphisms between automata A and B is denoted as HOM(A,B). For generalized homomorphisms input literals of the pre-image automaton A can be mapped into sequences of input symbols of increasing (finite) length of the image automaton B. Such homomorphisms are computationally reducible to *state homomorphisms* [3]. Therefore only state homomorphism algorithms are discussed in details in this paper. Generalized homomorphisms require a computation of the *characteristic semigroup* of the image automaton B. The characterisitic semigroup of an automaton A is the set of equivalence classes Σ^* with respect to Myhill relation, together with operation of their composition with respect to the Myhill relation, where Σ^* denotes the set of all input words except empty word λ. Unfortunately, for many finite automata the cardinality of the characteristic semigroup grows exponentially with number of states. These are automata which have computational power to simulate all other automata. Therefore the computation of the characteristic semigroup can be treated as a separate problem.

All other concepts concerning automata, used and not directly defined in this paper, are taken from Mikolajczak [8]. Concepts used in the paper for the first time are presented in italics independently whether definition is provided or quoted from references.

Paralellization of one of the two existing sequential algorithms has been undertaken in [9]. The algorithm relies on decomposition into autonomous factors. This approach reduces the automata homomorphism problem to study of autonomous factors' homomorphisms and to verification whether homomorphism for one autonomous factor can be extended to the remaining autonomous factors. The verification step can be accomplished in O(n) time on sequential computer and in O(1) time on parallel computer. Additional reason for decision in this direction was the fact that automata homomorphism problem can be treated as a complex computational problem, requiring coordination of several elementary graph and combinatorial algorithms. In this sense the parallelization of automata homomorphism algorithm is a challenging task comparing with parallelization of graph algorithms for basic properties such as such as connectivity. In [] author of this paper formulated the sequential algorithm computing the set of all generalized homomorphims between two finite complete deterministic automata. In other words, this algorithm is capable to generate all possible decompositions of the first automaton. The algorithm has practical applications in computational problems where program semantics is described by a huge state spaces (for instance communication protocols, combinatorial optimization problems, and collections of cooperating sequential programs described by means of Petri nets). In addition, the proof of NP-completeness of automata homomorphism has been formulated. Therefore one should not expect fast and efficient sequential and parallel algorithms for the automata homomorphisms problem. The special case of the generalized homomorphism sequential algorithm, called automata state homomorphisms problem, has been implemented [5, 6, 10].

The sequential algorithm has the following six major steps: selection of an autonomous factor, computation of connected components, computation of graphtheoretic characteristics of connected components, computation of the shapes of connected components, computation of all partial homomorphisms for connected components of autonomous factors, composition of partial homomorphisms.

Parallel state homomorphism algorithm of complete finite automata

Recently, the parallel algorithm computing all automata state homomorphisms has been formulated [9], and implemented [5, 6] using reconfigurable transputer-based multicomputer architectures and using distributed shared memory programming environment with Linda C. The algorithm, denoted here as PAHA (Parallel Automata Homomorphism Algorithm), applies, to a maximal degree permitted by several graph-theoretic structural properties of the automata involved, the process-based parallelism and data parallelism. Data decomposition over automata inputs is explored in a precomputation stage of the algorithm. Dependency graph of the parallel automata homomorphism algorithm [9] indicates that three fundamental stages of automata homomorphism algorithm: finding connected components, finding graph-theoretic characteristics of connected components, and checking whether mappings are state homomorphisms have to be executed sequentially. This creates a natural bottleneck in achieving high speedup of the algorithm.

Four necessary graph-theoretic structural properties of automata are exploited in PAHA to increase degree of parallelism and to improve algorithm's performance:

- *degree of connectedness of both automata*, i.e. how many connected components can be extracted from the original automata [1]

- *length cycle divisibility*, i.e. condition that lengths of all cycles of connected components involved in a mapping (being a candidate to state homomorphism) have to be mutually divisible

- *state level* , i.e. condition that any state of the image automaton has to be mapped on levels not higher than the level of a state in the pre-image automaton [2]

- *state distance* , i.e. condition that a distance between any two states in the pre-image automaton has to be preserved in the image automaton modulo length of cycle of the connected component of the image automaton [11, 12].

When all four necessary conditions are met for a mapping, then the binary relation between all implied states of the pre-image automaton and image automaton is created by means of respective extended transition functions of automata. This relation is created only for the sets of generators and states reachable from these generators. Finally the relation is checked whether it is a function or not. If yes, the function constitutes a state homomorphism for autonomous factors under consideration. Suitability of this state homomorphism for other autonomous factors is then checked in a deterministic manner. In Fig.1, 2, and 3 we present dependency graphs to compute connected components, to compute graph-theoretic characteristics of connected components, and to compute automata state homomorphisms for connected components with three different shapes, respectively. The parallel algorithm has to obey these dependencies.

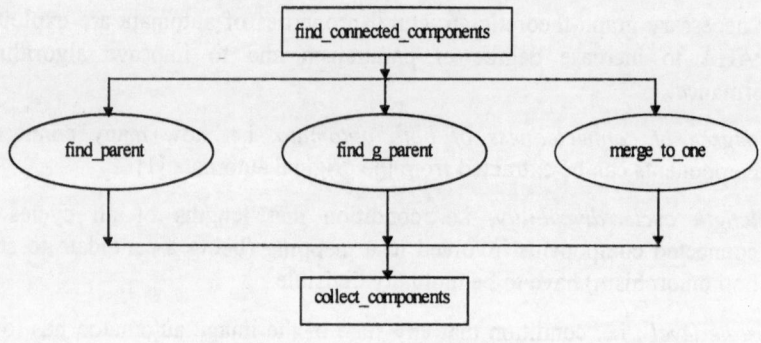

Fig.1. Dependency graph of parallel algorithm computing connected components

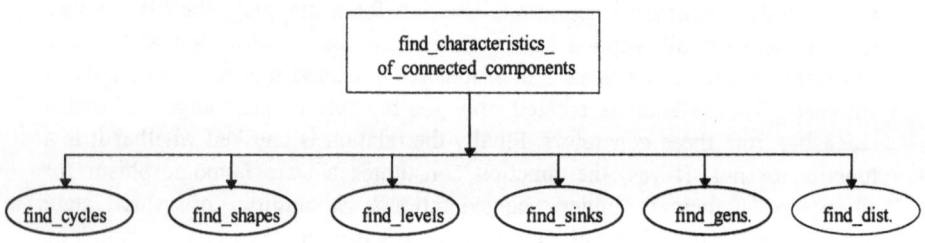

Fig. 2. Dependency graph of parallel algorithm computing graph-theoretic characterisitcs of connected components.

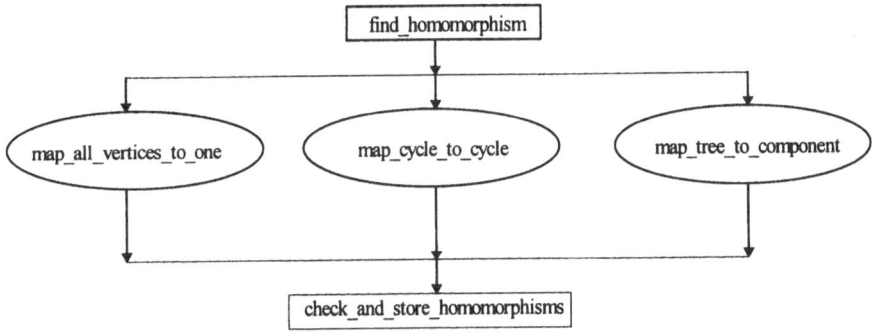

Fig.3. Dependency graph of parallel algorithm computing automata state homomorphisms.

The general structure of the parallel algorithm can be presented by the following steps:

Step 1: Select input literal σ for which computation of state homomorphisms between automata A and B will be carried out; this selection can be based on random choice or on a precomputation to minimize parallel execution time of the algorithm. The precomputation can be carried out in parallel for all autonomous factors. Structural properties of a graph include graph connectivity and a shape of connected components.

Step 2: Compute connected components of autonomous factors A_σ and B_σ.

   forall states of autonomous factors A_σ and B_σ **do**

   Set a parent for all states on the path from that state to the root as the root of the tree;

   Compute the root of the state in the forest of trees;

   Merge all trees into one single tree;

Step 3: Compute cycle lengths of each connected component of autonomous factors A_σ and B_σ.

   forall connected components of autonomous factors A_σ and B_σ **do**

   Compute cycle length;

   if cycle divisibility condition between connected components is not met **then** Hom(A_σ, B_σ)=$\varnothing$

   else

Step 4: Compute shape characterisitcs of each connected component of autonomous factors A_σ and B_σ

forall connected components of autonomous factors A_σ and B_σ **do**

Determine a shape of a connected component;

Compute a level of each state;

Compute a sink state of each state;

Compute a minimal set of generators;

Compute cardinality of the minimal set of generators;

Compute distances between the first generator and each other generator in the minimal set of

generators;

Compute distances between each pair of vertices in autonomous factor B_σ;

Step 5: Generate partial mappings between connected components of autonomous factors A_σ and B_σ and check whether these mappings are functions.

forall pairs of connected components of autonomous factors A_σ and B_σ **do**

Generate all partial mappings between the minimal set of generators in a connected component of A_σ

and all states of connected components in B_σ;

Extend each partial mapping to the set of all states in A_σ using transition functions δ_A δ_B ;

if the extended partial mapping is a partial function **then** record function;

Step 6: Combine partial functions generated in step 5 to form state homomorphisms between autonomous factors A_σ and B_σ. Check whether these state homomorphisms can be extended to the remaining autonomous factors of A and B.

forall connected components of autonomous factor A_σ **do**

Choose partial functions recorded in **Step 5**;

Combine partial functions into a total function for autonomous factors A_σ and B_σ;

Record the total function as an element of the set $HOM(A_\sigma, B_\sigma)$;

forall autonomous factors of automata A and B **do**

Check whether total functions can be extended to all autonomous factors;

PAHA's distributed and distributed shared memory implementations

PAHA's implementation is process-based and data parallel. Processes are running both synchronously and asynchronously. In asynchronous mode processes are attached to specific functions from the sequential algorithm. Functions were selected according to specific functionalities of the algorithm and with attention to approximately similar granularity of each function. Number of processes created and processors involved depends on degree of connectedness, number of states, and structural class from which automata come from.

PAHA has been implemented on a 17 node reconfigurable transputer architecture from Transtech, Ithaca, New York, attached to the PC 486DX2 66MHz, with 16MB of main memory and 256 kB of cache memory. The first node is a host (with 4 MB), the remaining 16 transputers (1 MB of memory each) can be software reconfigured into line, ring, mesh, tree and hypercube or any other reasonable architecture (for instance one of the many hypercubic architectures). This last feature creates enormous research potentials in experimentation of relationship between algorithms and architectures, especially for algorithms which theoretical parallel execution time is known to be exponential and for architectures having identical worst case communication overhead (for instance logarithmic in terms of the number of processors). In this study we explored this feature to the limit. We studied performance of our algorithm for every realistic architectures: pipeline, ring, mesh, tree, and several hypercubic networks. The reason for such extensive approach is simply an initial exploration of the algorithm which has not been well researched.

The second implementation of PAHA has been performed using distributed shared memory programming environment with Linda C. The original sequential source code was available in C [5]. This code has been adopted to Linda C [6]. Timing of the execution times has been accomplished using three Linda C functions: *start_timer()* that sets the time to 0 and starts timing of program execution, *split_timer(string)* – sets a break point and labels it with the 'string', *print_times()* – prints the legacy time and accumulation time from the beginning through every break points to the end.

There are four coordination operations in Linda that allow building a parallel program: **in, out, eval**, and **rd.** The **in()** operator attempts to remove a passive tuple from a tuple space by associatively searching for a data tuple that matches a template specified as arguments of **in()** operator. If no matching is found then the operator blocks execution of a process until a matching has been found. If there is one or more matching tuples then one of the matching tuples is removed nondeterministically. The matching tuple is removed from the tuple space and each formal in the template is set to the value of its corresponding field in the tuple. The **out()** operator adds a passive tuple to the tuple space. Prior to adding it, the **out()** operator evaluates all of its fields, resolving them to actual values. The **rd()** operator is identical in functionality to **in()** operator except that it does not remove the matching tuple from tuple space, just the value of the tuple is read. The **eval()** operator creates a process tuple (active tuple) consisting of the fileds specified as its arguments. If the field is a function call then this function is evaluated concurrently by a separate process that returns a resulting passive tuple to the tuple space. A function, being an argument of the **eval()** operator, can not use pointers as parameters. Therefore, the calling function can use **out()** operator to place needed arguments into the tuple space. The called function then can use **in()** operator to read those arguments.

In parallel Linda C implementation of the automata homomorphism algorithm we followed the agenda parallelism, called also coordinator-worker parallel programming paradigm. Separate workers were created to compute connected components, shapes, and graph-theoretic properties of autonomous factors. The resulting degree of concurrency depends on how many connected components automata A and B have.

The following quantitative factors have to be considered when testing performance of parallel automata homomorphism algorithm: number of states in automata A and B, number of connected components in automata A and B, shapes of connected components of automata A and B, number of CPUs per processors, and number of machines in a network environment. In our experiments we limited number of states in automata A and B to 32. This is motivated by two pragmatic factors: the sequential run time of such cases is large enough (several hours) and overflowing of the tuple space. The second factor can be eliminated by using the watermarking technique. This technique keeps actual size of the tuple space during the computation within limits of minimum and maximum.

For performance testing purposes three versions of automata homomorphism program have been developed: sequential version, parallel multithreaded version running on a single machine, parallel networked version. All three programs use Linda C compiler. The last two programs are identical except using different executing environments: **cds** environment for multithreaded version and **network** environment for the networked version.

PAHA's performance in distributed and distributed shared memory programming environments

Performance evaluation of PAHA is based on comparison with sequential implementation in C [5,6] using speedup and processor utilization (efficiency). The reason for such approach is that this is the only known parallel implementation of automata state homomorphims algorithm. Examples used in this evaluation have been selected from literature and classified into several categories in such a manner that the number of states grows for a given class of automata. Number of states is treated as a fundamental measure of automaton complexity. Number of inputs is treated as a constant coefficient. Time complexities (both sequential and parallel) are expressed as a function of the number of states for specific classes of automata.

However, during experiments it has been observed that from speedup point of view, the number of connected components of each automaton is more important than the number of states for all classes of automata studied. Speedup grows approximately linearly with increase in the number of connected components of each automaton for each structural class of automata studied. By a class of automata we mean classes which have the same graph-theoretic structural properties. Classes investigated were: permutation automata, asynchronous automata, k-asynchronous automata, (k,l)-asynchronous automata. These classes have tendency to have increasing number of state homomorphisms (as listed from left to right). It is important to mention here that for two randomly chosen automata the probability of having nonempty state homomorphism is very, very low. Therefore, searching spaces and execution times are enormous for this problem.

We studied relatively small textbook examples up to 40 states in the pre-image automaton and 20 states in the image automaton. Even for such small examples searching spaces reach millions of potential mappings (even after taking into account the necessary conditions stated above). For this reason we decided not store these mappings; we check them 'on the fly' and store only mappings which are state homomorphisms for all inputs.

To find the most suitable architecture for automata state homomorphism algorithm we used transputer system software reconfiguration capabilities. The following architectures were implemented: line, ring, binary tree, and hypercube.

The highest parallel execution time observed (experiments with the algorithm are still continued in the whole architectural space) was around 40 seconds for 16-node hypercube with maximal speedup achieved of 7.5 (no I/O operations are included in these values. This last result seems to be somewhat disappointing. On the other hand, the problem studied has very large and unstructured data domain which influence on algorithm's performance is mostly unknown.

Testing in Linda C environment comprises two kinds of machines and environments: 4-processor server UltraSPARC II 400 MHz with 512 MB of main memory each and 10 networked SPARCstation4 with 110 MHz processors and 64 MB of main memory. These hardware and software environments permit testing of sequential algorithm on a server, testing of sequential version running on one workstation, testing of a multithreaded parallel version running on a server, testing of a parallel version running on a network of workstations. Testing has been fully automated [] by writing scripts, preparing files of tested automata, and by sending results of computations to proper files.

First, we have run certain number of tests with automata having number of states smaller than 10 to check correctness of parallel versions of the algorithm. For these tests we actually got a slowdown in parallel execution time.

Secondly, we retained the structure of automata A and B from previous test and we increased number of states to 28 for automaton A and to 14 for automaton B. For a 4-processor server UltraSPARC II we got a spedup of 3.41 out of 4 or efficiency of 85.2%. The actual sequential execution time was 150.72 sec and parallel execution time was 44.19 sec. For a networked environment we got a speedup of 3.39 out of 4 or efficiency of 84.7%. The actual sequential execution time was 622.93 sec and parallel execution time was 183.42 sec. These results are very encouraging. However, running the multithreaded parallel program on a single processor workstation actually slows down the execution time (643.26 sec vs. 622.93 sec for sequential single machine workstation). The reason is an overhead to create child processes and the context switching time between processes.

Thirdly, we have retained the same structure of automata A and B and we have increased number of states to 32 and 16 for automata A and B, respectively. The speedup for a parallel algorithm running on a 4-processor server UltraSPARC II vs. sequential running on 1-processor server was 3.96 out of 4 with 5964.96 sec for sequential execution and 1502.81 sec for parallel execution. This implies 99% efficiency. For a networked environment we got a speedup of 3.98 out of 4 or efficiency of 99.5%. The actual sequential execution time was 24691.28 sec and parallel execution time was 6192.88 sec. These results are quite impressive. This almost perfect performance results can be attributed to the symmetric shapes of both automata. As a result work distribution among worker is also almost ideally symmetric. The overhead is in this case limited to process initialization and to collection of results.

In the next sequence of experiments we used exclusively and seperately automata with tree and quasi-tree structure of connected components. Execution times for both trees and quasi-trees are almost identical as in the first set of experiments. Increasing the number of states in automata with connected components being trees and quasitrees does not change significantly the execution times of sequential and parallel programs. This result leads us to a conclusion that number of different mappings generated by the algorithm is the key reason for increased execution time. Number of different mappings is limited to only several hundreds in case of automata with connected components being trees or quasitrees. This lead us to the second conclusion: there are two main factors affecting the number of mappings generated: number of connected components and shape of connected components. If both automata have connected components being cycles only and the cycles divisibility condition is met then the number of mappings generated by algorithm will be much larger than for automata with connected components being trees or quasi- trees. The second conclusion implies that from performance perspective it is sufficient to study automata with cycles only.

The purpose of the next sequence of experiments was to study an influence of the number of connected components of automaton A (pre-image) on execution time. Automata A were selected with 16 states and different number of connected components being all cycles of different length. Automaton B had fixed number of states equal 4 and connected components being cycles only. Experiments with parallel program running on a 4-processor server UltraSPARC II indicate that execution time is insensitive to the number of states in automaton A, it is very sensitive to the number of connected components in automaton A. In fact, with linear increase of the number of connected components from 12 to 16 the parallel execution time increased exponentially from ~10 sec for 12 connected components to ~2000 sec for 16 connected components.

The purpose of the next sequence of experiments was to study an influence of the number of connected components of automaton B (image) on the parallel execution time. We selected a fixed automaton A (pre-image) with 20 states and 10 cycles for one autonomous factor and one cycle for another autonomous factor. Automata B have been selected with fixed number of 8 states and variable number of connected components being cycles for one autonomous factor. Experiments with parallel program running on a 4-processor server UltraSPARC II indicate that the main factor that affects the execution time is the number of states in automaton B. Linear decrease in number of states in automaton B from 8 to 4 was accompanied by logarithmic reduction in parallel execution time from 438.37 sec for 8 states to 0.81 sec for 4 states. On the other hand, if the number of states in automaton B remained the same (n=8) and the number of connected components decreased from 8 to 4, then the parallel execution time shall remain in the same order of magnitude.

The purpose of the next sequence of experiments was to study performance of the networked parallel version of the algorithm. We selected fixed automaton A with 32 states and 8 cycles for one autonomous factor and 2 cycles for another autonomous factor. All automata B had 16 states and variable number of cycles changing from 16 to 8 and to 4 for one autonomous factor and fixed number of 2 cycles for another autonomous factor. Cycles are identical to connected components. Number of process workers used was identical to the number of connected components of of automaton B, i.e. 4, 8, 16. Number of workstations participating in experiment was 4, 8, 9 (Linda has licences for 10 and 20 workstations). The sequential execution time for number of 4, 8, 16 connected components was 26439.35 sec, 28873.78 sec, 34143.38 sec, respectively. The networked parallel version with 4, 8, 9 workstations had parallel execution time of 6723.55 sec, 4002.11, and 5190.12, respectively. These results imply speedups of 3.93 out of 4, 7.21 out of 8, and 6.57 out of 9 or efficiency of 98.3%, 90.18%, and 73.09%, respectively. The same experiments were repeated for the parallel algorithm running on a 4-processor server UltraSPARC II. For 4, 8, 16 connected components in automaton B the sequential execution times were: 5950.97 sec, 6219.89 sec, and 7316.84 sec, respectively. Parallel execution times were: 1622.73 sec, 1687.72, and 1879.72, respectively. This implies speedups of 3.66, 3.68, and 3.89, respectively, and efficiencies of 91.68%, 92.13%, and 97.31%.

Further research

Another approach, which requires modification in current implementation, takes into account influence of the data parallelism. In addition, parallelization of the automaton characterisitc semigroup algorithm could allow extension of the current algorithm to compute all generalized homomorphisms between two automata. We intend to study these problems using reconfigurable transputer architecture with line, ring, mesh, binary tree and hypercube architectures. An interesting question is whether there exist classes of automata which can achieve higher performance (speedup and efficiency) on certain architectures.

Acknowledgments

The author also wishes to thank Mary K. Moynihan, Xiaochang Hua, and Zheng-jie Kuo for their contribution to implementation of sequential and parallel versions of the automata homomorphism algorithms. Discussions with them during realizations of these projects, esp. those devoted to the issues of process vs. data parallelism, helped in better understanding the implementational issues of the algorithm.

References

[1]. Aggarval, A., Anderson, A.J., Kao, M., *Parallel depth-first search in general directed graphs,* SIAM J. of Computing, **19**, 2 (1989), pp. 397-409.

[2]. Chin F.Y., Lam J., Chen I-N., *Efficient parallel algorithms for some graph problems,* CACM, **25**, 9 (1982), pp. 659-665.

[3]. Grzymala-Busse, J.W., *Operation-preserving functions and autonomous factors of finite automata,* JCSS, **5** (1971), pp. 465-474.

[4]. Hirschberg D.S., Chandra A.K., Sarwate D.V., *Computing connected components on parallel computers,* CACM, **22**, 8 (1979), pp. 461-464.

[5]. Hua, Xiaochang, *Implementation of a parallel algorithm of automata homomorphisms problem on reconfigurable transputer architecture,* Master Research Project, Computer and Information Science Department, University of Massachusetts Dartmouth, January 1994.

[6]. Kuo, Zheng-jie, *Implementation of a parallel algorithm of automata homomorphisms problem in distributed programming environments,* Master Research Project, University of Massachuestts Dartmouth, Fall 1999

[7]. LaPoutre, J.A., *New Techniques for the Union-Find Problem,* Proc. of the First Annual ACM-SIAM Symp. on Discrete Algorithms, 1989, pp. 54-63.

[8]. Mikolajczak, B., (ed.), *Algebraic and Structural Automata Theory,* in series: Annals of Discrete Mathematics, vol. 44, North-Holland Publishing Company, 402 pp.,1991; ISBN 0-444-87458-5.

[9]. Mikolajczak, B., *Parallel Distributed Algorithm to Compute All Homomorphisms of Finite Automata,* DIMACS Series in Discrete Mathematics and Theoretical Computer Science, vol, 22, Parallel Processing of Discrete Optimization Problems, DIMACS Workshop April 28-29, 1994; edited by Panos M.Pardalos, Mauricio G.C. Resende, and K.G. Ramakrishnan, pp.233-258; American Mathematical Society; ISBN 0-8218-0240-2.

[10]. Moynihan, M. K., *Design and Implementation of a Sequential Algorithm for Computing All State Homomorphisms of Complete Deterministic Finite Automata Using Decomposition into Autonomous Factors,* Master Research Project, Computer and Information Science Department, University of Massachusetts Dartmouth, August 1992.

[11]. Shiloach, Y., Vishkin, U., *An O(log n) parallel connectivity algorithm,* J. of Algorithms, **3** (1982), pp. 57-67.

[12].Tarjan, R.E., *Efficiency of a good but not linear set union algorithm,* JACM, **22**, 2 (1975), pp. 215-225.

Methodology of Diagnostic Knowledge Acquisition from Databases of Examples

Wojciech Moczulski

Technical University of Silesia, PL 44-100 Gliwice, Poland

Abstract. The diagnostics of a critical machinery is nowadays aided by expert systems. Their knowledge bases contain knowledge on diagnostic relationships between a technical state of a given machine, its operating conditions and observable symptoms of this state. This knowledge may be acquired either from human experts or from databases containing examples. The paper focuses on problems of knowledge acquisition from examples. It concerns the whole range of problems starting from preparation of examples up to the verification and validation of the knowledge base at the end of the proceeding. To acquire diagnostic knowledge from a set of examples we apply both machine learning and knowledge discovery methods. An example of the application of described methods for the acquisition of knowledge suitable for diagnosing complex technical states of rotating machinery is also given.

Keywords: machinery diagnostics, complex technical states, knowledge acquisition, learning from examples, knowledge discovery

1 Introduction

A basic task of machinery diagnostics consists in diagnosing, i.e. recognition or identification of a technical state of a given machine that occurs by limited quantity of information. The essence of this activity depends on diagnostic reasoning which may be efficiently performed, if corresponding data that constitute premises of the reasoning process have been collected, possible technical states attributable to the diagnosed object have been known and the diagnostic system is equipped with sufficient knowledge which may be employed in the reasoning.

Recent computerized systems used commonly for monitoring of critical machinery collect plenty of data that describe inputs and outputs of a given machine. Input of the machine may be any action or influence of the environment onto the machine which includes control, supply and disturbances. Output of the machine is both useful/intended product or residual processes while the latter ones are unwanted yet unavoidable results of its operation [1]. There is a need to identify some diagnostic relationships [10] which combine features describing inputs, outputs and state of the object and thus representing domain knowledge. These relationships may be in a form of rules, decision trees etc.

There are two main knowledge sources: domain experts and databases of examples. Domain experts are primary sources of diagnostic knowledge. They may be directly engaged in the knowledge acquisition process or can act as indirect sources of knowledge if they are authors of professional literature, publications etc. whose contents have to be interpreted by other experts or special software. The participation of domain experts in the knowledge acquisition process is required in at least two stages: in the introductory stage where a description of the problem domain is created (which concerns: objects, classes of objects, attributes and their values etc.), as well as in the verification and validation stage.

Databases may contain results of diagnostic observations of the investigated object(s) or results of numerical experiments conducted with the application of a proper mathematical model. The latter examples may be generated according to some prior plan or they may be obtained in a closed-loop numerical experiment using some criterion which directs the generation process [2,10]. Such data sets may be used as training examples for knowledge acquisition by automated machine learning with the use of induction [8,16] or by discovering qualitative and functional dependencies in the data sets [13].

The paper concerns the methodology of acquisition of diagnostic knowledge from examples. It is based on the previous works of the author [10,11] and is organized as follows. In section 2 a brief description of the problem is given and a way of its solving is outlined. Section 3 deals with applied methods of knowledge acquisition and some methods of assessment (verification and validation) of previously acquired knowledge. An example of the application of the described methodology that concerns some problems frequently occurring in rotating machinery is described in section 4. The final section contains a brief recapitulation of more important results and conclusions.

2 Problem Description

As it has been already mentioned there is a need for acquisition of relevant knowledge concerning some well-defined diagnostic problem domain. In our research knowledge is represented by rules and/or decision trees. We assume that this knowledge is to be acquired by induction from data (so-called examples) described by diagnostic symptoms and features of operating conditions, that for the given object are pairs $< a, v >$ composed from attribute names and their values. For each example we also have the value of a deci sion attribute corresponding to the class of the technical state to which the example belongs. The set of learning examples may be collected during some diagnostic experiment. If we conduct series of active or passive diagnostics experiments, then the symptom values are usually features of vibro-acoustic signals observed on the diagnosed object during its functioning under some actual operating conditions. Other possibility is to perform a numerical experiment using simulations software. It is reasonable to represent all attribute values qualitatively, which usually requires discretization of real–valued ones. The way of preparation of the examples is crucial to the whole process.

Typical attempts to knowledge acquisition from examples assume a flat structure of the set of examples, i.e. no relationships between subsets of examples corresponding to the considered faults are taken into account. Such an approach is inadequate if we have to deal with complex technical states that are often observed e.g. on large scale rotating machinery. Thus there is a strong need for a method that would enable us to acquire knowledge suitable for diagnostic reasoning upon complex states.

The diagnostic concluding depends on the recognition of a class of the actual technical state (possibly complex) of the diagnosed object given the symptoms of this state and maybe some values of parameters of actual operating conditions. Such a task is equivalent to the classification. Hence the content of the knowledge base, regardless of the method of knowledge representation applied, determines some classifier. Therefore, the classifiers performance may be defined and used as an assessment criterion during verification and/or validation of this classifier.

Taking into account the problem outlined above, the author has undertaken the research on the methodology of acquisition of diagnostic knowledge [10]. Only selected results of this research are presented in this paper.

3 Methods Applied

Methods of acquisition of diagnostic knowledge are strongly related to knowledge sources (see Fig. 1) and can be divided into two groups: these connected with human experts (who may take active or passive part into the knowledge acquisition process) and 'automatic' ones, which are used for knowledge acquisition from databases. The latter group may be further classified into supervised Machine Learning (ML) methods and unsupervised methods of Data Mining (DM) and Knowledge Discovery (KD). As we mentioned in Section 1, domain experts are very valuable sources of diagnostic knowledge and cannot be eliminated in the knowledge acquisition process. However, direct methods of knowledge acquisition from experts are inefficient enough. Therefore it is advantageous to apply ML and KD methods that took place in the described research.

3.1 Methodology Developed

It has been decided to use both supervised and unsupervised methods. A more comprehensive research concerns an application of the supervised ML methods. We can use them if we have an access to a database containing previously classified examples. Databases applied in the process of diagnostic knowledge acquisition contain data sets that were collected in a diagnostic experiment performed either on a real object (as active and/or passive experiments, connected with measurements of several diagnostic signals), or on a model of some object (numerical experiment).

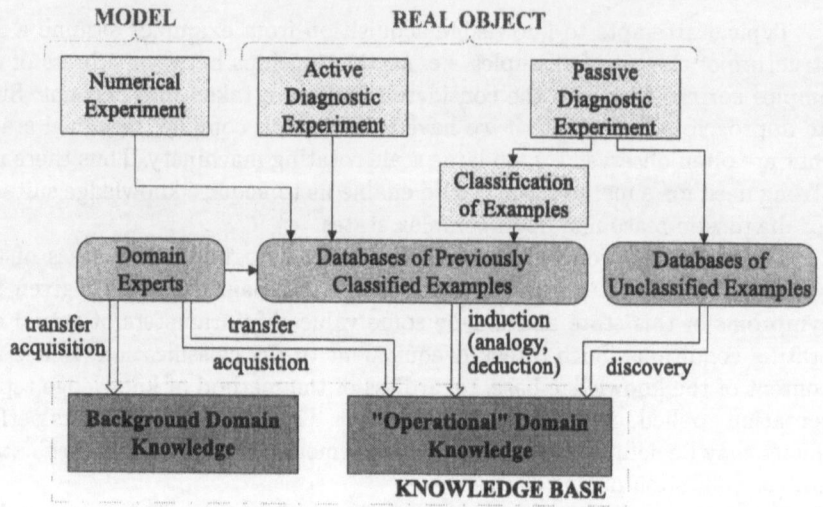

Fig. 1. Main sources of diagnostic knowledge [11]

The knowledge acquisition process consists of several steps (see Fig. 2) that will be briefly discussed below. The diagnostic experiment shall be conducted according to its plan which ought to take into account diagnostic knowledge referencing to the problem, which is to be solved. The proper plan of the experiment is crucial for the success of the whole process. During the experiment we are able to acquire signals that carry information on machinery malfunctions. If the experiment is numeric then signals are generated using model-based approach. Active and passive diagnostic experiments require measurements of needed diagnostic signals. It is reasonable to store acquired signals in digital form in the database. Such a solution enables us to extract qualitative features containing essential information on the condition of the diagnosed machine, and to optimize the set of features applied for learning (these problems are addressed in [7]). Then each example is represented by a record in the data set whose fields contain several values of conditional attributes and, since we have to deal with the supervised process, value(s) of at least one decision attribute denoting the class(es) where the classified example belongs. Each example is considered as positive for a concept that corresponds to some given technical state (malfunction) and as negative (counterexample) for all other concepts.

It is preferred to use qualitative values of conditional attributes. Hence respective discretization of quantitative values of signal features is required. There are two possible attempts [4]: supervised discretization and unsupervised one (see e.g. [14]). The author prefers the first kind of discretization since it takes into consideration experts knowledge on the machine to be diagnosed (see also [6]). The discretization process requires some set of cut-

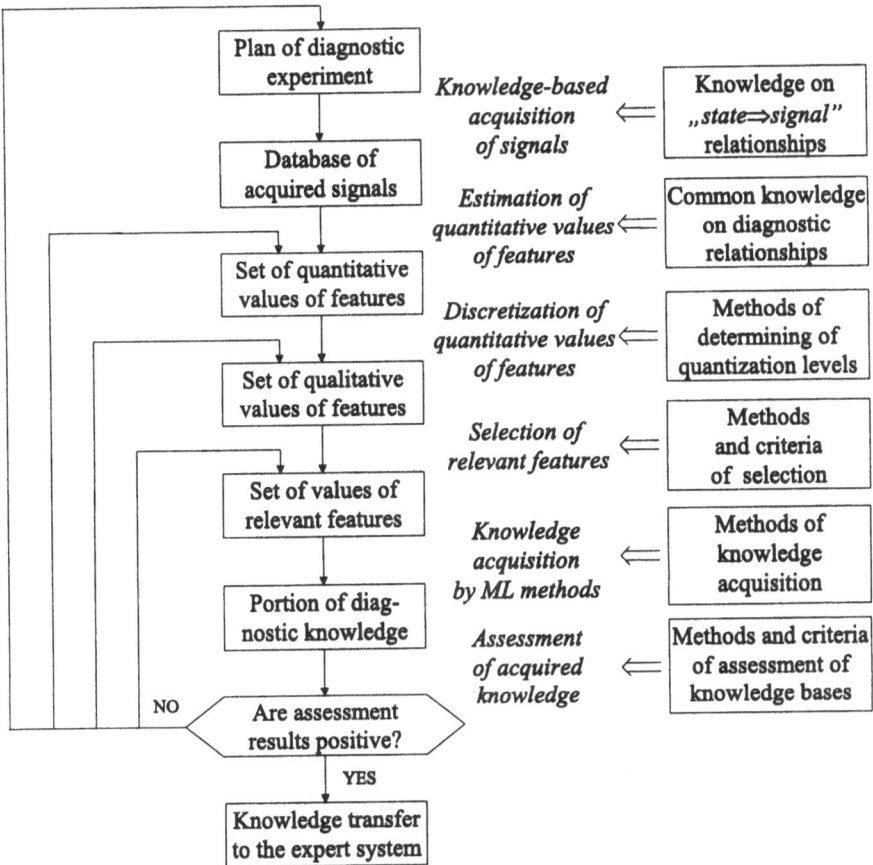

Fig. 2. Methodology of supervised knowledge acquisition using ML methods [12]

ting points for the domain of a given feature. The selection of these values is also vital for the whole process of automatic knowledge acquisition. We prefer such methods which give only a few cutting points. If we assign each discrete value to some linguistic value, an easy interpretation of the resulting qualitative values will be possible also by an untrained user. The more comprehensive discussion of the methods used for converting quantitative values of attributes into qualitative ones is contained in [11,3].

To make the whole process computationally effective a subset of relevant attributes should be selected. There are several methods of selection, e.g. based on minimal reducts using rough sets approach [15], or on correlation analysis of the values of attributes contained in the data set (see e.g. [3]). By the selection of relevant attributes and discretization of continuous ones we obtain the database of examples for knowledge acquisition using supervised ML methods.

To acquire knowledge from databases of examples we use the following well-known ML methods:

1. induction of rules using:
   - *STAR* general covering methodology [8],
   - rough sets approach [15,5];
2. induction of decision trees [16].

'Automatic' methods of assessment of the acquired knowledge depend on the application of either special set of testing examples or some resampling technique and then calculation of classification errors. The frequently used criterion concerns the overall empirical error rate (see next subsection). If the error rate obtained is unacceptable then the process may be repeated iteratively. There are some possibilities (see Fig. 2):

1. selection of a new subset of relevant attributes which can be obtained using other method of attributes selection;
2. determination of a new set of cutting points and new discretization of continuous attributes;
3. application of other signal features more sensitive to the considered malfunctions and more appropriate to distinguish different states;
4. modification of the plan of diagnostic experiment in order to collect new signals whose feature values will supplement the set of learning examples.

This iterative process is continued until the stop criterion (e.g. concerning the overall empirical error rate) is satisfied.

The author and J. M. Żytkow have also begun a research on applications of KD methods to machinery diagnostics [13]. The KD process included several steps. To discover qualitative (approximate) dependencies and estimate their strength, contingency tables were applied, which suggested very strong functional dependencies, but obtained results were imprecise. Contingency tables are suitable for identification of approximate dependencies, that may be refined by finding of equations. Continuous attributes were used and were discretized only for contingency tables - other analyses have been carried out using original data. Introductory results of this research were very promising, so it will be continued.

3.2 Methods of Knowledge Verification and Validation

To estimate classification errors, we use the overall empirical error rate $\epsilon_{ov} = n_{err}/n_t$, where n_{err} denotes number of classification errors and n_t is the total number of testing examples. With regard to the number of examples contained in the specific data sets, either *k-fold cross validation* or *random subsampling* techniques are applied.

An important problem concerns validation of acquired knowledge. We use special sets of examples prepared by independent experts or collected during measurements on the object whose technical state is known. Such testing examples enable us to detect and/or avoid an overfitting of knowledge to the learning examples that have been used.

4 Example of Application

Exemplary applications of the described methods and the means have been presented in [10]. These examples concerned rotordynamic problems related to diagnosing of some technical states of a rotating machine. The investigations were carried out using a material model called *Rotor Kit*.

To collect data we carried out an active diagnostic experiment on the *Rotor Kit*, whose task has been to find relationships between rotor vibrations and their causes as: imbalance, rubbing and overload. The object was observed by three rotating speeds of the rotor: sub-critical, critical and over-critical ones, that affect the response of the system to introduced malfunctions. Numbers of observations concerning several combinations of considered elementary technical states are shown in Table 1. Measurements and signal processing have been carried out by P. Kostka.

Table 1. Numbers of observations for different combinations of factors considered in the active experiment [10]

State of balancing	Additional factors				Total
	None	Rubbing	Overload	Rub+Ovld	
rough dynamic balancing	13	–	12	–	25
moment imbalance	7	–	–	–	7
quasistatic imbalance	16	98	23	9	146
Total	36	98	35	9	178

Since combinations of these factors caused complex technical states of the object, common ML methods gave poor results yielding the overall performance of the classifier $\eta_{ov} = 1 - \epsilon_{ov} = 0.65$. Therefore the author elaborated a novel attempt consisting in a decomposition of the set of examples according to the structure of the set of considered technical states [10,11]. It depends on learning hierarchical classifiers that make a sequential recognition of states possible. Therefore, both elementary and complex states can be recognized, where the latter are composed from several elementary states. Such a classifier is a collection of multiclass and/or binary classifiers. Its structure may be represented by a tree which is an expansion of the states tree (Fig. 3), where each node of the states tree has been assigned a 'portion' of knowledge (e.g. a set of rules or decision tree) that makes it possible to recognize the value of the given state attribute. These classifiers have been applied sequentially according to the order determined by the structure of the states tree (starting from the root).

The optimisation of the states tree with respect to the criterion of maximal classifier's performance has been carried out. Since the plan of the experiment was incomplete, the field of possible solutions contained 7 trees. The search of the optimum has been aided by the author's diagnostic knowledge. The structure of the optimal tree with values of the classification errors is shown in Fig. 3 where numbers in the blocks represent classification errors for each classifier. The crucial increase of the classifier's performance, especially with

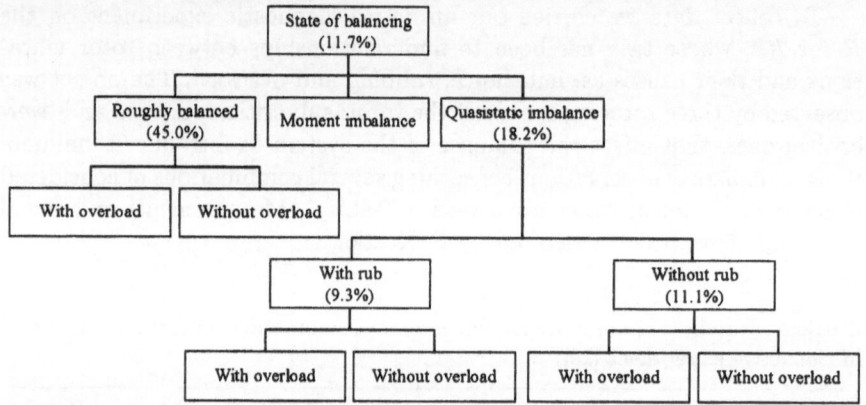

Fig. 3. Optimal tree of classifiers for diagnosing complex technical states [12]

respect to some subtrees as the one that starts from the node corresponding to the state 'quasi-static unbalance', has been achieved. Hence, it proved the usefulness of this method in typical diagnostic tasks where complex technical states are commonly observed. However, significant errors are encountered if we diagnose overload for roughly balanced rotor. They may be caused by too small overload magnitudes applied during the experiment, which did not cause vibration response that is typical in case of such malfunction.

5 Recapitulation and Conclusions

During the conducted research the comprehensive methodology of diagnostic knowledge acquisition has been elaborated, which includes many methods of knowledge acquisition from the most important sources of diagnostic knowledge and methods of knowledge assessment. These methods were implemented in several applications subsequently joined in the integral knowledge acquisition system [10,11]. This system gives intrinsically new opportunities in efficient acquisition of diagnostic knowledge from different sources and in mixed attempt to evaluate the acquired knowledge.

The research confirmed that the applied methods and tools make it possible to efficiently carry out the process of knowledge acquisition from the most valuable sources of diagnostic knowledge concerning typical rotordynamics problems. Results obtained yet enable us to conclude that the process is effective enough even in the case of complex technical states of considered objects. However, the problem of diagnosing complex technical states will focus our attention in the future, since in fact if we deal with complex machinery, we have to handle difficult situations with simultaneous occurrence of many faults, whose symptoms usually do not satisfy the superposition law.

A very interesting advantage of the approach described in the paper is the common knowledge representation format called *EMPREL* [10]. It enables us to combine expert-based and signal-based approach to knowledge acquisition and assessment (i.e. verification and/or validation).

However, all the described methodology needs further verification. Currently we are carrying out a comprehensive research concerning knowledge acquisition of large industrial turbine sets where we are faced with more complicated problems such as: nonlinear phenomena, complex technical states, many attributes of objects, complex problem of a right supervised data discretization connected with the selection of relevant attributes – both based on the domain knowledge, constructing of new attributes that better reveal the actual technical state of the diagnosed object, etc. This research has been initiated by the author in the Department of Machine Design Fundamentals, Technical University of Silesia. Some problems concerning this research subject are discussed in [6,7].

Acknowledgments

The author expresses his gratitude to Prof. W. Cholewa, Prof. R. S. Michalski and Prof. J. M. Żytkow for stimulating discussions concerning applications of machine learning and knowledge discovery methods to acquisition of diagnostic knowledge from examples.

A part of the presented research has been performed using software which has been kindly made accessible by R. S. Michalski (systems *AQ15c* [17] and *AQ17-HCI* [9]).

This research has been partly supported by the Polish Scientific Research Committee under grants No. 8T11F 020 09 and 7T07B 046 16.

References

1. Cempel Cz. (1989) Vibroacoustic Diagnostics of Machinery (in Polish), PWN, Warsaw
2. Cholewa W., Kiciński J. (1997) (Eds.) Machinery Diagnostics. Inverted Diagnostic Models (in Polish). Monographs - Machine Building and Exploitation, Technical University of Silesia, Gliwice

184

3. Ciupke K. (2000) Discretization of Real-Valued Diagnostic Symptoms. In: Intelligent Information Systems IX (this conference)
4. Dougherty J., Kohavi R., Sahami M. (1995) Supervised and Unsupervised Discretization of Continuous Features. In: A. Prieditis, S. Russell (Eds.), Machine Learning: Proceedings of the 12th International Conference, Morgan Kaufman, San Francisco, CA
5. Grzymala–Busse J. W., Wang A. (1997) Modified Algorithms LEM1 and LEM2 for Rule Induction from Data with Missing Attribute Values. In: Proceedings of the 5th International Workshop on Rough Sets and Soft Computing (RSSC'97) at the 3rd Joint Conference on Information Sciences (JCIS'97), Research Triangle Park, NC
6. Kostka P. (1998) Example of Application of Machine Learning Methods for Knowledge Acquistion on Rotating Machinery. In: Kłopotek M., Michalewicz M., Raś Z. (Eds.) Proceedings of the Workshop "Intelligent Information Systems" IIS'98, Malbork, 235-238, Institute of Computer Science PAS, Warsaw
7. Kostka P. (2000) Application of Machine Learning Methods to the Recognition of Shaft Bearing Misalignment. In: Intelligent Information Systems IX (this conference)
8. Michalski R. S. (1983) A Theory and Methodology of Inductive Learning. Artificial Intelligence 20:111-161
9. Michalski R. S. (1997) Machine Learning, Data Mining and Knowledge Discovery. Principles and Applications. Tutorial on the Workshop "Intelligent Information Systems" IIS'97, Zakopane. Institute of Computer Science PAS, Warsaw
10. Moczulski W. (1997) Methods of Knowledge Acquisition for the Needs of Machinery Diagnostics (in Polish). Series: Mechanics 130, Technical University of Silesia, Gliwice
11. Moczulski W. (1999) Acquisition of Diagnostic Knowledge from Examples Concerning Complex Technical States. In: Proceedings of the Workshop "Intelligent Information Systems" IIS'99, 80–91. Institute of Computer Science PAS, Warsaw
12. Moczulski W. (2000) Methodology of Diagnostic Knowledge Acquisition. Submitted to the Bulletin of the Polish Academy of Sciences, Technical Sciences.
13. Moczulski W., Żytkow J. M. (1997) Automated Search for Knowledge on Machinery Diagnostics. In: Kłopotek M., Michalewicz M., Raś Z. (Eds.) Proceedings of the Workshop "Intelligent Information Systems" IIS'97, Zakopane, 194-203, Institute of Computer Science PAS, Warsaw
14. Nguyen H. S. (1998) From Optimal Hyperplanes to Optimal Decision Trees. Fundamenta Informaticae 34:145–174
15. Pawlak Z. (1991) Rough Sets. Theoretical Aspects of Reasoning About Data. Kluwer Academic Publishers
16. Quinlan J. R. (1986) Induction of Decision Trees. Machine Learning 1:81-106
17. Wnek J., Kaufman K., Bloedorn E., Michalski R. S. (1995) Selective Induction Learning System AQ15c: The Method and User's Guide, Center for Machine Learning and Inference, George Mason University, Fairfax, VA

Verification of Rule Knowledge Bases Using Decision Units

Roman Siminski, Alicja Wakulicz-Deja

University of Silesia, Institute of Computer Science
41-200 Sosnowiec, Żeromskiego 3, Phone (+48 32) 2 918 945 ext. 38
email: {siminski l wakulicz}@us.edu.pl

Abstract. Expert systems are being developed and used in a wide variety of disciplines throughout the world. Much attention has been paid to check the reliability of expert systems. Verification of knowledge bases has emerged as a significant problem in the development of expert systems. We argue that knowledge bases verification can not be delayed until the final knowledge base realization and we suppose that verification should be performed incrementally and should be included into the development process. In this paper we introduce the main assumptions of decision unit conception and we briefly describe how we are going to apply decision units in knowledge bases verification and validation.

Keywords: expert systems, knowledge bases, verification, validation.

1 Introduction

Expert systems are being developed and used in a wide variety of disciplines throughout the word. Much attention has been paid to check the reliability of expert systems, because safety is usually the main goal in some application (e.g. medicine). Reliability of the expert systems has become a key factor in knowledge engineering. Consequently issues concerning validation and verification of knowledge bases become more and more important. Verification and validation of knowledge bases has emerged as a significant problem in development of knowledge-based systems.

Building complex knowledge bases requires encoding a large amount of domain knowledge. After acquiring this knowledge from domain experts, much of the effort in building a knowledge bases goes into verifying that the knowledge is encoded correctly. In general, verification and validation of any software system consist in checking that this system is fully operational and performs satisfactorily its intended function. Therefore, although the basic validation concepts are common for knowledge and software engineering, we encounter difficulties if we try to apply classical definitions of verification and validation (from software engineering) to knowledge engineering. The tasks performed by the expert systems usually can not be correctly and completely specified. These tasks are usually ill-structured and no efficient algorithmic approach is known from them.

2 Background of knowledge bases verification

Verification, validation and testing are terms that have been used for several year in classical software engineering (Adrin & Branstand & Cherniavsky 1982). A program is verified against its specification. Formal specifications are then vital to validation and verification in classical software. Sometimes knowledge engineering is compared to software engineering, but here many differences can be founded. Perhaps the crucial characteristic of knowledge engineering that distinguish it in an essential way from software engineering is the impossibility to obtain a correct and complete formal specification of expert system.

Expert systems are problem solvers for specialized domains of competence in which effective problem solving normally requires human experts. Expert systems are often intended for ill-defined problems and they need to work with incomplete or uncertain knowledge. Expert systems have proven to be an effective technology for solving ill-defined problems but from a software engineering point of view - when the problem is ill-defined then the user requirements are ill-defined, it leads to difficulties in determining whether the system meets its requirements. In some situation expert systems provides only the hope for a good solution.

Therefore, one of the main impediments to successful verification of expert system is the nature of expert systems themself. The second impediment are implementation methods and tools. Expert systems are usually implemented using declarative languages or specialized expert system shells. Rule-based languages are perhaps the most popular ones.

Therefore, although the basic verification concepts are shared by software engineering and knowledge engineering, verification methods of conventional software are not directly applicable to expert systems and the new, specific methods of verification are required. In (Siminski & Wakulicz–Deja 1998) we present some of the theoretical and practical information about verification and validation of knowledge bases.

3 Summarization of verification methods and tools

Many methods have been developed in order to obtain right knowledge bases, a variety of tools are described in references. These range from static tools that check for structural errors, to verifiers that include support for multilevel expert systems with uncertainty. In (Siminski 98) we present some of the best known methods and tools described in references.

The vast majority of current work in the verification of rule knowledge bases concerns the verification on some properties of the base separately considered, most of the validation approaches assume to work on fully implemented base. Verification is rather at the end of the knowledge base development process, where the consequence of any modification are not foreseeable.

We argue (Siminski & Wakulicz-Deja 1999) that knowledge bases verification can not be delayed until the final base realization. There is too high risk that errors will be found too late which may be very expensive to correct. We introduce the *dynamic verification* approach. The main assumption of this approach is as follow:

We suppose that verification should be included into the development process and that different types of verification should take place in different phases of development process. Verification has to be performed incrementally and can not be delayed until knowledge base is completed.

Verification should incorporate analysis of static and dynamic properties of knowledge base. Main goal of static analysis is demonstrating that a rule base is free from typical anomalies such as redundancy, contradiction, subsumption etc. Dynamic analysis depends on testing a knowledge base through its execution using run time subsystem that utilizes some inference engine algorithms and techniques.

4 The outline of the decision units conception

We assume, that *decision units* are the main tool for dynamic knowledge base verification. Let us present decision units conception using the following example. We consider the following rule base:

R1: C(2) if A(1) & B(1)
R2: C(1) if D(1) & B(3)
R3: F(1) if C(2) & E(1)

R4: C(2) if A(1) & B(1)
R5: F(2) if C(1)
R6: F(3) if C(2) & E(1)
R7: F(2) if D(1) & B(3)
R8: C(1) if D(1) & B(3) & E(3)
R9: B(3) if F(2)

The Arabic numerals represent values for the attributes A to F. The following figure 1 show in graphical way the example knowledge base.

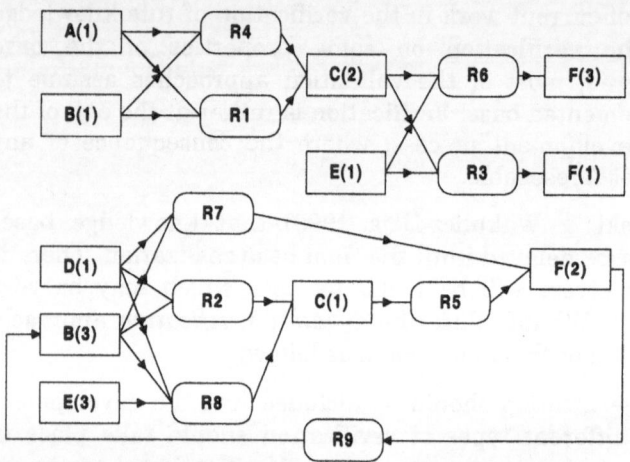

Figure 1: The graphic representation of an example knowledge base

We can identify a number of anomalies in the example knowledge base:

- Redundancy: duplicated rules – R1 and R4, subsumed rules – R2 and R8, compound subsumption – R2, R5 and R7.

- Ambivalence – R6 and R3.

- Circularity – R2, R5 and R9.

- Incompleteness.

We can show our example knowledge base in different way. All rules with the same attribute we can group together. This rule group we will called *decision unit*. Decision unit U_k contains the set of rules R_i with his same attribute in the decision part (conclusion) of each rule $r \in R_i$. All attribute-value pairs which appear in the conditional part of each R_i rule we will call input entry I_k. of decision unit U_k. All attribute-value pairs appearing in the decision part of each R_i rule we will call output entry O_k of decision unit U_k. Figure 2 presents the structure of the decision unit U_k.

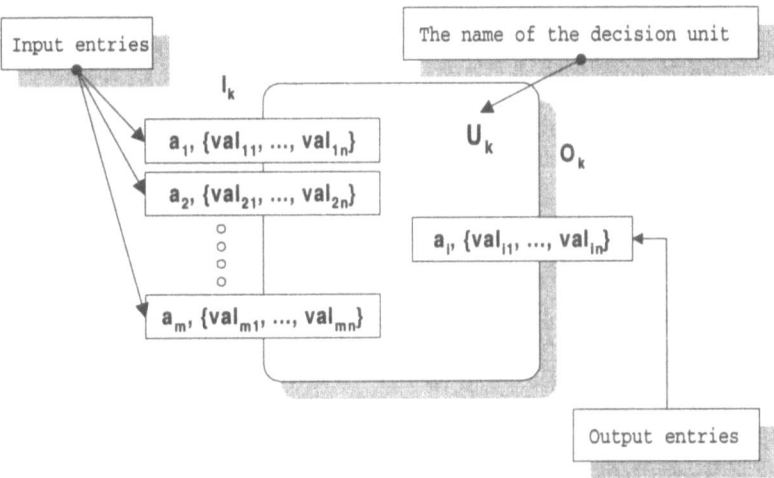

Figure 2: The structure of the decision unit

Our example knowledge base contains three sets of rules with the same attribute in the conclusion. Therefore we can show an example knowledge base using three decision units like on the following fig. 3.

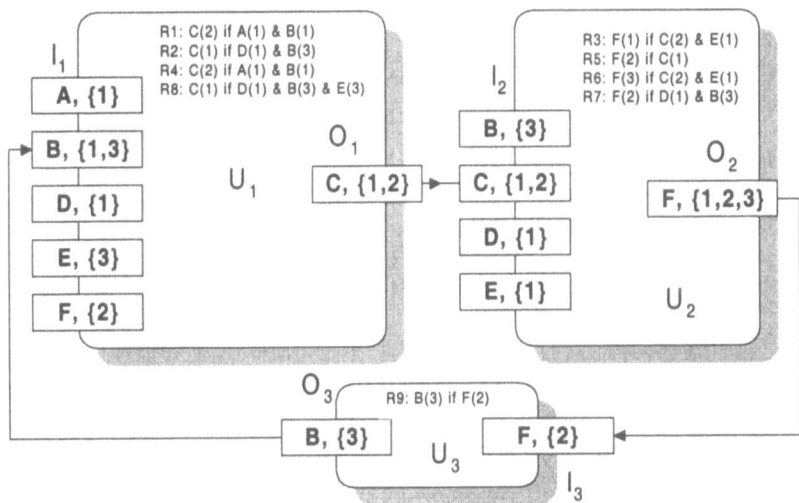

Figure 3: Decision units net for an example knowledge base

Basing on considered example we can briefly describe how decision units may be use in verification and validation issues.

Decision unit may be considered as a model of elementary decision produced by the system, therefore:

- decision unit separately considered a the way of verification and validation of knowledge base on the level of the local, elementary decision;

- apart from internal structure of the decision unit we can validate the base using testing techniques - basing on input entries we can choose appropriate input data;

- considering internal structure of decision unit we can validate the set of rules using known methods, e.g. decision tables approach.

The net of the decision units may be considered as a global model of decisions produced by the system, therefore:

- knowledge engineer may check if the current global decision model is consistent with intended model;

- unchained output entries represent main goals, chained output entries represent subgoals;

- unchained input entries represent the input data (facts) necessary to produce proper inference results;

- circularity dependencies are easy to detect on the decision net level.

In our opinion the decision units conception allows us to consider different verification and validation issues together. We can perform efficient static verification (based on anomalies detection on the level of decision unit) and dynamic validation (based on testing internal decision unit rule set). We can detect redundancy (duplication, subsumption), local inconsistency and local incompleteness. The net of the decision units is the tool for detecting circularity, dead end rules, auxiliary rules and global incompleteness. Graphical representation of knowledge base in the form of the decision units net is user friendly and is an efficient and useful way of presentation of current knowledge base contents. We suppose that verification should be included into the development process and that different types of verification should take place in different phases of development process. Thanks to properties of the decision units we can perform different verification and validation actions during knowledge base development and realization, based on one coherent approach. There is low risk that errors will be found too late which may be very expensive to correct.

5 Further works and concluding remarks

We are going to use a verification strategy base on decision units in the *kbBuilder* system (Siminski & Wakulicz-Deja 1999). The *kbBuilder* is a tool for interactive, incremental construction, validation and refinement of the PC-Shell's knowledge bases. The kbBuilder is implemented in C++ and works under the control of Windows 3.x/95. In the current version, system provides set of syntactic and structural validation functions. System detects:

- redundant and subsumend rules,

- contradictory and ambivalent rules,

- unused attributes and its values,

- missing rules for decision attributes (attributes for a goal statement).

Current works concern on designing and implementing a new verification subsystem based on decision units conception. In our opinion the decision units conception allows us to perform efficient static verification and dynamic validation. We think that the net of the decision units is a tool for detecting circularity, dead end rules, auxiliary rules and global incompleteness. Graphical representation of knowledge base in the form of the decision units net is the efficient and useful way of presentation of current knowledge base contents.

References

Adrion W.R., Branstad M.A., Cherniavsky J.C., 1982, „Validation, verification and testing of computer software", ACM Computing Surveys, June, 14(2) pp. 159-192.

Siminski R. (1998), Methods and Tools for Knowledge Bases Verification and Validation, *Proceedings of the CAI'98, Colloquia in Artificial Intelligence*, 28–30.09.1998, Poland, Łódź, pp. 273-291.

Siminski R., Wakulicz–Deja A. (1998) A., Principles and Practice in Knowledge Bases Verification, *Proceedings of the IIS VII, Intelligent Information Systems*, Poland, Malbork, 15–19.06.1998, pp. 203–211.

Siminski R., Wakulicz–Deja A. (1999) A., dynamic Verification of Knowledge Bases, , *Proceedings of the IIS VIII, Intelligent Information Systems*, Poland, Ustroń, 14–18.06.1999, pp.327–331.

Sound and Complete Propositional Nonmonotonic Logic of Hierarchically-Minimal Models

Marek A. Suchenek

California State University – Dominguez Hills

Carson, CA 90747 U.S.A.

e-mail addr: Suchenek@csudh.edu

Abstract

The subject of this talk is the semantics of stratified logic programs with negation in clauses' bodies. We present a sound and complete resolution based method for iterative evaluation of queries to such programs by means of, what we call, an *indefinite modeling*. To avoid unnecessary complications, we focus on propositional programs with two strata, although our method preserves the soundness and completeness when extended over clausal fragments of first-order languages and programs with arbitrary number of strata.

Our approach is based on some well known results of research in semantics of negation; particularly, closed-world assumption, circumscription, and minimal model theory.

Key words: *hierarchically-minimal semantics, indefinite deductive data bases, indefinite models, negation in clause's body, parallel positive resolution rule. prioritized circumscription, stratified logic programs.*

1 Introduction

In definite data bases and logic programs, negation is usually interpreted as a variant of non-provability, the so called *negation as finite failure to prove* (NAF), which approximates the original version of the closed-world assumption (cwa), first introduced in [Rei78]. In the indefinite case which allows disjunctive heads and/or occurrences of negation in clause's body neither seems adequate, as the following example testifies: $A \vee B \not\vdash A$ and $A \vee B \not\vdash B$, hence NAF, as well as cwa, when applied to $A \vee B$ proves $\neg A \wedge \neg B$, an obviously unwanted consequence. Therefore, in the indefinite case the interpretation of negation based on various versions of McCarthy's circumscription seems to prevail. In particular, one cannot derive the contradictory conclusion $\neg A \wedge \neg B$ from the circumscription of $A \vee B$.

In its simplest form, given a disjunctive deductive data base p, $\neg q$ expresses the falsehood of q in all minimal models of p. This fact is usually articulated by $p \vdash_{min} \neg q$ (p minimally entails $\neg q$). In the light of such an interpretation of negation, the *yes-or-no* answer to query $\neg q$ directed to indefinite data base p is reduced to the question whether $p \vdash_{min} \neg q$. Negation understood this way has the following neat characterization in terms of first-order provability (propositional, in this paper) of positive (i.e., negation-free) sentences:

$$p \vdash_{min} \neg q \text{ iff } Cn_{Pos}(\neg(p \supset q)) \subseteq Cn(p) \qquad (1)$$

where $Cn_{Pos}(X)$ is the set of all positive logical consequences of X, and Cn is the set of all logical consequences of X (see [YH85] for the proof of the case of q being a conjunction of positive ground literals, and [Suc89] for the proof of the general case with universal quantifier). Intuitively, the right-hand side of (1) means that every positive consequence of $\neg(p \supset q)$ is provable from p itself. In particular,

(**) if q is a positive sentence then $p \vdash_{min} q$ is equivalent to $p \vdash q$.

Characterization (1) extends over arbitrary clauses (not just of the form $\neg q$), and yields the following corollary: p and p' have the same positive consequences iff for every clause q, $p \vdash_{min} q$ and $p' \vdash_{min} q$ are equivalent.

The above fact gives rise to the following scheme of deciding $p \vdash_{min} q$. If p' is a formula equivalent to the conjunction of all positive consequences of p then decide $p' \vdash_{min} q$ instead of $p \vdash_{min} q$. It is being hoped that, at least in certain cases, one can find p' for which the decision problem $p' \vdash_{min} q$ is easier than $p \vdash_{min} q$. Of course, p' may be assumed to be a positive formula. In this paper we consider two forms of such alternate p': a positive reduced *disjunctive form* (DF), and a positive reduced *conjunctive form* (CF). The former constitutes, in fact, the familiar set of minimal Herbrand[1] models of p, and allows for straightforward algorithm of deciding $p' \vdash_{min} q$. We call the latter an *indefinite model* of p, and develop for it a method of deciding $p' \vdash_{min} q$ using a parallel positive variant of the resolution rule, complete with respect to positive conclusions. Both methods involve transformation of data base p into suitable DF or CF. Although in many cases, computing an indefinite model p' of p a program (also a CF-formula) seems quite easy, the problem $p' \vdash_{min} q$ for p' in a conjunctive form is far from being trivial, particularly for stratified p.

---

[1] In a Herbrand model only positive literals which are true in that model are specified; all other positive literals are assumed false in that model.

Example 1.1 Consider a program $p = \{A \lor B \leftarrow, C \lor D \leftarrow\}$ and a query $q = (\neg A \lor \neg B) \land (\neg C \lor \neg D)$. Program p is logically equivalent to $(A \lor B) \land (C \lor D)$ which, when converted to disjunctive form, yields

$$(A \land C) \lor (A \land D) \lor (B \land C) \lor (B \land D)$$

The latter determines the set

$$Mod_{min}(p) = \{\{A, C\}, \{A, D\}, \{B, C\}, \{B, D\}\}$$

of minimal Herbrand models of p. We have

$$(A \land C) \lor (A \land D) \lor (B \land C) \lor (B \land D) \vdash_{min} q \qquad (2)$$

iff q is true in all minimal models of

$$(A \land C) \lor (A \land D) \lor (B \land C) \lor (B \land D),$$

that is, iff

$$\{A, C\} \models q \text{ and } \{A, D\} \models q \text{ and } \{B, C\} \models q \text{ and } \{B, D\} \models q,$$

that is, iff (since the literals not specified in a Herbrand model, e.g., B in $\{A, C\}$, are assumed false)

$$A \land \neg B \land C \land \neg D \vdash q \text{ and } A \land \neg B \land \neg C \land D \vdash q$$

and

$$\neg A \land B \land C \land \neg D \vdash q \text{ and } \neg A \land B \land \neg C \land D \vdash q$$

The above statement is true, and so is (2). Therefore, query q to program p yields answer *yes* under the minimal model semantics. $\qquad\Box$

The property (**) of the minimal model semantics makes that semantics inadequate for certain cases of indefinite deductive data bases and general logic programs. For instance,

$$\{B \leftarrow \neg A\} \not\vdash_{Min} B, \qquad (3)$$

although one could argue that since A is considered false in every "adequate" minimal model of $\{B \leftarrow \neg A\}$, clause B should actually be entailed by $\{B \leftarrow \neg A\}$. Indeed, one of possible interpretations of the rule $B \leftarrow \neg A$ is that in the absence of evidence for A, clause B is assumed true. With such a goal in mind, the form of the clause on the left-hand side of (3), that is, the presence of negation in its body, has an essential impact on its semantics, to the effect that two logically equivalent clauses, $B \leftarrow \neg A$ and $A \lor B$ have different sets of "adequate" minimal models: the former has one "adequate" minimal Herbrand model, $\{\neg A, B\}$, while the latter has two, $\{A, \neg B\}$ and $\{\neg A, B\}$.

The above peculiarity has some rather profound consequences. Since the proof-theoretic methods of classical logic tend not to differentiate between logically equivalent forms of a formula, they can hardly be expected, as skeptics would argue, to completely characterize such an "adequate" minimal semantics. A rationale along these lines has often been used to dismiss up front any entailment based on classical logic, in particular, the minimal entailment, as not well suited to reason about logic programs with negation in clauses' bodies. To all its apparent logicality, such an argument is invalid in that it ignores a possibility of iterative applications of the minimal entailment, which, as opposed to the classical entailment, may produce more conclusions than any single (non-iterative, that is) application.

The method indefinite modeling we present here addresses the above problem by restricting semantics of indefinite data bases and stratified logic programs to hierarchically-minimal semantics of [SS90] characterized elsewhere in terms of second-order prioritized circumscription. It involves certain iterative applications of the right-hand side of criterion (1), and remedies the "weakness" of the minimal entailment indicated in the example (3). For instance, under the hierarchically-minimal semantics predicate A gets minimized first, with predicate B allowed to vary, yielding $\neg A$ as a consequence. Subsequent minimization of predicate B (vacuous, because now we have both $\neg A$ and $A \vee B$) yields the desired conclusion B. As a result, the unwanted property (3) no longer holds for the restricted semantics.

The decision algorithm for hierarchically-minimal entailment $\vdash_{Hmin}$ that we present here is based on the concept of *the weakest precondition* which in a way characteristic to abductive reasoning, allows for backward evaluation of queries without actually computing models for relevant strata. It turns out that our approach, by appropriate generalization of the concept of stratification eliminates the need of clauses with negation in the body.

2 Notation

We confine ourselves to a first-order language L without equality and variables (and, therefore, without quantifiers), with usual Boolean connectives $\vee, \wedge, \neg$ (we treat all other connectives as appropriate abbreviations), finitely many predicate symbols $A, B, ...$, and finitely many constants $1, 2, ..., M$. We denote formulas of L by $p, q, r, ...$. We call atomic formulas of L propositional variables (or simply variables) and place their arguments in subscripts rather than in parentheses (e.g., we write $B_{3,7}$ instead of $B(3,7)$). L has only finitely many distinct propositional variables; we denote their number by N. If φ is a set of formulas then $\wedge\varphi$ stands for $\wedge_{p \in \varphi} p$, with $\wedge 0$ interpreted as *true*, and dually for $\vee\varphi$, with $\vee 0$ interpreted as *false*. $\neg\varphi$ means $\{\neg p | p \in \varphi\}$. We extend the above convention over sets of sets of formulas in an obvious way; e.g. $\wedge\{\varphi_1, ..., \varphi_n\}$ means $\{\wedge\varphi_1, ..., \wedge\varphi_n\}$.

A *clause carrier* is a set of literals with every propositional variable occurring at most once. A *program carrier* is a set of clause carriers. We use small Greek letters to denote clause carriers, and capital Greek letters for program carriers. Both program and clause carriers are finite since L has only finitely many distinct variables. A *clause* is a formula of the form $\vee\varphi$, where φ is a clause carrier. A *program* (for simplicity we use this term instead of *indefinite deductive data base*) is a formula of the form $\vee\Phi$, where Φ is a program carrier, that is, a program is a finite set of clauses. Since the meaning of $\vee\Phi$ is the same as $\wedge\vee\Phi$, we will use $\vee\Phi$ and $\wedge\vee\Phi$ interchangeably. If X is a carrier, or a program or a clause, $|X|$ denotes the size of X measured as the number of occurrences of propositional variables in X, while $card(X)$ denotes the number of *elements* of X.

A *term* is a formula of the form $\wedge\varphi$, and is called a *minterm* if φ contains occurrences of all propositional variables of L. A conjunctive form formula (abbr: CF) is a formula of the form $\wedge\vee\Phi$. Similarly, a disjunctive form formula (abbr: DF) is a formula of the form $\vee\wedge\Phi$. If all elements of $\wedge\Phi$ are minterms then $\vee\wedge\Phi$ is called a disjunctive normal form formula (abbr: DNF). A set Y of subsets of X is called an *anti-chain* in X if no two distinct elements of Y are subsets one of another. If Φ is an anti-chain then $\wedge\vee\Phi$ is called a *reduced conjunctive form* formula (abbr: RCF), and $\vee\wedge\Phi$ a *reduced disjunctive form* formula (abbr: RDF).

Adjective *positive* refers to formulas and carriers without occurrences of negation, *negative* refers to those equivalent to negated positive ones. For instance, $A\vee B$ is a positive formula, while $\neg(\neg A\wedge\neg B)$ and $A\supset B$ are not ($A\supset B$ is an abbreviation for $\neg A\vee B$). Therefore, in the sense of this convention, positive clauses (or programs) are elsewhere called bodiless clauses (or programs). Bodiless definite programs constitute the easy case in traditional logic programming; they coincide with their minimal Herbrand models. Indefinite bodiless programs are much less trivial, and will serve as *indefinite models*. If φ is a clause carrier then φ^{Pos} denotes the set of all positive literals of φ. If Φ is a program carrier then $\Phi^{Pos} = \{\varphi\in\Phi|\varphi \text{ is positive}\}$ and $\Phi_{Pos} = \{\varphi^{Pos}|\varphi\in\Phi\}$. For instance, $\{\{A,\neg B\},\{C\}\}^{Pos} = \{\{C\}\}$, while $\{\{A,\neg B\},\{C\}\}_{Pos} = \{\{A\},\{C\}\}$. We use similar convention for Φ^{Neg} and Φ_{Neg}.

Sets of positive RCF formulas $\wedge\vee\Phi$ define *indefinite models* of formulas of L: $\vee\Phi$ is an indefinite model of formula p (notation: $Ind(p)$) iff $\wedge\vee\Phi$ is logically equivalent to the conjunction of all positive logical consequences of p (and therefore, to $\vee\wedge Mod_{min}(p)$). It follows from (1) that for any formulas p and q,

$$p\vdash_{min} q \text{ iff } Ind(p)\vdash_{min} q. \tag{4}$$

3 Indefinite Modeling

In this section we present and analyze algorithms for converting a program $\vee\Phi$ into its positive RDF-formula $Ind(\vee\Phi)$, and for deciding $Ind(\vee\Phi) \vdash_{min} q$. Both algorithms are based on the following *parallel positive* variant of the resolution rule:

$$\frac{q \vee \neg R_1 \vee ... \vee \neg R_n \mid p_1 \vee R_1 \mid ... \mid p_n \vee R_n}{q \vee p_1 \vee ... \vee p_n}, \tag{5}$$

where $n > 0$, R_i's are propositional variables, and q and p_i's are distinct positive clauses with no occurrences of variables $R_1, ..., R_n$.

Both algorithms use the operator of direct positive consequence $\mathcal{DPC}$, which assigns to a set of clauses $\vee\Phi$ the set $\mathcal{DPC}(\vee\Phi)$ of all positive clauses which can be derived from $\vee\Phi$ by subsumption and a *single* application of an instance of (5). Given a program $\vee\Phi$, Algorithm 3.1 computes $Ind(\vee\Phi)$.

Algorithm 3.1

> $K := min(\vee\Phi);\ I:=K^{Pos};J:=K \setminus I;$
> <u>while</u> $\mathcal{DPC}(I \cup J)$ is not subsumed by I <u>do</u>
> $\qquad I := min(I \cup \mathcal{DPC}(I \cup J));$
> $\{$At this point, all positive consequences $\}$
> $\{$of $\vee\Phi$ are subsumed by I $\}$
> $\{$Therefore, $I = Ind(\vee\Phi)$ $\}$
> return$(I);$

Here, $min(X)$ is the set of all clauses of X which are not subsumed by other clauses of X. The following lemma guarantees partial correctness of Algorithm 3.1 (and, in fact, the completeness of the parallel positive variant (5) of the resolution rule with respect to positive consequences).

Lemma 3.2 Let Φ be a program carrier. If there is a positive clause q which is a logical consequence of $\vee\Phi$ but is not subsumed by any of the clauses of $\vee\Phi^{Pos}$ then $\mathcal{DPC}(\vee\Phi)$ is not subsumed by $\vee\Phi^{Pos}$.

Proof. Let $\Psi = \Phi \setminus \Phi^{Pos}$. Assume that $\mathcal{DPC}(\vee\Phi)$ is subsumed by $\vee\Phi^{Pos}$, that is, for every $\psi \in \vee\Psi$, $\mathcal{DPC}(\vee\Phi^{Pos} \cup \{\psi\})$ is subsumed by $\vee\Phi^{Pos}$. Hence, $Mod(\vee\Phi^{Pos}) = Mod(\vee\Phi^{Pos}\cup\{\psi\}\cup\mathcal{DPC}(\vee\Phi^{Pos}\cup\{\psi\}))$, that is, $Mod_{min}(\vee\Phi^{Pos})$ $= Mod_{min}(\vee\Phi^{Pos} \cup \{\psi\} \cup \mathcal{DPC}(\vee\Phi^{Pos} \cup \{\psi\}))$. On the other hand, straightforward verification yields $Mod_{min}(\vee\Phi^{Pos} \cup \{\psi\}) = Mod_{min}(\vee\Phi^{Pos} \cup \{\psi\} \cup C(\vee\Phi^{Pos}\cup\{\psi\}))$. From this we conclude that $Mod_{min}(\vee\Phi^{Pos}) = Mod_{min}(\vee\Phi^{Pos}\cup \{\psi\}) = Mod_{min}(\vee\Psi^{Pos} \cup \vee\Psi) = Mod_{min}(\vee\Phi)$, that is, $\vee\Phi^{Pos} \vdash_{min} \wedge \vee \Phi$. Therefore, by thm. 4.3 in [Suc89], $\wedge \vee \Phi \in cwa_S(\vee\Phi^{Pos})$, that is, by definition of cwa_S (def. 3.1 in [Suc89]), all positive consequences of $\vee\Phi$ are provable from Φ^{Pos}. $\qquad\square$

Note. The completeness of the parallel positive variant (5) of the resolution rule with respect to positive conclusions has been proven in [Suc97] for the clausal fragment of first-order logic. The above proof which holds only for propositional case is considerably simpler than the one presented in [Suc97].

Algorithm 3.1 yields the decision algorithm for $\vdash_{min}$.

Theorem 3.3 For every positive program $\vee\Phi$ and every clause q, $Ind(\vee\Phi) \vdash_{min} q$ iff $Ind(\vee\Phi)$ subsumes $\mathcal{C}(Ind(\vee\Phi) \cup \{q\})$.

Proof. We inter from Lemma 3.2 that $\mathcal{C}(Ind(\vee\Phi) \cup \{q\})$ subsumes all positive clauses provable from $\vee\Phi \cup \{q\}$. By def 3.1 and thm. 4.3 in [Suc89], $Ind(\vee\Phi) \vdash_{min} q$ iff all positive clauses provable from $Ind(\vee\Phi) \cup \{q\}$ are subsumed by $Ind(\vee\Phi)$. From this we conclude the thesis. $\quad\square$

4 Layered Programs

The method of indefinite modeling generalizes nicely over stratified programs. Quite surprisingly, the concept of indefinite model does not need any modifications in this case. This is a considerable advantage of indefinite modeling over minimal modeling which requires recomputation of the set of minimal models after stratification has been imposed or changed.

In this section we require that $\vee\Phi$ be a minimally conservative extension of $\vee\Phi'$, that is, that every minimal model (in the usual, non-stratified sense) of $\vee\Phi'$ has an expansion to a minimal model of entire $\vee\Phi$. We call every such an expansion a *hierarchically-minimal model* of $\vee\Phi$, and the entailment $\vdash_{Hmin}$ induced by hierarchically minimal semantics a *hierarchically-minimal entailment*. Any program which satisfies the above requirement is called a *layered* program. One can verify with ease that hierarchically-minimal models are exactly the models of prioritized circumscription. It is also easy to check that every stratified program is layered, but not vice versa.

For each clause q of L', $\vee\Phi \vdash_{min} q$ and $\vee\Phi \vdash_{Hmin} q$ are equivalent, as they are for negated literals q of L. For other clauses from $L \setminus L'$ $\vdash_{Hmin}$ behaves differently than $\vdash_{min}$. For instance, for positive clauses q of $L \setminus L'$, $\vee\Phi \vdash_{Hmin} q$ and $\vee\Phi \vdash q$ need not be equivalent. In particular, there are layered programs $\vee\Phi$ and positive clauses q of $L \setminus L'$ with $\vee\Phi \vdash_{Hmin} q$ but not $\vee\Phi \vdash q$. For example, if R is a variable of L' and S is a variable of $L \setminus L'$ then $\{\neg R \supset S\} \vdash_{Hmin} S$. (Recall, that $\neg R \supset S$ is an abbreviation for $R \vee S$.) We will characterize $\vee\Phi \vdash_{Hmin} q$ in terms of $Ind(\Phi)$, $\vdash_{min}$, and q. To that end, we need the following concept.

Definition 4.1 Let $\vee\Phi$ be a layered program and let q be a formula of L. The *weakest precondition* $WP(\vee\Phi, q)$ for q relative to Φ is a set of clauses of L' which satisfies two conditions:

i. $\vee\Phi \cup WP(\vee\Phi, q) \vdash q;$

ii. for every sentence r of L', if $\vee\Phi \cup \{r\} \vdash q$ then $\{r\} \vdash \wedge WP(\vee\Phi, q)$. □

Intuitively, the weakest precondition for q relative to Φ is equivalent to the weakest formula of the smaller language L' which together with $\vee\Phi$ implies q, that is, $\wedge WP(\vee\Phi, q)$ is logically equivalent to $\vee\{r \in L' | \vee\Phi \cup \{r\} \vdash q\}$. In particular, if q is a formula of L' then $WP(\vee\Phi, q) = \{q\}$.

Theorem 4.2 Let $\vee\Phi$ be a set of positive clauses, let q be a positive clause in $L \setminus L'$, and let $s_1 \vee p_1, ..., s_n \vee p_n$ be all the clauses of $\vee\Phi$ such that each s_i is in $L \setminus L'$, each p_i is in L', and each s_i subsumes q. Then

$$WP(\vee\Phi, q \vee r) \equiv \{\neg p_1 \vee ... \vee \neg p_n \vee r\}. \tag{6}$$

(If $n=0$ then, by convention, $\neg p_1 \vee ... \vee p_n \vee r = r$).

Proof. Let us first prove that $\vdash \neg p_1 \vee ... \vee \neg p_n$ is the weakest precondition for q. Obviously, $\vee\Phi \cup \{\neg p_1 \vee ... \vee \neg p_n\} \vdash q \vee r$. Therefore, it suffices to demonstrate that for every ground clause x in L', if $\vee\Phi \cup \{x\} \vdash q$ then $\vee\Phi \cup \{x\} \vdash \neg p_1 \vee ... \vee \neg p_n$. Suppose to the contrary, that $\vee\Phi \cup \{x\} \nvdash \neg p_1 \vee ... \vee p_n$, that is, $\vee\Phi \cup \{x\} \cup \{p_1, ..., p_n\}$ is consistent. Because $\{p_1, ..., p_n\}$ subsumes $\{s_1 \vee p_1, ..., s_n \vee p_n\}$, $\vee\Phi \cup \{x\} \cup \{p_1, ..., p_n\}$ had the same models as $\vee\Phi' = \vee\Phi \setminus \{s_1 \vee p_1, ..., s_n \vee p_n\} \cup \{p_1, ..., p_n\}$. In particular, $\vee\Phi'$ is consistent. Let $\mathcal{M}$ be a model of $\vee\Phi'$. Because $\vee\Phi$ is positive, $\mathcal{M}' = \mathcal{M} \cup \{A | A$ is a positive literal of $L \setminus L'\}$ is also a model of $\vee\Phi'$. By the definition of $\{s_1 \vee p_1, ..., s_n \vee p_n\}$, all occurrences of q in $\vee\Phi'$ are in positive clauses involving literals of $L \setminus L'$ not in q, and all these literals are satisfied by $\mathcal{M}'$. Therefore, $\mathcal{M}'' = \mathcal{M}' \setminus \{B | B$ is a literal of $q\}$ is a model of $\vee\Phi'$. $\mathcal{M}'' \models \neg q$. Hence $\vee\Phi' \cup \{\neg q\}$ is consistent, and therefore, $\vee\Phi \cup \{x\} \cup \{p_1, ..., p_n\} \cup \{\neg q\}$ is consistent. From this, we conclude that $\vee\Phi \cup \{x\} \cup \{\neg q\}$ is consistent - a contradiction. Thus $\vee\Phi \cup \{x\} \vdash \{\neg p_1 \vee ... \vee \neg p_n\}$, and $\{\neg p_1 \vee ... \vee \neg p_n\}$ is the weakest precondition for q.

Now, let $\vee\Phi \cup \{x\} \vdash q \vee r$. We get $\vee\Phi \cup \{x \wedge \neg r\} \vdash q$, that is, $\vee\Phi \cup \{x \wedge \neg r\} \vdash \neg p_1 \vee ... \vee \neg p_n$, so $\vee\Phi \cup \{x\} \vdash \neg p_1 \vee ... \vee \neg p_n \vee r$, that is, $\neg p_1 \vee ... \vee \neg p_n \vee r$ is the weakest precondition for $q \vee r$. □

Because $WP(\vee\Phi, p \wedge q) = WP(\vee\Phi, p) \cup WP(\vee\Phi, q)$, Theorem 4.2 yields the following straightforward algorithm to compute WP for positive programs and positive clauses.

Algorithm 4.3

```
function WP(∨Φ:  {positive} program; t:  {positive} clause):  program;
type
    simple_clause = stack of positive_literal;
                    {the head or the body of a clause}
    clause =        record
```

```
                        head,  {positive part}
                        body:  simple_clause
                                 {negative part}
                   end;
program =          stack of clause;
                   {conjunction of clauses}
cmplx_program = stack of program;
                   {disjunction of conjunctions of}
                   {clauses}
```

var

```
q, r,          {clauses of Lemma 4.2}
C, D: clause;
Y: program; {output stack}
W: cmplx_program; {accumulation stack} begin {WP}
q := t.head∩(L \ L⁻);       {a part of t from L \ L⁻}
r := t.head ∩ L⁻;           {a part of t from L⁻}
{t.body is empty since t is positive}
W := NULL; {a stack for the weakest precondition}
            {in conjunctive normal form}
PUSH({r}, W); {the last clause of (6)}
for C ∈ ∨ (Φ∩L) do
      if C \ q ∈ L⁻ and C \L⁻ ⊆ q {⊑ and ⊆}
                   {coincide on positive clauses}
```

then

```
            {∨(C \q) is πᵢ of Lemma 4.2}
            PUSH(¬ ∨(C \q), W);
{Now, by (6), the entire weakest precondition is on W}
Y := CNF(W);
{conjunctive normal form; represented by set of clauses}
for C ∈ Y do
      for D ∈ ∨(Φ∩L) do
            if D ⊆ C then DELETE(C, Y);
{Now, Y does not contain clauses entailed by ∨Φ}
return(CNF(W));
{conjunctive normal form; represented by a set of clauses}
end {WP}
```

For every program $\vee\Phi$ and clause q,

$$\vee\Phi \vdash_{Hmin} q \text{ iff } Ind(\vee\Phi) \vdash_{Hmin} q. \tag{7}$$

This property follows from the fact, that if p and r have the same minimal models then they also have the same hierarchically-minimal models. Hence the following theorem.

Theorem 4.4 For every program $\lor\Phi$ and clause q, $\lor\Phi \vdash_{Hmin} q$ iff $Ind(\lor\Phi)'$ subsumes $\mathcal{DPC}(Ind(\lor\Phi)' \cup WP(Ind(\lor\Phi), \land\mathcal{DPC}(Ind(\lor\Phi) \cup \{q\})))$.

Proof. First, let's notice that, for every positive layered program Φ and every positive formula q of L,

$$\lor\Phi \vdash_{Hmin} q \text{ iff } \lor\Phi' \vdash_{min} \land WP(\lor\Phi, q). \tag{8}$$

Indeed, $\lor\Phi \vdash_{Hmin} q$ iff [by [SS90], thm. 5.5] $q \in cwa_S(\lor\Phi \cup cwa_S(\lor\Phi'))$ iff [by [Suc89], thm. 4.3] $\lor\Phi \cup cwa_S(\lor\Phi') \vdash_{min} q$ iff [by positiveness of q and thm. 2.7 of [Suc90]] $\lor\Phi \cup cwa_S(\lor\Phi') \vdash q$ iff [by definition 4.1 of WP] $cwa_S(\lor\Phi') \vdash \land WP(\lor\Phi, q)$ iff [by [Suc89], thm. 4.3] $\lor\Phi' \vdash_{min} \land WP(\lor\Phi, q)$.

Next, let's notice that, for every positive program $\lor\Phi$ and every clause q,

$$\lor\Phi \vdash_{Hmin} q \text{ iff } \lor\Phi \vdash_{Hmin} \land\mathcal{DPC}(\lor\Phi \cup \{q\}). \tag{9}$$

Indeed, ($\Rightarrow$) is obvious. ($\Leftarrow$) $\lor\Phi \vdash_{Hmin} \land\mathcal{DPC}(\lor\Phi \cup \{q\})$ **implies** [by [SS90], thm. 5.5] $\land\mathcal{DPC}(\lor\Phi \cup \{q\}) \in cwa_S(\lor\Phi \cup cwa_S(\lor\Phi'))$ **implies** [by thm. 4.3 of [Suc89]] $\lor\Phi \cup cwa_S(\lor\Phi') \vdash_{min} \land\mathcal{DPC}(\lor\Phi \cup \{q\})$ **implies** [by positiveness of $\land\mathcal{DPC}(\lor\Phi \cup \{q\})$ and thm 2.7 of [Suc90]] $\lor\Phi \cup cwa_S(\lor\Phi') \vdash \land\mathcal{DPC}(\lor\Phi \cup \{q\})$ **implies** [by positiveness of $\lor\Phi$ and Lemma 3.2] $\lor\Phi \cup cwa_S(\lor\Phi')$ proves all positive consequences of $\Phi \cup \{q\}$ **implies** [by [Suc89], thm. 4.3] for every minimal model $\mathcal{M}$ of $\lor\Phi \cup cwa_S(\lor\Phi')$ there exists a minimal model $\mathcal{N}$ of $\lor\Phi \cup \{q\}$ with $\mathcal{N} \subseteq \mathcal{M}$ **implies** [by [SS90], thm 5.4, every model of $cwa_S(\lor\Phi')$ is a minimal model of $\lor\Phi'$, therefore, $\mathcal{M} \restriction L'$ is a minimal model of $\lor\Phi'$; also, $\mathcal{N} \restriction L' \subseteq \mathcal{M} \restriction L'$, and $\mathcal{N} \restriction L' \models \lor\Phi'$] $\mathcal{N} \restriction L' = \mathcal{M} \restriction L'$ **implies** $\mathcal{N} \restriction L'$ is a model of $cwa_S(\lor\Phi')$ **implies** for every minimal model $\mathcal{M}$ of $\lor\Phi \cup cwa_S(\lor\Phi')$ there exists a minimal model $\mathcal{N}$ of $\lor\Phi \cup \{q\} \cup cwa_S(\lor\Phi')$ with $\mathcal{N} \subseteq \mathcal{M}$ **implies** [by [Suc89], thm. 4.3] $\lor\Phi \cup cwa_S(\lor\Phi')$ proves all positive consequences of $\lor\Phi \cup cwa_S(\lor\Phi') \cup \{q\}$ **implies** [by [Suc89], df. 3.1] $q \in cwa_S(\lor\Phi \cup cwa_S(\lor\Phi'))$ **implies** [by [SS90], thm. 5.5] $\lor\Phi \vdash_{Hmin} q$.

Now, $\lor\Phi \vdash_{Hmin} q$ iff [by (7)] $Ind(\lor\Phi) \vdash_{Hmin} q$ iff [by (9)] $Ind(\lor\Phi) \vdash_{Hmin} \land\mathcal{DPC}(Ind(\lor\Phi) \cup \{q\})$ iff [by (8)] $Ind(\lor\Phi)' \vdash_{min} WP(Ind(\lor\Phi)), \land\mathcal{DPC}(Ind(\lor\Phi) \cup \{q\}))$ iff [by Theorem 3.3] $Ind(\lor\Phi)'$ subsumes $\mathcal{DPC}(Ind(\lor\Phi)' \cup WP(Ind(\lor\Phi), \land\mathcal{DPC}(Ind(\lor\Phi) \cup \{q\})))$. □

Given the Algorithm 4.3 for computing WP, Theorem 4.4 yields a straightforward decision algorithm for $\vdash_{Hmin}$. Its iterative applications decide queries to programs with arbitrary finite number of strata

Example 4.5 Let $L' = \{A, B\}$, $L = \{A, B, C, D\}$, $\lor\Phi = \{A \lor B, A \lor C \lor D, B \lor C \lor D\}$, and $q = C \lor D$. We have: $Ind(\lor\Phi) = \lor\Phi$; $\lor\Phi' = \{A \lor B\}$; Φ is a minimal conservative extension of $\lor\Phi'$; $\mathcal{DPC}(Ind(\lor\Phi) \cup \{q\}) = \{C \lor D\}$; $WP(\lor\Phi, C \lor D) = \{\neg A \lor \neg B\}$; $\mathcal{DPC}(\lor\Phi' \cup \{\neg A \lor \neg B\}) = B \lor A$; Φ' subsumes $\mathcal{DPC}(\lor\Phi' \cup \{\neg A \lor \neg B\})$. Hence, $\Phi \vdash_{Hmin} q$. □

5 Speed-ups

The pigeonhole principle is an example of propositional tautology that, as it has been demonstrated in [CR79], has an exponentially complex resolution proof. This fact leaves no hope for a complete and fast resolution-based derivation algorithm. Consequently, the resolution-based algorithms we presented so far must perform at least exponentially badly in the worst case. In this section we briefly discuss to what extent the indefinite modeling may be faster than the minimal modeling and vice versa.

First, let us notice that for every anti-chain Φ in the set of sets of variables of L, $\vee\Phi$ is its own indefinite model, and $\wedge\Phi$ is the set of minimal models of $\vee\wedge\Phi$. Therefore, if there are programs for which the indefinite model is smaller than the set of minimal models, there must be equally many others for which the converse is true. This fact suggests that a parallel application of both methods while deciding $\vee\Phi \vdash_{min} q$ may result in a considerable speed-up in some cases, while the slow-down factor, if any, will not exceed 2. Also the converse is true: there are programs $\vee\Phi$ with $|Mod_{min}(\vee\Phi)|$ polynomial in $|\vee\Phi|$ but $|Ind(\vee\Phi)|$ exponential in $|\vee\Phi|$. (Even if both are polynomial, any resolution-based conversion of one onto another may require exponential number of steps). This parallel strategy, however, cannot improve the worst-case performance of these methods, since there are programs $\vee\Phi$ for which both $|Mod_{min}(\vee\Phi)|$ and $|Ind(\vee\Phi)|$ are exponential in the size of $|\Phi|$. Moreover, the carrier of $Mod_{min}(\vee\Phi)$ coincides with the carrier of $Ind(\vee\Phi)$ in worst cases, which means that the improvement achieved by parallelization of the two method is limited to some non-worst cases.

Example 5.1 Let $N = 2n - 1$ and let $\Phi = \{\varphi \mid \varphi$ is a set of n distinct literals of $L\}$. Φ is an anti-chain. Obviously, $Ind(\vee\Phi) = \vee\Phi$. Also, $Mod_{min}(\vee\Phi) = \wedge\Phi$. The size of Φ is maximal: $\begin{pmatrix} N \\ \lceil\frac{N}{2}\rceil \end{pmatrix}$ elements with $\lceil\frac{N}{2}\rceil$ literals each, which totals in $\lceil\frac{N}{2}\rceil \times \begin{pmatrix} N \\ \lceil\frac{N}{2}\rceil \end{pmatrix} \approx \frac{2^N}{\sqrt{2N}}$ occurrences of literals. $\quad\square$

We conclude this section with rough estimation of the average ratio $R_{avg}^{D,C}$ of the sizes of the indefinite model and of the set of minimal models of a program with N variables. For that purpose, we will use the *Shannon's counting argument*. Let $\mathcal{M}$ be a set of m elements, $\mathcal{N}$ be the set of n shortest sequences of elements of $\mathcal{M}$, and k be the length of the longest element of $\mathcal{N}$. For every $i < k$, $\mathcal{N}$ contains m^i sequences of length i and at most m^k sequences of length k. Therefore,

$$\sum_{i=0}^{k-1} m^i < n \le \sum_{i=0}^{k} m^i.$$

The total length l of all sequences of $\mathcal{N}$ is

$$\sum_{i=1}^{k-1} i \times m^i + k \le l \le \sum_{i=1}^{k} i \times m^i.$$

Elementary calculations show that the average length $\frac{l}{n}$ of an element of $\mathcal{N}$ satisfies

$$log_m \frac{n}{4} < \frac{l}{n} < log_m n$$

From this we conclude that the average length of a sequence in any finite set of n (not necessarily shortest) sequences of elements of $\mathcal{M}$ is greater than $\frac{log_2 n - 2}{log_2 m}$.

Let κ be the number of indefinite models in N variables (which, as we noted above, is the same as the number of sets of minimal models) and let $\gamma = \begin{pmatrix} N \\ \lceil \frac{N}{2} \rceil \end{pmatrix}$ be the cardinality of the longest antichain with N elements. Because a subset of an anti-chain is an anti-chain, $\kappa \ge 2^\gamma$. Using the Shannon's counting argument we conclude that the average size of a set of minimal models (each of them being a sequence of up to N literals and curly braces { and }) is at least $\frac{log_2 \kappa - 2}{log_2 (N+2)} \ge \frac{\gamma - 2}{log_2 (N+2)}$. Hence

$$R_{avg}^{D,C} = \frac{1}{\kappa} \times \sum_{i=1}^{\kappa} \frac{d_i}{c_i} \ge \frac{1}{\kappa} \times \frac{\sum_{i=1}^{\kappa} d_i}{\lceil \frac{N}{2} \rceil \times \gamma} = \frac{1}{\lceil \frac{N}{2} \rceil \times \gamma} \times \frac{\sum_{i=1}^{\kappa} d_i}{\kappa} \ge$$

$$\ge \frac{\gamma - 2}{N \times log_2(N+2) \times \gamma} \approx \frac{1}{N \times log_2 N},$$

where c_i's and d_i's are the sizes of all indefinite models and sets of their minimal models. Symmetric argument shows that the average $R_{avg}^{C,D}$ of the converse ratio has the same lower bound. Therefore, on average, the cost of minimal modeling and indefinite modeling are very close to each other. Their closer relationship, for instance, the average ratio $\frac{d_i}{c_i}$ with averaging restricted to cases when the smaller of c_i, d_i is polynomial in N, requires further study.

References

[CR79] Stephen A. Cook and Robert A. Reckhow. The relative efficiency of propositional proof systems. *The Journal of Symbolic Logic*, 44(1):36–50, 1979.

[Rei78] Raymond Reiter. On closed world data bases. In Hervé Gallaire and Jack Minker, editors, *Logic and Data Bases*, pages 55–76. Plenum Press, 1978.

[SS90] Marek A. Suchenek and Rajshekhar Sunderraman. Minimal models for closed world data bases with views. In Zbigniew W. Ras, editor, *Methodologies for Intelligent Systems, 5*, pages 182–193, New York, 1990. North-Holland.

[Suc89] Marek A. Suchenek. A syntactic characterization of minimal entailment. In Ewing L. Lusk and Ross A. Overbeek, editors, *Logic Programming, North American Conference 1989*, pages 81–91, Cambridge, MA, October 16–20 1989. MIT Press.

[Suc90] Marek A. Suchenek. Applications of Lyndon homomorphism theorems to the theory of minimal models. *International Journal of Foundations of Computer Science*, 1(1):49–59, 1990.

[Suc97] Marek A. Suchenek. Evaluation of queries under the closed-world assumption. *Journal of Automated Reasoning*, 18:357–398, 1997.

[YH85] A. Yahya and L. Henschen. Deduction in non-Horn databases. *Journal of Automated Reasoning*, 1:141–160, 1985.

Artificial Neural Network for Multiprocessor Tasks Scheduling

Ireneusz Czarnowski, Piotr Jędrzejowicz

Computer Science Department, Gdynia Maritime Academy,
Morska 83, 81-225 Gdynia, Poland

Abstract. The paper deals with scheduling problems where tasks have to be processed on more than one processor at a time. The discussed optimization problems belong, in general, to NP-hard class and it is very likely that no polynomial-time exact algorithm solving them could ever be found. Hence, a dedicated artificial neural network has been proposed as a tool for solving multiprocessor tasks scheduling problems. The paper presents the proposed neural network structure and algorithms used to train it. Efficiency of the approach has been evaluated experimentally. Examples and computational experiment results are also shown.

1 Introduction

As it was pointed out by [3] and [4], there exist scheduling problems where tasks have to be processed on more than one processor at a time. During the execution of these multiple-processor tasks communication among processors working on the same task is implicitly hidden in a "black box" denoting an assignment of this task to a subset of processors during some time interval. To represent m-p tasks a $size_j$ parameter denoting processor requirement of a task j is used. In our case a $size$ of the task corresponds to the number of its redundant variants. Scheduling multiple-processor tasks does not require an assumption of variant independence. Hence, failures of variants belonging to a task can be positively correlated. The goal is to allocate multiple-processor tasks to processors in such a way that schedule dependability is maximized and time constraints are kept.

One of the potential application areas for m-p tasks scheduling algorithms is the fault-tolerant computing under time constraints. A unit of software is said to be fault-tolerant if it can continue delivering the required service after dormant imperfections, called software faults, have been activated by producing errors. To make simplex software units fault-tolerant, the corresponding solution is to add one, two or more program variants to form a set of $N \geq 2$ units. The redundant units are intended to compensate for, or mask the failed software unit.

Among several techniques used to achieve software fault tolerance, some best known include N-version programming (NVP) [1], recovery blocks (RB) [18], [14], and N-version self-checking programming (NSCP) [21], [17]. In all the above listed techniques, the required fault tolerance is achieved by increasing the number of independently developed program variants, which in turn leads to higher reliability at a cost of the additional resources used.

It should be noted that the concept of m-p tasks could be used to model variety of the fault-tolerant structures, since all require processing of redundant variants. Moreover, a multiple-processor task can be used as a convenient tool to model not only a structure with redundancy but also a structure involving internal communication and execution of an adjudication algorithm.

Unfortunately, the discussed scheduling problems belong, in general, to NP-hard class, and it is very likely that no polynomial-time exact algorithm solving them could ever be found. Hence, approximate algorithms and heuristic approaches, producing satisfactory solutions within reasonable time, could be of interest as tools for solving multiprocessor tasks scheduling problems.

The idea of using an artificial neural network to solve NP-hard class problems was proposed in [9]. Neural networks applied to job-shop scheduling were presented in [22] and [10]. An expert system for trucks scheduling based on neural network was proposed in [2].

In this paper a multi-layered, backpropagation model-based, artificial neural network for scheduling m-p tasks is proposed. Its architecture, including a number of layers, depends on features of the scheduling problem. To train the discussed network two algorithms are used. Some of its layers are trained using an evolutionary algorithm [19] and some are trained using a simulated annealing algorithm (see for example [15]). The actual choice between the algorithms is based on the decision of the internal expert system.

The paper is organised as follows: Section 2 presents problem formulation. In Section 3 neural network architecture is discussed and learning algorithms are presented. Section 4 shows an example schedule produced by the proposed neural network. Finally, in Section 5 computational experiment results are presented and commented upon.

2   Problem formulation

The problem of scheduling a set N of multiple-processor tasks under hard time constraints is considered. It is assumed that the following information, with respect to each m-p task in N, is available:

- time of readiness - a_j, $j = 1, \ldots, N$;
- deadline - d_j, $j = 1, \ldots, N$;
- maximum *size* - $M_j = max\{size_j\}$, $j = 1, \ldots, N$;
- processing time - p_{ji}, $j = 1, \ldots, n$, $i = 1, \ldots, M_j$;
- for each possible size of the task its reliability -
  $R_{ji}, j = 1, \ldots, N, i = 1, \ldots, M_j$.

Two problems of scheduling multiple-processor tasks are considered, The first problem, denoted using Graham's [7] notation as $P|a_j, size_j|R$, is characterized by a set of multiple, identical processors P, and a set of multiple-variant tasks N. Each task has the maximum size$=M_j$, and the minimum size equal to 1. Tasks are independent and non-preemptable with ready times and deadlines differing per task. Tasks have arbitrary processing times, which may differ per size chosen. Task j of the $size_j = M$ requires M parallel processors for processing. Optimization criterion is schedule reliability calculated as:

$$R = \prod_{j=1}^{N} R_{jk_j} \tag{1}$$

where k_j is a selected *size* of the task j, $1 \leq k_j \leq M_j$.

Task reliabilities are statistically independent. Decision variables include assignment of tasks to processors and size of each task. Tasks can not be delayed.

The second problem, denoted using Graham's notation as $P|a_j, size_j|V$ is similar to the first one, except for the optimization criterion which now is the total of the executed task sizes -V ($V = \sum size_j$), where $size_j$ is the *size* task j, used to construct a schedule.

3   Neural network for scheduling multiprocessor tasks

3.1   Network architecture

The proposed network architecture depends on task characteristics and varies for different problems. Set N of multiprocessor tasks is partitioned into subsets of tasks with identical ready times. A number of subsets thus created correspond to a number of layers in the respective network. Cardinality of each subset corresponds to a number of neurons representing tasks in a layer.

The neural network architecture has been additionally extended to include the so-called adders. Adders are placed in each layer and a number of adders in a layer correspond to a number of processors.

Neurons representing tasks in a layer send their signals to adders. Signals between layers pass through the decision block (or decoder). The decision block role is to accept signals received from adders. The block may adjust the weights of connections between neurons and adders in a layer, if signals from adders need to be corrected. If the changes do not bring the expected results the decision block may stimulate similar action within a previous layer, if such a layer is available.

Decision block of the layer controls values of signals received from adders which, in turn, depend on signals from neurons representing tasks. While scheduling m-p tasks, output signals from adders cannot exceed task deadlines transferred from adders attached to neurons.

When the decision block needs to adjust the respective connection weights, a learning process is activated. This process is based on two different methods – evolutionary computations and simulated annealing. Weights are adjusted at the end of an epoch, which is one cycle through the entire set of patterns

210

under consideration. This method is known as a batch training procedure [6].

The choice of the algorithm used in a learning process is based on a simple set of rules and depends on a layer structure. The algorithms chosen may differ between layers. More complex layers are trained using evolutionary algorithm, otherwise simulated annealing meta-heuristic is used.

Scheduling m−p tasks using the proposed neural network involves executing the following steps:

- Step 1: Decide on a number of layers by partitioning a set of tasks.
- Step 2: Construct a network placing the required number of neurons, adders andthedecision block at each layer.
- Step 3: Train the network using evolutionary algorithm and simulated annealing.
- Step 4: Decode representation of the solution.

3.2 Representation of the solution and evaluation function

A solution of the m−p tasks scheduling problem is derived from the values of connection weights. Values of weights are binary (zero−one). Active connections have weights equal to one. A number of active connections, leading from a neuron, have to be equal or greater then 1 and equal or smaller then the respective maximum *size* of the task represented by this neuron. The decision block of each layer controls these constraints. Values of the connection weights define an allocation of processors to tasks. Such an allocation can be used to calculate the evaluation function value.

To represent connection weights within a layer, a matrix structure could be used. For example, with two neurons in a layer and each task of the maximum size equal to 4, and altogether 5 processors represented by 5 adders, the respective matrix representing an example feasible solution is shown in Fig. 1.

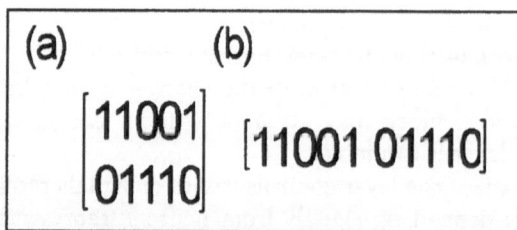

Fig. 1. Example of connection matrix (a) and connections vector (b).

The matrix (Fig. 1a) has two rows and five columns. Binary digits point to active and dormant connections. Total of active connections gives the evaluation function value for the $P|a_j, size_j|V$ problem. For the second of the analyzed problems— $P|a_j, size_j|R$, evaluation function is also easily calculated from the connection matrix (or vector).

3.3 Training method

The network is trained using either evolutionary computations or simulated annealing. Basic steps for both of these approaches is shown in Fig. 2.

```
procedure evolutionary_algorithm;        procedure simulated_annealing;
begin                                     begin
 i := 0;                                   initial T;
initial population P (0);                 generate random configuration X
calculate function V (R) for P (0);       calculate energy V (R) for X;
while (no_termination_condition_occur)    repeat
 do i := i + 1;                            generate new configuration X_new;
initial P (i) - elitist selection, one point  calculate energy V_new (R_new);
crossover, mutation;                      calculate energy
calculate function V (R) for P (i);        ΔV = V − V_new (orΔR);
end while;                                 if Δ V < 0
end procedure;                             or random < exp{−ΔV (R) /T}
                                           then X := X_new;
                                           reduce T;
                                           until (termination_condition_occur);
                                           end procedure;

where i-number of iteration.             where X-represents vector
                                         of connection, T-is a control parameter
```

Fig. 2. Pseudocode of training methods.

4 Example

Consider the following example $P|a_j, size_j|R$ problem. It is assumed that 5 m-p tasks are to be scheduled on 3 processors with a view to maximize schedule reliability. Each task can be run in one out of the 3 possible *sizes*. The respective data set for the example problem is shown in Table 1.

For the discussed example the respective neural network parameters as well as learning techniques used is shown in Table 2. The network has three layers corresponding to three subsets of the identical ready times. The number of adders (i.e. neurons with specific function) is identical for each layer.

The architecture of the resulting neural network is shown in Fig. 3. The arrows represent the connections between neurons and adders. Values of the final connection weights are given as chromosomes for layers 1 and 2 and as

Table 1. Data set for the example problem.

Task number	a_j	d_j	p_j for size $= 1$	p_j for size $= 2$	p_j for size $= 3$	R_j for size $= 1$	R_j for size=1	R_j for size=1
1	0	2	1	2	2	0,9349	0,9933	0,9995
2	0	10	5	5	6	0,8144	0,9884	0,9997
3	3	15	6	8	10	0,8408	0,9792	0,9966
4	3	15	6	7	8	0,8184	0,9664	0,9948
5	6	10	1	1	2	0,9180	0,9848	0,9993

Table 2. Breakdown of parameters for the neural network example.

Layer number	1 2 3
Number of neuron in layer	2 2 1
Total number of neurons	5
Number of adders	3 3 3
Lenght of connections vector	6 6 3

the connections vector for layer 3. The schedule produced by the network is shown in a form of the Gantt's Chart in Fig.4. The value of the respective schedule reliability is 0,7369.

5 Computational experiment results

The proposed neural network for scheduling multiprocessor tasks has been evaluated by means of computational experiment. For both optimization problems 50 sets of data have been randomly generated. Each set involves scheduling of 10-20 tasks, each task with the maximum size equal to 4. Tasks have had to be scheduled on 3-10 processors. The results produced by the neural network have been compared with other results obtained by using evolution algorithm [13], social learning algorithm (SLA) [12] and hybrid algorithm [5].

In Tables 2 and 3 relative errors from the best-known solutions for both problems are shown. Obtained solutions aren't optimal but in comparison with other solutions values. In case of the $P|a_j, size_j|V$ problem the neural network performance has not been particularly impressive. However, in case of the $P|a_j, size_j|R$ the neural network approach has been clearly a winner with only 2,27% of mean relative error. It should be also noted that the proposed network time performance is comparable to those of the other approaches.

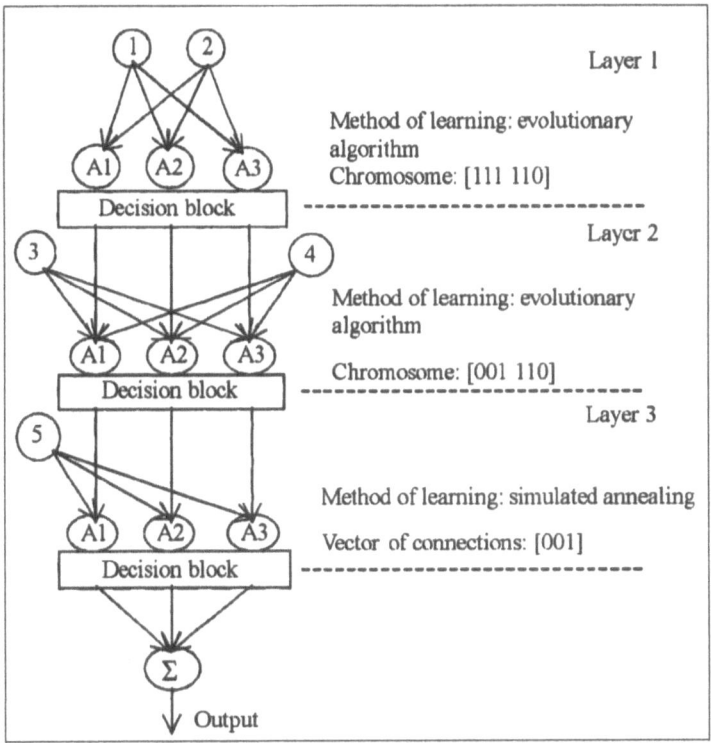

Fig. 3. Architecture of the example network.

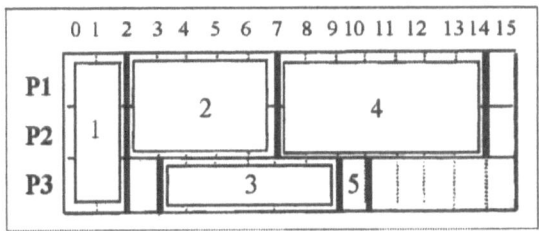

Fig. 4. The schedule produced by the network.

Table 3. Mean relative errors (in %) from the best solution found for $P|a_j, size_j|V$ problem.

No of proc.	Artifical Neural Network	Evolution Algorithm	SLA Algorithm	Hybrid Algorithm
4	7,00	6,00	3,8	4,25
5	5,75	9,25	3,43	4,73
6	2,33	15,17	3,38	6,64
7	12,00	23,14	3,71	12,29
8	11,14	20,29	3,25	10,07
9	15,00	23,20	2,67	11,36
10	11,75	20,00	2,25	10,88
Overall	9,28	16,72	3,21	8,6

Table 4. Mean relative errors (in %) from the best solution found for $P|a_j, size_j|R$ problem.

No of proc.	Artifical Neural Network	Evolution Algorithm	SLA Algorithm	Hybrid Algorithm
4	0,00	18,82	10,50	8,88
5	0,00	15,42	7,82	4,67
6	0,00	15,67	13,86	3,42
7	2,86	19,67	17,00	9,64
8	6,71	20,13	13,67	11,54
9	4,17	17,47	15,42	11,50
10	2,17	17,20	15,70	11,00
Overall	2,27	17,77	13,42	8,66

6 Conclusions

It has been demonstrated that neural networks could serve as an effective and competitive tool for solving difficult combinatorial optimization problems. The concept of the dedicated network which architecture directly depends on some features of the problem to be solved seems very promising.

Future research will concentrate on different learning schemes and algorithms as well as on considering some hybrid algorithms combining neural network approach with effective improvement strategies. The approach should also be tested against a wider spectrum of scheduling problems.

References

[1] Avizienis, A., Chen, L. (1977): On the Implementation of the N-version Programming for Software Fault Tolerance During Execution. IEEE COMPSAC 77, 149-155

[2] Biagioni, E., Abe, T., Ishii, S. (1989): Applying Neural Network to Scheduling Problems. Conference of the Information Processing Society of Japan, Tokyo

[3] Błażewicz, J., Drabowski, M., Węglarz, J. (1986): Scheduling Multiprocessor Tasks to Minimize Schedule Length. IEEE Transactions on Computers 35, 389 - 393

[4] Błażewicz, J., Ecker, K.H., Pesch, E., Schmidt, G., Węglarz, J. (1986): Scheduling Computer and Manufacturing Processes. Springer, Berlin

[5] Czarnowski, I., Skakowski, A. (1999): Hybrydowy Model Szeregowania Programów Tolerujących Błędy. Algorytmy Ewolucyjne i Optymalizacja Globalna Potok Złoty, 83−90

[6] Duch W., Korczak, J. (1998):Optimization and Global Minimization Method Suitable for Neural Networks. Neural Computing Surveys 2, http://www.icsi.berceley.edu/ jagopta/NCS

[7] Graham, R.L., Lawler, E.L., Lenstra, J.K., Rinnooy Kan, A.H.G. (1979): Optimization and Approximation in Deterministic Sequencing and Scheduling. Annals Discrete Math., 287-326

[8] Hertz, J., Krogh, A., Palmer, R.G. (1995): Wstęp do Teorii Obliczeń Neuronowych. WNT Warszawa

[9] Hppfield, J.J., Tank, D.W. (1985): "Neural" Computations of Depencision in Optimisations Problems. Biological Cybernetics 52, 141-152

[10] Janiak, A. (1999): Wybrane Problemy i Algorytmy Szeregowania Zadań i Rozdziału Zasobów. Akademicka Oficyna Wydawnicza PLJ, Warszawa

[11] Jędrzejowicz, P. (1997): Scheduling Fault−Tolerant Programs. Research Reports Nr 3 KI97 WSM Gdynia

[12] Jędrzejowicz, P. (1999): Social Learning Algorithm. Research Reports Nr 7 KI98, WSM Gdynia

[13] Jędrzejowicz, P., Czarnowski, I., Szreder, H., Skakowski, A. (1999): Evolution−Based Scheduling of Fault−Tolerant Programs on Multiple Processor. Lecture Note in Computer Science 1586, Springer, 210−219

[14] Kim, K.H. (1984): Distributed Execution of Recovery Blocks: an Approach to Uniform Treatment of Hardware and Software Faults, Proc. 4th International Conference on Distributed Computing Systems. IEEE Computer Society Press, 526-532

[15] Kirpatrick, S., Gellett, C.D., Vecci, M.P. (1983): Optimisation by Simulated Annealing. Science 22, 671-680

[16] Koza, J., Rice, J.P. (1991): Genetic Generation of Both The Weights and Architecture for a Neural Network. Seatle WA, USA

[17] Laprie, J.C., Arlat, J., Beounes, C., Kanoun, K. (1990): Definition and Analysis of Hardware−and−Software Fault−Tolerant Architectures. IEEE Computer23(7), 39-51

[18] Melliar−Smith, P.M., Randell, B. (1977): Software Reliability the Role of Programmed Exception Handling. SIGPLAN Notice 12(3), 195-100.

[19] Michalewicz, Z. (1992): Genetic Algorithm+Data Structures=Evolution Programs. Spring-Verlag

[20] Whitley, D. (1995): Genetic Algorithm and Neural Networks. In: Winter, G., Periaux, J., Galan, M., Cuesta, P. (Eds): Genetic Algorithm and Computer Science. John Wiley, 203-216

[21] Yau, S.S., Cheung, R.C. (1975): Design of Self−Checking Software. Proc. Int. Conf. on Reliable Software, IEEE Computer Society Press, 450-457

216

[22] Zohu, D.N., Cherkassky, V., Balwin, T.R., Olson, D.E. (1991): A Neural Approach to Job Shop Scheduling. IEEE Transactions on Neural Networks, vol 2, 175-179

Probabilistic Neural Nets in Knowledge Intense Learning Tasks

Mieczysław A. Kłopotek

Institute of Computer Science, Polish Academy of Sciences, Warsaw, Poland, also

Institute of Computer Science, University of Podlasie, Siedlce, Poland

e-mail: klopotek@ipipan.waw.pl

Abstract: In this paper an idea of modeling technical processes for purposes of process optimization with restricted amount of experimental data is described. It is based on tuning micro-models to reflect real-world data. Quickly learning probabilistic neural networks are used as a vehicle to invert independent parameters of micro-models into ones depending on macro-statistics of a simulated process.

Keywords: Artificial Neural Networks, technical process design

1. Introduction

Many practical problems, e.g. in engineering, consist in searching a model for a process, finding optimal process conditions in this model and / or optimal process control. For example in chemical engineering, given laboratory experiments, optimal synthesis conditions are sought yielding maximal gain and selectivity while reducing negative side effects. The results have to be moved, in appropriate steps, to industrial scale production where the production process has to be controlled in such a way as to keep the maximum productivity while avoiding dangerous or risky situations Another example is optimal macro-control of social and economic processes.

Usually, no explicit nor implicit analytical model combining control with its effects is available. Under these conditions the mathematical experiment planning is a well-founded methodology for search of optimum. However, high costs of planned experiments and non-linearity of the process under consideration make frequently it impossible to find an optimum in this way.

Hence another type of model of the phenomenon under consideration has to be found that would

- allow for process optimization and

- require a restricted number of experiments.

2. General Idea

Neural networks with hidden layers are frequently considered as an effective method of modeling non-linear behavior [6,13]. On the one hand they are equivalent with some methods of statistical estimation, on the other hand they possess a nice method of learning by presentation of input and expected output data of the model to be created. However, for purposes of applications considered here, most types of neural networks offer severe disadvantages:

1. they require relatively large sample sizes - unacceptable due to high costs (e.g. of industrial scale experiments) or unavailability of data (few countries with comparable economies)

2. they have long training times - which excludes applications with real-time learning

3. results of learning depend on presentation sequence

4. they have significant learning parameters (e.g. number of hidden layers) that have no direct relation to the application problem

Probabilistic neural networks (PNN) [12] seem to an exception to this rule. They learn quickly, even with a small sample, and the number of net-specific parameters is limited (e.g. AINET [1] has only one such parameter).

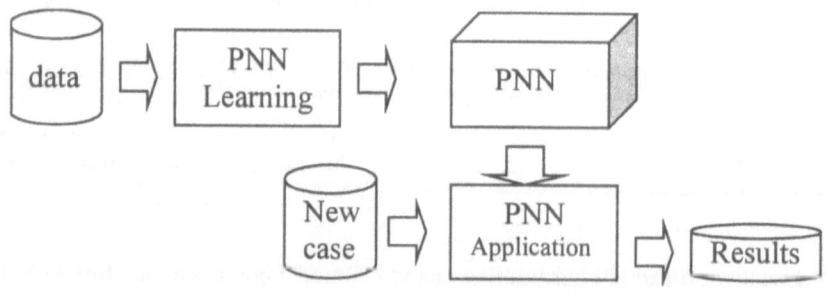

Fig. 1 Typical application of PNN

However, these networks are feed-forward ones so that optimization tasks cannot be carried out by them (see fig.1). In particular, also their own parameters cannot be automatically optimized.

Therefore, an additional component for finding optima is needed. We suggest usage of Evolutionsstrategien (ES) [10] for this purpose (see fig.2).

Subsequent sections will explain in detail PNN and ES.

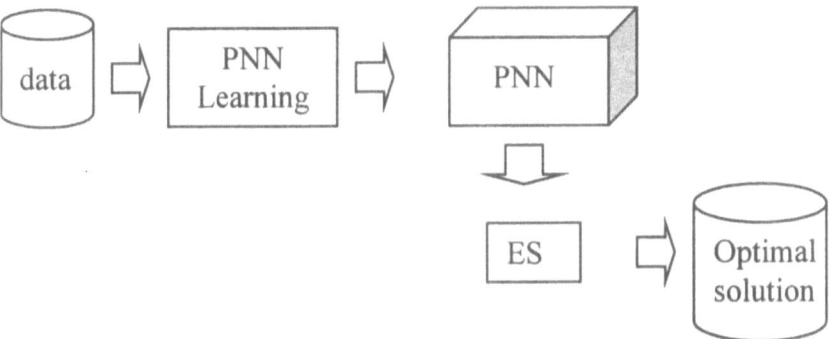

Fig. 2 ES cooperating with PNN for finding an optimal solution

Usually, the optimum will be relative only to the current model and therefore needs to be verified empirically, so that an iterative process will take place - enhancng the PNN model based on the empirical data. (see fig.3)

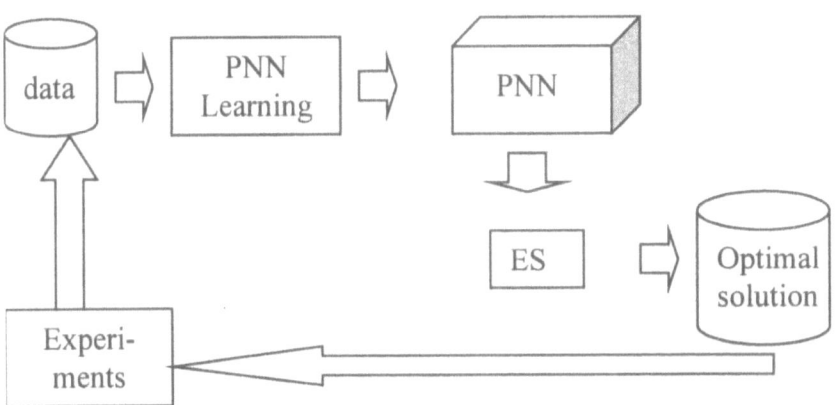

Fig. 3 ES cooperating with PNN in an optimization loop

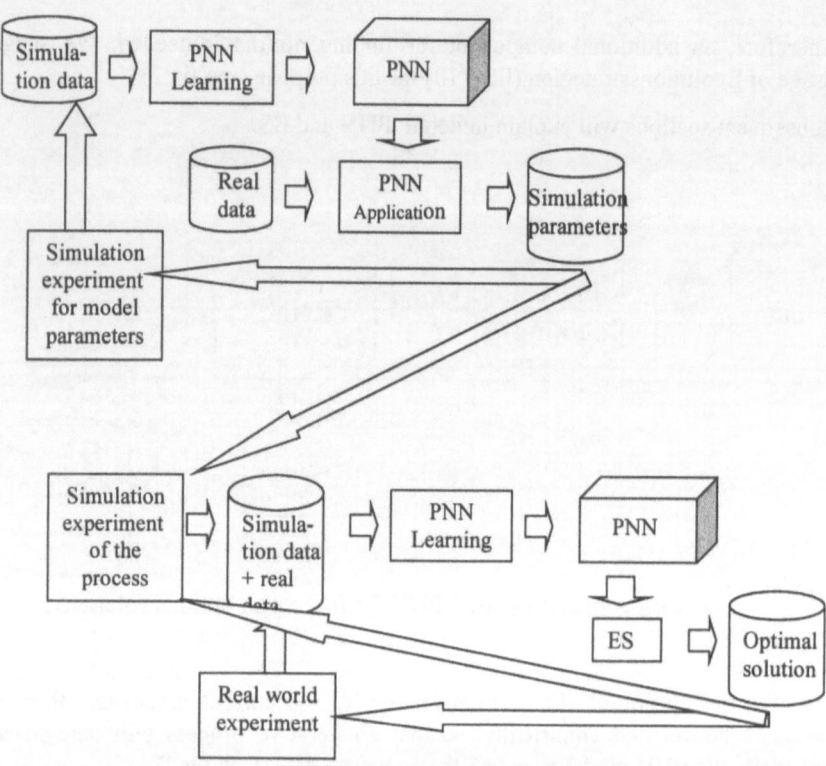

Fig. 4 Exploitation of simulation models

However, frequently the costs of experiments are prohibitive. But there exist models of the process of interest, e.g. the ChemCad [5] for chemical processes. Such models, being general in nature, usually are not prepared for simulation of our particular case, especially if the chemical process under consideration is a new invention. Usually, the models have some parameters (e.g. the coefficients of synthesis speed) that need to be adjusted for a particular process. These parameters are in general micro-scale dynamic parameters, that is they are not observable directly. Only the total input and output of the process can be traced. In this case the PNN can be exploited in the way described in fig.4. First some trial simulations with guessed micro-parameters are carried out and the macro-effects are resulting from a process simulation. Then with PNN learning a mapping from macro-effects to micro-parameters is sought (inversion of the simulation process). Then using the real world data available micro-parameters can be estimated. Usually repeated simulations with the acquired micro-parameters are to be carried out to achieve good agreement with empirical observations. Once the micro-parameters are tuned, a simulation study of the process considered may start, optimal process conditions can be calculated as previously described using ES and repeated (real and/or simulated) experiments.

Notice that a qualitative jump is achieved with architectures presented above. Neural networks are usually associated with black boxes, where one tries to create a real-world model in case of missing theoretical knowledge. However, if neural networks are coupled with evolutionsstrategien and with some simulation models, they can in fact make use of domain knowledge incorporated in the simulation model and in the constraints of evolutionsstrategien.

3. Probabilistic Neural Network

PNN or "Probabilistic Neural Network" is Specht's [12] term for kernel discriminant analysis. (Kernels are also called "Parzen windows".) One can think of it as a normalized RBF (radial basis function) network in which there is a hidden unit centered at every training case. These RBF units are called "kernels" and are usually probability density functions such as the Gaussian. The hidden-to-output weights are usually 1 or 0; for each hidden unit, a weight of 1 is used for the connection going to the output that the case belongs to, while all other connections are given weights of 0. Alternatively, you can adjust these weights for the prior probabilities of each class. So the only weights that need to be learned are the widths of the RBF units. These widths (often a single width is used) are called "smoothing parameters" or "bandwidths" and are usually chosen by cross-validation or by some other method. Gradient descent is not used.

Specht claims that a PNN trains 100,000 times faster than backpropagation network. While they are not iterative in the same sense as backpropagation, kernel methods require apriorical estimation of the kernel bandwidth, and this requires accessing the data many times. Furthermore, computing a single output value with kernel methods requires either accessing the entire training data or clever programming, and either way is much slower than computing an output with a feed-forward net. PNN is just faster when the amount of training data is low. This is the case when usually backpropagation fails, as in the applications considered.

PNN is a universal approximator for smooth class-conditional densities, so it should be able to solve any smooth classification problem given enough data. The main drawback of PNN is that, like kernel methods in general, it suffers badly from the curse of dimensionality. PNN cannot ignore irrelevant inputs without major modifications to the basic algorithm. So PNN is not likely to be the top choice if there are more than 5 or 6 nonredundant inputs. 5-10 variables are in fact maximum number of independent inputs in technical applications under consideration.

There exist also modified algorithms that deal with irrelevant inputs, see [7,8].

If all inputs are relevant, PNN has the very useful ability to tell you whether a test case is similar (i.e. has a high density) to any of the training data.

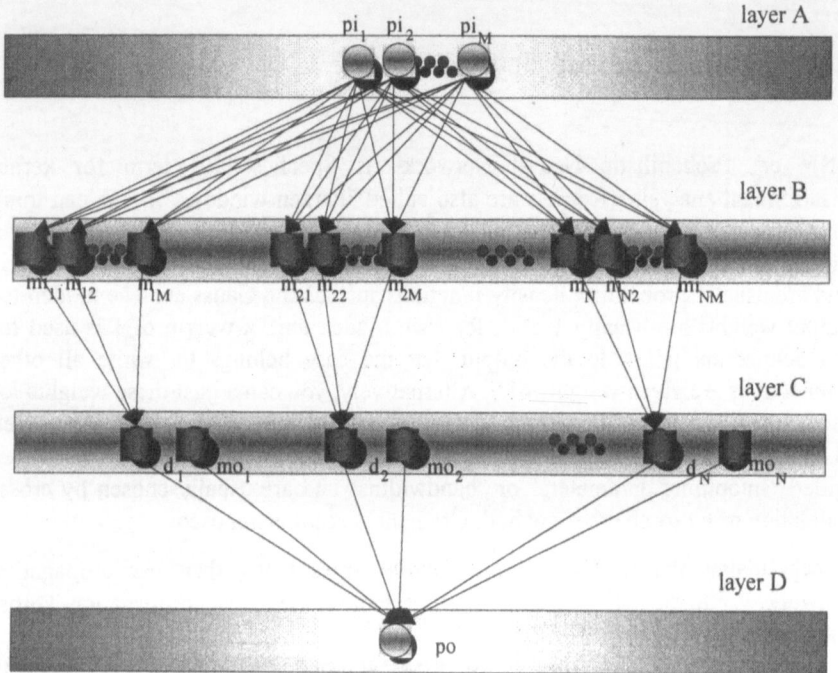

Fig. 5 A model of a PNN

In Fig.5 an example of a PNN (so-called AiNet [1]) is visible. Denotation:

- p   prediction vector,
- m   model vector,
- i   indicates the neuron, belonging to the input variable,
- o   indicates the neuron, belonging to the output variable.
- N   number of model vectors,

- M   number of input variables of the phenomenon,
- K   number of output variables of the phenomenon (K is equal to 1 in presented case, and is omitted),
- pc   penalty coefficient

The weights on connections are either equal to one or equal to zero. The expression for weight adaptation can be written as:

$$w_{ij} = \overline{w}_{ij} \delta_{kj},$$

where $\overline{w}_{ij}$ is equal to 1.0, and δij is defined :

$$\delta_{ij} = \begin{cases} 1; i = j \\ 0; i \neq j \end{cases}$$

Network works in prediction mode according to the following scheme:

- *layer A:*   value of the neuron: $X_i^A = p_i,$

  transfer function: *linear*

  output value of the neuron:

  $$Y_i^A = f(X_i^A) = X_i^A.$$

- *layer B:*   value of the neuron:

  $$X_{ij}^B = \sum_{k=1}^{M} \left(Y_k^A - mi_{ij} \right) \delta_{kj}$$

  transfer function: *linear*

  output value of the neuron:

  $$Y_{ij}^B = f\left(X_{ij}^B \right) = \left(X_{ij}^B \right)^2$$

- *layer C:*   value of the neurons type d: $X_i^C = \sum_{j=1}^{M} Y_{ij}^B$

  transfer function: *linear*

  output value of the neuron:

  $$Y_i^C = f\left(X_i^C, pc \right) = e^{\frac{-X_i^C}{pc}}$$

value of the neuron <u>type mo</u>: $\overline{X}_i^C = mo_i,$

transfer function: *linear*

output value of the neuron:

$$\overline{Y}_i^C = f(\overline{X}_i^C) = \overline{X}_i^C = mo_i.$$

• *layer D:*   value of the neuron: $X^D = \sum_{i=1}^{N} Y_i^C ,$

$$\overline{X}^D = \sum_{i=1}^{N} Y_i^C \, \overline{Y}_i^C$$

transfer function: *linear*

output value of the neuron:

$$po = Y^D = f\left(X^D, \overline{X}^D\right) = \frac{X^D}{\overline{X}^D}$$

4. Evolution Strategy (ES)

Evolutionsstrategien [10,11] were invented to solve technical optimization problems like e.g. constructing an optimal flashing nozzle, and until recently ES were predominantly used by civil engineers, as an alternative to standard solutions. Usually no closed form analytical objective function is available for technical optimization problems and hence, no applicable optimization method exists, but the engineer's intuition.

In a two-membered or (1+1) ES, one parent generates one offspring per generation by applying normally distributed mutations, i.e. smaller steps occur more likely than big ones, until a child performs better than its ancestor and takes its place. Because of this simple structure, theoretical results for stepsize control and convergence velocity could be derived. The first algorithm, using mutation only, has then been enhanced to a (m+1) strategy which incorporated recombination due to several, i e. m parents being available. The mutation scheme and the exogenous stepsize control were taken across unchanged from (1+1) ESs. Schwefel later generalized these strategies to the multimembered ES now denoted by (m+l) and (m,l) which imitates the following basic principles of organic evolution: a population, leading to the possibility of recombination with random mating, mutation and selection. These strategies are termed plus strategy and comma strategy, respectively: in the plus case, the parental generation is taken into account during selection, while in the comma case only the offspring undergoes selection, and the parents die off.

Notice that also evolutionary programs could be used for optimization problems [9].

5. Conclusions

In the paper an architecture for engaging neural networks into knowledge-intense learning tasks has been proposed. Neural networks are usually associated with black boxes, where one tries to create a real-world model in case of missing theoretical knowledge. However, if neural networks are coupled with evolutionsstrategien and with some simulation models, they can in fact make use of domain knowledge incorporated in the simulation model and in the constraints of evolutionsstrategien.

The proposed architecture could be used e.g.

- for introductory analysis of costs of implementing a technology [3]

- for evaluation of usefulness of changes in an existing technology [2,4]

- for identification of simulation parameters of newly elaborated technologies,

- for optimal real-time control of technological processes

Bibliography

1. AINET - documentation URL http://www.ainet-sp.si/aiNetNN.htm

2. Adamska-Rutkowska D.: Modelowanie złożonych procesów chemicz-nych za pomocą sieci neuronowych, *Przemysł Chemiczny* 77/7(1998), 247-250

3. Adamska-Rutkowska D., Rejewski P.: Szacowanie kosztów inwestycyj-nych I eksploatacyjnych technologii chemicznych za pomocą sieci neuronoweej na wstępie cyklu badawczo-wdrożeniowego, *Przemysł Chemiczny* 78/3(1999), 83-86

4. Adamska-Rutkowska D.: Wykorzystanie sieci neuronowych do esty-macji parametrów matematycznego modelu procesu chemicznego, *Przemysł Chemiczny* 77/12(1998), 446-448

5. ChemCad by Chemstations http://www.chemstations.net/

6. Gately E. Ed . *Sieci neuronowe. Prognozowanie finansowe i projektowanie systemów transakcyjnych.* Tłum. z ang. Warszawa 1999 WIG-Press

7. Lowe, D.G., Similarity metric learning for a variable-kernel classifier, *Neural Computation,* 7, (1995) 72-85, http://www.cs.ubc.ca/spider/lowe/pubs.html

8. Masters, T. *Advanced Algorithms for Neural Networks: A C++ Sourcebook,* NY: John Wiley and Sons, (1995)

9. Michalewicz Z.::. *Algorytmy genetyczne + struktury danych = programy ewolucyjne.* Tłum. z ang. Warszawa 1996 WN-T

10. Rechenberg, I.: *Evolutionsstrategie: Optimierung technischer Systeme nach Prinzipien der biologischen Evolution,* Stuttgart: Fromman-Holzboog. (1973)

11. Schwefel, H.-P:. *Numerische Optimierung von Computermodellen mittels der Evolutionsstrategie,* Basel: Birkhäuser. (1977)

12. Specht, D.F.: Probabilistic neural networks, *Neural Networks,* 3, (1990) 110-118.

13. Tadeusiewicz R.: *Sieci neuronowe.* Warszawa 1993, Akad. Oficyna. Wydawnicza.

Evolutionary Real-Time Optimization System for Ecological Power Control

Maciej Michalewicz[1], Katarzyna Juda-Rezler[2], Krzysztof Trojanowski[1], Andrzej Matuszewski[1], Zbigniew Michalewicz[1,3], Michał Trojanowski[4]

[1] Institute of Computer Science, Polish Academy of Sciences, Warsaw, Poland (michalew@ipipan.waw.pl, trojanow@ipipan.waw.pl)

[2] Institute of Environmental Engineering Systems, Warsaw University of Technology, Warsaw, Poland (kasiajr@pegaz.iis.pw.edu.pl)

[3] University of North Carolina at Charlotte, Charlotte, USA (zbyszek@uncc.edu)

[4] Institute of Computer Science, Faculty of Electronics and Information Technology, Warsaw University of Technology, Warsaw, Poland (mtrojano@elka.pw.edu.pl)

Summary: In this paper, Evolutionary Real-time Optimization System for Ecological Power Control for the area of Poland is presented. We describe the modeling issues of the problem, provide discussion on data used for the developed system, and introduce statistical methodology incorporated in the system. Finally, we describe evolutionary optimization system EROS and some experimental results.

Keywords: evolutionary computation, air pollution control, sulphur dioxide concentration, energy supply systems

1. Introduction

The aim of the work described in this paper was to develop an Evolutionary Real-time Optimization System for Ecological Power Control for the area of Poland. The system belongs to the family of Integrated Assessment Models (IAMs) which provide a framework for bringing together disparate information related to a particular environmental problem. IAMs were used to help formulate the second sulphur protocol [UN-ECE EB.AIR/R.84, 1994] which derived cost-effective strategies for reducing SO_2 emissions from coal-fired power stations across

Europe. Similar methodologies were used to derive abatement strategies for the heavy polluted *Black Triangle* region of eastern Europe (Lowles *et al.*, 1998).

In this current work the aim was to derive recommended level of produced energy for each particular pollution source from the public power generation sector (power plants and cogeneration plants) in Poland, with respect to actual country energy demand, which would minimize the sulphur dioxide exposure to ecosystems. Such a solution is possible as the country has an oversupply of the installed power with respect to the energy demand.

System includes input data (data on emission sources, meteorological data, land-cover data), atmospheric pollution dispersion and deposition models as well as data on the capacity of the ecosystem to sustain certain level of concentration, so called critical levels. Evolutionary computation techniques (extended by genetic memory structures) are used for optimization process.

The paper is organized as follows. Section 2 describes the modeling issues of the problem. Section 3 provides discussion on data used for the developed system. Section 4 introduces statistical methodology incorporated in the system. Section 5 describes evolutionary optimization system EROS and some experimental results. The final section concludes the paper.

2. Modeling issues

The modeling area covers the territory of Poland (900 km x 750 km). The adopted computational grid constitutes a part of the MSC-W EMEP (Meteorological Syntesizing Centre-West, Co-operative Programme for Monitoring and Evaluation of the Long Range Transmission of Air Pollutants in Europe) model grid, only with finer spatial resolution (30 km x 30 km). The polar stereographic projection is applied. A grid designated in such a way facilitates comparison of the results obtained with other European models results.

Sulphur dioxide atmospheric dispersion and deposition have been modeled by two different models: the POLSOX-I Eulerian grid model and the REGFOR Lagrangian trajectory model. Model's codes combine transport, diffusion, chemistry and deposition processes (dry and wet) in the study area. Two chemical compounds has been modeled: SO_2 and SO_4^{2-}.

The necessity of applying two different models arises form the fact that sulphur dioxide concentrations in Poland are caused by three group of emission sources:

1. sources from abroad (mainly from Germany and the Czech Republic),

2. Polish sources from industrial and municipal sectors,

3. Polish sources from the public power generation sector (power plants and cogeneration plants).

SO_2 concentrations caused by first two groups of sources are defined in the system as *background concentrations*; these sources and are not subjected for control procedure. The third group of sources is subjected for real-time energy production control procedure. Resulting concentration of SO_2 in each computational grid element is the sum of background concentration and concentration caused by third group of sources.

Annual mean values of background SO_2 concentration have been calculated for the expanded computational grid (1050 km x 900 km) with resolution of 30 km x 30 km. Calculations have been made by the use air pollution dispersion model POLSOX-I (see Juda-Rezler *et al.*, 1997). The POLSOX-I model belongs to the family of numerical two-dimensional Eulerian grid (K-theory) models, developed at the Institute of Environmental Engineering Systems, Warsaw University of Technology. Input meteorological data were taken from ECMWF (European Centre for Medium-Range Weather Forecasts, Reading, UK). Input emission data were prepared for Polish industrial and municipal emission sources as well as for sources from neighborhood countries (Czech Republic and Germany). These emission data were taken from the EASE Database (*Copernicus Project*).

For the sources from the public power generation sector (power plants and cogeneration plants) the REGFOR Lagrangian trajectory model developed at the System Research Institute of the Polish Academy of Sciences (see Holnicki *et al.* 1993, 1994) has been applied. Input meteorological data were taken from the Institute of Meteorology and Water Management in Warsaw.

In order to improve the predictions of REGFOR model the dry deposition submodel has been built in. The SO_2 concentrations are strongly dependent on dry deposition process, so its parameterization is essential for the model results. The dry deposition submodel for sulphur species have been developed and tested based on the original multi-species RIVM's (National Institute of Public Health and Environmental Protection, Bilthoven, the Netherlands) dry deposition model. The land-cover data are needed for dry deposition submodel.

For the sources from the public power generation sector daily mean *source-receptor transmission matrixes* have been calculated. The matrix for a given emission source gives the SO_2 daily mean concentration in each receptor (grid element) resulting from unit emission from that source. Actual concentration is then calculated by multiplying the source-receptor matrixes by the actual emission levels (nominal emission, optimized emission).

3. Data for the emission sources and land cover

For the purpose of current work the actual data for the public power generation sector emission sources (power plants and cogeneration plants), which are included in the real-time control system, have been prepared. The data are used for actual sulphur compounds concentration calculations.

The analysis of possibilities of power control in Poland have been undertaken. The subject of analysis was country energy demands in the context of existing power burden and energy production on the yearly basis. From the country power disposal point of view, the following data for 90 power plants and cogeneration plants sources have been taken into account: energy production efficiency, energy production costs, long-term contracts concluded with Polish Power Grid Company, existing and planned ecological installations. As a results of performed analysis, 83 sources have been chosen for power optimization procedure.

For each source the following data have been prepared: source name, source (stack) number, geographical source co-ordinates, stack height, stack diameter, exhaust gas temperature and velocity, nominal power and nominal annual sulphur dioxide emission. Emission data have been calculated on the base of real amount of burned fuel, characteristic of technological combustion process and sulphur content in the fuel.

The land-cover data for Poland are essential for the presented work. The land covers in each computational grid are needed as a input to the dry deposition submodel as well as to the area valorization model.

The land-cover map for the territory of Poland in the adopted computational grid have been prepared on the base of RIVM's original data (with geographical resolution of 10' x 10'). A Geographical Information System (Arc/Info) was used to convert original data into a projection and resolution suitable for the adopted computational grid (with resolution 30 km x 30 km). The following land-use categories are included in original data: coniferous and mixed forest, deciduous forest, permanent crops, grassland, urban areas, arable land, inland water, sea and „other". Additional category: „high mountain forest" have been introduced and added to the land-cover prepared for the current work.

4. Statistical methodology

Area valorization model estimates the capacity of the ecosystem to sustain certain level of concentration. The risk to ecosystems was evaluated through an standardized *sten* value, which estimated a region's sensitivity to pollution based on UN-ECE guideline values for mean-annual critical levels of SO_2 (Ashmore and

Wilson, 1993). The critical levels is defined as "the concentrations of pollutants in the atmosphere above which direct adverse effects on receptor such as plants, ecosystems or materials, may occur according to present knowledge".

The following table shows critical levels of SO_2 corresponding to all types of land (use)-covers. They are expressed in $\mu g/m^3$.

P1: grassland	30
P2: deciduous forest	20/15*
P3: coniferous and mixed forest	20/15*
P4: arable land	30
P5: permanent crops	30
P6: inland water	50
P7: urban areas	50
P8: 'other'	40
P9: sea	50

* lower value if there exist mountain forests within the grid element

The following three types of descriptive parameters are considered within the statistical science as characteristics of a given population and/or sample.

1. Location parameters
2. Dispersion parameters
3. Quantiles.

We use these parameters to characterize computational grid elements in aspect of their "sensitivity" to the high SO_2 concentration in atmosphere.

Let us consider as a basic location parameter of a grid element K, the following mean:

$$m(K) = \Sigma \, p_i(K) \, d_i / 100$$

where: $p_i(K)$ is a percent of i-th land-cover within the grid element K

d_i is the critical level of i-th land-cover within the grid element K

Actually there is only 4 point in the distribution of the critical levels, so it is difficult to consider quantiles of that distribution. We will propose a new method

232

for the generalized percentiles calculation therefore. The formula that connect those percentiles with a dispersion parameter will be derived either.

We introduce the notion of "neighborhood" of grid element. This notion has an empirical meaning. To define this meaning a statistical analysis was performed. Information basis of that analysis was the Polish land-cover data set representing percentage shares.

Neighborhoods and generalized percentile critical levels were derived through the cluster analysis performed on the grid elements, which are most sensitive. Through the subsequent regression analysis the relation between those percentiles and the following dispersion parameter was established.

$$D(K) = \Sigma \, p_i \, \text{abs}(m(K) - d_i)/100$$

It is well known that the actual concentration of SO_2 in atmosphere has the lognormal distribution. Parameter sigma of that distribution can serve as an "error" of the measurements of logarithms of the actual concentration value. It would be important if we can treat this error as constant for the territory of Poland.

For estimation of the parameter sigma of that distribution, a statistical study was performed. The measurement data for Poland i.e. available concentration measurements of the daily mean concentration for different measurement stations were taken into account. Estimated sigma equal to 0.35 refers to he distribution of the daily means over year.

To adjust the actual concentration of SO_2 in atmosphere to the structure of land-cover of a grid element, a notion of standardized concentration was introduced. This notion simplifies the practical interpretation of the actual data whether they are real or followed the appropriate theoretical model.

The sten (standard ten) scale was introduced within psychometry i,e. a branch of psychology dedicated to the methodology of the psychological measurement (tests, questionnaires etc.). Sten scale, like any other standardized scale, allows making the so-called norms of a given psychological test (variable, factor, dimension etc.) for a population the test is aimed.

The scale, like many other standard scales, is based on the normal (statistical) distribution. This distribution is divided in 10 parts, which also are called stens. The mean (expectation, average) of the observed (non-standardized) value – roughly speaking – corresponds to the common limit:

- Upper limit of the 5-th sten
- Lower limit of the 6-th sten.

From other point of view one can say that the expectation of stens is equal to 5.5.

The length of each sten, excluding the two extreme, is equal to the half of the standard deviation. That has the following interpretation within our application: Once the SO_2 concentration in the atmosphere grows 0.35 on the logarithmic scale, standardized scores should grow roughly 2 stens.

We made some changes in the definition of the sten scale. The proposed changes take into account several differences that exist between psychological measurement and the standardization of the actual concentration of SO_2 in atmosphere to the structure of land-cover of a given grid element.

First of all our stens correspond linearly to the logarithms of the original scale. Two other changes reflect the fact that interpretation of a certain difference between two low concentrations has less significance within ecology than the same difference if we are beyond the critical levels that correspond to a given grid element.

Once the actual concentration of SO_2 crossed the critical level we change the mean of the scale. Instead of $m(K)$ it become the generalized 10-th percentile. One can treat this change as an additional reason why the cluster analysis described above was based on most sensitive grid elements within the area of Poland only.

We defined also 11-th sten (the highest), which reflects the highest part of the lognormal distribution of SO_2 concentration in atmosphere i.e. that part, which is above the 99.8 percentile limit. That limit can be crossed for a 30-minute period only. All these episodes can last less than 1 day yearly.

To standardize the actual concentration of SO_2 in atmosphere for a given element of the grid, one needs to know how to calculate the limits between subsequent stens. If we call those limits g_j – the common: upper limit of j-th sten and lower limit of (j+1)-th sten, then the formulas for them are as follows.

$g_1 = \ln m(K) - 2*0.35$

$g_2 = \ln m(K) - 1.5*0.35$

$g_3 = \ln m(K) - 0.35$

$g_4 = \ln m(K) - 0.5*0.35$

$g_5 = \ln m(K)$

$g_6 = \ln(m(K) - 0.08*D(K)) + 0.5*0.35$

$g_7 = \ln(m(K) - 0.16*D(K)) + 0.35$

$g_8 = \ln(m(K) - 0.16*D(K)) + 1.5*0.35$

$g_9 = \ln(m(K) - 0.16*D(K)) + 2*0.35$

$g_{10} = \ln(m(K) - 0.16*D(K)) + 2.9*0.35$

The above limits must be applied to the logarithm of the actual value of concentration of SO_2 in atmosphere within the grid element K.

There are several statistical procedures that operate on the sten data. One can check if the series of the SO_2 concentration measurements has statistically higher value than given sten.

This latter procedure is based on: μl and σl, i.e. mean and standard deviation calculated from logarithms of a given series of measurements of SO_2 concentration.

Another procedure can be applied for stens and/or logarithms only. This procedure assesses if two series of concentrations differ significantly.

Third statistical procedure gives indication if there is an alarm concentration in a given grid element. Such an indication is very useful to establish a radical change in the SO_2 emission.

5. Evolutionary optimization

For searching for optimal levels of produced energy for the pollution sources, we have selected one modern heuristic method of global optimum search, namely: evolutionary computation technique (Michalewicz, 1996). In contrast to classic methods, evolutionary computation technique of optimum search allows for incorporation of knowledge of the environment to be embedded in the algorithm structure, and enables the search to continue (no breaks) in case of environment changes. In evolutionary algorithms, optimal solutions cannot be guaranteed to be found all the time, on the other hand many reasonable suboptimal solutions could be reached.

In evolutionary process a group of individuals compete with each other to survive and reproduce. Fitness of an individual controls chances of its sexual reproduction and chances of selection to the next generation of its offspring. Briefly, evolution is an iterated process of reproduction and selection. In the evolutionary algorithms, a group of solutions from the domain of the problem is represented by a group of individuals. A new group of offspring individuals is generated with the search operators, and then the next generation of solution is selected. In fact, it is the same iterated process of reproduction and selection, as in natural evolution.

The main purpose of the system is to reduce pollution in the area of the whole Poland. The outcome of the system would indicate the recommended level of produced energy for each particular pollution source. First, we need to define the problem for optimization. We discuss three main components of the problem, i.e., a domain, an evaluation function, and a set of constraints (Trojanowski and Michalewicz, 1999):

The domain of the problem: n-dimensional search space D (n is a number of controlled sources of pollution). A solution represents a vector of recommended power control levels for pollution sources (emission of pollution for i-th source is a function of i-th power control level).

The evaluation function: the main goal is to minimize the relative level of pollution in the area of the country.

The resulting vector represents a list of recommended power control levels for which relative levels of pollution in all regions in the country are least and the pollution is distributed to protect regions with more sensitive environment (e.g., natural ecosystems, especially forests). Every day the vector can be different depending on current weather conditions.

Set of constraints:

1. Avoidance of long expositions on high sulphur dioxide concentration of the area units. The level of maximum available exposition of a unit depends on the type of terrain,

2. current value of energy demand in the country

Constraints divide solutions into feasible and infeasible ones. To handle constraints in the algorithm we used a method based on preserving feasibility of solutions. The idea is based on specialized operators, which transform infeasible solutions into feasible ones only.

The system is also ready for continuous optimization of pollution sources in the country, day by day. Every morning a new set of weather reports and forecast makes changes in the optimized environment. However, in that case the system does not start the search from scratch but incorporates information about changes and continues optimization. This type of optimization is a form of adaptation to changes in the environment. One of the most important skills in adaptation to changes is reasoning from previous experiences. If we want to reason from the past, a place to collect experiences is needed. Therefore, we added memory structures to increase evolutionary algorithm efficiency.

A redundant genetic material was introduced into an individual, resulting in a new polyploid representation and a dominance function, which controlled transfer of information between chromosomes inside the individual (Trojanowski and Michalewicz, 1999[2]).

Polyploidy can be viewed as a way to incorporate *memory* into the individual's structure. Instead of single chromosome (haploid structure) representing a precise information about an individual, a diploid structure is made up of a pair of chromosomes: the choice between two values is made by some dominance function. The diploid (polyploid) structures are of particular significance in evolutionary optimization of non-stationary environments. In such an algorithm, each individual consists of more than one chromosome (each chromosome still represents a single solution). The dominance function determines one chromosome as the current representative of the individual, which then participates in the evaluation process. The other chromosomes in the structure are ``inactive'' and play the role of memory: a set with past experiences.

Memory structure and content: in our approach, we used exact memory with individual level structures. An individual consists of an *active chromosome*, which represents a solution and a *memory buffer*, which may contain several chromosomes inherited from the individual's ancestors. The size of the memory buffer is constant during the time of evolutionary process.

Process of remembering: the first generation of populations has empty memory buffers. Then, each time after a new individual is generated, if it is included in the next generation of population, the active chromosome of its parent (or a better parent - in case there are two parents) is added to its memory buffer. In addition, it will inherit the chromosomes in the memory buffer of its parent or a better parent. Thus, what is remembered (i.e. the content of memory buffers) increases as the generation number increases. Each memory buffer is a FIFO queue such that when it is full, the oldest chromosome is deleted to make room for a new one.

Process of recalling: in our implementations, memory is recalled every time the change appears in the environment.
Note, that this is the time when all the individuals in the current population are re-evaluated (to take into account the effect of changes). During this re-evaluation process, the chromosomes in the memory buffer of an individual become active and are also re-evaluated together with the active chromosome of the individual. After the re-evaluation, if any of the remembered chromosomes is better than the currently active chromosome of the individual, then it is swapped with the current one to become active, while the latter becomes inactive and is placed in the memory.

5.1 The EROS System

EROS is a visual application dedicated for Windows 95/98/NT/2000 platform. It was implemented and compiled in Borland C++ Builder 4 environment. Major part of data used by the program is stored in a Microsoft Access relational database. Program realizes connections with database through an ODBC driver.

System EROS integrates three main modules: (1) Regfor++, (2) evolutionary optimizer, and (3) visualization tools. Regfor++ computes forecasted transport of pollution depending on weather reports, weather forecast and emissions of sources during last two days. The second module finds optimal vector of produced energy levels for pollution sources. Third module is a visual application that shows maps illustrating disposition of stens and concentrations over area of Poland.

Each experiment executed by the system is composed of two main steps:

1.   Preparation of input data, execution of Regfor++ (forecasted transport of SO_2 concentrations over Poland's area is then computed) and storing of all output data in the database.

2.   Preparation of input data, execution of evolutionary optimizer (the optimal vector of sources power percentages is found; matrices of stens and concentrations for that vector are computed) and storing of all output data in the database.

After finishing the experiment it's results may be presented on maps generated by the system.

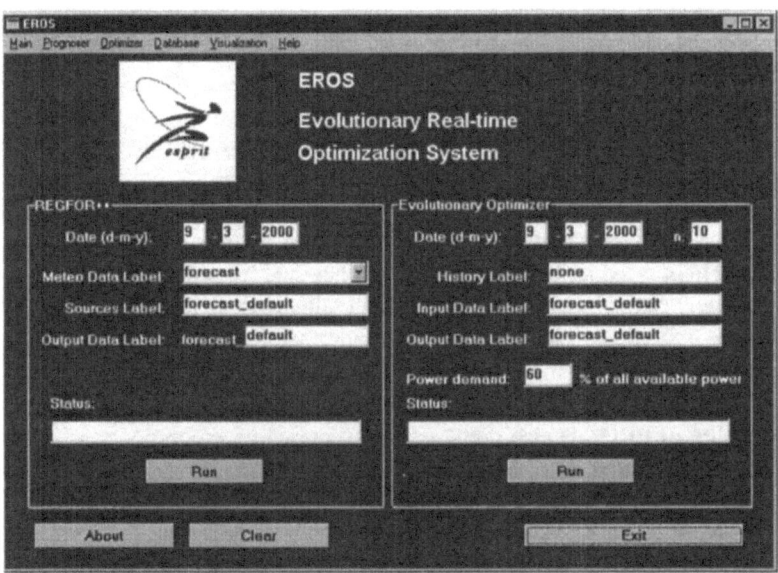

Fig. 1. The EROS system – main screen

Input and output data of the system are kept in two ways. One of them is flat text file: data are stored in text file if they don't change during experiments (e.g. data stored in text file are Poland's map, coordinates and names of meteorological sites, or parameters for evolutionary optimizer, etc). Major part of data is stored in a relational database. All data stored in the database are individual for each experiment (e.g. weather circumstances or stens and concentrations for given day). All data stored in the database are identified by date and label which means that there can exist multiple sets of data describing one day. All input and output data are presented below:

Set of input data for Regfor++ includes (1) weather data for last two days and weather forecast for the next day, (2) list of sources and their parameters including emissions of each source for last two days and (3) land cover (for each square of 30 x 30 km).

Output data of Regfor++ consists of (1) matrices (25 rows x 30 columns) with expected unitary emission for the next day for each source, and (2) a matrix containing concentration created by emissions of the sources during last two days (so called "tail" concentration).

Input data for the evolutionary optimizer contains (1) a matrix with background concentration calculated by the use of the air pollution dispersion model POLSOX-I, (2) a matrix with "tail" concentration created by emissions of sources during last two days, (3) a set of matrices with unitary emissions of sources for the day of experiment, (4) a set of sources that are to be optimized in the experiment, (5) a set of sources that have constant power levels in the experiment, i.e. that will not be optimized and power levels of these sources, (6) power demand as a percentage of all available power, (7) land cover and (8) parameters of evolutionary optimizer.

Output data of evolutionary optimizer is (1) a vector of power percentages for all sources and (2) a matrix of stens and a matrix of concentrations for the given vector.

The system provides functions for importing and managing data stored in the database. There is a possibility to import weather data for any number of days, and to import new set of sources. There exists an edit window that contains all tables of database and allows viewing and modifying them. Operations of import of all input data stored in the database are provided by the system EROS.

Functionality of EROS is also prepared for execution of experiments with various combinations of input data. Moreover Regfor++ and optimizer can be executed independently of each other.

There are two kinds of weather data possible – real weather and weather forecast. System gives possibility to run Regfor++ as well on weather forecast – then forecasted pollution transport is computed – as on real weather – so as to compute real pollution transport. From the other side, there is a possibility to execute Regfor++ with any previously computed emissions of sources during last two days. Emissions of sources during last two days create "tail" concentration, such function gives possibility to compare the influence of different "tails". But what is most important, emissions of sources can be included to input data independently of weather data. This allows executing experiments with the same weather and different emissions, for example experiments with optimization and with constant control vector and then comparing the differences. Finally, each output data of Regfor++ is identified by date and label, so for each day any number of results of experiments with different labels can be stored in the database.

After getting the results of Regfor++ the next part of experiment is optimization. To run optimizer all input data must be prepared. Sources that will be optimized must be chosen and all other sources must have defined their power percentages.

Such set of sources is identified by date and label and is explicitly placed as input data for the optimizer. Other input data are the output data of Regfor++ and their label must also be defined. There is one more data, which can be but doesn't have to be taken into account in optimization. There is a possibility to make the optimization dependent on the situation from previous days. It means, that for each square on the map its history (stens in that square in previous days) will be also taken into account. The system allows defining which history will be analyzed (for example disposition of stens with or without optimization) and defining number of days that will be analyzed. After executing the optimization its results are stored with the same label as the one defining a set of sources for this optimization.

5.2 Experiments and results

Results of experiment may be presented in a few ways. One of them is a map presenting area of Poland with lines representing successive levels of concentrations. Such map may show concentrations caused by all sources or by sources chosen by a user.

The other way of visualization of results is a VisiTool window. It can generate maps depicting stens or concentrations for any experiment stored in the database and maps of terrain sensitivity or localization of weather sites.

VisiTool can present one or two maps. When one map is presented more information about experiment is available. When the "brief description" option is chosen, there is some information at the right side available. These are: date, label, average, minimal and maximal concentration, average sten, average emission and average energy produced. Below there is a frame that shows information about a square pointed by a mouse. There are square's coordinates, concentration, a list of sources in that square and their power percentages. After choosing "full description" option the frame is replaced by additional information about weather circumstances (see the Figure 2).

When two maps are presented only "brief description" option is available. Presenting two maps in one window gives possibility to compare two different experiments (Figure 3).

Each map depicting stens of concentration has many parameters. There are four ways of presenting colors on that map – color stens, color stens but stens 1 to 5 are not taken into account, grayscale and grayscale but stens 1 to 5 are not taken into account. Besides, the names of sources can be placed on the map, their localization may be placed or removed and finally information about sources in pointed square can be listed in the frame at the right or it can be disabled. When a

"Concentration" option is chosen there is a possibility to **define scale** in [μg/m³] for that map.

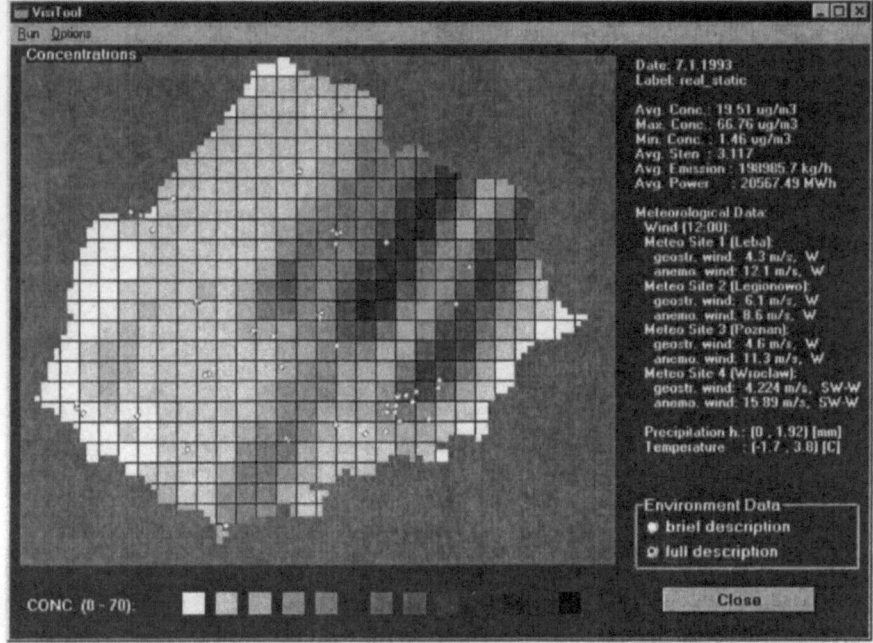

Fig. 2. Example of map generated by VisiTool – with full description

After clicking any square with right button of a mouse some additional functions are available. One of them is detailed information about square's sensitivity – values in [μg/m³] that are border values between successive stens for that square. The other function is a histogram of pointed square. It shows stens from previous days for that square. The length of period for the histogram can be defined by a user.

Several experiments with real data (meteorological real data and weather forecasts, and real emission data for chosen summer and winter periods) have been conducted.

Initially real concentrations and stens have been calculated for each chosen experimental period (see Figure 2). Then the optimization process has been applied and results were compared with initial results (see Figure 3).

From the performed experiments, the following conclusions can be drawn:

1. according to our assumptions the amount of produced energy was equal in both cases,

2. average emission and average concentration in the country decreased substantially (12-15%) after optimization process,

3. results, obtained when applying real meteorological data instead to weather forecast, were practically identical (less than 1% differences).

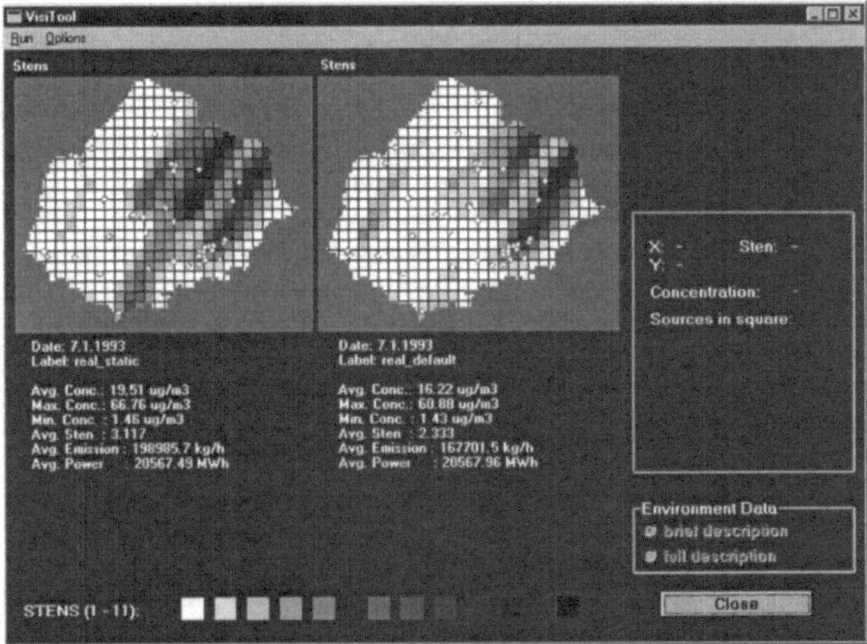

Fig. 3. Example of maps generated by VisiTool – comparising of experiments

6. Summary and further research

The results provide experimental evidence that EROS is a promising tool for a real-time ecological power control.

In the near future we plan to extend the system (in corporation with Polish Power Grid Company) to include real financial and industrial constraints. The next version of the system would be tested in the real daily power control process in Poland.

Acknowledgements

This research was partially supported by the ESPRIT Project 20288 Cooperation Research in Information Technology (CRIT-2): "Evolutionary Real-Time Optimization System for Ecological Power Control".

References

Ashmore M.R., and Wilson R.B. (eds.), 1993. Critical Levels of Air Pollutants for Europe. *Report from the UN ECE Workshop on Critical Levels, Egham, UK, March 23-26, 1992.* Creative Press, Reading, UK, p. 209.

Holnicki P., Kałuszko A., Żochowski A., Multilayer Computer Model for Air Quality Forecasting in Urban/Regional Scale, *Control and Cybernetics*, Vol 22, nr 3, 1993, pp 5-28.

Holnicki P., Kałuszko A., Żochowski A., A Microcomputer Implementation of An Urban-Scale Air Quality Forecasting System, *Microcomputer Applications*, Vol 13, nr 2, 1994, pp 76-85.

Juda-Rezler K., Budziński K., Abert K., Warchałowski A., Dobija J., Matuszewski A. and M. Szumanowska, 1997. Description of the POLSOX-I model. In: *Emission Abatement Strategies and the Environment (EASE) - Final Report,* Imperial College of Science, Technology and Medicine, London, pp. 381-387.

Lowles I., ApSimon H., Juda-Rezler K., Abert K., Brechler J., Holpuch J. and A. Grossinho, 1998. Integrated Assessment Models - tools for developing emission abatement strategies for the *Black Triangle* Region. *Journal of Hazardous Material,* 61, 229-237.

Michalewicz Z., *Genetic Algorithms + Data Structures = Evolution Programs*, 3rd Revised and Extended Edition, Springer-Verlag, 1996.

Trojanowski K., and Michalewicz Z., Evolutionary Approach to Non-Stationary Optimization Tasks, Proceedings of 11th ISMIS, 1999, vol 1609 in LNAI, Springer, pp. 538-546.

Trojanowski K., and Michalewicz Z., Searching for Optima in Non-Stationary Environments", Proceedings of IEEE CEC, 1999, IEEE Publishing, pp. 1843-1850.

Speeding Up Evolution through Learning: LEM

Ryszard S. Michalski*, Guido Cervone and Kenneth Kaufman
Machine Learning and Inference Laboratory
George Mason University, Fairfax, Virginia
Phone: (703) 993-1558 or 764-9142 Email: michalski@gmu.edu
Fax: (703) 993-3729 or (703) 764-9142

*Also, Institute of Computer Science
Polish Academy of Sciences, Warsaw, Poland

Abstract: This paper reports briefly on the development of a new approach to evolutionary computation, called the Learnable Evolution Model *or* LEM. *In contrast to conventional Darwinian-type evolutionary algorithms that employ mutation and/or recombination, LEM employs machine learning to generate new populations. At each step of evolution, LEM determines hypotheses explaining why certain individuals in the population are superior to others in performing the designated class of tasks. These hypotheses are then instantiated to create a next generation. In the testing studies described here, we compared a program implementing LEM with selected evolutionary computation algorithms on a range optimization problems and a filter design problem. In these studies, LEM significantly outperformed the evolutionary computation algorithms, sometimes speeding up the evolution by two or more orders of magnitude in the number of evolutionary steps (births). LEM was also applied to a real-world problem of designing optimized heat exchangers. The resulting designs matched or - outperformed the best human designs.*

1   Introduction

Recent years have witnessed significant progress in the development of machine learning methods and in scaling them up to cope with large datasets (e.g., Cohen, 1995; Dietterich, 1997; Mitchell T., 1997; Michalski, 2000b). There has also been significant progress in the area of evolutionary computation (e.g., Baeck, Fogel and Michalewicz, 1997; Koza, 1994; Banzhaf, 1999; Michalewicz et al., 1999). As symbolic learning and evolutionary computation have complementary capabilities and strengths, a question arises as to whether they can be integrated in a way that will lead to a new, more powerful model of evolutionary computation. This paper presents some early results from the efforts toward such a goal.

Specifically, we briefly describe the *Learnable Evolution Model*, LEM, which employs machine learning to guide evolutionary computation and then report a few results from its testing on selected problems.

2   What is Learnable Evolution Model?

The central engine of evolution in LEM is *Machine Learning* mode which generates hypotheses about differences between high fitness and low fitness individuals, and then uses these hypotheses to generate new individuals. New individuals are thus generated not by a semi-blind process of mutation and/or recombination, as in conventional evolutionary algorithms, but rather by a deliberate process of inference. LEM can be viewed as a form of genetic engineering. Below is a simplified form of LEM (a full version is in Michalski, 2000):

1. *Generate a population.*

2. *Execute Machine Learning mode:*

    2a Derive a training set: Select from a population (either the current one or a union of the current and selected past populations) a *high performance group*, or briefly *H-group*, and *Low performance group*, or briefly *L-group*, according to the fitness function.

    2b Create a hypothesis: Apply a machine learning method to create a description of the H-group that differentiates it from the L-group.

    2c Generate a new population: Instantiate the hypothesis in different ways to generate new individuals, and combine them with those in the H-group. Create a new population from the resulting set by some form of selection operation.

    2d Go to step 2a, and continue repeating Machine Learning mode until the *Machine Learning mode termination condition* is met. When this termination condition is met, take one of the following actions:

    A. If the *LEM termination condition* is met, go to step 5.

    B. Repeat the process from step 1. This is called a *start-over* operation.

    C. Go to step 3.

3. *Execute Darwinian Evolution mode:*

    Apply some form of mutation, crossover (optionally) and selection operators to generate a new population. Continue this mode until the *Darwinian Evolution mode termination condition* is met.

4. *Alternate:*

Go to step 2, and then continue alternating between step 2 and step 3 until the *LEM termination condition* is met (e.g., the generated solution is satisfactory, or the allocated computational resources are exhausted), in which case the control goes to step 5.

5. *End:*

The best individual or individuals obtained are the result of the evolutionary process.

If LEM executes repeatedly only step 2, or steps 1 and 2, then it is called *uniLEM*; otherwise, it is called *duoLEM*. The full description of the LEM algorithm includes some additional features and a few control parameters (Michalski, 2000a). When variables describing individuals are continuous, they have to be quantized. In Problem 1 we used an adaptive anchoring quatization method (Michalski and Cervone, 2000) and in Problem 2 we applied a fixed quantization method (Michalski and Zhang, 1999). The LEM methodology can employ, in principle, in step 2 any machine learning method that can generate discriminant descriptions (Michalski, 1983), and in step 3 any existing evolutionary algorithm.

3   LEM as Progressive Partitioning of the Search Space

The search conducted in Machine Learning mode can be interpreted as a progressive partitioning of the search space. An H-group description hypothesizes a region or regions that likely contain the optimal individual. Each subsequent H-group description hypothesizes a new, typically more specialized, partition of the search space. Due to this effect, the LEM evolution process may converge to the optimum (local or global) much more rapidly than Darwinian-type evolutionary algorithms. Since partitioning is guided by inductive inference, this process may miss the area with the global optimum. In such cases, LEM executes a start-over operation or temporarily switches to the Darwinian Evolution mode.

The next sections briefly describe a selection of results from preliminary studies (Michalski, 1998; Michalski and Zhang, 1999; Cervone and Michalski, 2000; Cervone, Kaufman and Michalski, 2000).

4   Pilot Study: Optimization Problems

This study applied rudimentary implementations of LEM (LEM1 and LEM2) and several evolutionary computation algorithms to problems of optimizing five functions f_1, f_2, f_3, f_4, and f_5, described in (De Jong, 1975), which have been used by researchers for testing evolutionary algorithms. For the sake of space, we present here only a small selection of results. Other results followed the same pattern as those presented here (Michalski, 1999; Cervone, 1999; Cervone and Michalski, 2000).

Problem 1: Find the minimum of the Rosenbrook function, f_2, of 5 variables bound between -10.1 and 10.1 (an inverted 2D graph of f_2 is presented in Figure 1).

$$f_2(\mathbf{x}) = \sum_{i=0}^{5}(100 \cdot (x_{i+1} - x_i)^2 + (x_i - 1)^2)$$

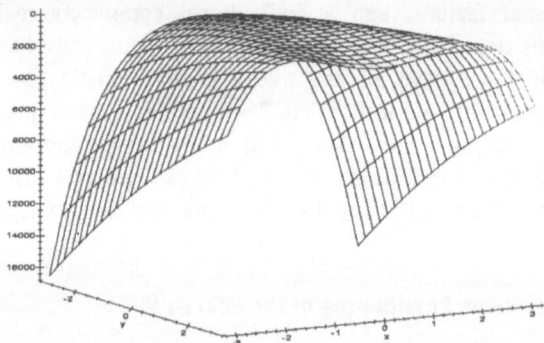

Figure 1. Inverted 2D graph of function f_2.

This function represents a non-trivial minimization problem because it has a very narrow ridge and variables are interdependent. The tip of the ridge is very sharp, and runs along a parabola. Algorithms that are not able to discover good directions underperform in this problem. Although the function looks symmetric, it is not.

In this experiment, LEM2 and a conventional evolutionary computation algorithm, EV, were run with different values of parameters to test the sensitivity of the methods to the parameter values. The EV algorithm is an exact reimplementation within the LEM2 program of the EV3 program developed by Ken De Jong. EV selects randomly individuals from the population and then mutates each of them in several ways (the number of mutations is defined by the brood parameter). The mutated individuals compete in a binary tournament with randomly selected individuals from the original population and the winner becomes a member of the new population. The mutation is done according to a Gaussian distribution in which the mean equals the value being mutated and the standard devation (mutation rate) is a program parameter.

Figure 2 presents typical results from experiments.

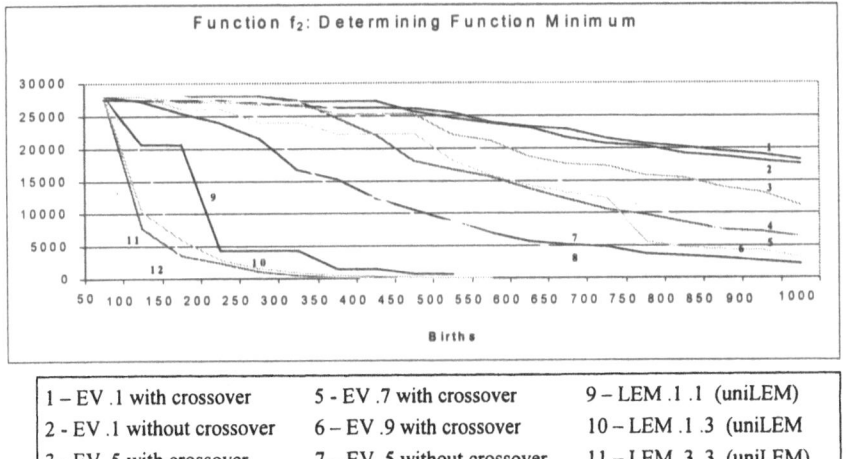

1 – EV .1 with crossover	5 - EV .7 with crossover	9 – LEM .1 .1 (uniLEM)
2 - EV .1 without crossover	6 – EV .9 with crossover	10 – LEM .1 .3 (uniLEM
3 - EV .5 with crossover	7 – EV .5 without crossover	11 – LEM .3 .3 (uniLEM)
4 - EV .3 without crossover	8 – EV .7 without crossover	12 – LEM .3 .1 (uniLEM)

Figure 2. An example of results from applying LEM2 and EV to the
problem of minimizing Rosenbrook function.

Each curve in Figure 2 represents the average of 10 runs, each starting with a
different initial population (which was the same for LEM2 and EV). Curves 1, 3, 5
and 6 represent runs with a uniform crossover; the remaining runs of EV did not
use crossover. All runs used elitism. The initial population was 100 and kept
constant in all the experiments. In the caption of Figure 3, the value after EV
represents the mutation rate, and a pair of values after LEM represents the high
(HPT) and low (LPT) population threshold, respectively.

In this experiment LEM2 was relatively insensitive to its basic parameters, HPT
and LPH (a similar behavior was observed in other experiments too, including
cases when the number of variables was increased to 100). LEM2 found the global
minimum in almost all cases. EV was quite sensitive to its parameters and was
unable to find the global minimum within the limit of 1000 births for any of the
parameter values that were tried.

Problem 2. Find the minimum of function f_3 of 100 continuous variables   (an
inverted 2D graph of f_3 is presented in Figure 3).

$$f_3(x_1, x_2, x_3, ..., x_{100}) = \sum_{i=1}^{100} \text{integer}(x_i) \quad -5.12 \leq x_i \leq 5.12$$

248

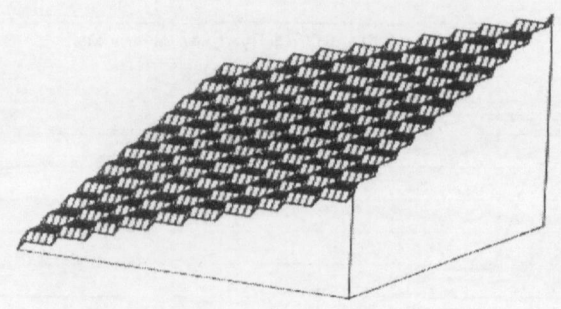

Figure 3. Inverted two-dimensional graph of f_3.
(Reprinted with permission of Kenneth De Jong)

In this experiment, the number of variables in function f_3 was increased from the original 5 to 100 in order to test LEM2's scalability. Results from applying LEM2 and three evolutionary computation methods EV, EP and ES with different mutation rates are presented in Figure 4. These three algorithms were implemented in the EV3 program, developed by Kenneth De Jong.

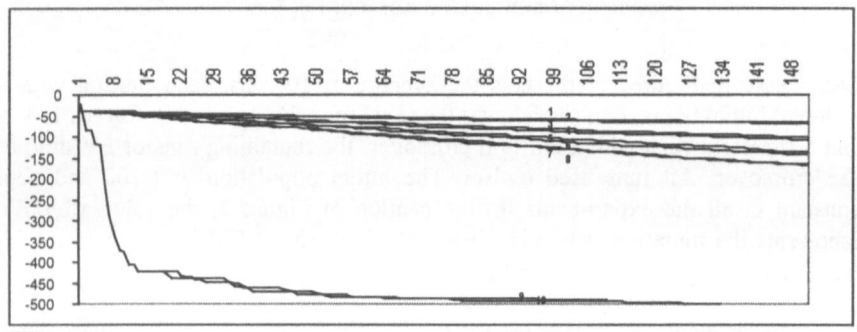

1 - EP 100, 10, 0.1;   2 - EV 100, 10, 0.1;   3 - EP 100, 10, 0.5;   4 - ES 100, 0.5;
5 - EP 100, 10, 0.9;   6 - ES 100, 0.9;   7 - EV 100, 10, 0.5;   8 - EV 100, 10, 0.9;
9 – uniLEM2 (AQ18 ; HFT & LFT 30%) 10 - duoLEM2 (AQ18 + EV 100,10, 0.5)

Figure 4.   An evolutionary process for finding the minimum of f_3 with 100 variables using EP, EV and ES evolutionary computation methods and LEM2 in uniLEM and duoLEM versions.

The horizontal axis in Figure 4 represents the number of births in thousands, and the vertical axis represents the function value. In the caption of Figure 4, EP p, c, m; EV p, c, m; and ES p, m stand respectively for "Evolutionary Program," "Evolutionary Algorithm," and "Evolutionary Strategy," where p denotes the number of parents, c denotes the number of children. and m is the mutation rate. LEM2 was run in uniLEM mode (i.e., using only Machine Learning mode), and in duoLEM mode (i.e., using both Machine Learning and Darwinian Evolution). As seen in Figure 4, LEM2 dramatically outperformed the tested evolutionary algorithms. Both variants of LEM (uniLEM and duoLEM) performed similarly (graphs 9 and 10 in Figure 4).

The results presented above represent only a sample of experimental; results. In all experiments, LEM1 and LEM2 have consistently outperformed selected evolutionary computation algorithms in terms of the number of evolutionary steps, sometimes by a wide margin, and exhibited a relatively low sensitivity to the initial population and its parameters (for details, see Cervone, 1999; Michalski and Zhang 1999; Michalski, 2000a; Cervone and Michalski, 2000). These experiments were repeated many times and results consistently exhibited a similar pattern of performance.

It should be noted, however, that operations of hypothesis generation and instantiation are computationally more complex than operations of mutation and recombination used in conventional evolutionary computation algorithms. In these studies we concentrated on measuring the number of generations needed to achieve the global solution in different problems, and have not investigated the total time of achieving the solution. Such a time depends, in general, on the time of generating new populations and the time of evaluating individuals in the population. The latter depends on the type of problem at hand. It is believed that LEM may be particularly useful for problems in which the fitness evaluation is highly time-consuming, such as engineering design, considered in the next section.

5   An Exploratory Application to Heat Exchanger Design

To test LEM on a complex engineering design problem, we started a collaboration with the National Institute of Standards and Technology (NIST). In this research, we applied LEM to problems of optimizing heat exchangers. The problem is how to design heat exchangers that have maximal capacity for any given set of environmental and technical constraints. Such constraints include the outside air temperature and humidity, the flow of air through the heat exchanger, the number of rows of tubes and the number of tubes per row in the exchanger, the refrigerant used, etc.

Below is a highly abbreviated illustration of one of our initial experiments. A population consists of a set of heat exchanger design structures. Each structure is represented by a vector of numbers characterizing the connections between tubes. The vector is associated with capacity of that design, determined by a simulator.

```
Exchanger Size: 16 x 3
Population Size: 15    Generations: 40
Operator Persistence: 5(# of unsuccessful trials of a
structure modifying operator)
Mode Persistence: Dar-probe=2 and Learn=probe=1.

Initial population:
Structure #0.3:   17  1  2  3  4  5  6  7  8  9 12 13 29 15 31 I
                  18 33 20 36 22 38 24 40 26 42 11  2  7 45 14 47 16
```

```
        34 35 19 37 21 39 23 41 25 43 44 28 46 30 48 32:
        5.5376
Structure #0.8:  17 1 20 3 4 22 6 24 8 26 10 28 27 15
        16 32 33 2 18 19 5 38 7 40 9 42 11 44 13 46 30
        48 34 35 36 I 21 37 23 39 25 41 27 43 29 45 31
        47:  Capacity = 5.2099
and 13 others

Selected Members:  3, 2, 3, 7, 9, 3, 9, 3, 6, 9, 9, 6,
8, 1, 7
Operations: NS(23, 39), SWAP(8), SWAP(28), SWAP(19),
SWAP(1), SWAP(27),
            SWAP(40), SWAP(43), SWAP(15), SWAP(25),
SWAP(7), SWAP(36),
            SWAP(29), SWAP(25), SWAP(1)
```

Below is one of the structures created by the application of a SM operator in Machine Learning algorithm mode (by swapping the two tubes following tube 29 in Structure #0.8)

Generation 1:

```
Structure #1.13: 17 1 20 3 4 22 6 24 8 26 10 28 27 15
        16 32 33 2 18 19 5 38 7 40 9 42 11 4 13 45 30 48
        34 35 36 I 21 37 23 39 25 41 27 43 46 29 31 47:
        Capacity=5.2093
(15 structures in a population)

Selected Members:  6, 15, 11, 3, 13, 1, 10, 6, 12, 10,
        5, 4, 13, 1, 3
.....
```

Generation 5: Machine Learning mode
```
A learned rule:
Rule:
        [x1.x2.x3.x4.x5.x6.x7.x8.x9.x11.x12.x13.x14.x15.x
        17.x18.x19.x20.x21.x22.x23.x24.x25.
        x26.x27.x28.x29.x30.x31.x32.x33.x34.x35.x36.x37.x
        38.x39.x40.x41.x42.x43.x44.x45.x46.
        x47.x48=regular] & [x10=outlet] & [x16=inlet]
                        (t:7, u:7, q:1)

An example of a generated structure:
Structure #5.1:   17 1 2 3 4 5 6 7 8 9 12 29 45 30 31 I
        18 33 20 36 22 38 24 40 26 42 11 27 13 15 47 48
        34 35 19 37 21 39 23 41 25 43 44 28 46 14 32 16:
        Capacity=5.5377
```

Below are examples of structures from the 21st generation:
.....

Generation 21: Machine Learning mode

Structure #21.7: 18 1 4 2 6 3 5 7 8 9 12 13 45 15 31 I
      33 17 35 36 22 39 24 40 42 25 11 44 30 46 32 47
      34 19 20 37 21 23 44 41 26 43 28 27 29 14 48 16:
      4.1702
Structure #21.15 2 18 4 1 6 3 5 7 8 9 12 13 45 15 31 I
      33 17 35 36 22 39 24 40 42 25 11 44 30 46 32 47
      34 19 20 37 21 23 38 41 26 43 28 27 29 14 48 16:
      5.5387
and 13 others

Selected Members: 11, 4, 4, 13, 15, 10, 12, 13, 15,
15, 12, 2, 3, 5, 10.
.....

Generation 40:

Structure #40.15: 33 17 2 41 4 5 6 9 7 8 12 29 46 45 47
      I 1 34 20 36 22 38 24 3 42 43 44 27 13 15 32 16
      18 11 19 37 21 32 23 25 40 26 28 35 30 14 48 31:
      Capacity=6.3686
.....

As shown above, the initial designs evolved to better designs (as measured by the capacity). In these experiments, LEM explored many different architectures, reaching heat capacities comparable to the best human designs in the case of uniform flow. In the case non-uniform flow, LEM designs were judged by collaborating experts as superior to best human designs. For details on this work, see (Kaufman and Michalski, 2000).

6   Relation to Other Research

The proposed LEM methodology was introduced originally in Michalski (1998). To our knowledge, it is an original development. In searching through the literature, we found several papers describing efforts to apply machine learning to evolutionary computation, but they are substantially different from LEM. Work has also been done on the application of evolutionary computation to machine learning. A brief review of some of this work is below.

Sebag and Schoenauer (1994) applied machine learning to adaptively control the crossover operation in genetic algorithms (implementing their own version of AQ-type learning). In their system, a machine learning method develops rules characterizing relevant crossovers. These rules are then used to bias the selection of crossover operators. Sebag, Schoneauer and Ravise (1997a) used inductive learning to determine mutation step-size in evolutionary parameter optimization. Ravise and Sabag (1996) described a method for using rules to prevent new generations from repeating past errors. In a follow-up work, Sebag, Schoenauer and Ravise (1997) proposed keeping track of past evolution failures by using templates of unfit individuals, called "virtual losers." An evolution operator, called "flee-mutation," aims at creating individuals different from the virtual losers. Grefenstette (1991) developed a genetic learning system, SAMUEL, that implements a form of Lamarckian evolution. The system was designed for sequential decision making in a multi-agent environment. A strategy, in the form of *if-then* control rules, is applied to a given world state and certain actions are performed. This strategy is then modified either directly, based on the interaction with the environment, or indirectly by changing the rules' strength within the strategy. The changes in a strategy are passed to its offspring. This is a Lamarckian-type process that takes into consideration the performance of a single individual when evolving new individuals.

Reynolds (1994) proposed cultural algorithms, which are dual inheritance systems that provide a cooperation between a cultural and population-based levels of evolution. The cultural level is represented by a belief space that contains global knowledge in the form of beliefs. The beliefs constrain the way in which individuals are modified by genetic operators. Cultural algorithms relate to LEM (developed independently) in that they utilize top individuals in the population, but do it differently, namely they vote for the beliefs to be accepted into the belief space (e.g., Rychtyckyj and Reynolds, 1999). Baluja and Caruana (1995) described a method called "population-based incremental learning" that explicitly maintains statistics about the evolving ppopulation and uses this statistics to generate new individuals.

As to the application of evolutionary computation to machine learning, most research has concerned the improvement of propositional concept learning. An indirect form of such application is to evolve the "best" subset of attributes from a collection of original attributes in order to improve concept learning (Forsburg, 1976; Vafaie and De Jong, 1992). Another form concerns an improvement of the learning method itself (e.g., Vafaie and De Jong, 1991; De Jong, Spears, and Gordon, 1993; Giordana and Neri, 1995; Greene and Smith 1993; Janikow, 1993; Hekanaho, 1997).

There have also been efforts to use genetic algorithms to evolve a population of biases for a machine learning algorithm. For example, Turney (1995) applied a genetic algorithm to evolve weights assigned to attributes in the C4.5 program in order to derive the minimum cost decision tree. Evolutionary algorithms have also been applied to improve relational learning, e.g. (Augier, Venturini and Kodratoff, 1995; Hekanaho, 1998).

7   Conclusion

Although the results obtained in the pilot studies are highly encouraging, there are many unanswered questions and desirable directions for further research. These include a systematic theoretical and practical investigation of the methodology, determining its trade-offs, indentifying best methods for implementing both modes of operation, and a determination of the type of tasks for which it will likely be successful. One emerging pattern in performance of LEM in comparison with the evolutionary computation methods is that LEM typically needs far fewer generations (or births) to reach the global solution, and tends to be less sensitive to the values of its parameters and the choice of initial population.

As mentioned earlier, in these studies we investigated the problem of evaluating the number of births (or generations) that LEM requires to achieve the global solution. We were not concerned with the total time of the evolutionary process, because it depends, in general, on the time of generating new individuals and on the time of their evaluation (the time of determining their fitness). The latter time is highly problem-dependent. It should be noted, however, that generating new individuals through hypothesis generation and instantiation, as done in LEM, is significantly more complex and time-consuming than through operations of mutation and recombination, than in the Darwinian type evolutionary algorithms.

Since LEM usually requires a much lower number of births but involves more complex computation in generating new individuals, it appears that it may be particularly attractive in problem domains with a high cost of determining the fitness function. It may also be worth noting that in the current LEM implementations (LEM1 and LEM2), we used off-the-shelf general purpose learning programs (AQ15 and AQ18, respectively), which were not planned for such applications. These programs were chosen for the Machine Learning mode because that appear to be particularly suitable for LEM (Michalski, 2000). There is a significant potential for speeding-up the AQ-type learning programs, if practical applications would require this.

Acknowledgments

Authors would like to thank Dr. Ken De Jong for providing the EV3 program used in some of the experiments. This research was conducted in the Machine Learning and Inference Laboratory at George Mason University. The Laboratory's research related to the work presented in the paper has been supported in part by the National Science Foundation under Grants No. IIS-9904078 and IRI-9510644, in part by the Defense Advanced Research Projects Agency under Grant No. F49620-95-1-0462 administered by the Air Force Office of Scientific Research, and in part by the Office of Naval Research under Grant No. N00014-91-J-1351. This research was also supported in part by International Intelligent Systems, Inc.

References

1. Augier, S., Venturini, G. and Kodratoff, Y., "Learning First Order Logic Rules with a Genetic Algorithm," *Proceedings of the First International Conference on Knowledge Discovery and Data Mining*, pp. 21-26, Montreal, Canada, AAAI Press, 1995.

2. Baeck, T., Fogel, D.B., and Michalewicz, Z., (Eds.), *Handbook of Evolutionary Computation*, Oxford University Press, 1997.

3. Baluja, S. and Caruana R., Removing the Genetics from the Standard Genetic Algorithm, *Proceedings of the 12th International Conference on Machine Learning*, Tahoe City, California, July 9-12, 1995.

4. Banzhaf, W., Daida, J., Eiben, A.E., Garzon, M.H., Honavar, V., Jakiela, M. and Smith, R.E. (eds.), *Proceedings of the 1999 Genetic and Evolutionary Computation Conference* (GECCO), Orlando, Florida, July 13-17, 1999.

5. Cervone, G., "An Experimental Validation of the Learnable Evolution Model to Selected Optimization Problems," Master's Thesis, Department of Computer Science, George Mason University, Fairfax, VA, November 1999.

6. Cervone, G. and Coletti, M, R., "ECC^{++}: A Generic C++ Library for Evolutionary Computation," *Reports of the Machine Learning and Inference Laboratory*, George Mason University, Fairfax, VA, 2000 (to appear).

7. Cervone, G., Kaufman, K. and Michalski, R.S., "Experimental Validations of the Learnable Evolution Model," *2000 Congress on Evolutionary Computation*, San Diego CA, July, 2000 (to appear).

8. Cervone and Michalski, "Design and Experiments with the LEM2 Implementation of the Learnable Evolution Model," *Reports of the Machine Learning and Inference Laboratory*, George Mason University, 2000 (to appear).

9. Coletti, M., Lash, T., Mandsager C., Michalski, R.S., and Moustafa, R., "Comparing Performance of the Learnable Evolution Model and Genetic Algorithms on Problems in Digital Signal Filter Design." *Proceedings of Genetic and Evolutionary Computation Conference* (GECCO), Orlando, Florida, July 14-17, 1999 (an extended version was published in *Reports of the Machine Learning and Inference Laboratory*, MLI 99-5, 1999).

10. De Jong, K.A., "An Analysis of the Behavior of a Class of Genetic Adaptive Systems", Ph.D. thesis, Department of Computer and Communication Sciences, University of Michigan, Ann Arbor, 1975.

11. De Jong, K. A., Spears, W. M., and Gordon, F. D., "Using Genetic Algorithms for Concept Learning," Machine Learning, 13, pp. 161-188, 1993.

12. Dietterich, T.G., "Machine-Learning Research: Four Current Directions," *AI Magazine*, 18, No.4, 1997.

13. Forsburg, S., "AQPLUS: "An Adaptive Random Search Method for Selecting a Best Set of Attributes from a Large Collection of Candidates," *Internal Technical Report*, Department of Computer Science, University of Illinois, Urbana, 1976.

14. Giordana A. and Neri, F., "Search-intensive Concept Induction," *Evolutionary Computation*, 3(4), pp.375-416, 1995.

15. Grefenstette, J. "Lamarckian Learning in Multi-agent Environment," *Proceedings of the Fourth International Conference on Genetic Algorithms*, R. Belew and L. Booker (Eds.), San Mateo, CA: Morgan Kaufmann, pp. 303-310, 1991.

16. Greene D. P. and Smith, S.F., "Competition-based Induction of Decision Models from Examples," *Machine Learning*, 13, pp. 229-257, 1993.

17. Hekanaho, J, "GA-based Rule Enhancement Concept Learning," *Proceedings of the Third International Conference on Knowledge Discovery and Data Mining*, pp. 183-186, Newport Beach, CA, AAAI Press, 1997

18. Hekanaho, J., "DOGMA: A GA-based Relational Learner,: *TUCS Technical Reports Series*, Report No. 168, March 1998.

19. Janikow, C. Z., "A Knowledge-intensive Genetic Algorithm for Supervised Learning," *Machine Learning*, 13, pp. 189-228, 1993.

20. Kaufman K. and Michalski, R.S., "Applying Learnable Evolution Model to Heat Exchanger Design," *Twelfth International Conference on Innovative Applications of Artificial Intelligence*, Austin, TX, August, 2000 (to appear).

21. Koza, J.R., *Genetic Programming II: Automatic Discovery of Reusable Programs*, The MIT Press, 1994.

22. Michalewicz, Z., *Genetic Algorithms + Data Structures = Evolution Programs*, Springer Verlag, third edition, 1996.

23. Michalewicz, Z., Schoenauer, M.. Yao, X., and Zazala, A. (eds.), *Proceedings of the Congress on Evolutionary Computation*, Washington, DC, July 6-9, 1999.

24. Michalski, R.S., "A Theory and Methodology of Inductive Learning," *Artificial Intelligence*, 20(2), pp. 111-161, 1983.

25. Michalski, R.S., "Learnable Evolution: Combining Symbolic and Evolutionary Learning," *Proceedings of the Fourth International Workshop on Multistrategy Learning*, Desenzano del Garda, Italy, pp. 14-20, June, 1998.

26. Michalski, R.S., "LEARNABLE EVOLUTION MODEL: Evolutionary Processes Guided by Machine Learning," *Machine Learning*, 38(1-2), pp. 9-40, January/February, 2000.

27. Michalski, R.S., "NATURAL INDUCTION: Theory, Methodology, and Applications to Machine Learning and Knowledge Mining," *Reports of the Machine Learning and Inference Laboratory*, George Mason University, 2000 (to appear).

28. Michalski R.S. and Zhang, Q., "Initial Experiments with the LEM1 Learnable Evolutionary Model: An Application to Function Optimization and Evolvable Hardware," *Reports of the Machine Learning and Inference Laboratory*, George Mason University, MLI 99-4, 1999.

29. Mitchell, M. *An Introduction to Genetic Algorithms*, Cambridge, MA, MIT Press, 1996.

30. Mitchell, T. M., "Does Machine Learning Really Work," *AI Magazine*, 18(3), 1997.

31. Ravise, C. and Sebag, M., "An Advanced Evolution Should Not Repeat Its Past Errors," *Proceedings of the 13th International Conference on Machine Learning*, L. Saitta (ed.), pp. 400-408, 1996.

32. Reynolds, R.G., "An Introduction to Cultural Algorithms," *Proceedings of the 3rd Annual Conference on Evolutionary Programming*, Selbak, A.V. Fogel L.J. (eds.), River Edge, NJ World Scientific Publishing, pp 131-139, 1994.

33. Rychtyckyj, N. and Reynolds, R.G., "Using Cultural Algorithms to Improve Performance in Semantic Networks," *Proceedings of the Congress on Evolutionary Computation*, Washington, DC, pp. 1651-1663, 1999.

34. Sebag, M. and Schoenauer, M., "Controlling Crossover Through Inductive Learning," in Davidor, Y., Schwefel, H.P. and Manner, R. (eds.), *Proceedings of the Third Conference on Parallel Problem Solving from Nature*, Springer-Verlag, LNVS 866, pp. 209-218, 1994.

35. Sebag, M., Schoenauer M., and Ravise C., "Inductive Learning of Multation Step-size in Evolutionary Parameter Optimization," *Proceedings of the Eighth Annual Conference on Evolutionary Programming*, LNCS 1213, pp. 247-261, Indianapolis, April 1997.

36. Sebag, M., Shoenauer, M., and Ravise, C., "Toward Civilized Evolution: Developing Inhibitions," *Proceedings of the Seventh International Conference on Genetic Algorithms*, pp.291-298, 1997.

37. Vafaie, H. and De Jong, K.A., "Improving the Performance of a Rule Induction System Using Genetic Algorithms," *Proceedings of the First International Workshop on Multistrategy Learning (MSL-91)*, Harpers Ferry, WV, November 7-9, 1991.

Evolutionary Search with Erosion of Quality Peaks

Andrzej Obuchowicz

Technical University of Zielona Góra, Institute of Robotics and Software
Engineering, ul. Podgórna 50, 65–246 Zielona Góra, Poland

Abstract. The aim of this note is to find effective evolutionary algorithm specialized in landscape saddle crossing. Emphasis is put on the modification of the
Evolutionary Search with Soft Selection algorithm which is enriched by a mechanism called the Deterioration of the Objective Function. Formal analysis is used in
order to find the best approximation of the local peak which has to be eroded by
the trapped population. Simulation results confirm the assumed effectiveness of the
method.

1 Introduction

The applicability of evolutionary inspiration in global optimization is not qu-
estionable. The main advantage of evolutionary processes is their capability
of saddle crossing in multimodal surfaces. In contrast to conventional optimization methods, an evolutionary search does not get stuck (potentially) in a
local optimum trap, which is a crucial characteristic of global optimization.

It is easy to prove that the Darwinian-type evolution has a cyclic nature
in multimodal adaptation landscapes [3]. Each cycle consists of two phases:
active and latent. In relative short active phases the population of individuals
climbs on an adaptation slope to the neighbourhood of a local peak. The
latent phase is a quasi-stationary state with sporadic fluctuations. If the
occupied hill possesses a higher neighbour, then fluctuations can contribute
to the crossing of a saddle and new active phase starts.

In the case of global optimization problems without constraints a searching procedure has to reconcile the optimum localization with the capability
of saddle crossing. Application of two specialized algorithms is a good solution
to this problem. However, although there are many specialized algorithms of
local optimization, the algorithms specialized in saddle crossing are scarce.
Pure Darwinian evolution is, of course, a compromise method, but its aim is
adaptation, not optimization. Consequently, its saddle crossing mechanisms
are more interesting.

The idea of natural evolution is applied in several well-known algorithms,
e.g. Evolutionary Strategies [11], Evolutionary Programming [1], Genetic Algorithms [4], and some unfamiliar Evolutionary Search with Soft Selection
(ESSS) [2]. The last one is considered in this paper. Numerical tests of the
ESSS algorithm [3] proved essential advantages of soft selection over hard

selection which reaches only a local optimum. The ESSS possesses a good capability of saddle crossing, thus it gives a chance to find a global optimum of the objective function. On the other hand, it is an adaptive method, rather than an optimization one. This feature suggests that a hybrid method, which combines it with a local optimization algorithm, can be an efficient global optimization procedure.

The aim of this work is to carry out some formal analysis of the ESSS algorithm in order to increase its effectiveness of saddle crossing.

The paper is organized as follows. At first, an outline of the ESSS algorithm is given. Some formal analysis of the ESSS is presented in the next section. As a result of this analysis, a new modified algorithm is proposed and tested. Concluding remarks and some areas of future research are summarized in the last section.

2 Evolutionary Search with Soft Selection Algorithm

A basic phenotype evolution model was proposed by Galar [2]. The relevant assumptions can be formalized by the numerical ESSS algorithm (Tab.1). Some results of the investigations regarding the efficiency of the ESSS algorithm are presented in [3]. Numerical tests proved essential advantages of soft selection over selection which reaches only a local optimum. The ESSS algorithm is not an optimization algorithm in the sense of reaching an optimum with a desired accuracy. Evolution is not asymptotically convergent to an optimum and the interpolation efficiency of the soft selection is weak. Evolution leads next generations to an elevated response surface, rather than to maxima. Evolution which started from a high and narrow peak could terminate on a lower and wider peak. In spite of that, search advantages of the ESSS algorithm suggest that this algorithm can be used in numerical packages for global numerical optimization, especially when combined with local optimization algorithms. The ESSS efficiency depends on some exogenous parameters, e.g.:

1. parameters of normal distribution (an expectation vector m and a standard deviation σ which is used to generate a new population,
2. a topology of an objective function,
3. a population size η of searching points.

There exist some modified algorithms which try to adapt the above parameters during the searching process in order to increase its effectiveness:

- ESSS with Simple Variance Adaptation (ESSS-SVA) [10],
- ESSS with Forced Direction of Mutation (ESSS-FDM) [8],
- ESSS with Varying Population Size (ESSS-VPS) [9],
- ESSS with Deterioration of the Objective Function (ESSS-DOF) [7].

Table 1. The outline of the ESSS algorithm

Input data

    η – the size of population;

    $t_{\max}$ – the maximum number of iterations (epochs);

    σ – the standard deviation of the normal distribution;

    $\Phi : \mathbb{R}^n \to \mathbb{R}_+$ – the non-negative fitness function (adaptation landscape),
       n is a feature number;

    x_0^0 – the initial point of searching

I. Initiation

A. $P(0) = \{x_1^0, x_2^0, \dots, x_\eta^0\}$ $(x_k^0)_i = (x_0^0)_i + N(0, \sigma)$ (1)
   $i = 1, 2, \dots, n;$ $k = 1, 2, \dots, \eta$

B. $q_0^0 = \Phi(x_0^0)$ (2)

II.Repeat:

A. *Estimation*
   $P(t) \to \Phi(P(t)) = \{q_1^t, q_2^t, \dots, q_\eta^t\}$ $q_k^N = \Phi(x_k^t)$ $k = 1, 2, \dots, \eta.$ (3)

B. *Choice of the best element in the history*
   $\{x_0^t, x_1^t, x_2^t, \dots, x_\eta^t\} \to x_0^{t+1}$ $q_0^{t+1} = \max\{q_k^t\}$ $k = 0, 1, \dots, \eta.$ (4)

C. *Selection*
$$\Phi(P(t)) \to \{h_1, h_2, \dots, h_\eta\} \quad h_k = \min\left\{h : \frac{\sum_{l=1}^h q_l^t}{\sum_{l=1}^\eta q_l^t} > \zeta_k\right\}, \qquad (5)$$
   where $\{\zeta_k\}_{k=1}^\eta$ are random variables uniformly distributed
   on the interval $[0, 1)$.

D. *Modification*
   $P(t) \to P(t+1)$
   $(x_k^{t+1})_i = (x_{h_k}^t)_i + N(0, \sigma)$ $i = 1, 2, \dots, n;$ $k = 1, 2, \dots, \eta$ (6)
   where $N(m, \sigma)$ is a normally-distributed random variable
   with expectation m and a given variance σ.

Until $t > t_{\max}$.

The ESSS-SVA algorithm accelerates the saddle crossing by adaptation of the modification radius. The ESSS-FDM speeds up the local optimum localization and saddle crossing by adaptation of the mutation expectation, which is parallel to the latest trends of population drift. This algorithm has been successfully implemented in the case of an objective function which changes in time. The value of population size η is adapted in the ESSS-VPS algorithm. An individual element x_k^t in the ESSS-VPS algorithm is extended by adding one component: the life-time τ_k^t.

The ESSS-DOF influences the topology of an objective function. It contains an additional step which is composed of the following procedures:

- *Trap test* – the aim of this procedure is to determine whether the population quality changed substantially for a given number of epochs.
- *Erosion* – this procedure transforms the objective function $\Phi(x)$ as follows:

$$\Phi(x) = \begin{cases} \Phi(x) - G(x) & \text{for } \Phi(x) \geq G(x), \\ 0 & \text{for } \Phi(x) < G(x), \end{cases} \tag{7}$$

where $G(x)$ is the distribution of population points

$$G(x) = q_{\max}^t \exp\left(-\frac{1}{2}\left(x - \langle x^t \rangle\right)^T \mathbb{C}^{-1}\left(x - \langle x^t \rangle\right)\right), \tag{8}$$

$\mathbb{C}$ is the covariance matrix of population $P(t)$, $\langle x^t \rangle$ is the expectation vector of $P(t)$.

The ESSS-DOF algorithm has a much greater convergence rate than other algorithms from the ESSS family. If the population gets stuck in an evolutionary trap, then the process of local peak erosion is started. This effect decreases the average fitness of the population. The population fitness reduces to a saddle level and running away towards other quality peaks is possible. The deteriorated peak will never be attractive for the searching population. The disadvantage of the ESSS-DOF is its numerical complexity.

3 Elements of Convergence Analysis

The convergence analysis of evolutionary algorithms is very difficult or, sometimes, impossible to be performed, because of their nonlinear, stochastic or heuristic nature. Standard tools of dynamic systems analysis are not effective, even though simple models are used. A first attempt at the ESSS convergence analysis was presented in [5,6]. In order to analyze simplification, let us assume an infinite size of the population. The population state can be represented by a distribution function $p_t(x)$ defined on the phenotype space at a discrete time moment t [5]. Let $\Phi(x)$ be a nonnegative fitness function and $g(x - y)$ be a modification function which describes the transformation of an element y into x:

$$g(x - y) = \left(\frac{1}{\sqrt{2\pi}\sigma} \right)^n \exp\left(-\frac{\|x - y\|^2}{2\sigma^2} \right).$$ (9)

The population distribution after selection (5) can be calculated from the formula

$$p'_t(x) = \frac{\Phi(x)p_t(x)}{\int \cdots \int_{\mathbb{R}^n} \Phi(z)p_t(z)dz} = \frac{\Phi(x)p_t(x)}{\langle \Phi(z) \rangle}$$ (10)

and after mutation

$$p_{t+1}(x) = \int \cdots \int_{\mathbb{R}^n} p'_t(y)g(x - y)dy$$ (11)

Equations (10) and (11) do not possess, in general, closed-form solutions. Let us consider the fitness function in the Gaussian peak form with the maximum localized in the centre of the reference frame:

$$\Phi(x) = \exp\left(-\frac{1}{2}x^T \mathbb{T}^{-1} x \right),$$ (12)

where $\mathbb{T}$ defines the ellipsoidal cross-section of the peak. Similarly, let us assume that the population distribution at t is of normal form

$$p_t(x) = \left(\frac{1}{\sqrt{2\pi \det \mathbb{C}_t}} \right)^n \exp\left(-\frac{1}{2}\left(x - \langle x^t \rangle \right)^T \mathbb{C}_t^{-1} \left(x - \langle x^t \rangle \right) \right),$$ (13)

where $\mathbb{C}_t$ is the population covariance matrix and $\langle x^t \rangle$ is the population expectation vector at t. If the initial population has isotropic symmetry, e.g. $P(0)$ is obtained by normal mutations of a given phenotype $\langle x^0 \rangle$, then we may expect that, after some epochs, the matrices $\mathbb{C}$ (13) and $\mathbb{T}$ (12) have the same set of eigenvectors. Hence, after a similarity transformation, equations (12) and (13) have the forms

$$\Phi(x) = \prod_{i=1}^{n} \exp\left(-\frac{x_i^2}{2\tau_i^2} \right)$$ (14)

and

$$p_t(x) = \prod_{i=1}^{n} \frac{1}{\sqrt{2\pi}\nu_{ti}} \exp\left(-\frac{(x_i - \langle x_i^t \rangle)^2}{2\nu_{ti}^2} \right)$$ (15)

If we use the above formulae in (10) and (11), then the population distribution at time $t + 1$ is normal with the expectation vector

$$\langle x_i^{t+1} \rangle = \langle x_i^t \rangle \frac{\tau_i^2}{\nu_{ti}^2 + \tau_i^2}, \qquad i = 1, 2, \ldots, n$$ (16)

and the variance vector

$$\nu_{t+1,i} = \sqrt{\sigma^2 + \frac{\tau_i^2 \nu_{ti}^2}{\nu_{ti}^2 + \tau_i^2}}, \qquad i = 1, 2, \ldots, n. \tag{17}$$

It is easy to see that $\lim_{t\to\infty} \|\langle x^t \rangle\| = 0$, so the ESSS algorithm, in the case of an infinite population size, is convergent to fitness function optimum. In latent phase, the system is stable $p_{t+1}(x) = p_t(x)$ and has the normal distribution form with the expectation vector equals to zero and the variance vector:

$$\nu_{\infty,i} = \sigma \sqrt{\frac{1}{2}\left(1 + \sqrt{1 + \left(\frac{2\tau_i}{\sigma}\right)}\right)}, \qquad i = 1, 2, \ldots, n, \tag{18}$$

Analyzing the formulae (18) one can deduce the following characteristics:

- If $\tau_i \ll \sigma$, then the variance of the population distribution can be approximated by the variance of the modification function $\nu_{\infty,i} \approx \sigma$. This is the proof that the optimum point is an attractor which does not allow the population to disperse.
- If $\tau_i \approx \sigma$, then $\nu_{\infty,i}^2 \approx \sigma^2(1 + \sqrt{5})/2 \approx 1.618\sigma^2$, so there are no quality differences between this case and that described above.
- If $\tau_i \gg \sigma$, then the variance of the population distribution can be approximated by the geometric mean of modification and fitness functions variances $\nu_{\infty,i} \approx \sqrt{\tau_i \sigma}$.

4 The ESSS-DOF* Algorithm

Althogh, the ESSS-DOF algorithm is the most efficient in saddle crossing when compared with other methods based on ESSS, it possesses one main disadvantage: the deterioration function (8) does not approximate the current quality peak with the sufficient accuracy. If an evolutionary trap is detected, then the modified quality peak looks like a crater with steep slopes. The deterioration mechanism should be performed several times until the population starts scouring another landscape area. A large number of deterioration peaks used by the algorithm influences the computation time and space complexity.

In this paper a modified ESSS-DOF algorithm, named ESSS-DOF*, is proposed. The covariance matrix of the deterioration Gaussian peak (8) is approximated using (18). This part of the algorithms consists of four steps:

1. Calculate the covariance matrix $\mathbb{C}_t$ of the actual population;
2. Find all the eigenvectors and eigenvalues of the matrix $\mathbb{C}_t$ in order to define an orthonormal matrix $\mathbb{U}$ and a diagonal matrix $\mathrm{diag}(\nu_{ti}^2 | i = 1, 2, \ldots, n)$ such that

$$\mathbb{C}_t = \mathbb{U}\,\mathrm{diag}(\nu_{ti}^2 | i = 1, 2, \ldots, n)\mathbb{U}^T; \tag{19}$$

3. Calculate the variances of the deterioration peak (18):

$$\tau_i^2 = \nu_{ti}^2 \left(\frac{\nu_{ti}^2}{\sigma^2} - 1 \right);$$

(20)

4. Calculate the covariance matrix $\mathbb{T}$ of the deterioration peak:

$$\mathbb{T} = \mathbb{U} \operatorname{diag}(\tau_i^2 | i = 1, 2, \ldots, n) \mathbb{U}^T.$$

(21)

If the fitness is a multimodal function which consists of regular peaks then the above method seems to be a very good global optimization algorithm.

5 Saddle Crossing – Simulation Results

Numerous simulation runs (almost 100) with various objective functions (about 10) have served us as tests of the delivered technique. Examples of bivariate functions used during simulations are presented below:

- the sum of two 2D Gaussian peaks:

$$f_1(x_1, x_2) = \exp\left(- 5x_1^2 - 3x_2^2 \right) + \frac{1}{2} \exp\left(- 5(x_1 - 1.4)^2 - 3x_2^2 \right);$$

(22)

- Rosenbrock's function:

$$f_2(x_1, x_2) = 500 - 100(x_1^2 - x_2)^2 - (1 - x_1)^2, \qquad -2 \leq x_i \leq 2,$$

(23)

- Rastring's function:

$$f_3(x_1, x_2) = 100 - (x_1^2 + x_2^2) - 10(\cos(2\pi x_1) + \cos(2\pi x_2)).$$

(24)

The fitness function was chosen in the form

$$\Phi(x_k^t) = f(x_k^t) - f_{\min}^t + \left(\frac{1}{\eta} \right)^2,$$

(25)

where $f_{\min}^t = \min(f(x_k^t) | k = 1, \ldots, \eta)$ is the minimal value of f taken over all elements in the actual population. Such a fitness function is non-negative and its relative values in the actual population make the proportional selection effective.

Comparison of two algorithms: ESSS-DOF and ESSS-DOF* is presented in Fig. 1. It is easy to see that the deterioration peak of the ESSS-DOF* algorithm approximates the peaks of the local objective function better than the ESSS's one. This explains, why the ESSS-DOF* algorithm is more effective in saddle crossing and scours the widest area of the landscape in a given time interval.

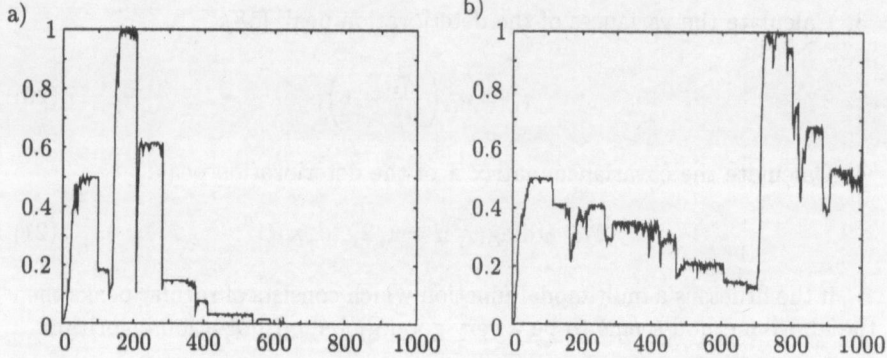

Fig. 1. Fitness of the best individuals in the population vs. time (epochs) in the ESSS-DOF* (a) and ESSS-DOF (b) algorithms for objective function f_1 (22) with the following parameters: population size = 20; standard deviation of mutation = 0.05; time interval for the trap test = 20; number of iterations = 1000

6 Conclusions

The aim of this note has been to construct an evolutionary method of global optimization for which the scoured area of the searching space in a given time interval would be as large as possible. The proposed method is based on the Evolutionary Search with Soft Selection algorithm [2], which is enriched by a mechanizm called the Deterioration of the Objective Function [7]. In this algorithm the population trapped on the local peak erodes it. This effect decreases the average population fitness which reduces to a saddle level and running away towards other quality peak is possible. The modification of the ESSS-DOF, called ESSS-DOF*, is also proposed. The ESSS-DOF* accelerates the erosion process by better approximating of the local quality peaks.

It will be interesting to compare the proposed algorithm with other algorithms from the ESSS family known from the literature [10,8,9] and other evolutionary algorithms extended by the DOF feature. These problem constitutes a subject of further research.

References

1. Fogel L.G., Owens A.J. and Walsh M.J. (1996) Artificial intelligence through simulated evolution. Wiley, New York
2. Galar R. (1985) Handicapped individua in evolutionary processes. Biol. Cybern., **51**, 1–9
3. Galar R. (1990) Soft selection in random global adaptation in R^n. A biocybernetic model of development. Technical University Press, Wrocław (in Polish)
4. Holland J.H. (1975) Adaptation in natural and artificial systems. The University of Michigan Press, Ann Arbor, MI

5. Karcz-Dulęba I. (1992) Simulation of evolutionary processes as a tool of global optimization in $\mathbb{R}^n$. Ph.D. Thesis, Technical University of Wrocław, Wrocław (in Polish)

6. Karcz-Dulęba I. (1997) Some convergence aspects of evolutionary search with soft selection method. In: Evolutionary Algorithms and Global Optimization, 2nd Conference at Rytro, Poland, September 15–19, 1997, Warsaw University of Technology Press, Warsaw, 113–120

7. Obuchowicz A. (1997) The evolutionary search with soft selection and deterioration of the objective fuction. In: Kłopotek M., Michalewicz M. (Eds.) Intelligent Information Systems IIS'97, 6th International Symposium at Zakopane, Poland, June 9–15, 1997, Polish Academy of Sciences Press, Warsaw, 288–295

8. Obuchowicz A. and Korbicz J. (1998) Evolutionary search with soft selection and forced direction of mutation.In: Kłopotek M., Michalewicz M. (Eds.) Intelligent Information Systems IIS'97, 6th International Symposium at Malbork, Poland,June 15-19, 1998, Polish Academy of Sciences Press, Warsaw, 300–309

9. Obuchowicz A. and Korbicz J. (1999) Evolutionary search with soft selection algorithms in parameter optimization. In: Wyrzykowski R., Mochnacki B., Piech H., Szopa J. (Eds.) Parallel Processing and Applied Mathematics PPAM'99, 3rd International Conference at Kazimierz Dolny, Poland, September 14–19, 1999, Technical University of Czestochowa Press, Czestochowa, 578-586

10. Obuchowicz A. and Patan K. (1997) About some Modification of Evolutionary Search with Soft Selection Algorithm. In: Evolutionary Algorithms and Global Optimization, 2nd Conference at Rytro, Poland, September 15–19, 1997, Warsaw University of Technology Press, Warsaw, 193–200

11. Rechenberg I. (1965) Cybernetic solution path of an experimental problem. Roy. Aircr. Establ., libr. Transl. 1122, Farnborough, Hants., UK

Brain Differently Changes its Algorithms in Parallel Processing of Visual Information

Andrzej W. Przybyszewski[1,2] and Daniel A. Pollen[1]

[1] Dept. of Neurology, UMass Medical Center, Worcester, MA 01655
[2] Center for Adaptive Systems, Boston University, Boston, MA 02155

Abstract. Feedback from the visual cortex (V1) to the Lateral Geniculate Nucleus (LGN) in macaque monkey increase contrast gain of LGN neurons for black and white (B&W) and for color (C) stimuli. LGN parvocellular cells responses to B&W gratings are enhanced by feedback multiplicatively and in contrast independent manner. However, in magnocellular neurons corticofugal pathways enhance cells responses in a contrast-dependent non-linear manner. For C stimuli cortical feedback enhances parvocellular neurons responses in a very strong contrast-dependent manner. Based on these results [13] we propose a model which includes excitatory and inhibitory effects on cells activity (shunting equations) in retina and LGN while taking into account the anatomy of cortical feedback connections. The main mechanisms related to different algorithms of the data processing in the visual brain are differences in feedback properties from V1 to parvocellular (PC) and to magnocellular (MC) neurons. Descending pathways from V1 change differently receptive field (RF) structure of PC and MC cells. For B&W stimuli, in PC cells feedback changes gain similarly in the RF center and in the RF surround, leaving PC RF structure invariant. However, feedback influence MC cells in two ways: directly and through LGN interneurons, which together changes gain and sizes of their RF center differently than gain and size of the RF surround. For C stimuli PC cells operate like MC cells for B&W. The first mechanism extracts from the stimulus an important features in a independent way from other stimulus parameters, whereas the second channel changes its tuning properties as a function of other stimulus attributes like contrast and/or spatial extension. The model suggests novel idea about the possible functional role of PC and MC pathways.

Keywords: lateral geniculate nucleus, visual cortex V1, parvocellular, magnocellular

1 Introduction

The retina has at least two types of outputs (ganglion cells), which send signals to parvocellular (PC) or magnocellular (MC) neurons in the LGN which is the second stage of the pathway which transmits visual information to the brain. Midget ganglion cells (P-cells) in primate (corresponding to X-type cells in cats) project to PC lamine of LGN and primates parasol (M-cells) cells project to MC lamine of LGN. P- and M-cells like X- and Y-type cells have a different organizations of their receptive fields (RF). Photoreceptors with strong nonlinear properties, send signals to bipolar cells which converge almost in equilibrium on the RF center and on the RF surround of X-type ganglion cells. In a consequence X-type cells using push-pull mechanism which compensates photoreceptors' nonlinearities, sum input signals in a linear way [2]1. The push-pull mechanism in Y-cells is far away from equilibrium and therefore signal summation is strongly nonlinear with different dynamics than X-cells [3,4]. In LGN the different organization of the RF in PC and MC neurons helps to extract different properties of visual stimuli. PC channels extract certain stimulus features locally in a relative invariant way, however MC channels change tuning properties in a more flexible way. It seems that the first channel gives a dense, invariant matrix which could be the basis for a dynamic changes and for tuning in many different ways of the second channel. Interactions between these channels would give precision and flexibility to our visual system. The neurophysiological model based on experiments of both channels is presented below.

2 Materials and Methods

Standard surgical and anesthetic procedures were used [9]. After initial anesthesia (Ketamine 10-15 mg/kg, Brevital in increments of 3 mg/kg, respiration with a mixture of 70% nitrous oxide and 30% oxygen) and loading with a bolus of sufenta (Sufentanil) (2 μg/kg) in individual doses, we infused at a rate starting at 2 μg/kg/hr, with upward adjustments in dose whenever any significant increases in arterial blood pressure or heart rate were observed. Doses greater than 2 μg/kg/hr were generally needed, but we started with this dose to avoid severe hypotension. Monkeys were paralyzed by continuous infusion of Pavulon (pancuronium bromide) (0.2 mg/kg per hr) in 5% dextrose and saline. Extracellular action potentials were recorded from LGN using parylene-coated tungsten microelectrodes, amplified and saved in PC. All visual stimuli were presented on RGB monitor controlled by PC. Background luminance was between 80 and 90cd/m^2. First, RF position and neuron's spatial frequency and temporal frequency were determined by using drifting achromatic sine-wave gratings. Color selectivity of neurons was determined according to method of [11] using drifting sine-wave gratings. **Cryogenic blockade of V1** and back-projecting activity was achieved with a silver plate with an appropriate shape attached to a device that cooled electrically through the application of the Peltier principle. The cooling power of the device was adjusted by changing the electric current. Re-warming of the cortex was achieved by reversing the current polarity in the device. Temperature was measured continuously on the cooling plate surface. The cortex was cooled for at least 3 minutes until its surface was at a temperature of between 9 and 12°C.

2.1 Model's assumptions and equations

Retina. Each retinal cell's position is denoted by (i, j), and visual input in position (p,q) on the retina has intensity $I_{p,q}$. On-center and off-center retinal ganglion cells (rGC's) obey the shunting equations [6]

$$\frac{d}{dt}x_{ij} = -Dx_{ij} + (U - x_{ij})\sum_{p,q} C_{pqij}I_{pq} - (x_{ij} + L)\sum_{p,q} S_{pqij}I_{pq} \quad (1)$$

where U and L are upper and lower limits of (dimensionless) cell activities, $U = 1, D = 1, L = 1$, and

$$C_{pqij} = Cg(p, q, i, j, \sigma_c) \quad (2)$$

$$S_{pqij} = Sg(p, q, i, j, \sigma_s) \quad (3)$$

where the two dimensional Gaussian function g is defined as

$$g(p, q, i, j, \sigma) = \frac{1}{2\pi\sigma^2} exp(-\frac{(p-i)^2 + (q-j)^2}{2\sigma^2}) \quad (4)$$

In a steady-state condition, on-center and off-center rGC activities

$$x_{ij} = \frac{\sum_{p,q}(UC_{pqij} - LS_{pqij})I_{pq}}{D + \sum_{p,q}(C_{pqij} + S_{pqij})I_{p,q}} \quad (5)$$

LGN and V1 influence. We assumed [5,7] that responses (r_{ij}) of LGN on-center and off-center relay cells obey the same equation:

$$\frac{d}{dt}r_{ij} = -Dr_{ij} + (U - r_{ij})[x_{ij}^+](1 + \sum_{p,q} C_{pqij}E_{pq}) - (r_{ij} + L)\sum_{p,q} S_{pqij}M_{pq} \quad (6)$$

where feedback from cortical hypercomplex cells at position (p, q) in layer 6 of V1 is given by E_{pq} and M_{pq}. U, D, L - constants as above. C_{pqij}, S_{pqij} as above Gaussian related to excitatory (center) and inhibitory (surround) influences. The bracket notation $[x_{ij}^+]$ signifies half-wave rectification; $[x_{ij}^+] = max(x_{ij}^+, 0)$, and x_{ij} input from retina. We have simplified this equation in many way for example, by suppress the half-wave rectification notation, assuming we are always in a regime where all arguments are non-negative. At steady state the on-center and off-center LGN relay cell activities is defined by:

$$r_{ij} = \frac{U[x_{ij}^+](1 + \sum_{p,q} C_{pqij}E_{pq}) - L\sum_{p,q} S_{pqij}M_{pq}}{D + [x_{ij}^+](1 + \sum_{p,q} C_{pqij}E_{pq}) + \sum_{p,q} S_{pqij}M_{pq}} \quad (7)$$

In the FACADE model [7,5] detailed analysis and description of the simple, complex, hypercomplex, higher order cells and their connections is given. Here we have concentrated on the LGN relay cells' characteristics without consideration orientation selectivity but with adding the influence of the stimulus contrast on the activity of each cell.

270

3 Results

3.1 Different properties of the LGN magnocellular and parvocellular neurons

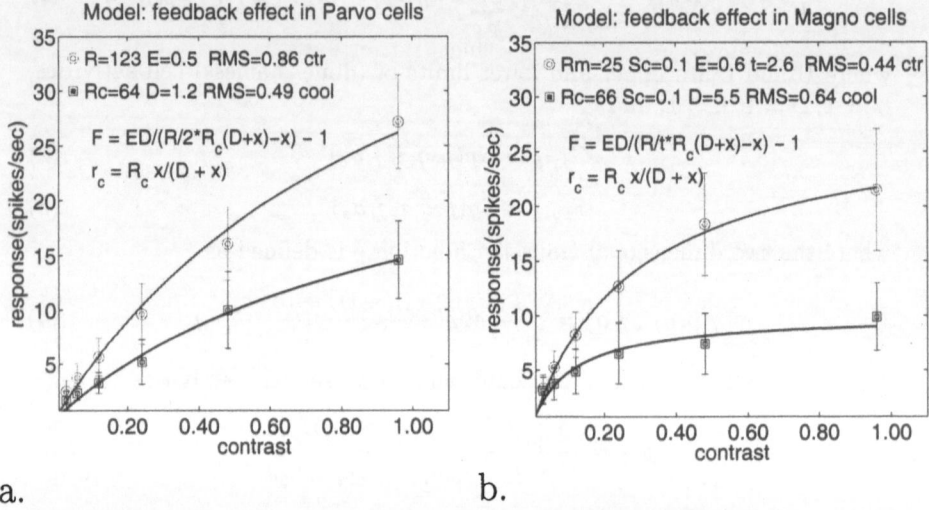

Fig. 1. Averaged responses +/- SEM of ten parvocellular neurons (a) and ten magnocellular neurons (b) plotted as a function of contrast before (circles, ctr) and during (squares, cool) cooling of V1. In the model lower curves were simulated as relay cell response during cooling r_c - formula showed in the figures. r_c are function of x which is output of the retina described with the Naka-Rushton equations with the half saturation coefficients 1.74 for parvo-cells and 0.13 for magno-cells (see text). Upper curves were modeled with eq.8 and the same feedback F as showed in figures. The mean values for each population were obtained by summation of average responses of each individual cell at each stimulus contrast.

In the following section we will analyze our experimental data eq. 8 was approximated as following:

$$r - (Ux(1+F) - S)/(D + x(1+F) + S) \qquad (8)$$

, where $F \sim \sum_{p,q} C_{pqij} E_{pq}$ describes center-to-center excitatory feedback from cortex to LGN, and
$S \sim \sum_{p,q} S_{pqij} M_{pq}$, $L = 1$ describes inhibitory surround effect from the cortex. Let assume, at first, that for LGN relay cells the dominant effect on firing rate comes from stimulation of the RF in the retina, and that there is no influence ($S = 0$) of the cortical inhibitory feedback related to the cortical surround, and constant $U = 1$, then eq. 8 become:

$$r = x(1+F)/(D + x(1+F)) \qquad (9)$$

We can rewrite eq. 9 as:

$$r = x/(\frac{D}{(1+F)} + x) \qquad (10)$$

which shows that for $F = 0$, i.e., in the absence of feedback from cortex, the LGN cell obeys a simple Naka-Rushton equation. Feedback from cortex changes the of value D (semi-saturation constant) in this equation. Increase in feedback's amplitude decreases D, which will decrease the amplitude of LGN response and it will increase its nonlinearity. Therefore, cortical feedback, could increase or compensate retinal nonlinearities. In the next part, we will define feedback functions for parvo- and magno-cellular neurons on the basis of our experimental findings.

In Fig. 1 we plot parvo and magno LGN cells' experimental contrast responses before and during V1 cooling. During V1 cooling the shapes of these curves are dominated by P and M-cells retinal properties [10] with response amplitudes (contrast sensitivity) smaller than in the retina. This reduction could be related to the several mechanisms, like shunting inhibition from interneurons, different positions of synapses on relay cells and involvment of ionotropic and metabotropic receptors (see discussion in [13]).

Parvocellular neurons By using experimental results [10] describing activity of the retinal P-cells as a function of the stimulus contrast, we have converted, in our model, stimulus contrast c to retinal ganglion cell (rGC) output signal x. We will now show that, for the parvocellular neurons during V1 cooling, the experimental responses can be explained as due primarily to the effect of the RF stimulation. Following [10] we fit P-projecting rGCs' (midget cells') contrast responses to Naka-Rushton functions $x = R_{max}c/(d + c)$, where c is stimulus contrast, R_{max} = amplitude of maximum response, and d is semi-saturation constant. Mean d for P-cells is d=1.74 [10]. Eq. (10), during V1 inactivation, takes the Naka-Rushton form,

$$r_c = R_c x/(D + x) \qquad (11)$$

where x is input to PC LGN cells from P-retinal cells and D is a constant related to semi-saturation for the retinal and LGN cells together, R_c - amplitude of maximum response during V1 cooling.

In order to determine the feedback as a function of contrast we make use of the results of our experiments [12,13] that PC cells response in the presence of the feedback can be approximated by equation: $r = 10^{1.45}c^{0.72}$ which is a scaled version of their response during V1 cooling ($r_c = 10^{1.11}c^{0.72}$, therefore we can assume that $r = t*r_c$, where r = response with feedback, r_c = response during cooling, t - scaling factor. Coming back to our model, we can describe experimental responses of parvo cells with feedback as following:

$$r = Rx(1 + F)/(D + x(1 + F)) \qquad (11a)$$

where constant R is related to amplitude of the response. From eq. 11a, we will find the feedback function as:

$$F = \frac{D}{x} \frac{(r/R)}{1 - r/R} - 1 \tag{12a}$$

and by using $r = t * r_c$ and eq. 11 we get:

$$F = \frac{ED}{\frac{R}{t*R_c}(D + x) - x} - 1 \tag{12b}$$

Eq. 12b can be interpreted that the cortical feedback compensates suppressive nonlinearities of the retina. The fit to the data is shown in Fig. 1a. (In order to fit experimental data we scaled the feedback F by constant E, as shown in equation in Fig. 1a for averaged responses of ten parvo cells.)

Magnocellular neurons Magnocellular neurons responses to drifting grating show stronger nonlinearities in compare to parvocellular cell responses as a function of contrast (Fig. 1b), which corresponds to a small coefficient D. This is similar to M-cells characteristics in retina, where mean D was found to be 0.13 [10]. We have simulated these properties assuming anatomical connections between retina and LGN on the basis of cat experiments [8]. We assume triadic synaptic connection between retinal axons, LGN relay cells and LGN interneurons (Fig. 2). As shown in this figure, we assumed that all interneurons receive excitatory connections from the cortex and inhibitory connections from other interneurons. Only some of interneurons receive excitatory connections from both the cortex and retina (rGC's) and inhibitory connections from many other interneurons. We will call such interneurons D-interneurons because they receive direct excitation from retina and also they directly inhibit LGN relay cells. A single LGN interneuron receives excitation from the cortex and also an indirect inhibition from cortex through many other LGN interneurons. We will assume that this last effect can be described as a surround inhibition in the interneuron. All these influences obey the differential shunting equation which in equilibrium and after simplifications is defined as:

$$i = \frac{Ux + F - S}{D + x + F + S} \tag{13}$$

The LGN magnocellular responses r are modeled as follows. The LGN relay cell gets excitatory input from the retina x, excitatory, multiplicative feedback from cortex F, and inhibitory input from interneuron i. The feedforward connection from retina to interneuron to relay cell is responsible for the modification of the direct connection from retina to relay cell. The explicit inclusion here of the LGN interneurons is an addition to previous FACADE versions. In steady state responses of the relay cell can be described as:

$$r = \frac{Ux(1 + F) - S_c i}{D + x(1 + F) + S_c i} \tag{14}$$

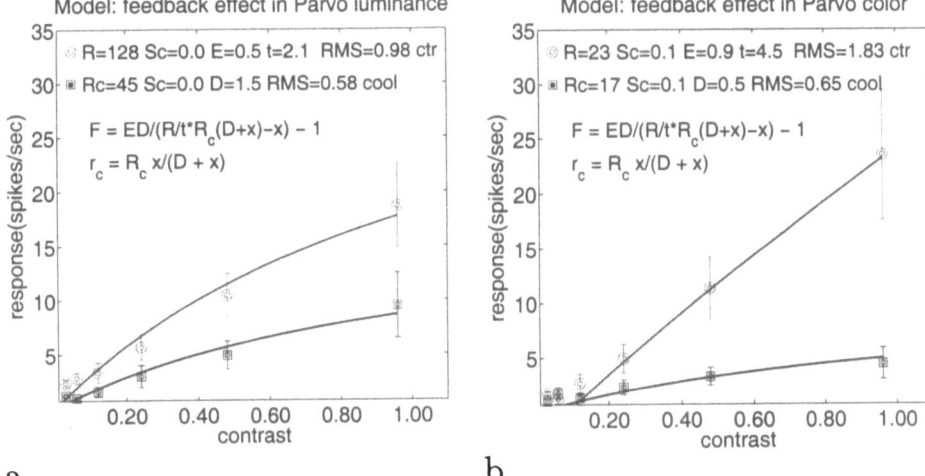

Fig. 2. Connections between retina, relay cell and interneurons in LGN, and cortical cells described in the model. Two feedback pathways are shown in the figure. On the right side, it is shown a direct feedback from V1 layer 6 neurons to LGN relay cells. On the left side indirect feedback is presented, where cortex influence LGN interneurons. There are shown two kinds of interneurons: direct interneurons, which receive input from cortex and build triad with retinal axon and relay cells, and other interneurons receiving input from cortex and inhibiting other interneurons (for details see text).

This differs from eq.10a, in which feedback is limited only to the CRF—the inhibitory surround influence was assumed to be negligible in that case. Here, instead, inhibition from interneurons plays significant role, with an amplitude S_c (as limited to CRF). By putting eq. 13a into 14 and setting $U = 1$, $D = 1$ we obtain:

$$r = (Ux(1+F) - S_c\frac{x+F-S}{1+x+F+S})/(D+x(1+F))(1+S_c\frac{x+F-S}{1+x+F+S})$$
$$(14a)$$

$$r = \frac{Ux(1+F)(1+x+F+S) - S_c(x+F-S)}{D(1+x+F+S) + x(1+F)(1+x+F+S) + S_c(x+F-S)} \quad (14b)$$

Under cooled conditions, F=0, and relay cell responses r_c are

$$r_c = \frac{Ux(1+x+S) - S_c(x-S)}{D(1+x+S) + x(1+x+S) + S_c(x-S)} \quad (14c)$$

We have assumed in our simulations that the cortical feedback F to the magno cells has the same form as for the parvocellular neurons (eq. 12b) but could have a different amplitude E. From model simulations, the mean strength of the feedback for ten magno cells is $E = 0.6$ (Fig. 1b), near the mean value of $E = 0.5$ for the parvo cells (Fig. 1a). By changing the strength of feedback F from LGN interneurons to LGN relay cells, we can explain the contrast responses functions of relay cells during stimulation of RF center alone as well as during combined RF center-and-surround stimulation. Simulations of the MC cells responses showed that during stimulation of the RF center alone the influence of the inhibitory interneurons is very small. During combined stimulation of the RF center and surround, interneurons play in MC cells a significant role. During V1 cooling, when feedback is inactivated, the influence of interneurons actually increases because so-called "direct" interneurons (D-interneurons), which receive input from the retina and directly contact relay cells, are normally (with intact cortex) strongly inhibited by other interneurons which are controlled by cortex (Fig. 2). In order to simulate our experimental results, we assumed that an inhibitory surround must influence D-interneurons. This means that the same cortical feedback could show multiple effects (Fig. 2). Interactions between interneurons can change the strength and the sign of the descending influence from V1 (Fig. 2). Simulation of experimental data in fact suggests such case, that during V1 cooling the net surround of the direct interneurons (D-interneurons) could be in some cases excitatory. This in turn indicates that during normal conditions direct interneurons receive a strong inhibition. In order to simulate MC neurons responses to different stimulus contrast with and without feedback from V1 (Fig. 1b) we have to assume influence of interneurons ($S_c = 0.1$). It was not necessary for PC neurons (Fig. 1a) where $S_c = 0$. In summary, on the basis of our model we have found an important role played by LGN interneurons which, depending on the situation, can change the slope (gain), dynamic range, and shape of the relay cells' contrast responses. Interneurons and feedback can thus in complex ways change the information transmitted by LGN, as well as the CRF structure of LGN cells.

3.2 Model of the chromatic properties of parvocellular LGN neurons.

We have analyzed chromatic properties of cells in LGN using a technique proposed by Derrington et al. (1984). The color-opponency strength of a cell is defined as the magnitude in 3D color space of the projection of the cell's maximum response vector onto the normalized equiluminant plane. We classify cells from which recordings are made using the fact that parvocellular surround-center color-opponency strength is near unity, while magnocellular neurons exhibit color-opponency strength near zero. (This classification was confirmed by noting the position of the recording electrode.)

Effect of the back-projection on luminance and color contrast responses of LGN cells. Cooling depressed the contrast-response function for parvocellular neurons tested with full-field chromatically opponent isolu-

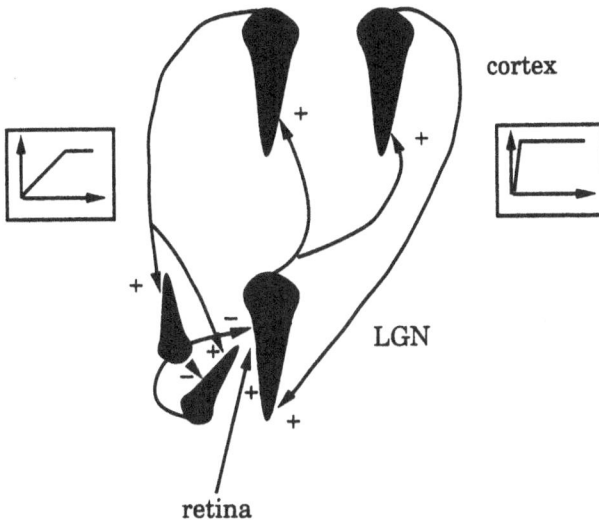

Fig. 3. Averaged responses +/- SEM of five parvocellular neurons plotted as a function of luminance (a) or chromatic contrast before (circles) and during (squares) cooling of V1. In (a,b) curve fitting to experimental results of the power function and log-log plots. In (c,d) model fitted to the same experimental data. Input to the model was from retina which output was described with Naka-Rushton equation with semi-saturation coefficient equal 1.74 for luminance and 3.7 for chromatic stimuli. Parvo cell responses to luminance can be described by a pure central mechanism (in (c) S_c =0), whereas in color responses the influence of interneurons is significant (in (d) S_c =0.1).

minant stimuli that were strongly tuned along either the red-green or blue-yellow axes. A subset of five such neurons were tested over the contrast range both with gratings modulated in luminance (Fig. 3a) and with gratings of low spatial frequency modulated selectively in chromaticity in the isolumi-nant plane (Fig. 3b). Parvo cells showed stronger responses to contrast color in the equiluminant plan than to luminance. V1 inactivation produced a slope change in the color contrast response curves (Fig. 5b) whereas responses to luminance changes were only shifted as a result of V1 inactivation. Using our model to simulate of both situations, we found that the difference is related to the role of interneurons. For luminance contrast, the model can explain our experimental results by feedback mechanism to relay cells (Fig. 2, loop on the right side). The amplitude of the interneuron inhibition was negligible (S_c =0) both with normal and with cooled cortex. On the other hand, in the presence of color stimuli, the role of interneurons becomes significant. We simulated experimentally observed changes in the color contrast response curves by introducing an inhibitory interneuron influence with strength S_c = 0.1. This is similar to the mechanism in magnocellular neurons (Fig. 1b).

4 Conclusions

We propose that the descending pathways, by incorporating higher level computations into the lower levels, change contrast gain for color and for luminance in the classical receptive field (CRF) center and in CRF surround. The spatial grouping of similar attributes by the interneurons and by horizontal connections within each area can be changed by still higher areas, which modulate interneurons and/or horizontal connections and directly change responsiveness of center-to-center cells.

References

1. Derrington, A. M., Lennie, P. (1984). Spatial and temporal contrast sensitivity of neurons in lateral geniculate nucleus of macaque. J. Physiol. **357**, 219-240
2. Enroth-Cugell, C., Robson, J. G. (1966) The contrast sensitivity of retinal ganglion cells of the cat. J. Physiol. **187**, 517-552
3. Gaudiano P. (1982) A unified neural network [corrected] model of spatiotemporal processing in X and Y retinal ganglion cells. I. Analytical results. Biol Cybern **67**, 11-21
4. Gaudiano, P., Przybyszewski, A. W., van Wezel, R. J., van de Grind, W. A. (1998) Spatial asymmetries in cat retinal ganglion cell responses. Biol Cybern **79**,151-9
5. Gove, A., Grossberg, S., Mingolla, E.. (1995) Brightness, perception, illusory contours, and corticogeniculate feedback. Visual Neuroscience **12**, 1027-1052
6. Grossberg, S., (1980) How does the brain build a cognitive code? Psychol. Rev. **87**,1-51
7. Grossberg, S., Mingolla, E. (1985) Neural dynamics of perceptual grouping: Textures, boundaries, and emergent segmentations. Perception and Psychophysics **38**, 141-117
8. Hamos, J. E., Van Horn, S. C., Raczkowski, D., Uhlrich, D. J., Sherman, S. M. (1985) Synaptic connectivity of a local circuit neuron in lateral geniculate nucleus of the cat. Nature **317**. 618-21
9. Jacobson, L. D., Gaska, J. P., Chen, H.-W. and Pollen, D. A. (1993). Structural testing of multi-input linear-nonlinear cascade models for cells in macaque striate cortex. Vision Research, **33**, 609-626
10. Kaplan, E., Shapley, R. M.. (1982) X and Y cells in the lateral geniculate nucleus of macaque monkeys. J. Physiol. **330**, 125-143
11. Lennie, P., Krauskoff, J., Sclar, G..(1990) Color mechanisms in the striate cortex of Macaque. J Neurosci **10**, 649-669
12. Przybyszewski, A. W., Foote, W., and Pollen, D. A. (1998) Contrast gain control of LGN neurons by V1. Investigative Opthamology and Visual Science, **39**, S238
13. Przybyszewski, A. W., Foote, W., and Pollen, D. A. (2000) Striate cortex increases Contrast gain control of macaque LGN neurons. Visual Neurosci., in press

Discovery of Bayesian Networks from Data with Maintenance of Partially Oriented Graphs[*]

Mieczysław A. Kłopotek and Sławomir T. Wierzchoń

Institute of Computer Science, Polish Academy of Sciences

ul. Ordona 21, PL 01-237 Warsaw, Poland

klopotek@ipipan.waw.pl, stw@ipipan.waw.pl

Abstract: The paper presents a concept of a new class of algorithms for discovery of Bayesian networks from data. The basic difficulty of many incremental discovery algorithms in this area is the increasing number of potentially equivalent orientations of edges while an improper choice at the given stage may have dramatic impact on the final network structure. As a remedy, usage of so-called partially oriented graphs at intermediate stages is recommended for which the property of partial dependency separation has been proven. Such partially oriented graphs may maintain in a single structure all equivalent consistent Bayesian networks.

Keywords: Bayesian networks, learning

Introduction

Currently, Bayesian networks (Pearl, 1988) appear to be quite a popular method of representation of uncertain knowledge. They can represent concisely a joint multivariate discrete probability distribution exploiting properties of conditional independence. A Bayesian network is an acyclic directed graph (dag) nodes of which are labeled with variables and conditional probability tables of the node variable given its parents in the graph.

The joint probability distribution is then expressed by the formula:

$$P(x_1,\ldots\ldots,x_n)= \Pi_{i=1\ldots n} P(x_i \,|\,\pi(x_i))$$

[*] Research partially sponsored under EU project CRIT-2, workpackage Nr.3

where $\pi(x_i)$ is the set of parents of the variable (node) x_i.

E.g. in Fig.1 we have:

$$P(a,b,c,d,e,f) = P(a)\ P(b|a)\ P(c|a)\ P(d|b,c)\ P(e|b,c)\ P(f|e)$$

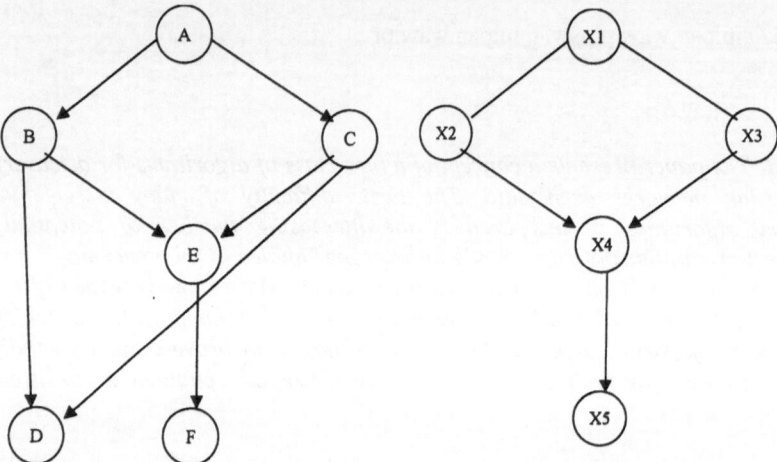

Fig.1. Bayesian network   Fig.2. Partially oriented graph

On the one hand, Bayesian networks allow for efficient reasoning, and on the other they contain information on conditional independences among variables. Geiger, Verma and Pearl (1990) demonstrated that the so-called d-separation property in a dag implies conditional statistical independence, and missing d-separation (except for a set of networks with zero measure, that means highly improbable ones) implies missing conditional independence. Beside this, if edges of a network reflect causal relationships among variables, then the network is minimal. This last property suggests that the Bayesian network can be reconstructed if at least part of conditional independence properties is known.

Detailed methods of discovery of Bayesian networks from data based on this suggestion have been elaborated in the past. Among them are the algorithms by Spirtes, Glymour and Scheines (1993): SGS, PC, PC+, CI and FCI.

However, it is general statistical knowledge that one has to be careful about when drawing causal conclusions from statistical analysis. This is in particular valid for Bayesian networks. Bayesian networks, while representing conditional independence, are not uniquely determined by the relation of conditional and marginal dependence and independence. For example in dags in Fig.3 and 4 relations of d-separation are identical in spite of the fact that in Fig.4 the edge (X2,X1) has different orientation from that in Fig.3.

This behavior not only implies impossibility of complete determination of edge orientations in the final dag that is we usually cannot recover the intrinsic "causal" dag because statistical tests would be insufficient to identify causal relations. It also has consequences for the construction of Bayesian networks from data (network discovery) especially if the discovery process is an incremental one. Not only in the final product, but also in intermediate stage networks of the discovery process there exist many equivalent possibilities of edge orientations. A "wrong" choice at an intermediate stage may prevent from finding a minimal network for the data. This is particularly true for algorithms based on the measures of distances between the Bayesian network and the empirical distribution, e.g. the algorithms K2 of Cooper/Herskovits (1992), Lam/Bacchus (1994), Acid/Lopez (1996), Urban/Kaempke (1999) and other.

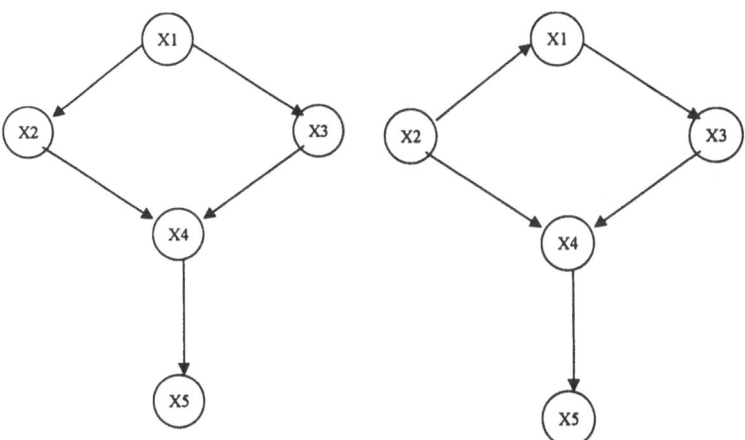

Fig.3. Bayesian network   Fig.4. Bayesian network

Under these circumstances a common practice is to assume the knowledge of the ordering of nodes compatible with the intrinsic Bayesian network (Acid & Lopez, 1996, Cooper & Herskovits, 1992). Though sequencing of events related to many variables e.g. in a time sequence is frequently possible, the complete ordering may prove a too strong requirement.

In this research we considered the possibility of overcoming the need for a total node ordering. We propose basing of the algorithms on the concept of partial dependency separation (p-d-separation). P-d-separation allows maintaining in a single structure many alternative orientations of edges of a Bayesian network.

P-d-separation

The notion of p-d-separation has been originally introduced while seeking for an alternative proof of the Conjecture of Spirtes, Glymour and Scheines (1990) concerning the possibility of reconstruction of the global Bayesian network structure from local conditional independence tests (Kłopotek, 1998, Klopotek 1999). The correctness of this Conjecture implies the correctness of the SGS algorithm for Bayesian network discovery (and derivatives like PC, PC*). The "pog-from-data" algorithm together with the "pog-to-dag" algorithm recalled below is a result of this research (The "pog-from-data" algorithm may be viewed as a version of the PC algorithm).

The SGS algorithm was of particular interest for us because at intermediate stages and in the final product part of the edges is oriented and the other are not. Let us call a graph with some edges oriented and some not a partially oriented graph, pog. (See Fig. 2).

> **Definition:** A *partially oriented graph (pog)* is a graph with some edges oriented and some not, such that the oriented subgraph is a directed acyclic graph.

Note that a dag is a special case of a pog.

Geiger et al (1990) introduced d-separation to describe dag properties where "isolating" (d-separating) nodes in a dag implies statistical independence. P-d-separation has been introduced for the very same reason in partially oriented graphs. The concept of p-d-separation is an extension of the d-separation onto the pogs. This concept and the auxiliary ones defined below are designed so that their definitions coincide with those for dags in case that a pog is in fact a dag. So p-d-separation in a dag is a d-separation, an active p-trail in a dag is an active trail in a dag, p-descendant in a dag is a descendant in a dag etc.

After (Kłopotek, 1998) let us introduce the concept of p-d-separation. We need several auxiliary concepts defined below to introduce p-d-separation. Intuitively, a p-d-separation between two nodes is achieved if all p-trails between them are not active.

Definition: A *p-trail* in a pog is a sequence of links that form a path in the underlying undirected graph. A node b is called a head-to-head node with respect to a p-trail t if there are two consecutive links a→b and b←c on that t. A p-trail is minimal iff no two of its succeeding links on the p-trail are bridged in the graph. (A bridge of two links is a link connecting the beginning of the first with the end of the second one.).

A p-tral is not active among others when its head-to-head nodes are not blocked at their p-descendants. We need hence the following definition:

Definition: A *p-descendent* of a node n in a pog is any node m such that there exists a minimal p-trail from n to m such that every oriented link on the p-trail is oriented from n to m and an oriented edge (m,n) does not exist in the graph.

We can define now what an active p-trail is.

Definition: A p-trail t connecting nodes a and b is said to be *active* given a set of nodes L, if

(1) every head-to-head-node wrt t either is or has a p-descendent in L and

(2) every other node on t is outside L.

Otherwise t is said to be *blocked}* (given L).

We are ready now to say what we precisely mean by p-d-separation:

Definition: If J,K and L are three disjoint sets of nodes in a pog H, then L is said to *p-d-separate* J from K, denoted I(J,K | L)_H, iff no minimal p-trail between a node in J and a node in K is active given L.

For example in Fig. 4 nodes {X2,X3} p-d-separate node X1 from X4.

The following theorem defines an important property of p-d-separation on simplification of p-d-separation testing:

Theorem: Let L be a set of nodes in a pog H, and let a,b ∉ L be two additional nodes in H. Then a and b are connected via an active p-trail (given L) iff a and b are connected via a simple (i.e. not possessing cycles in the underlying undirected graph) active p-trail (given L).

282

The above concepts allow us to formulate the following algorithm for reconstruction of pog structure from data.

"pog-from-data-algorithm"

Let SV be a given set of variables

Let H become a complete unoriented graph over SV.

1. Initialize the variable k:=0 indicating the maximum number of conditioning variables in the steps below:.

2. For each pair of nodes $X,Y \in SV$, connected in H by an egde and possessing more than k neighbors each let us check if for any subset of neighbors of X with cardinality exactly k, the variables X,Y are conditionally independent. If so, let us save this set as SS(X,Y) and let us remove the link (X,Y) from H.

3. k:=k+1. If there exists a pair of nodes $X,Y \in SV$, connected in H with an edge and having in H more than k neighbors each, go to step 2. Otherwise go to step 4.

4. For each three variables $X,Y,Z \in SV$, such that in H there exist edges (X,Y) and (Y,Z), but not (X,Z) and SS(X,Z) does not contain Y, orient edges resp. from X to Y and from Z to Y.

5. For each three variables $X,Y,Z \in SV$, such that in H there exist edges (X,Y) and (Y,Z), but not (X,Z), the edge (X,Y) is oriented from X to Y, and edge (Y,Z) is not oriented, orient (Y,Z) from Y to Z.

6. For each unoriented edge (X,Y) in H, if there exists in H a path from X to Y consisting of oriented edges each of them pointing from X towards Y, then orient edge (X,Y) from X to Y

7. For each four variables $X,Y,Z,T \in SV$, for which in H edges {X,Y}, {Z,Y} are oriented head-to-head (towards Y) and there is no edge (X,Z) in H and both edges {X,T}, {Y,T} or both edges {Z,T}, {Y,T}, or all edges {X,T}, {Z,T}, {Y,T} are unoriented, orient edge {Y,T} from T to Y.

8. If steps 5, 6, or 7 managed to orient at least one previously unoriented edge, go to step 5. Otherwise **THE END**

Let's formulate an algorithm deriving all dags based on a pog. First let us introduce the notion of legitimate removal of a node from pog.

> **Definition:** A node can be *removed legitimately* from a pog iff all the oriented edges it meets are oriented towards it, and all pairs of edges meeting at it for which at least one is unoriented are bridged.

Pog-to-dag algorithm

1. Find a legitimately removable node in the pog, remove it with edges meeting it while marking the edges as oriented towards this node.

2. Proceed with Step.1 until all the nodes are removed.

3. Orient the edges of the original pog so as they were marked in step 1. **THE END**

Notice that the algorithm is non-deterministic: At step 1 we can have several candidate legitimately removable nodes. Selecting any of them may lead to different, though statistically equivalent dags. We claim that:

> **Theorem** Let pog G be obtained using the "**pog-from-data-algorithm**". Then every dag obtained from the pog G by the above "**pog-to-dag-algorithm**" is a dag reflecting all d-separation properties of the data. For any dag reflecting all d-separation properties of the data there exists a derivation from G via the "**pog-to-dag-algorithm**".
>
> **Proof: (the general idea)** On the one hand each dag has a legitimately removable node, on the other hand the derivations of "**pog-from-data-algorithm**".do not induce conflicts with d-separation principles (that is no edge orientations conflicting with preceding statistical tests are introduced).

For example from the pog in Fig.2 one can derive three different Bayesian networks (dags) including those in Fig.3 and Fig.4.

New class of algorithms

Undoubtedly the SGS-like algorithms have a strong theoretical foundation justifying their correctness. However the analysis of complexity of these algorithms carried our by Kłopotek (1998) pessimistically sees their potential speed. Therefore search for heuristic methods allowing to speed up the Bayesian network discovery process is highly advisable.

We have already pointed at lowered efficiency of known heuristic incremental algorithms caused by explosion of equivalent structures of Bayesian networks that either have to be all maintained or arbitrarily chosen at risk of subsequent suboptimal (or even totally unoptimal) solutions.

From the previous considerations on p-d-separation we see that:

*   Pog structure allows to save partial knowledge about Bayesian network without commitment to a particular Bayesian network

- The p-d-separation property implies equivalence of all compatible alternative derived dag structures and therefore any of them can be used to evaluate the distance between the pog and the empirical probability distribution.

These properties let us hope to restrict the combinatorial explosion on the one hand and to reuse the constructions of the existent constructions of known heuristic algorithms on the other hand.

We propose the following framework algorithm exploiting p-d-separation to enhance known algorithms. Essentially it is a kind of metacode of algorithms like K2 or BENEDICT, where we can exploit the measures of agreement from those known algorithms, combined with the maintenance of the Bayesian network structure in form of a dag which is expanded into a proper dag whenever the agreement measure is to be calculated.

Framework algorithm:

1. Create an empty pog H (that is without edges) over the set of all variables SV.
2. For each still unconnected pair of nodes P,Q in H:
   a) add undirected edge between P and Q,
   b) apply steps 4-8 of the algorithm "pog-from-data" and then "pog-to-dag"
   c) if no contradiction appeared (no cycles), then calculate the measure of agreement between the resulting dag and the real distribution.
   d) recall all changes implied by steps a)-c) in pog H
   e) if P (Q) is entered by an edge {S,P} (edge (S,Q}) oriented towards P (towards Q) or
      unoriented and there exists no edge (Q,S) (no edge (P,S)) then

      - add edge (P,Q) and orient both edges (P,Q) and (S,P) towards P ((P,Q) and (S,Q) towards Q)
      - apply steps 4-8 of the algorithm "pog-from-data" and then "pog-to-dag"
      - if no contradiction appeared (no cycles), then calculate the measure of agreement between the resulting dag and the real distribution.
      - recall all changes implied by step e) in pog H so far

3. Add to H the edge (unoriented or oriented with additional orientation of the other existing edge)for which no contradiction appeared and which gave the best matching with the empirical distribution.
4. If a new edge has been successfully added in step 3 and termination criteria are not met, goto step 2, otherwise **THE END**

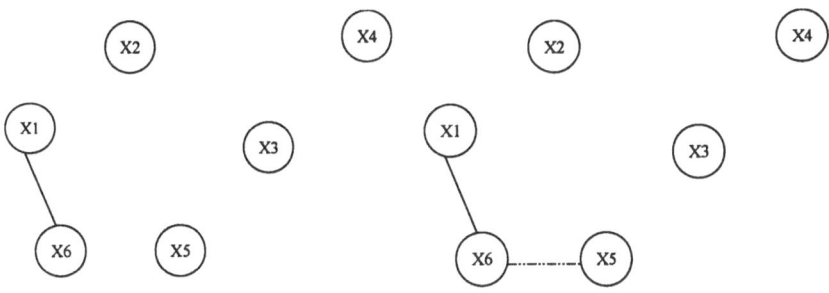

Fig.5. Partially oriented graph (pog)   Fig.6. Partially oriented graph (pog) -
     first edge added   second edge added

We have carried out initial experimental evaluation of the framework algorithm. Figures 5-12 illustrate a sample behavior of a group of 6 variables. Starting with an empty graph, in Fig.5-7 edges with no orientation proved to be best choices when adding new edge. In Fig.8 we see that an oriented edge (X3➔X2) met best the evaluation conditions. The edge X1-X2 has been at this step oriented as X1➔X2. In Fig. 9 again an unoriented edge was added. This edge has been oriented as X4➔X3 at the next stage that gave rise to the new oriented edge X5➔X3.

At this point the process of edge inserting has been aborted as the entropy did not increase significantly. The graph has been left with two unoriented edges (X1-X6 and X6-X5). Now, using Pog-to-dag algorithm, the edges can be oriented in three different ways, two of them being shown in Figs 11,12.

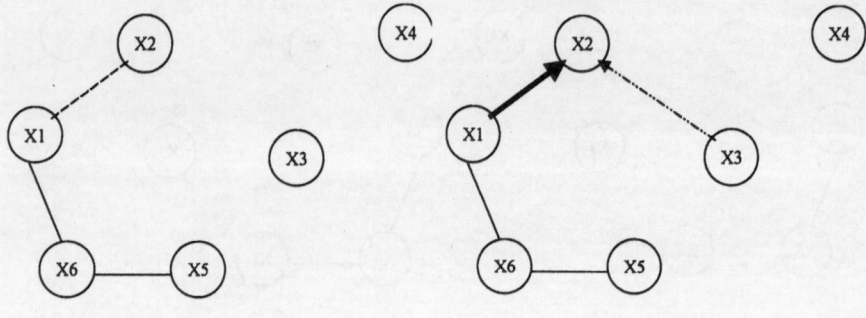

Fig.7. Partially oriented graph (pog) - next unoriented edge

Fig.8. Partially oriented graph (pog) - adding an oriented edge with changing an existent unoriented edge into oriented one

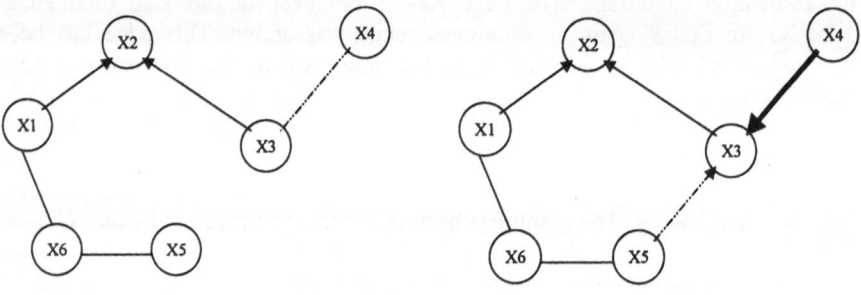

Fig.9. Partially oriented graph (pog)

Fig.10. Partially oriented graph (pog)

Conclusion

The paper presented a new framework algorithm for construction of Bayesian networks from data allowing overcoming the requirement of apriorical knowledge of a compatible ordering of the variables.

The new framework algorithm makes use of partially oriented graph structure and p-d-separation properties to reduce the number of alternative equivalent paths of incremental Bayesian network construction. This allows avoiding disadvantages of known algorithms.

It should be however notified that this new algorithm does not avoid the pitfall of XOR dependencies which have to be treated separately as suggested by Xiang et al., (1997).

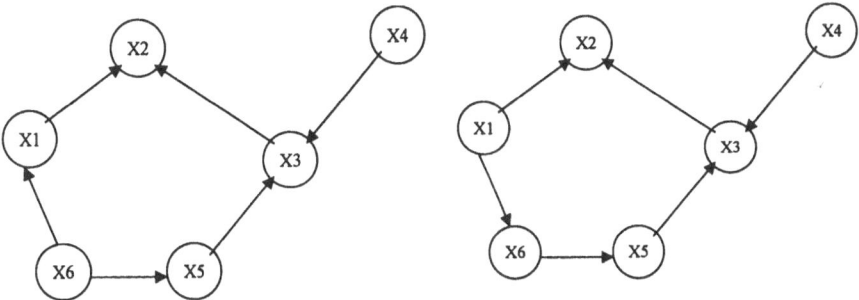

Fig.11. Possible Bayesian network   Fig.12. Possible Bayesian network

References

1. S. Acid, L.M. de Campos: An algorithm for finding minimum d-separating sets in belief networks, forthcoming, 1996..
2. G.F.Cooper, E.Herskovits: A Bayesian method for the induction of probabilistic networks from data. *Machine Learning* 9 (1992), 309-347
3. D.Geiger, T.Verma, J. Pearl: d-Separation: From theorems to algorithms. W: M.Henrion, R.D.Shachter, L.N.Kamal, J.F.Lemmer (eds): *Uncertainty in Artificial Intelligence* 5, Elsevier Science Publishers B.V. (North-Holland), 1990, 139-148

4. M.A.Kłopotek: Partial Dependency Separation - a new concept for expressing dependence/ independence relations in causal networks. Demonstratio Mathematica. Vol XXXII No 1,1999, pp. 207-226.

5. M.A.Kłopotek: Methods of Identification and Interpretations of Belief Distributions in the Dempster-Shafer Theory (in Polish), IPI PAN Publisher, Warsaw 1998, ISBN 83-900820-8-x.

6. W. Lam and F. Bacchus: Learning Bayesian Belief Networks: An Approach based on the MDL Principle, *Computational Intelligence*, vol. 10, pages 269--293, 1994.

7. J. Pearl: *Probabilistic Reasoning in Intelligent Systems: Networks of Plausible Inference*, Morgan Kaufmann, San Mateo CA, 1988

8. P. Spirtes, C. Glymour, R. Scheines: Causality from probability. In: G. McKee ed.: *Evolving knowledge in natural and artificial intelligence*, London: Pitman, 1990, 181-199

9. P. Spirtes, C. Glymour, R. Scheines: *Causation, Prediction and Search*, Lecture Notes in Statistics 81, Springer-Verlag, 1993.

10. T. Urban, T. Kaempke: Recovering dependency graph in uncertain data. M. Mohammadian, ed: Computational Intelligence for Modelling, Control and Automation. Evolutionary Computing & Fuzzy Logic for Intelligent Control, Knowledge Acquisition & Information Retrieval. Concurrent Systems Engineering Series Vol. 55. IOS Press Amsterdam, Berlin, Oxford 1999. pp. 476-481.

11. Y. Xiang, S.K.M. Wong and N. Cercone: A 'Microscopic' study of minimum entropy search in learning decomposable Markov networks. *Machine Learning*, Vol. 26, No.1, 65-92, 1997.

Visualization in Prediction Based on Grade Correspondence Analysis

Olaf Matyja [1] and Wiesław Szczesny [1], [2]

[1] Institute of Computer Science, Polish Academy of Science, Ordona 21, 01-237 Warsaw, Poland

[2] Department of Econometry and Computer Science, Warsaw Agricultural University, Nowoursynowska 166, 02-787 Warsaw, Poland

Abstract:

The grade correspondence analysis (GCA) is used to form a solution of predictive problems with a binary response variable and a vector of nonnegative explanatory variables. At first, the GCA is applied to the matrix of values of explanatory variables corresponding to objects belonging to the training set. Then, this analysis is repeated under the restriction that two non-overlapping blocks are formed, each gathering objects of a common value of the response variable. The results provide a general information on the joint behavior of explanatory variables and their link with the response variable. Moreover, the second analysis produces a GCA based discriminant function, used subsequently to classify new objects or objects belonging to a test set. Each phase of this process is clearly visualized by means of suitable over-representation maps. All stages of predicting are illustrated in the paper by simulated university drop-out problem.

Key words:

classification, correspondence analysis, explanatory variable, grade parameters, latent structure, response variable, stochastic dependence, visual intelligent information system.

1. Introduction

We presume that the reader is acquainted with typical approaches to binary predictive problems [cf. eg. Hand 1986] and with classical correspondence analysis [cf. eg. van der Heijden 1987] .

This knowledge is however not necessarily required to understand the approach proposed by us, since all stages of predicting are illustrated step by step on simulated data concerning a university drop-out problem. Correspondence analysis and prediction working together provide not only a clearly visualized solution for the predictive problem, but also help to recognize the latent structure of the whole set of variables. They also give new opportunities while looking for outliers [Szczesny W. 1999]. The grade correspondence analysis, introduced recently by the Statistical Data Analysis Group from the Institute of Computer Science PAS, works better than the classical CA, but an application of GCA from contingency tables to data matrices faces with difficulties [cf Ciok. et al. 1998 for a concise information, and also Szczesny 1991 for a grade approach to standard discriminant problems]. This problem is explained in a detailed study, prepared for publication [Szczesny W. 2000], and will not be discussed in our paper.

Technically, GCA can be applied to any matrix of non-negative variables, which often leads to well interpretable results in spite of theoretical limitations. In practice it has to be supported by a diligent search for outliers (among objects and among variables) and for suitable weights assigned to particular variables. Then it should be followed by a cross-validation and by other methods checking quality of the GCA based on discriminant functions. However, this is not considered in the present paper, devoted mainly to present visualization. This type of visualization can be easily adopted in intelligent information systems.

2. Simulated data for an university drop-out problem

Cox and Wermuth (1996, p.142-150) considered determinants of university drop-out. They wanted to develop a psycho-diagnostic instrument for counseling prospective students when they choose a field of study. 3500 students were investigated and values of nine explanatory variables registered jointly with the value of the response variable A: drop-out from university. The explanatory variables concerned psychological predispositions, school career and demographic background. As the data matrix used by Cox and Wermuth has been not published and thus could be not used to demonstrate our approach to predicting a drop-out, we prepared a simulated data set using the names of six explanatory variables appearing in the Cox and Wermuth study. They are:

X - motivation

Y - expected achievement

U - average grade during last three years at school

B - change of school (1 - no, 2 - yes)

C - integration into school class, last year

D - class repeated (1 - no, 2 - yes).

Variables X, Y, C describe results of psychological tests valued 1-10, average grade U is rescaled to the interval 4 -10.

The 40×7 data matrix forming a training set is presented in Table 1 (with students and explanatory variables ordered according to GCA). Ten additional "new" students, labeled new 1, ... new 10, constitute a test set and inserted into data from Table 1 form Table 2 (their places are chosen by the GCA based discriminant function constructed from the data matrix of the training set).

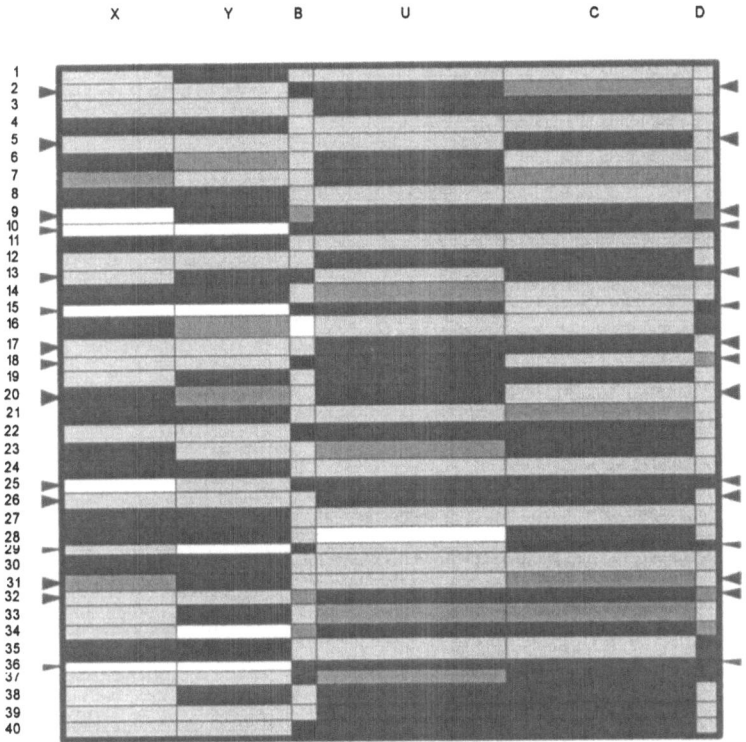

Fig. 1. Simulated university drop-out data: the over-representation map for 40 students in the training set (in an initial order), each described by variables X, ..., D. The indicated rows correspond to students dropped out.

To create both data matrices, a special model consisting of seven interdependent normal or exponential variables has been built. Then, the variables were suitably discretized, a random sample of size 50 was drawn and divided into the training set (first 40 elements) and test set (last 10 elements). The training and test sets contain respectively 15 and 3 drop-outs, indicated on the tables by arrows attached to respective rows. An early version of the generator was proposed by T. Goetzendorf-Grabowski and W. Szczesny (1992).

The generator has been adapted to form samples consisting of subsamples, drawn independently from the multivariate distribution according to separately chosen parameter sets. This enabled a simultaneous preparation of many sets of simulated data according to a preliminary plan.

The multivariate model and its random sample generator details will not be described here, but may be delivered on request.

#	Y	X	C	U	D	B		#	Y	X	C	U	D	B	
28	7	7	9	4	1	1		19	5	4	8	8	1	1	
35	10	9	7	7	2	1		39	5	5	9	9	1	1	
24	8	7	8	7	1	1		37	4	4	8	7	1	1	
30	8	7	8	8	1	1		12	5	5	10	10	1	1	
8	8	8	8	9	1	1		26	5	4	9	9	1	1	←
11	6	8	6	8	1	1		9	5	3	8	8	1	1	←
4	7	7	8	9	1	1		17	4	5	10	9	1	1	←
27	7	7	9	9	1	1		32	4	4	8	8	1	1	←
1	7	5	8	8	1	1		7	4	5	8	9	1	1	
31	6	5	8	7	1	1	←	3	4	5	10	10	1	1	
21	6	6	9	8	1	1		22	5	5	10	10	1	2	
14	7	7	10	10	1	1		18	4	4	7	8	1	2	←
16	7	9	10	10	2	1		40	4	5	10	10	1	2	
33	7	6	10	10	1	1		2	4	4	8	9	1	2	←
6	6	7	9	10	1	1		34	3	4	8	9	1	1	
20	6	7	9	10	1	1	←	29	2	3	6	4	1	2	←
38	7	4	10	10	1	1		25	3	2	7	8	1	1	←
5	5	5	9	8	1	1	←	10	2	2	6	7	2	1	←
13	4	3	8	5	1	1	←	36	1	2	7	6	2	1	←
23	5	6	10	9	1	1		15	1	2	6	9	2	2	←

Table 1. Data matrix for the training set with students ordered due to the GCA Seriation Index as presented in Fig. 3. Arrows indicate drop-outs.

#	Y	X	C	U	D	B	
new 5	10	10	4	3	2	1	
28	7	7	9	4	1	1	
35	10	9	7	7	2	1	
24	8	7	8	7	1	1	
30	8	7	8	8	1	1	
new10	8	7	8	8	1	1	
8	8	8	8	9	1	1	
11	6	8	6	8	1	1	
4	7	7	8	9	1	1	
27	7	7	9	9	1	1	
1	7	5	8	8	1	1	
31	6	5	8	7	1	1	←
21	6	6	9	8	1	1	
14	7	7	10	10	1	1	
16	7	9	10	10	2	1	
33	7	6	10	10	1	1	
new 1	7	6	10	10	1	1	
6	6	7	9	10	1	1	
20	6	7	9	10	1	1	←
38	7	4	10	10	1	1	
5	5	5	9	8	1	1	←
13	4	3	8	5	1	1	←
new 7	6	5	4	8	2	1	
23	5	6	10	9	1	1	
19	5	4	8	8	1	1	
new 6	5	5	10	9	1	1	
39	5	5	9	9	1	1	
new 9	6	3	9	9	1	1	←
37	4	4	8	7	1	1	
new 2	5	4	10	9	1	1	
12	5	5	10	10	1	1	
26	5	4	9	9	1	1	←
9	5	3	8	8	1	1	←
17	4	5	10	9	1	1	←
32	4	4	8	8	1	1	←
new 4	4	4	8	8	1	1	←
7	4	5	8	9	1	1	
new 3	5	4	10	10	1	1	
3	4	5	10	10	1	1	
22	5	5	10	10	1	2	
18	4	4	7	8	1	2	←
40	4	5	10	10	1	2	
2	4	4	8	9	1	2	←
34	3	4	8	9	1	1	
29	2	3	6	4	1	2	←
25	3	2	7	8	1	1	←
new 8	2	4	9	10	1	1	←
10	2	2	6	7	2	1	←
36	1	2	7	6	2	1	←
15	1	2	6	9	2	2	←

Table 2. The GCA for the training and test sets. Arrows indicate drop-outs.

3. Construction and visualization of the GCA based discriminant function

Any $m \times k$ data matrix with non-negative values can be visualized as an over-representation map in the same way as a contingency table [cf Ciok et al 1998]. The frequency n_{ij} is then replaced by the value of j-th variable for i-th object. It is compared in a contingency table with the corresponding "fair representation" $n_{i\bullet} \times n_{\bullet j} / \sum \sum n_{ij}$, where $n_{i\bullet} = \sum_j n_{ij}, n_{\bullet j} = \sum_i n_{ij}$. The ratio of the first and second expression is called the over-representation ratio. An over-representation surface over a unit square is divided onto $m \times k$ rectangles situated in m rows and k columns, the area of rectangle placed in row i and column j being equal to "fair representation" of normalized n_{ij}. A surface ideally expressing fair representation is constant and equal to one. Four thresholds of this index have been chosen: 2/3, 99/100, 100/99, 3/2. The respective intervals of the index were called: strong under-representation, weak under-representation, almost fair representation, weak over-representation, strong over-representation. The shades of grayness are:

below 2/3	strong under-representation
2/3 - 99/100	weak under-representation
99/100 - 100/99	almost fair representation
100/99 - 3/2	weak over-representation
above 3/2	strong over-representation

The respective chart with five shades of grayness from white to black is called the over-representation map. Fig.1 presents such a map for 40 students in the training set, described by variables X, Y, U, B, C, D. The drop-outs are indicated by arrows. This map preserves the initial orderings of variables and students as obtained in the random sample being drawn from the model. As expected, this map provides no clear pattern of interdependencies among the seven variables, or of similarities among the students. Such a pattern is clarified when students and variables are reordered according to the GCA which maximizes the value of the grade correlation coefficient ρ^*: from 0.0093 for the initial table visualized in Fig 1 to 0.1495 for the GCA table visualized in Fig 2. Order of variables is changed from X, Y, U, B, C, D into Y, X, C, U, B, D while the initial order of students is strongly changed by the GCA. Table 3 shows how the over-representation map approximates an over-representation surface. The values of the over-representation ratio are provided for the ten initial and ten final rows. These may be confronted with the corresponding shades of grayness in Fig. 2.

#	Y	X	C	U	D	B
28	1.363561	1.370148	1.085283	0.486694	0.900383	0.88081
35	1.569177	1.419082	0.679977	0.686103	1.450617	0.709541
24	1.41226	1.241697	0.874256	0.771866	0.815972	0.798234
30	1.369464	1.20407	0.847763	0.855401	0.791246	0.774045
8	1.291209	1.297447	0.79932	0.907336	0.746032	0.729814
11	1.129808	1.513688	0.699405	0.940941	0.87037	0.851449
4	1.198281	1.20407	0.847763	0.962326	0.791246	0.774045
27	1.163037	1.168656	0.925683	0.934022	0.767974	0.751279
1	1.318109	0.946055	0.93254	0.940941	0.87037	0.851449
31	1.210508	1.01363	0.99915	0.882132	0.93254	0.912267
⋮	⋮	⋮	⋮	⋮	⋮	⋮
22	0.855915	0.86005	1.059704	1.069251	0.791246	1.54809
18	0.869083	0.873281	0.941506	1.085701	1.004274	1.964883
40	0.70613	0.886926	1.09282	1.102665	0.815972	1.596467
2	0.807005	0.810904	0.99915	1.13417	0.93254	1.824534
34	0.651812	0.873281	1.076007	1.221414	1.004274	0.982441
29	0.627671	0.946055	1.165675	0.784117	1.450617	2.838164
25	0.770323	0.51603	1.112689	1.283101	1.186869	1.161067
10	0.564904	0.567633	1.049107	1.234985	2.611111	1.277174
36	0.297318	0.597508	1.288377	1.114272	2.748538	1.344394
15	0.256774	0.51603	0.953734	1.443489	2.373737	2.322134

Table 3. The over-representation surface for Table 1 (first ten and last ten rows).

296

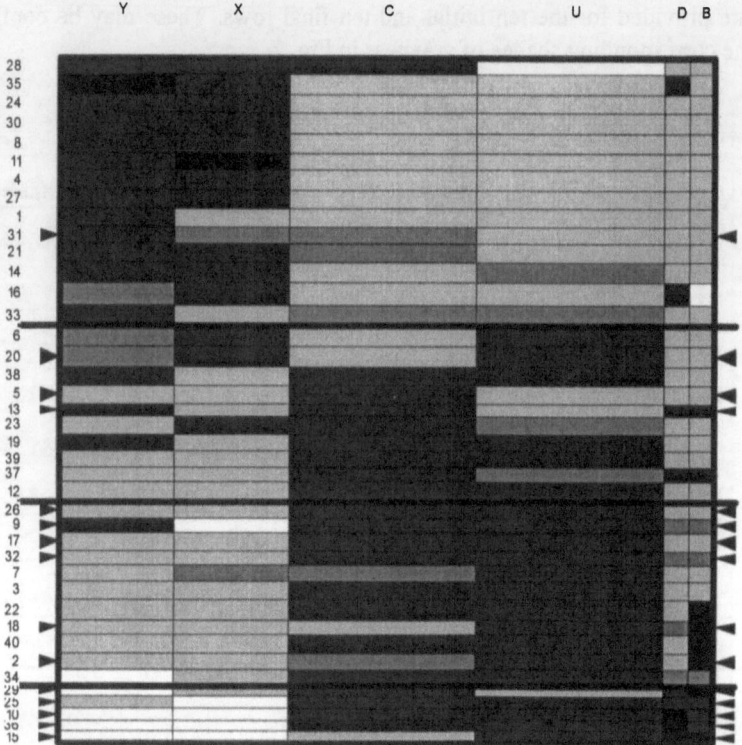

Fig. 2. The GCA transform of the over-representation map from Fig. 1. (Visualization of Table 1) The indicated rows correspond to students dropped out.

The set of students is divided in Table 1 and Fig 2 onto four non-overlapping subsets. The first consists of 14 students who have strongly over-represented expectations and motivation as compared with C (integration) and U (average grade); only one of this group turned to be a drop-out. The last subset consists of five students, all of them drop-outs, which have very small expectations and motivation as compared with not too bad marks for C and U; three of them repeated school class, two changed school. The two other subsets (10 and 11 students each students with three and six drop-outs) tend respectively towards the first and the last subset; the third contains four cases of changing school. It is important to look simultaneously at Table 1 and Fig 2 since "black" or "white" may be misleading: the over-representation map compares relative influences of variables and not necessarily indicates directly which values are high and which ones are small. In any case, the GCA provided four ordered and rather homogeneous clusters, which by chance are also ordered according to the proportion of drop-outs. The first subset may be treated as a pattern of successful students, and the next subsets form patterns for students who are "rather successful", "rather dropped out", and "decidedly dropped out". It is also clear which variables are especially important in making a prediction.

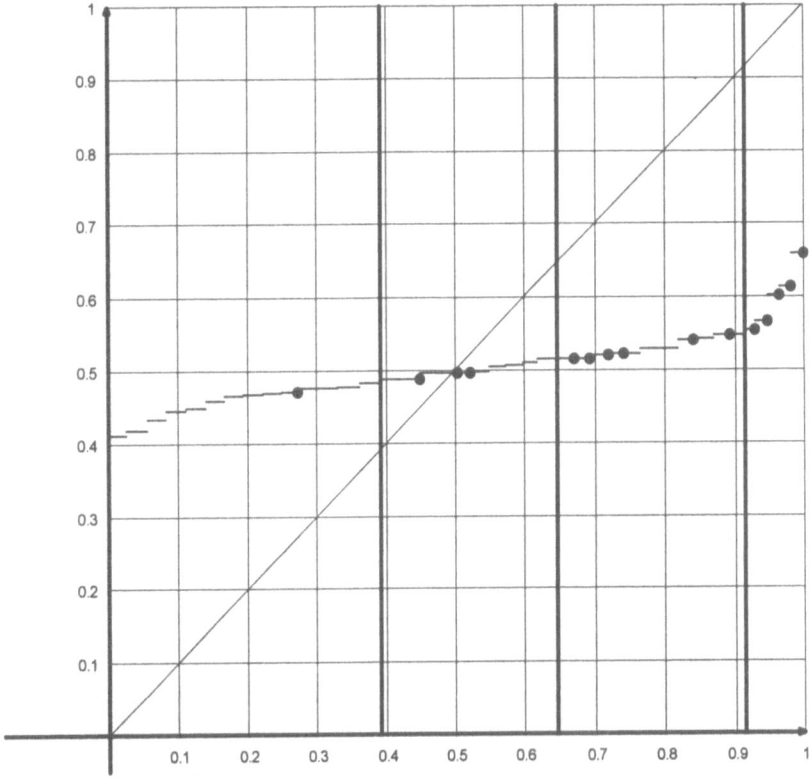

Fig. 3. The GCA Seriation Index for rows (students) in Table 1. The black circles correspond to students dropped out.

Fig 3 visualizes the seriation index, which arranges students in the training set. The black circles in this chart denote drop-outs. The thick vertical lines indicate the boundaries of the four clusters. This function increases more quickly in the first and the last cluster and is nearly constant in the other two. The values of the seriation function are constant on intervals corresponding to subsequent rows (i.e. students) and indicate to which extent a "mass" of the vector of over-representation ratios is distributed in the left part of the table. This function is normalized to the interval <0,1).

In our example we choose the model so that intensity of drop-outs tends to increase with the GCA seriation index and therefore this index can directly serve as a discriminant function in predicting university drop-out. In general the discriminant function based on GCA is constructed in a more sophisticated way.

On Fig 4 we have the results of GCA executed under the restriction that all drop-outs have to form a separate block. In this case the order of variables can differ from that obtained by the GCA with no restrictions and hence other variables may be indicated as particularly influential in predicting a drop-out. The object seriation index derived by the constrained GCA is presented in Fig 5: it increases on each block, but not on the whole set. Fixing the order of variables provided by the constrained GCA, we can find the order of students which maximizes ρ^*, and this seriation function is taken as the GCA based discriminant function.

When the order of variables is the same after processing by the unconstrained and the constrained GCA (as occurred in our example), the GCA seriation index is taken as the discriminant function.

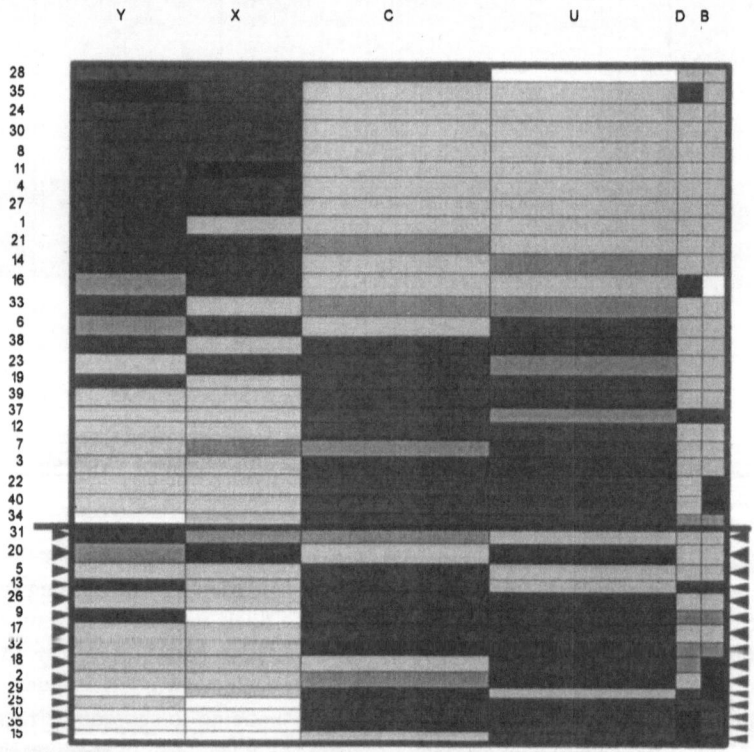

Fig. 4. The GCA transform of the over-representation map from Fig. 1. under the restriction that the dropped out students form a separate block.

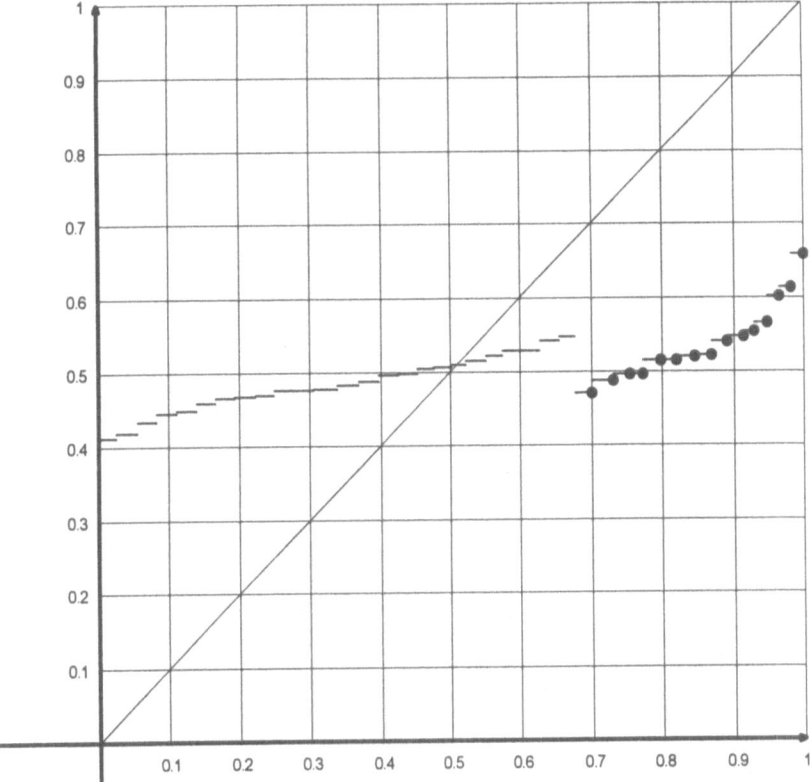

Fig. 5. The GCA Seriation Index for rows (students) in the table visualized at Fig. 4. The black circles correspond to students dropped out.

4.Prediction applied to the elements of the test set

We have now to insert the elements of the test set into the training set transformed by the GCA. First of all we reorder variables in the test set in the same way as in the training set. Then we check to which extent a "mass" of the vector of over-representation ratios is distributed in the left part of the table for each element in the test set as compared with the marginal distribution in the training set. In case of elements from the training set this procedure is equivalent to comparing the vector of over-representation ratios with the fair representation. Therefore we extend in this way the definition of our discriminant function so that it can be applied to elements from outside of the training set.

300

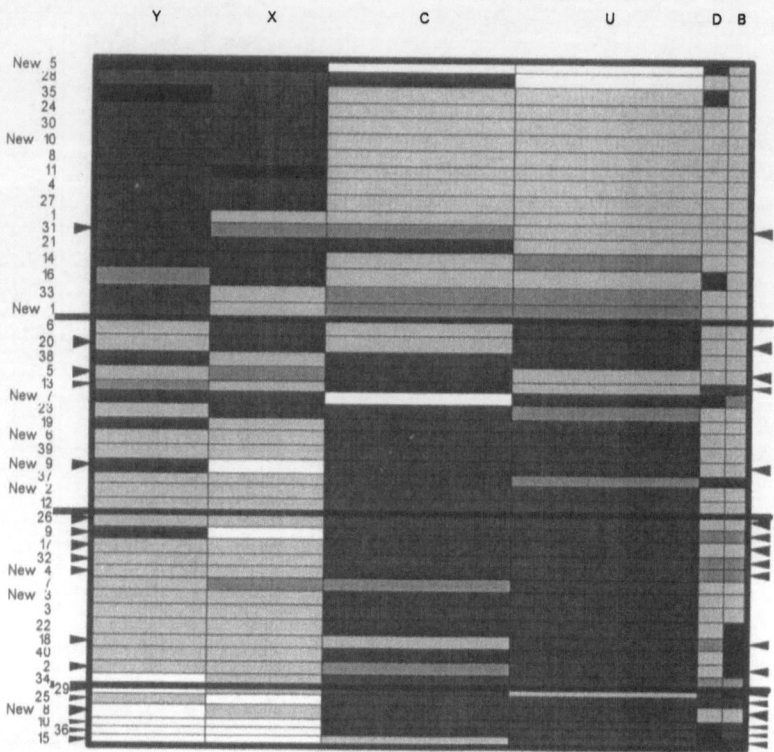

Fig. 6. The over-representation map for data in Table 2. Arrows indicate students dropped out Students from the test set are labeled "New".

The results are presented in Fig 6. We can see ten elements denoted new dispersed in the four clusters in a practically random way. Three new drop-outs are included to the fourth, third, and second cluster, and are classified respectively as "a drop-out", "rather a drop-out", and "rather not a drop-out". Three of seven new successful students are included to the first cluster, and another three to the second cluster. And are classified respectively as "not a drop-out" and "rather not a drop-out", just one new successful student is in the third cluster classified as "rather a drop-out". So we make correct decisions in case of four (all) new students belonging to the edge clusters, and correct suggestions in case of four out of the six new students belonging to the intermediate clusters of deferred decision.

It is convenient for an investigator to inspect each new student at the background of all other and compare it with its neighbors in order to catch trends and interpret the possible reasons of failure.

5. References

1. Ciok A., Kowalczyk T., Pleszczyńska T.: How a New Statistical Infrastructure Induced a New Computing Trend in Data Analysis, In: Polkowski L., Skowron A. (Eds.) Rough Sets and Current Trends in Computing, Lecture Notes in Artificial Intelligence 1424 Proceedings of the First International Conference, RSCTC'98, Warsaw, Poland June 22-26, 1998, Springer, 1998, 75-82.

2. Cox D. R., Wermuth N.: Multivariate Dependencies. Models, analysis and interpretation, Chapman and Hall, London 1996.

3. Goetzendorf-Grabowski T., Szczesny W.: Multivariate Data Generator "UNIV" (User's guide), ICS PAS Reports No 723, Warsaw 1992

4. Hand D. J.: Discrimination and Classification, John Wiley and Sons, New York 1986

5. van der Heijden P. G. M., Correspondence Analysis of Longitudinal Categorical Data, DSWO Press, Leiden, 1987.

6. Szczesny W.: Grade Analysis of Multivariate Data, prepared for publication in 2000.

7. Szczesny W.: On the performance of discriminant function, Journal of Classification, 1991, 8, 201-215.

8. Szczesny W.: Outliers in grade correspondence analysis, In: Michalewicz M., Kłopotek M. (Eds.) Intelligent Information Systems IIS'99, Proceedings of the Workshop held in Ustroń, Poland, 14-18 June 1999, Institute of Computer Science PAS, Warsaw 1999.

Extension of the HEPAR II Model to Multiple-Disorder Diagnosis

Agnieszka Onińsko[1], Marek J. Druzdzel[2], and Hanna Wasyluk[3]

[1] Institute of Computer Science, Białystok University of Technology, Ul. Wiejska 45-A, 15–351 Białystok, Poland, aonisko@ii.pb.bialystok.pl
[2] Decision Systems Laboratory, School of Information Sciences, Intelligent Systems Program, and Center for Biomedical Informatics, University of Pittsburgh, Pittsburgh, PA 15260, USA, marek@sis.pitt.edu
[3] The Medical Center of Postgraduate Education, and Institute of Biocybernetics and Biomedical Engineering, Polish Academy of Sciences, Marymoncka 99, 01-813 Warsaw, Poland, hwasyluk@cmkp.edu.pl

Abstract. The HEPAR II system is based on a Bayesian network model of a subset of the domain of hepatology in which the structure of the network is elicited from an expert diagnostician and the parameters are learned from a database of medical cases. The model follows the assumption made in the database that each patient case is diagnosed with a single disorder, i.e., disorders are mutually exclusive.

In this paper, we describe an extension of the HEPAR II system to multiple-disorder diagnosis. We show that our network transforms readily to a network that can perform multiple-disorder diagnosis with some benefits to the quality of numerical parameters learned from the database. We demonstrate empirically that the diagnostic performance in terms of single-disorder diagnosis improves under this transformation. The new model is more realistic and we expect that it will be of higher value in clinical practice.

1 Introduction

Decision analysis has had a major influence on computer-based diagnostic systems. The field of Uncertainty in Artificial Intelligence, through which this influence was funneled, has developed practical modeling tools based on probabilistic graphical models, such as Bayesian networks [9] (also called belief networks or causal networks) and influence diagrams [4] (also called relevance diagrams or decision networks). Bayesian networks are directed acyclic graphs modeling probabilistic dependencies among variables. The graphical part of a Bayesian network reflects the structure of a problem, while local interactions among neighboring variables are quantified by conditional probability distributions. One of the main advantages of Bayesian networks over other schemes for reasoning under uncertainty is that they readily combine existing frequency data with expert judgment within the probabilistic framework. Often, for example, hospitals and clinics collect patient data, which over time allow for discovering statistical dependencies and potentially improving the overall quality of diagnosis. When incorporated into a model, they can provide a valuable enhancement to the subjective knowledge obtained from an expert. Bayesian networks have been employed in practice in a variety of fields, including engineering, science, and medicine (for examples of successful real world applications of Bayesian networks, see March 1995 special issue of the journal *Communications of the ACM*) with some models reaching the size of hundreds of variables.

Bayesian networks can be extremely valuable in medical diagnosis. A major advantage of Bayesian networks, compared to other modeling tools, is that they readily model simultaneous presence of multiple disorders. Many approaches, such as those based on classification methods, assume that in each diagnostic case only one disorder is possible, i.e., various disorders are mutually exclusive. This is often an unnecessarily restrictive assumption. It happens fairly often that a patient suffers from multiple disorders and a single disorder may not account for all observed symptoms. Worse even, a situation can arise that a single disorder offers a better explanation for all observations than any other single disorder, while the true diagnosis consists of, for example, two other disorders appearing simultaneously.

In this paper we focus on multiple-disorder diagnosis in the context of the HEPAR II system [6–8]. Our work on the HEPAR II system is continuation of the HEPAR project [1,10], conducted in the Institute of Biocybernetics and Biomedical Engineering of the Polish Academy of Sciences in collaboration with physicians at the Medical Center of Postgraduate Education in Warsaw. The HEPAR system was designed for gathering and processing of clinical data on patients with liver disorders and aimed at reducing the need for hepatic biopsy by modern computer-based diagnostic tools. An integral part of the HEPAR system is its database, created in 1990 and thoroughly maintained since then at the Gastroentorogical Clinic of the Institute of Food and Feeding in Warsaw. The current database contains over 800 patient records and its size is steadily growing. Each hepatological case is described by over 200 different medical findings, such as patient self-reported data, results of physical examination, laboratory tests, and finally a histopathologically verified diagnosis. One of the assumptions made in the database that was available to us is that every patient case is ultimately diagnosed with only one disorder. This assumption, while imposed on us by the data, is not necessary — in reality a patient can be suffering from multiple disorders at the same time and a diagnostic system should consider this possibility.

We describe an extension of our Bayesian network model that relaxes this assumption. We have modified the structure of the network using expert knowledge and subsequently learned the parameters of the new network from the database. While we had to make some assumptions about the data (please note that the data assumed mutual exclusivity of disorders), we show that the diagnostic performance of the modified model on the single-disorder diagnosis is better than that of the original model. The new model is more realistic and we expect that it will be of higher value in clinical practice.

The remainder of this paper is structured as follows. Section 2 summarizes the single-disorder version of the HEPAR II model. Section 3 describes the structural modifications that we performed on the model in order to be able to perform multiple-disorder diagnosis. Section 4 describes the details of learning of the conditional probability distributions of the enhanced model from the database and compares them in terms of their complexity and reliability. Section 5 compares the single-disorder and the multiple-disorder models in terms of their diagnostic accuracy. Finally, Section 6 discusses general issues related to the performed study and directions for further work.

2 The Single-Disorder Diagnosis Version of the HEPAR II Model

The HEPAR II project aims at applying decision-theoretic techniques to diagnosis of liver disorders. Its main component is a Bayesian network model involving a subset of variables included in the HEPAR database. The version of the database used in our project consists of 570 patient cases described by 119 medical findings and classified into 16 different classes (15 disorder classes and one class that represents the hepatologically normal state). One limitation of the data set that we have been using is that it assumes that all disorders are mutually exclusive, i.e., each diagnosed patient suffers from at most one disorder. This limitation led us to the original single-disorder diagnosis model. We selected from this database 94 variables that we judged to be the most important in diagnosis and built a causal Bayesian network. We elicited the structure of the model, i.e., dependencies among the variables, based on medical literature and conversations with our domain expert, a hepatologist Dr. Hanna Wasyluk (third author) and two American experts, a pathologist, Dr. Daniel Schwartz, and a specialist in infections diseases, Dr. John N. Dowling from the University of Pittsburgh. We estimate that elicitation of the structure took approximately 40 hours with the experts, of which roughly 30 hours were spent with Dr. Wasyluk and roughly 10 hours spent with Drs. Schwartz and Dowling. This includes model refinement sessions, where previously elicited structure was reevaluated in a group setting.

The numerical parameters of the model, i.e., the prior and conditional probability distributions, were extracted from the HEPAR database. Prior probability distributions are simply relative counts of various outcomes for each of the variables in question. Conditional probability distributions are relative counts of various outcomes in those data records that fulfill the conditions described by every combination of the outcomes of the predecessors. While prior probabilities can be learned reasonably accurately from a database of consisting of a few hundred records, conditional probabilities present more of a challenge. In cases where there are several variables directly preceding a variable in question, individual combinations of their values may be very unlikely to the point of being absent from the data file. In such cases, we made an arbitrary assumption that the distribution is uniform, i.e., the combination is completely uninformative. The restructuring effort described in this paper has as one of its long-term goals addressing this problem.

Given a patient's case, i.e., values of some of the modeled variables, such as symptoms or test results, the model derives the posterior probability distribution over the possible liver disorders. This probability distribution can be directly used in diagnostic decision support. We measured the performance of our model by how well it can predict the disorder in each of the available patient cases. To this effect, we applied the standard leave-one-out approach [5], i.e., using repeatedly all but one record in the database to learn the parameters and then using the remaining record to test the prediction. We were interested in both (1) whether the most probable diagnosis indicated by the model is indeed the correct diagnosis, and (2) whether the set of k most probable diagnoses contains the correct diagnosis for small values of k (we chose a "window" of $k=1$, 2, 3, and 4). Results were approximately 34%, 47%, 56%, and 67% for $k=1$, 2, 3, and 4 respectively. In other words, the most likely diagnosis indicated by the model was the correct diagnosis in 34% of the cases. The correct diagnosis was among the four most probable diagnoses as indicated by the model in 67% of the cases. Our experts considered this performance to be in the right ballpark given the inherent difficulty of the problem, small size of the data set, and many missing values. Please note that given 16 states of the disorder node, mean performance based on random guessing would barely exceed 6%. More details on the tests performed can be found in [8].

3 Structural Changes to the HEPAR II Model

We have identified several problems with the HEPAR II model. The first problem is that all disorders in the network were modeled as distinct states of one node. This is equivalent to the assumption of mutual exclusivity of disorders. As we mentioned in the previous section, this structure was implied by the data set available to us that had one final diagnosis for each of the patient cases. This assumption is not very realistic in medicine. Presence of a disorder often weakens a patient's immune system and as a result the patient may develop multiple disorders. Since one of the applications of our model is training novice diagnosticians, we would like to model the interactions between disorders and symptoms correctly.

The second problem is still suboptimal diagnostic performance of the HEPAR II network. We believe that the diagnostic performance of the model can be further improved by improving both the structure and the quality of the numerical parameters. Our long-term plans are to use parametric probability distributions, such as Noisy-OR gates [2,3,9], to enhance the quality of the conditional probability distributions learned from data. In order to be able to apply parametric probability distributions, we had to restructure the network in such a way that various nodes express either propositions or various grades of intensity of some quantity. The disorder node in the HEPAR II model is a categorical variable with 16 outcomes that is not suitable for a parametric probability distribution. One way of preparing the structure for these distributions is by breaking the disorder node into separate nodes for each of the disorders. This modification takes care of two problems: it relaxes the assumption of mutual exclusivity of disorders and it makes the nodes more amenable to parametric quantification.

We have concentrated the structural changes on the disorders. In our initial approach, we reduced the number of disorders modeled from 15 to 9. The six disorders excluded were either represented by very few records in the data base (*Acute hepatitis, Subacute hepatitis, HBV, Alcoholic cirrhosis*) or were later stages of other disorders (*Fibrosis hepatis, Carcinoma*). We plan to add the excluded disorders to our model in the future. The 9 modeled disorders were five binary nodes (*Toxic hepatitis, Reactive hepatitis, Steatosis, Hyperbilirubinemia, PBC*) and two nodes with three outcomes each (*Chronic hepatits, Cirrhosis*). The nodes that we originally modeled as causes/effects of the liver disorder variable were broken down into several groups, specific to each of the 9 disorders. In order to be able to compare the performance of the single-disorder to the multiple-disorder versions of the model, we created a single-disorder version of the original HEPAR II model consisting of the same 9 disorders and precisely the same feature variables as the newly developed multiple-disorder model. As a result, we worked with 66 features and 505 records (65 records of the 570 available to us belonged to the omitted disorder classes) in the database. The resulting models consisted of 67 nodes (66 feature nodes and one disorder node in the single-disorder model) and 73 nodes (66 feature nodes and 7 disorder nodes in the multiple-disorder model) respectively.

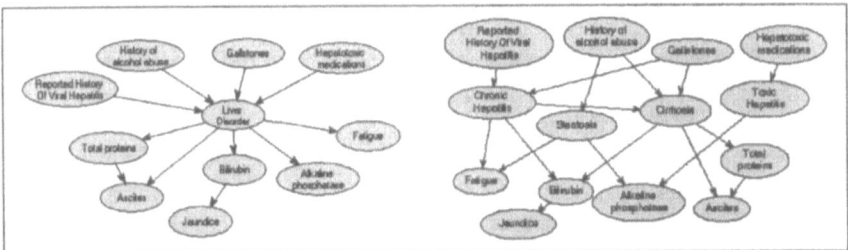

Fig. 1. A simplified fragment of the HEPAR II network: single-disorder diagnosis (left) and multiple-disorder diagnosis (right) version

Fig. 1 shows a simplified fragment of both models and gives an idea of the structural changes performed in the transition from the single-disorder to the multiple-disorder versions of the model. In particular, the models share each of the four risk factors (*Reported history of viral hepatitis, History of alcohol abuse, Gallstones,* and *Hepatotoxic medications*) and six symptoms and test results (*Fatigue, Jaundice, Bilirubin, Alkaline phosphatase, Ascites* and *Total proteins*). The single *Liver disorder* node is replaced by four disorder nodes (*Chronic hepatitis, Steatosis, Cirrhosis* and *Toxic hepatitis*). The main difference between the models is that some of the four new disorder nodes are not connected with the risk factors and symptoms. This leads to a significant reduction in the number of numerical parameters necessary to quantify the network.

4 Parameters of the HEPAR II Model

In order to compare the single-disorder to the multiple-disorder versions of the model, we used the same data to extract the numerical parameters (i.e., still each patient was described by only one disorder). The data set contained 505 patient records classified in 9 different disorder classes. A side-effect of our structural changes is that they have decreased the number of numerical parameters in the model. We have mentioned in Section 2 that it is quite common in learning the conditional probability distributions from data that there are too few records corresponding to a given combination of parents of a node. Breaking the original disorder node into several nodes representing individual disorders decreases the size of conditional probability tables and, hence, increases the average number of records for each combination of parents in a conditional probability distribution table. Indeed, the multiple-disorder version of the model required only 1,488 parameters (we counted $\mu = 87.8$ data records per conditional probability distribution) compared to the 3,714 ($\mu = 16.8$ data records per conditional probability distribution) parameters needed for the single-disorder version of the model. With an increase in the average number of records per conditional probability distribution, the quality of the model parameters improves.

Fig. 2 shows the distribution over the number of data records per parent combination for the single-disorder and the multiple-disorder models. We can see that over 50% of the conditional probability distributions in the single-disorder model contained zero records. In the multiple-disorder model this number is dramatically smaller — only 0.5% of all cases involved zero records and there is quite a high proportion of conditional probability distributions for which tens of records were available.

The fact that we used a data set in which each patient record had a single-disorder diagnosis placed us before a difficulty in assessing conditional probabilities of nodes that had several disorder nodes as parents — there were no records in the database for conditions involving combinations of various disorders. We applied a simple solution, in which we included in the calculation all records that described the disorders present in the condition. For example (see Fig. 1), when computing the conditional probability distribu-

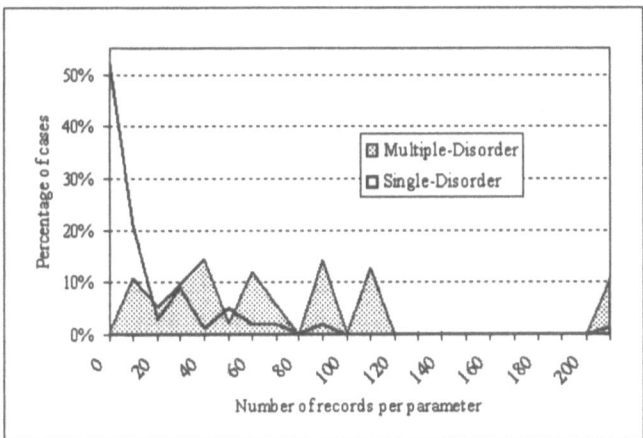

Fig. 2. Distribution over the number of data records per parent combination for the single-disorder and the multiple-disorder models

tion of node *Fatigue* given presence of both *Chronic hepatitis* and *Steatosis*, we used both: records that were diagnosed as *Chronic hepatitis* and records that were diagnosed as *Steatosis*. This amounted to averaging the effect of various disorders. We also tried taking the maximum effect of all disorders present in the condition with a very modest improvement in performance. Another limitation of the HEPAR data that has a serious implication on our work is that mutual exclusivity of disorders did not allow us to extract dependencies among disorders. Hepatology often deals with disorders that are consequences of the previous disorders, e.g., a chronic liver disorder implies *Fibrosis hepatis* which can further cause *Cirrhosis*. In the future we plan to model and quantify these dependencies by combining data with expert judgment.

5   Diagnostic Accuracy of the Multiple-Disorder Model

Our first empirical test focused on the overall performance of the model in terms of classification accuracy (each of the disorders was viewed as a separate class that the program predicted based on the values of all the other variables). This test is very conservative towards the multiple-disorder model, as this is the task for which the single-disorder version of the model was designed. We applied again the leave-one-out approach. Essentially, given $n=505$ data records, we used $n-1$ of them for learning model parameters and the remaining one record to test the model. This procedure was repeated n times, each time with a different data record.

One of the assumptions that we used in learning the model parameters was that missing values for discrete finding variables corresponded to state *absent* (e.g., a missing value for *Jaundice* was interpreted as *absent*). In case of continuous variables, a missing value corresponded to a normal value, elicited from the expert (e.g., a missing value for *Bilirubin* was interpreted as being in the range of 0–5), which included the typical value for a healthy patient. In our tests, we used as observations only those findings that have actually been reported in the data (i.e., we did not use the values that were missing, even though we used their assumed values in learning). Similarly to the tests performed on the original HEPAR II model, we used window sizes of $k=1$, 2, 3, and 4. Results (pictured graphically in Fig. 3) were for the multiple-disorder version of the model approximately 44% (compared to 42% for the single-disorder version), 59% (57%), 68% (68%), and 77% (78%) for $k=1$, 2, 3, and 4 respectively. In other words, the most likely diagnosis indicated by the model was the correct diagnosis in 44% of the cases. The correct diagnosis was among the four most probable diagnoses as indicated by the model in 77% of the cases. The performance of both versions of the model was very similar, with the multiple-disorder version being slightly more accurate. Please note that the diagnostic accuracy of the single-disorder model in our test is significantly higher than the accuracy reported for the original Hepar II model. This is an effect of the fact that the new version of the model had fewer disorders and most disorders considered were well represented in the database.

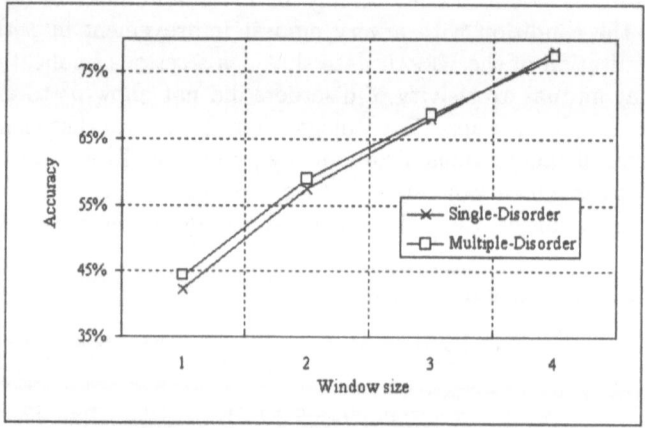

Fig. 3. Diagnostic accuracy of the single-disorder and the multiple-disorder models

Performance for each of the 9 disorders individually is pictured graphically in Fig. 4. We can see that in case of some of the disorders, the multiple-disorder version of the model performed significantly better than the single-disorder version. In order to gain some insight into when multiple-disorder version of the model is better, we focused our second test on the relationship between the number of records in the database for each class and the diagnostic accuracy within that class.

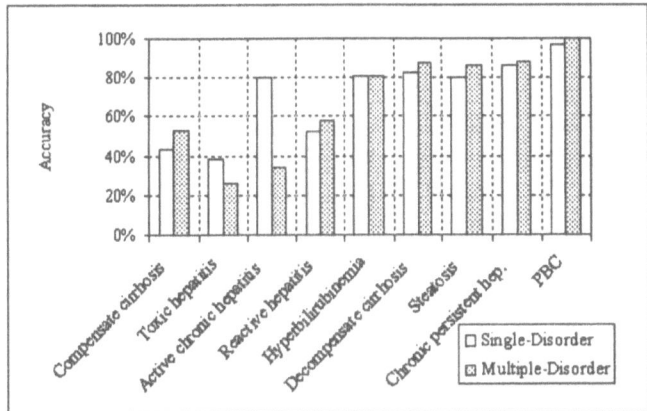

Fig. 4. Diagnostic accuracy per disorder of the single-disorder and the multiple-disorder models

Fig. 5 shows the relationship between the number of records for a particular disorder and the system accuracy in diagnosing this disorder for windows of size 1 (i.e., the most likely disorder) and 4 (the true diagnosis is among the four most likely diagnoses). It is clear that accuracy increases significantly with the number of data records. Disorders with more than 50 records present in the database showed quite high diagnostic accuracy. Another interesting result is that the multiple-disorder model performed often better than the single-disorder model for those disorders that have many records. This promises a higher diagnostic value of our approach when the available data set is sufficiently large, i.e., when the quality of parameters is high.

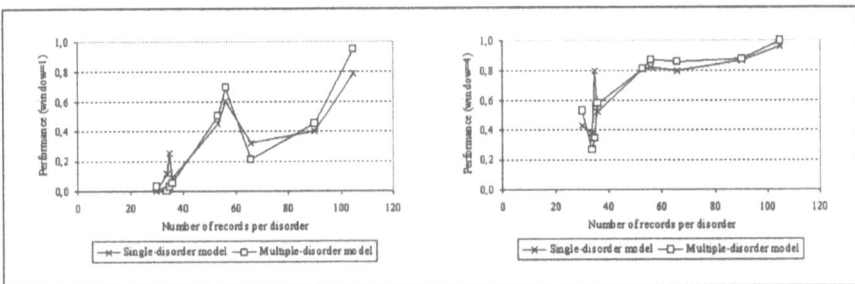

Fig. 5. Diagnostic accuracy as a function of the number of disorder cases in the database (class size) of the single-disorder and the multiple-disorder models for the one-disorder (left) and four-disorder (right) window cases

6 Discussion

The exercise that we went through shows that Bayesian network models readily accommodate multiple-disorder diagnoses. It was relatively easy to derive the multiple-disorder version of the model from the existing single-disorder version. We estimate that the total time spent with the expert was less than 10 hours. Of course, some of the reduction in time, compared to the original model, can be explained by our increased modeling proficiency.

While the performance of the multiple-disorder diagnosis version of the model is only slightly better than the single-disorder diagnosis version, we should keep in mind that the two models were compared on a task for which the latter is specialized. Furthermore, the data that we learned our parameters from were single-disorder data.

We believe that pure diagnostic performance, in terms of the percentage of correct diagnoses, is in itself not an adequate measure of quality of a medical decision support system. In the domain of medicine, the physician user carries the ultimate responsibility for the patient and he or she will be unwilling to accept a system's advice without understanding it. The effort described in this paper is a further step towards making our model mimic the causal structure of the domain. While a causal model may perform worse in numerical terms than a regression-based model (if it does at all; this remains an empirical question), it offers three important advantages: (1) its intuitive and meaningful graphical structure can be examined by the user, (2) the system can automatically generate explanations of its advice that will follow the model structure and will be reasonably understandable, and (3) the model can be enhanced with expert opinion; interactions absent from the database can be added based on knowledge of local causal interactions with the existing parts and can be parameterized by expert judgment.

Our future work includes expert verification of the probability distributions of those nodes that have several disorder nodes as parents. As we mentioned above, these parameters cannot be learned from our data and the arbitrary assumptions that we made in the learning process may have had a negative effect on diagnostic performance of the system. At a later stage, we plan to replace most of the interactions by parametric probability distributions, such as Noisy-OR gates. We expect that this will increase the model performance even further. We also plan to elaborate on the disorder-to-disorder dependencies. This information is lacking from the database, so here again we will have to rely on expert judgment.

Acknowledgments

This research was supported by the Air Force Office of Scientific Research, grants F49620–97–1–0225 and F49620–00–1–0112, by the National Science Foundation under Faculty Early Career Development (CAREER) Program, grant IRI–9624629, by the Polish Committee for Scientific Research, grant 8T11E02917, by the Medical Centre of Postgraduate Education of Poland grant 501-2-1-02-18/00, and by the Institute of Biocybernetics and Biomedical Engineering Polish Academy of Sciences, grant 16/ST/2000. The HEPAR II model was created and tested using SMILE, an inference engine, and GeNIe, a development environment for reasoning in graphical probabilistic models, both developed at the Decision Systems Laboratory and available at http://www2.sis.pitt.edu/~genie.

References

1. Bobrowski, L. (1992): HEPAR: Computer system for diagnosis support and data analysis. Prace IBIB 31, Institute of Biocybernetics and Biomedical Engineering, Polish Academy of Sciences, Warsaw, Poland
2. Diez, F. J. (1993): Parameter adjustment in Bayes networks. The generalized Noisy-OR gate. In: Proceedings of the 9th Annual Conference on Uncertainty in Artificial Intelligence (UAI–93), Washington, D.C., 99–105
3. Henrion, M. (1989): Some practical issues in constructing belief networks. In: Kanal, L. N., Levitt, T. S., Lemmer J. F., editors, Uncertainty in Artificial Intelligence 3, Elsevier Science Publishers B.V., North Holland, 161–173
4. Howard, R. A., Matheson, J. E. (1984): Influence diagrams. In: Howard, R. A., Matheson, J. E., editors, The Principles and Applications of Decision Analysis, Strategic Decisions Group, Menlo Park, CA, 719–762
5. Moore A. W., Lee M. S. (1994): Efficient algorithms for minimizing cross validation error. In: Proceedings of the 11th International Conference on Machine Learning, Morgan Kaufmann, San Francisco
6. Onisko, A., Druzdzel, M. J., Wasyluk H. (1997): Application of Bayesian belief networks to diagnosis of liver disorders. In: Proceedings of the 3rd Conference on Neural Networks and Their Applications, Kule, Poland, 730–736
7. Onisko, A., Druzdzel, M. J., Wasyluk H. (1998): A probabilistic causal model for diagnosis of liver disorders. In: Proceedings of the 7th International Symposium on Intelligent Information Systems (IIS–98), Malbork, Poland, 379–387
8. Onisko, A., Druzdzel, M. J., Wasyluk H. (1999): A Bayesian network model for diagnosis of liver disorders. In: Proceedings of the 11th Conference on Biocybernetics and Biomedical Engineering, volume 2, Warszawa, Poland, 842–846
9. Pearl J. (1988): Probabilistic Reasoning in Intelligent Systems: Networks of Plausible Inference. Morgan Kaufmann Publishers, Inc., San Mateo, CA
10. Wasyluk, H. (1995): The four year's experience with HEPAR-computer assisted diagnostic program. In: Proceedings of the 8th World Congress on Medical Informatics (MEDINFO–95), Vancouver, BC, Canada, 1033–1034

Evaluation of Bank Transactions Correctness with Method of 2-Dimensional Projection of High-Dimensional Fuzzy Membership Functions

Marcin Pluciński, Andrzej Piegat

Faculty of Computer Science and Infornation Systems, Technical University of Szczecin, Żołnierska 49, Pl-71210 Szczecin, tel.(+4891) 48 764 85, e-mail: Marcin.Plucinski@wi.tuniv.szczecin.pl , Andrzej.Piegat@wi.tuniv.szczecin.pl

Abstract. Larger and larger part of bank transactions is realized by means of telecommunication (Home Banking). Particular transactions ordered this way can and should be checked by the bank to reveal shady and dubious ones, which will be further on called incorrect transactions. Correctness of transactions is a fuzzy notion. It can be evaluated by an intelligent fuzzy system learned with hitherto realized transactions of the bank. Such system has to extract the bank experience and convert it into appropriately shaped and parameterized high-dimensional membership functions of diversified correctness classes. Learning of the system for transaction evaluation is based on features of transactions made hitherto by the bank contractors. The paper describes transaction features and a special method of a high-dimensional fuzzy clustering which yields a good solution of a very difficult classification task.

Keywords: safety of bank transactions, fuzzy classification, high-dimensional clustering.

1 Introduction

Particular bank contractors have their customs and habits, which can be referred to as features of transactions ordered by them to the bank. Knowledge of these features enables probability evaluation of how the transactions are correct or not.

Feature 1 – transaction sum

The bank cooperates with a certain number of contractors. Every now and again they order transactions of different height. But usually transactions sums ordered by a particular contractor C_i vary within certain limits depending on how big is the contractor firm. If the ordered transaction sum goes outside these limits, then the probability of the transaction being shady (incorrect) increases and it is to be checked.

Feature 2 – contractor number

Feature 3 – transaction hour

Particular contractors order their transactions usually in special hours of day resulting from the work organization in their firms or works. Therefore other hours can be treated as more or less incorrect (dubious).

Feature 4 – authorizing person

In each firm only limited number of persons are allowed to authorize transactions, e.g. manager, deputy manager, main bookkeeper, etc. Also sometimes the highest transactions may be allowed to be authorized only by e.g. one person as the manager. The persons validated to authorization can be numbered 1,2,3,4 etc.

Feature 5 – transaction day

Particular bank contractors order their transactions usually on a special weekday, e.g. Tuesday. Other weekdays may be treated as incorrect (dubious).

Feature 6 – holiday

Certain contractors order sometimes transactions on holidays as Saturdays or Sundays. Other contractors don't. Therefore a holiday transaction may be in their case treated as unusual and at least partially incorrect.

The bank practice has revealed existence of distinct specific habits (features) of transactions ordered by particular firms. Features of incorrect (shady) transactions ordered by a given contractor can be determined from data of the hitherto transactions ordered by the contractor (transactions history). Exemplary features of such transactions are given in Table 1.

Table 1. Exemplary features data of transactions ordered to the bank by contractors

No.	Transaction sum	Contractor number	Transaction hour	Authoriz. person no.	Week day	Holiday	Trans. correctness
1	480	2	10	2	1	0	100%
⋮	⋮	⋮	⋮	⋮	⋮	⋮	⋮
14	3500	10	13	1	2	0	75%
⋮	⋮	⋮	⋮	⋮	⋮	⋮	⋮
75	5000	20	23	5	6	1	0%
⋮	⋮	⋮	⋮	⋮	⋮	⋮	⋮
100	3000	2	15	2	6	1	50%
⋮	⋮	⋮	⋮	⋮	⋮	⋮	⋮
106	1000	2	18	5	6	1	25%
⋮	⋮	⋮	⋮	⋮	⋮	⋮	⋮

The last column of Table 1 includes the evaluation of the transaction correctness [%] made by the bank expert. Particular values of the correctness have meaning as follows.

100 % – correct transaction – no checking,

75 % – slightly incorrect transaction – this fact is recorded into the bank computer memory. At next connection with the contractor he will be inform about it.

50 % – on an average incorrect transaction – the bank realizes it only after a second validated person of the contractor-firm has authorized it.

25 % – very incorrect (shady) transaction – the bank contacts the contractor by phone to get a direct transaction confirmation.

0 % – fully incorrect (false) transaction (e.g. authorized by a not validated person). The bank inform the contractor about the transaction incorrectness. After the transaction has been checked and corrected by the contractor, it is realized.

The problem of the transaction correctness evaluation can be shown in the black box form as depicted on Fig. 1.

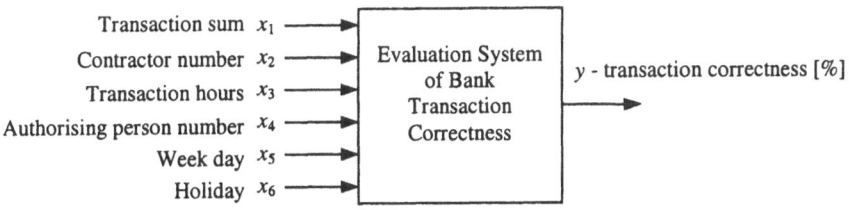

Fig. 1. Inputs and output of the evaluation system of the bank transaction correctness

To determine the evaluation of the transactions correctness the method of 2-dimensional projection of high dimensional fuzzy membership functions elaborated by A. Piegat has been applied.

2 Method of 2-Dimensional Projection of High-Dimensional Fuzzy Membership Functions

Learning samples (e.g. points determining features of the bank contractors) create in the feature space $X_1 \times X_2 \times, \ldots, \times X_n$ a cluster of a given class, e.g. of the 100% – correct bank transactions. An example is shown in Fig. 2.

The 2-dimensional projection method bases on assumption that, if a certain sample belongs to the cluster of the given class in the n-dimensional space, then its projection belongs also to the cluster projection on each of 2-dimensional component subspaces $X_i \times X_j$, $i,j \leq n$. Therefore to determine the n-dimensional

318

membership function $\mu_i(x_1, x_2, \ldots, x_n)$ of the given class i, membership functions of the cluster projections on particular subspaces have to be determined (1):

$$\mu_i(x_1, x_2), \quad \mu_i(x_1, x_3), \quad \ldots, \mu_i(x_2, x_n), \quad \ldots, \mu_i(x_{n-1}, x_n), \quad (1)$$

and next, applying one of the union operators of fuzzy sets (t-norms), e.g. PROD [3] the n-dimensional membership function (2) is found.

$$\mu_i(x_1, x_2, \ldots, x_n) = \mu_i(x_1, x_2) \cdot \mu_i(x_1, x_3) \cdot \ldots \cdot \mu_i(x_2, x_n) \cdot \ldots \cdot \mu_i(x_{n-1}, x_n) \quad (2)$$

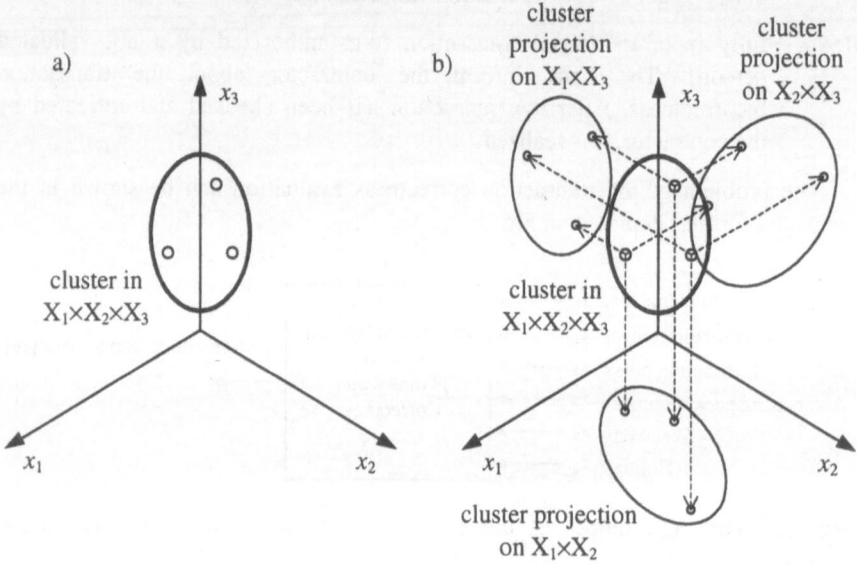

Fig. 2. Cluster of learning samples of the given class (a) and its projection on 2-dimensional subspaces (b)

Because clusters shapes and their orientations can be very different in each subspace employment of regular, symmetrical membership functions which are characteristic for e.g. commonly used c-means clustering method [1] decreases modeling effectiveness. Therefor the authors have used as cluster membership functions generalized, non-symmetric and rotary Gaussian functions expressed by (3).

$$x_i^* = (x_i - m_i)\cos\alpha_{ij} + (x_j - m_j)\sin\alpha_{ij}, \quad x_j^* = -(x_i - m_i)\sin\alpha_{ij} + (x_j - m_j)\cos\alpha_{ij}$$

$$\mu(x_i^*, x_j^*) = \exp\left[-\left|\frac{x_i^*}{v_{ij} \cdot c_{i1} + (1 - v_{ij}) \cdot c_{i2}}\right|^{l_{ij1}} - \left|\frac{x_j^*}{w_{ij} \cdot c_{i1} + (1 - w_{ij}) \cdot c_{i2}}\right|^{l_{ij2}}\right] \quad (3)$$

where:

m_i – center coordinate of the Gaussian function respectively to the x_i axis,

m_j – center coordinate of the Gaussian function respectively to the x_j axis,

α_i – angle of the main axis of a cut of the Gaussian function, see Fig. 4,

l_i, l_j – exponents,

v_{ij}, w_{ij} – logical variables (0 or 1) activating different widths $c_{i1}, c_{i2}, c_{j1}, c_{j2}$ of the non-symmetric Gaussian function, see Fig. 4,

c_{i1}, c_{i2} – different widths of the non-symmetric Gaussian function.

Fig.3 depicts a 3-dimensional Gaussian membership function. The 3-dimensional membership function can be shown on 2-dimensional inputs-plane with use of cuts (contour lines) made at different heights, Fig. 4.

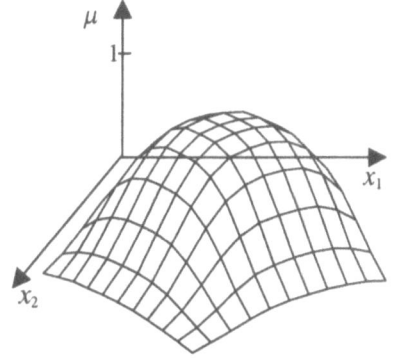

Fig. 3. 3-dimensional Gaussian membership function

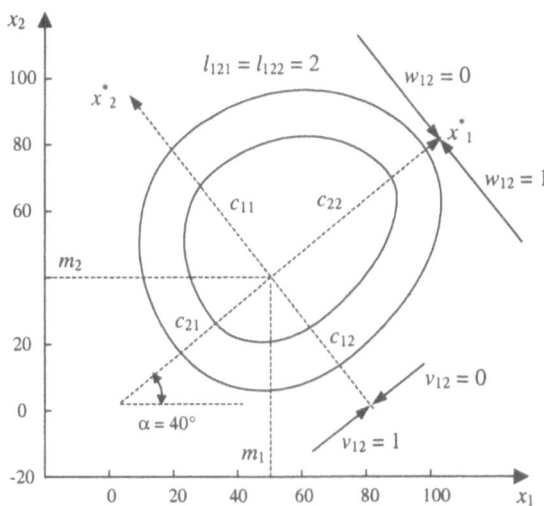

Fig. 4. Cuts (contour lines) of the generalized, non-symmetric Gaussian function projected on subspace $X_i \times X_j$, for $i = 1, j = 2$

Variation of parameters m_i, m_j causes the Gaussian function to move along axes, variation of ∞_i causes rotation of the function, parameters c_{i1}, c_{i2} change non-symmetrically the function width, and l_{ij1}, l_{ij2} its shape. Owing to these parameters features the Gaussian function can be visually moved in neighborhood of the measurement samples center of the given class and next rotated and shaped to encircle all or most samples of the class, Fig. 5.

In the sequel an application of the 2-dimensional projection method to evaluation of the bank transactions correctness will be presented.

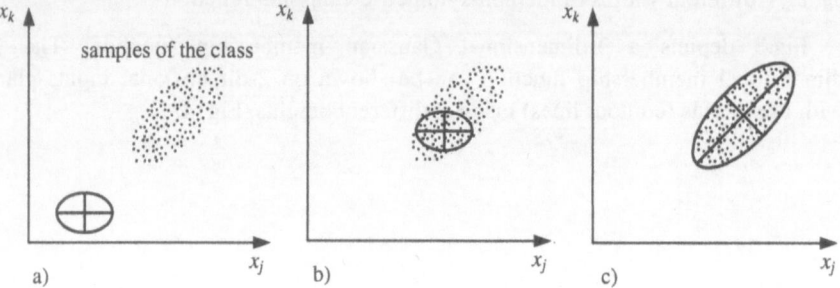

Fig. 5. Start position of the membership function tuned (a), putting the function center over the samples center (b), rotating and adjusting the function to the samples distribution

3   Evaluation of the Bank Transaction Correctness with the 2-Dimensional Projection Method

The authors had at disposal 128 learning samples presenting history of transactions ordered to the bank by 10 contractors. Exemplary data of the transactions are given in Table 1. Fig. 6, 7 and 8 show projections of the 7-dimensional transaction samples on particular subspaces $X_i \times X_j$, $i,j = 1 \div 6$.

Only analysis of the sample projections on 2-dimensional subspaces shows how much the samples representing particular classes are mixed. Certain samples of different classes often lie one over another and cover themselves accurately. For this reason membership functions of particular classes also more or less (sometimes very strong) overlap themselves. It is particularly visible on Fig. 8 for the subspace $X_5 \times X_6$. Covering of different classes means increased difficulty in distinction of these classes because of their great similarity in this subspace. However, in the 2-dimensional projection method special generalized, rotary and non-symmetric Gaussian function have been used. Thanks to their different orientations, shapes, widths and lengths in projection on many subspaces distinction of very similar classes becomes possible after we create one full-dimensional classes membership functions as fuzzy-logical union of component membership functions determined in 2-dimensional subspaces. And so membership function of the 75% – transaction correctness class is constructed as follows:

$$\mu_{75\%}\left(x_1,x_2,x_3,x_4,x_5,x_6\right) = \begin{aligned}&\mu_{75\%}\left(x_1,x_2\right)\cdot\mu_{75\%}\left(x_1,x_3\right)\cdot\mu_{75\%}\left(x_2,x_3\right)\cdot\\&\mu_{75\%}\left(x_4,x_5\right)\cdot\mu_{75\%}\left(x_4,x_6\right)\cdot\mu_{75\%}\left(x_5,x_6\right)\end{aligned} \quad (4)$$

where particular 2-input membership functions of this class are given by formulae (5÷10).

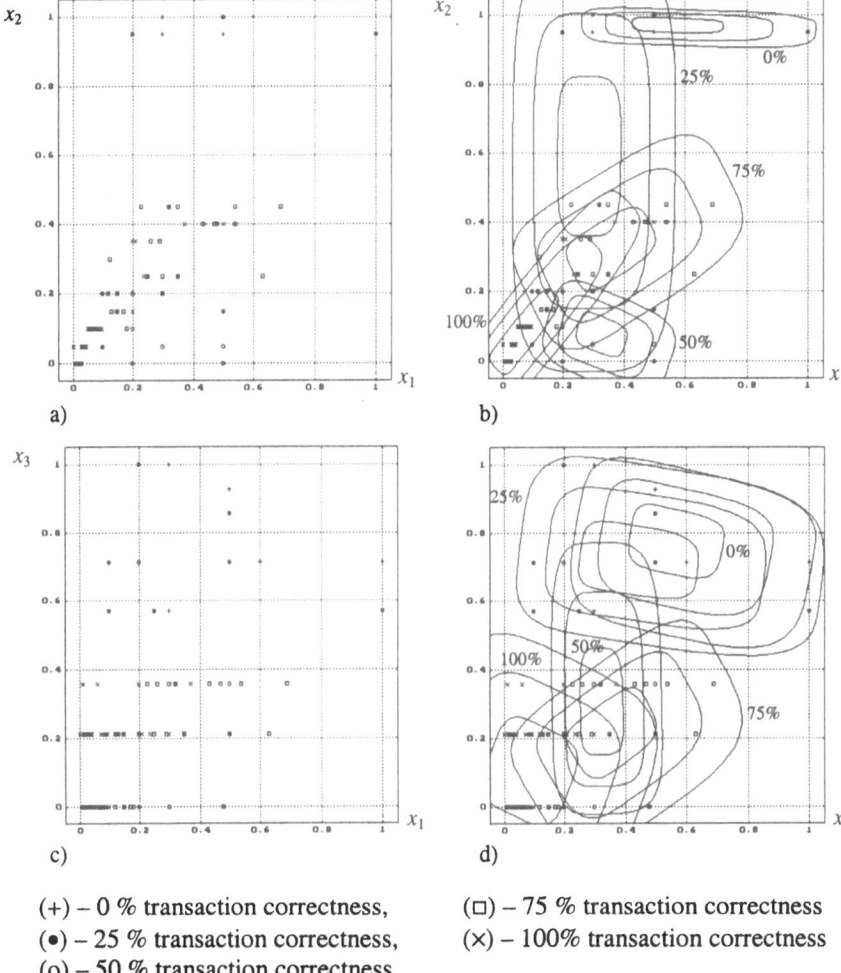

(+) – 0 % transaction correctness,   (□) – 75 % transaction correctness
(•) – 25 % transaction correctness,   (×) – 100% transaction correctness
(o) – 50 % transaction correctness,

Fig. 6. Projections of 7-dimensional measurement samples of the transaction features on particular subspaces (a,b,c,d) and cuts of membership functions of particular classes made at heights 0.9, 0.3, 0.01

$$x_1^* = (x_1 - 0.322)\cos 28.98 + (x_2 - 0.309)\sin 28.98, \quad x_2^* = -(x_1 - 0.322)\sin 28.98 + (x_2 - 0.309)\cos 28.98$$

$$\mu_{75\%}\left(x_1^*, x_2^*\right) = \exp\left[-\left|\frac{x_1^*}{v_{12} \cdot 0.184 + (1 - v_{12}) \cdot 0.322}\right|^4 - \left|\frac{x_2^*}{w_{12} \cdot 0.150 + (1 - w_{12}) \cdot 0.139}\right|^4\right] \tag{5}$$

$$x_1^* = (x_1 - 0.322)\cos 36.65 + (x_3 - 0.224)\sin 36.65, \quad x_3^* = -(x_1 - 0.322)\sin 36.65 + (x_3 - 0.224)\cos 36.65$$

$$\mu_{75\%}\left(x_1^*, x_3^*\right) = \exp\left[-\left|\frac{x_1^*}{v_{13} \cdot 0.206 + (1 - v_{13}) \cdot 0.236}\right|^4 - \left|\frac{x_3^*}{w_{13} \cdot 0.210 + (1 - w_{13}) \cdot 0.115}\right|^4\right] \tag{6}$$

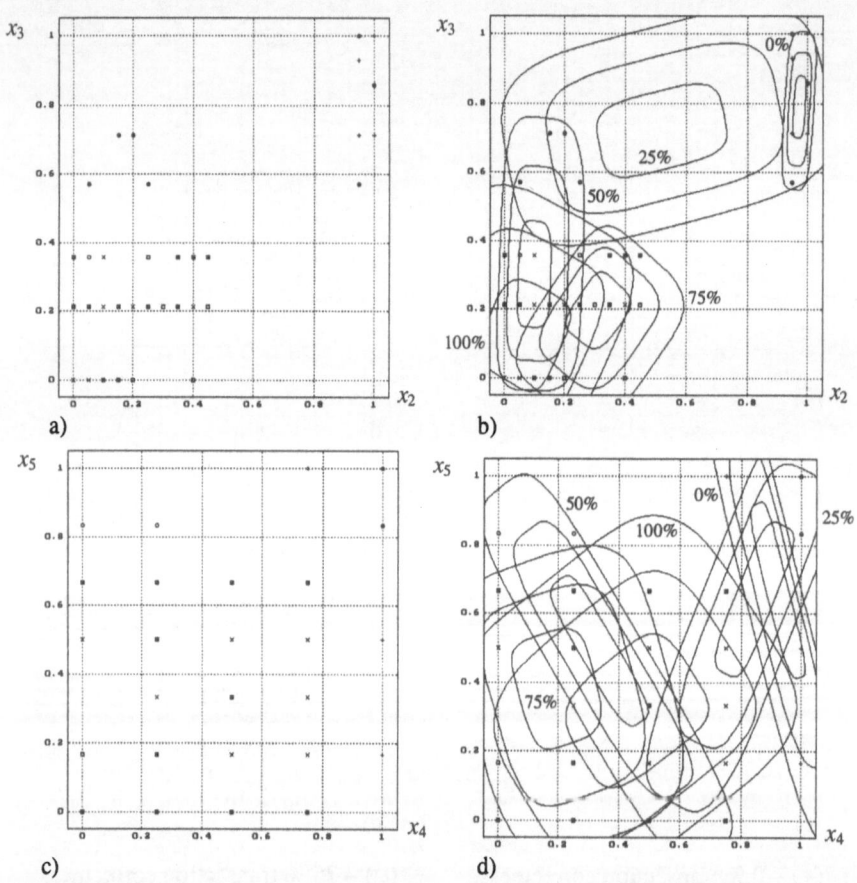

Fig. 7. Projections of 7-dimensional measurement samples of the transaction features on particular subspaces (a,b,c,d) and cuts of membership functions of particular classes made at heights 0.9, 0.3, 0.01

$$x_2^* = (x_2 - 0.309)\cos(-37.59) + (x_3 - 0.224)\sin(-37.59), \quad x_3^* = -(x_2 - 0.309)\sin(-37.59) + (x_3 - 0.224)\cos(-37.59)$$

$$\mu_{75\%}(x_2^*, x_3^*) = \exp\left[-\left|\frac{x_2^*}{v_{23} \cdot 0.099 + (1 - v_{23}) \cdot 0.176}\right|^4 - \left|\frac{x_3^*}{w_{23} \cdot 0.224 + (1 - w_{23}) \cdot 0.144}\right|^4\right] \tag{7}$$

$$x_4^* = (x_4 - 0.170)\cos 17.61 + (x_5 - 0.402)\sin 17.61, \quad x_5^* = -(x_4 - 0.170)\sin 17.61 + (x_5 - 0.402)\cos 17.61$$

$$\mu_{75\%}(x_4^*, x_5^*) = \exp\left[-\left|\frac{x_4^*}{v_{45} \cdot 0.190 + (1 - v_{45}) \cdot 0.259}\right|^4 - \left|\frac{x_5^*}{w_{45} \cdot 0.335 + (1 - w_{45}) \cdot 0.234}\right|^4\right] \tag{8}$$

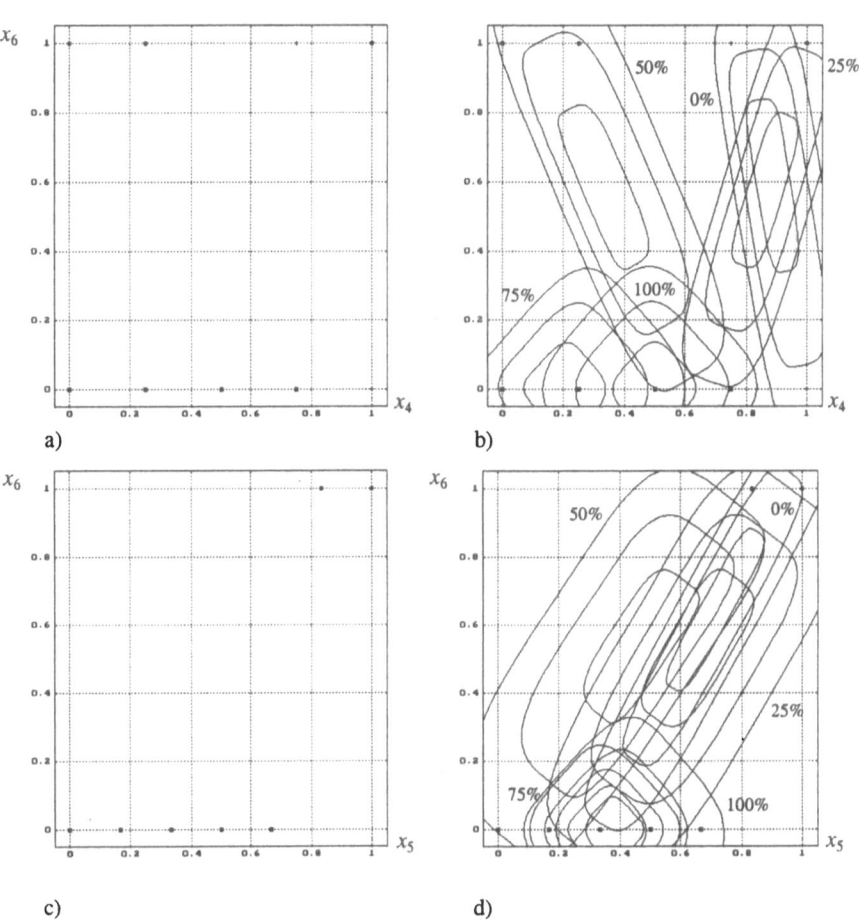

Fig. 8. Projections of 7-dimensional measurement samples of the transaction features on particular subspaces (a,b,c,d) and cuts of membership functions of particular classes made at heights 0.9, 0.3, 0.01

$$x_4^* = (x_4 - 0.170)\cos(-45) + (x_6)\sin(-45), \quad x_6^* = -(x_4 - 0.152)\sin(-45) + (x_6)\cos(-45)$$

$$\mu_{75\%}\left(x_4^*, x_6^*\right) = \exp\left[-\left|\frac{x_4^*}{v_{46} \cdot 0.152 + (1 - v_{46}) \cdot 0.246}\right|^4 - \left|\frac{x_6^*}{w_{46} \cdot 0.142 + (1 - w_{46}) \cdot 0.246}\right|^4\right] \tag{9}$$

$$x_5^* = (x_5 - 0.402)\cos(-45) + (x_6)\sin(-45), \quad x_6^* = -(x_5 - 0.402)\sin(-45) + (x_6)\cos(-45)$$

$$\mu_{75\%}\left(x_5^*, x_6^*\right) = \exp\left[-\left|\frac{x_5^*}{v_{56} \cdot 0.170 + (1 - v_{56}) \cdot 0.112}\right|^4 - \left|\frac{x_6^*}{w_{56} \cdot 0.170 + (1 - w_{56}) \cdot 0.112}\right|^4\right] \tag{10}$$

Results of the experiment carried out have shown that the average percent evaluation difference between the bank expert and the 2-dimensional projection method equals 3.32% only. The method evaluated 17 of the total 128 differently than the expert. However its error was equal only 0.25 % each time and was the smallest evaluation error possible. The method hasn't made big errors e.g. 75% or 100% ones. Therefore its accuracy may be considered as very good, because the expert himself couldn't evaluate the particular transactions precisely and without errors.

4 Conclusions

The presented method of 2-dimensional projection of high-dimensional membership functions, owing to visualization of the tuning process of the functions and employment of generalized, rotary and non-symmetric Gaussian functions enables obtainment of high classification precision. Confirmation of this are results of the method application to a very difficult task of bank transanction correctness evaluation where learning samples of particular classes are strongly mixed (big similarity of classes).

References

[1] Bezdek J.C., Ehrlich R., Full W. (1984) FCM: the fuzzy c-means clustering algorithm. Computer and Geosciences, No. 10, pp. 191–203

[2] Kocan M. (1999) Nowoczesne technologie zabiezpieczeń w systemach Home Banking (New safety technologies in Home Banking systems). Diploma thesis on Faculty of Computer Science and Information Systems, Technical University of Szczecin

[3] Piegat A. (1999) Modelowanie i Sterowanie Rozmyte (Fuzzy Modeling and Control), Akademicka Oficyna Wydawnicza EXIT, Warsaw, Poland

Consensus-Based Methods for Restoring Consistency of Replicated Data

Czesław Daniłowicz, Ngoc Thanh Nguyen

Wrocław University of Technology, Department of Information Systems
Wybrzeże S. Wyspiańskiego 27, 50-370 Wrocław, Poland
{danilowicz, thanh}@zsi.pwr.wroc.pl

Abstract. In this paper a consensus model for restoring consistency of replicated data is presented. It is assumed that after some time of functioning of a
distributed system, versions of replicated data stored in different servers may
differ from each other, and the only basis for recreating the proper data version
is the set of these versions. The authors propose to determine the consensus of
data versions and take it as the proper version. In this work the consensus structure as a metric space, consensus choice and its analysis, and algorithms for determining most often used consensus functions are presented.

Key words: consensus methods, data consistency, data replication

1 Introduction

Computer networks and distributed information systems (DISs) enable us to obtain conformity of information systems to the organisation and location of departments of enterprises in which these systems work. It concerns not only big companies, which function in several countries or towns, but also smaller institutions,
which occupy only several buildings in a town. As an example let us take a clinic
or hospital which is serviced by a DIS in the way that each ward and laboratory
have access to its own server and a local database. Depending on the specificity of
a unit, in its database may be stored not only unique data which are not used by
others units, but also replicated data which are also used by other units.

Unique and replicated data are usually combined into structures suitable for a
given unit. Thank to this concept it is possible to decrease the number of data
transmission and limit the initial data processing. As a result, an access to data is
faster than in the case when they are stored in one server only [28]. Apart from it,
replication increases data safety because the larger is the number of replications
the smaller is the probability of data loss as the consequence of server damage or
viruses.

The positive effects of data replication are obtained when the database management system (DBMS) ensures data consistency, that is their identity on every
server at any moment of time. Among others, so-called *replication protocol con-*
trol methods serve for this purpose. We distinguish *optimistic* and *pessimistic*
protocols. Optimistic protocols allow a temporary data inconsistency during actu-

alisation. Elimination of the inconsistency takes place when the data management system obtains access to these servers which were inaccessible before. And the pessimistic protocols protect against data inconsistency by locking inconsistent data till actualisation is accomplished on all concerned servers [30]. Another methods for avoiding data inconsistency are presented in work [9], in which the authors assume storing copies of replicated data in all servers.

However, neither replication protocol control methods nor two-phase transaction committing [6,7] ensure data consistency of replicated data. We cannot take as impossible a wrong decision of a DBMS, transmission errors or a fault of the server on which we edit data. In addition, external factors, like unauthorised access or viruses, can change or damage some data what would also lead to inconsistency.

When detected, inconsistency of replicated data should be of course eliminated. Sometimes we can do it by referring to the original data source, that is re-enter and re-replicate data from traditional documents. Nevertheless, in practice it is not always possible: in some cases it is too expensive, in others too time-consuming. Especially in case when replicated data are used by real-time processing systems, re-entering data cannot be used to resolve the problem of data inconsistency. It also happens that we cannot use the original data source at all. It concerns observations and experiments, which cannot be repeated in the same conditions, for example medical examinations, meteorological or hydrological measurements, traffic analysis, etc.

So if we cannot restore the data consistency on the basis of original data and we cannot admit data loss, everything what we can do is to analyse these inconsistent data that we have. Knowing the meaning of the data we can develop and apply some semantic-based methods of restoring data consistency. For example, we could restore text data by means of some software using linguistic analysis. We could also try to correct some date on the basis of logical analysis of other dates which are related.

Unfortunately, these methods are not general enough to propose them for restoring of consistency of replicated data. Modifications and errors can occur at different times and in different data areas on different servers. So, it can concern data, interpretation of which is not possible without thorough analysis.

Taking this it into account, we assume in this work that data are binary sequences of unknown semantics. It is the most general and natural approach. In computer systems data are represented and processed mainly by binary sequences. It concerns such different kinds of data as numbers, tables, charts, pictures, video sequences, and so on. Binary are data and control messages transmitted in computer networks. Binary are also data stored on servers, what remains true if some of these data are replicated.

In this work we consider situation where there are given n binary sequences, which represent the same but inconsistent data coming from n servers. To the analysis of these data we shall apply the consensus methods. Knowing neither servers nor positions in binary sequences where errors occurred, we shall restore the consistency of data only on the basis of these inconsistent data. Although consensus methods does not assure perfectly accurate restoring of data, a consensus is the most reliable result, and we can use it for correcting inconsistency when we do not want to lose any data.

2 Related works

Consensus theory has a root in the theory of choice. A choice from some set A is based on a relation called a preference relation. Owing to it the choice function may be defined as follows

$$C(A)=\{x \in A: (\forall y \in A)((x,y) \in \alpha)\}.$$

Many works have dealt with the special case, where the basis of determining preference relation is a linear order on A. The most popular were the Condorcet choice functions. A choice function is called a Condorcet function if

$$(\forall A \subseteq U)[x \in C(A) \Leftrightarrow (\forall y \in A)(x \in C(\{x,y\}))].$$

Fishburn [16] has analyzed 9 Condorcet functions.

In the consensus-based researches, it is assumed that the chosen alternatives do not have to be included in the set presented for choice. Thus $C(A)$ must not be a subset of A, but naturally $C(A) \subseteq U$. An element of set $C(A)$ is called a consensus of set A, and $C(A)$ is called a representation of set A. In the beginning of this research only simple structures of set A (named *macrostructure*) , such as linear or partial order, were concerned. Later with the development of computing techniques the structures of each alternative (named *microstructure*) have also been investigated. Authors still assume that all the alternatives have the same structure. On the basis of the microstructure one can determine a macrostructure of the set A. The following microstructures were investigated: linear orders [1,17], ordered set partitions [10], ordered coverings [21], non–ordered set partitions [13], n–trees [14], time intervals [27]. The investigated macrostructures are: linear orders and distance (or similarity) functions. Representation of set A is most often determined on the basis of its macrostructure by some optimality rules. If the macrostructure is a distance (or similarity) function then very often the Kemeny median is used to choose the consensus. According to Kemeny rule the consensus should be nearest to the elements of set A. In work [22,23] the author proposed 5 axioms for consensus choice functions, two of them are dependent from the distance function. The analysis of these axioms presents very interesting properties of Kemeny median.

Consensus choice is often used to acquire a homogeneous profile for given heterogeneous situations. The aim of such processes is, for example, to achieve minimal replicated data design cost [30], to determine common value for given processes in fault-tolerant distributed computing [8,18], to specify a common scenario at presence of process failures in distributed computing [3], to work out common goals with minimal cost of realization for agents in multiagent systems [15], or to unify the agents' knowledge profile about dynamic populations [24]. Another research direction refers to statistic aspects of Condorset's model [2]. The authors of these works in a statistic way have simulated situations that require consensus and applied them to anthropology. The methods worked out are used for the analysis of statistic data that are results of experiments or public opinions.

3 Structure of consensus

In this paper we assume that the data which are replicated on different servers have one common logical structure which is a binary sequence of finite length. Such a form of data is most often processed and transmitted, therefore most often may be distorted. By D we denote the set of all possible evaluations of this structure. For example if the structure is a binary sequence of length 8, then set D should have 256 elements. Thus the *microstructure* of set D is binary sequence of some length. We may notice that set D is finite. By S we denote the set of K servers, on which the data are replicated, $S=\{s_1,...,s_K\}$. Generally *replication* of single data is a function $R: S \rightarrow D$. Value of this function, $R(s_i)$ we call a *version* of the replicated data. Data replication is in inconsistency state if in some moment of time several versions are different from one another, that is $R(s_i) \neq R(s_j)$ for some $i,j \in \{1,...,K\}$.

We assume that there is possibility to define a distance function between versions (elements of set D). It should be a function

$$\delta: D \times D \rightarrow R_+$$

which satisfies the following conditions:

a) *Nonnegative*: $(\forall x,y \in D)[\delta(x,y) \geq 0]$
b) *Reflective*: $(\forall x,y \in D)[(\delta(x,y)=0) \text{ iff } x=y]$
c) *Symmetric*: $(\forall x,y \in D)[\delta(x,y)=\delta(y,x)]$

Notice that the above conditions are a part of metric conditions. Metric is a good measure of distance, but its conditions are too strong [5]. Space (D,δ) could also be interpreted as the conflict space defined by Pawlak [29]. A general consensus model for solving conflicts in distributed systems is proposed in [25].

The distance function δ is then a *macrostructure* of set D.

On the basis of the distance function a replication R is inconsistent if there exist 2 versions $R(s_i)$ and $R(s_j)$ such that $\delta(R(s_i),R(s_j))>0$.

Assume that there are defined two distance functions for set D, let them be denoted by δ_1 and δ_2. Function δ_2 is *dependent* from function δ_1 if the following condition is satisfied: for any $x,x',y,y' \in D$ if $\delta_1(x,x') \geq \delta_1(y,y')$ then $\delta_2(x,x') \geq \delta_2(y,y')$. Functions δ_1 and δ_2 are dependent from each other if δ_2 is dependent from δ_1 and vice versa.

Remark 1. *For any* $x,x',y,y' \in D$

1. *If function δ_2 is dependent from function δ_1 then from inequality $\delta_2(x,x')>\delta_2(y,y')$ implies inequality $\delta_1(x,x')>\delta_1(y,y')$,*

2. *If functions δ_1 and δ_2 are dependent from each other then equality $\delta_2(x,x')=\delta_2(y,y')$ occurs if and only if equality $\delta_1(x,x')=\delta_1(y,y')$ occurs.*

Above remark implies that if for the set D there are defined 2 distance functions which are dependent of each other, then only one of them should be used because the second does not bring any new quality to the consensus choice.

Consensus problem for resolving inconsistency of replicated data should be formulated as follows:

Giving K versions $R(s_i)$, $(i=1,...,K)$, of replicated data, one should choose one version which could best represent these ones.

Below we present 8 postulates for "the best representation" choice of given versions.

4 Postulates for consensus choice

4.1 Consensus postulates

Notice that some of the given replicated data versions presented for consensus choice may be identical, in short we present the algebra of *sets with repetitions*, which is needed for this work. The notions and formalism are adopted from the Lipski and Marek work [19]. Expression $A=(a,a,b,b,b,c)$ is called a set with repetitions, in which element a occurs 2 times, b-3 times and c-1 time. Set A can also be expressed as $A=(2*a,3*b,1*c)$. The sum of sets with repetitions is denoted by symbol $\cup$ and has following interpretation: if element x occurs in set A n times, in B n' times, then in their sum $A \cup B$ it should occurs $n+n'$ times. For example, if $A=(2*a,3*b,1*c)$ and $B=(4*a,2*b)$, then $A \cup B=(6*a,5*b,1*c)$. Set A with repetitions is a subset of set B with repetitions $(A \subseteq B)$ if every element has in A not greater number of occurrence than in B.

For example $(2*a,3*b,1*c) \subseteq (2*a,4*b,1*c)$.

Let D_O be the set of all nonempty, finite subsets with repetitions of D, $X,X_1,X_2 \in D_O$, $x \in D$, and

$$\delta(x,X)= \sum_{y \in X} \delta(x,y),$$

$$\delta^2(x,X) = \sum_{y \in X} [\delta(x,y)]^2,$$

$$\overline{\delta}(x, X) = \sum_{y \in X} [\delta(x, y) - \frac{1}{card(X)} \delta(x, X)]^2 .$$

Definition 1. By *a consensus function in space* (D,δ) we call a function

$$C: D_O \rightarrow 2^D$$

which satisfies 1 or more of the following postulates:

P1. $C(X) \subseteq X$

P2. $C(X) \neq \emptyset$

P3. $(C(X_1) \cap C(X_2) \neq \emptyset) \Rightarrow (C(X_1 \cup X_2)=C(X_1) \cap C(X_2))$

P4. $\forall i \in N[(\forall x \in X (x_i=\lambda)) \Rightarrow (\forall x \in C(X) (x_i= \lambda))]$
   where x_i is the value on i-th position of sequence x and $\lambda \in \{0,1\}$

P5. $\forall x \in D \; [(x \notin C(X)) \Rightarrow ((\exists n \in N)(x \in C(X \cup (n*x))))]$

P6. $(X_1 \subseteq X_2 \wedge x \in C(X_1) \wedge y \in C(X_2)) \Rightarrow (\delta(x,X_1) \leq \delta(y,X_2))$

P7. $x \in C(X) \Rightarrow \delta(x,X) = \min\limits_{y \in D} \delta(y,X)$

P8. $x \in C(X) \Rightarrow \delta^2(x,X) = \min\limits_{y \in D} \delta^2(y,X)$.

An element of set $C(X)$ is called a *consensus* of set X.

Commentary. The above postulates are conditions for consensus choice function. Although they are intuitive we try to give their interpretation. According to postulate P1 the domain of consensus choice should be the set X. It is the assumption that at least one of given data versions is correct. From the practical point of view it is well-founded assumption, if the verifying process for data consistency is often made. Such condition should also take place if there exist the majority of versions which are identical to each other. Postulate P2 requires that there always exists a consensus for each nonempty set of versions. Postulate P3 states that if some sequence x is simultaneously a consensus of X_1 and X_2 then it should also be a consensus of their sum. This condition is also good for other cases of consensus choice, for example, if a place is suitable for building a warehouse for both shops nets X_1 and X_2 then it should be suitable for the net being the connection of X_1 and X_2. According to postulate P4, if number 1 (or 0) occurs in all binary sequences (data versions) on the same position, then in the consensus the number should also occurs on this position. It is very intuitive condition. Postulate P5 states that if some sequence x is not a consensus of set X then it should be the consensus of set X' containing X and n elements x for some n. In other words, each sequence has a chance to be chosen as the consensus of given sequences if there exists a enough number of data versions which are identical to this sequence. Postulate P6 is a natural condition for the structure of set D. Attention should be paid to 2 final postulates. Postulate P7 requires that the consensus be as near as possible to the data versions. Postulate P8, on the other hand, states that the sum of squared distances between the consensus and versions should be minimal. Defining postulate P8 has the following aim: notice that number $\overline{\delta}$ defined above is a measure of uniformity of distances between some sequence x to given versions. It is also an intuitive condition that the consensus should not only be nearest to the versions, but also generates uniform distances to them. As shown below, postulate P8 specifies consensus choice functions, which to a certain degree satisfy this condition.

Each of *above* axioms treated as a characteristic property of consensus choice function would specify in space C of all functions $C: D_0 \rightarrow 2^D$ a region (domain) denoted as $C_1, C_2, ..., C_8$ respectively. Complement in C to region C_i will be denoted as $\overline{C}_i$ for $i=1,...,8$.

Notice that the first 5 postulates (P1-P5) are independent from the structure of D (i.e. the distance *function* δ), while the postulates P6-P8 are formulated on the basis of this function. Postulates P1-P5 are in some sense very "natural" conditions which are often required to be satisfied in general task of consensus choice. We may show that the set $C_1 \cap C_2 \cap ... \cap C_5$ (including all consensus functions which satisfy postulates P1-P5) is not empty and includes for example the following function $C_1(X) = \{x \in X: \delta(x,X) = \min_{y \in X} \delta(y,X)\}$. The set $C_2 \cap C_3 \cap ... \cap C_6$ also is not empty and includes for example the following consensus function $C_2(X) = \{x \in D: \delta(x,X) = \min_{y \in D} \delta(y,X)\}$. Some interesting aspects of using distance spaces to determining consensus of versions of replicated data are given in [12].

4.2 Some results of postulates analysis

Theorem 1. *The following dependencies are held*

a) $C_i \not\subset C_j$ *for all* $i,j=1,...,8$ *and* $i \neq j$.

b) $C_1 \cap C_2 \cap ... \cap C_8 = \varnothing$.

c) $C_2 \cap C_3 \cap ... \cap C_6 \neq \varnothing$.

Theorem 2. *The following dependencies are held*

a) $C_7 \backslash \overline{C}_2 \subseteq C_4$.

b) $C_7 \backslash \overline{C}_2 = C_2 \cap C_4 \cap C_5 \cap C_6$.

c) $C_2 \cap C_3 \cap ... \cap C_6 \subseteq C_7 \backslash \overline{C}_2$.

Theorem 3. *The following dependencies are held*

a) $C_8 \backslash \overline{C}_2 \subseteq C_4 \cap C_5$.

b) $C_7 \cap C_8 = \varnothing$.

Theorem 4. *Let* $C \in C_8$, $X \in D_o$, $x \in C(X)$, *then for each* $y \in D$ *there must be held one of the following inequalities:*

a) $\delta(x,X) < \delta(y,X)$ *or*

b) $\overline{\delta}(x,X) \leq \overline{\delta}(y,X)$.

The proof of Theorem 2b is given in [23], of Theorem 4 in [11], and of other theorems in [26].

Commentary. Theorem 1 shows that all regions are independent, they do not have any element in common. It is the consequence of the fact that $C_7 \cap C_8 = \varnothing$, but there exist a function which belongs to regions C_2, C_3, C_4, C_5 and C_6. As it is shown in Theorem 2, this common function is specified by postulate P7. It means that a nonempty function specified by P7 satisfies each of postulates P2, P3, P4, P5 and P6. Functions specified by postulate P8 satisfies postulates P4 and P5 only (Theorem 3).

Theorem 4 shows very important property of a consensus chosen on the basis of a function from C_8. Notice that if x is a consensus of set X chosen by a C_8 function, then in relationship to any sequence y of set D consensus x has either smaller sum of distances from it to given versions, or the uniformity measure $\overline{\delta}$ for x is smaller than for y. It means that there may exist a sequence z which has smaller sum of distances to given versions than x, but the value of $\overline{\delta}$ for z will be greater.

In relationship to a consensus chosen by functions from C_7, the most often used functions, a consensus chosen by C_8 functions always has smaller value of $\overline{\delta}$, that means the distances from this consensus to given versions are more uniformly distributed.

Some attentions should be paid for postulate P1. As stated above, this consensus choice criterion has practical application. Of course we have $(C_1 \cap C_i) \setminus \overline{C}_2 = \varnothing$ for all $i=2,3,...,8$, it means that the nonempty consensus which satisfies simultaneously postulates P1 and any other does not exist. But if we assume "partial satisfying" of postulates (e.g. P1 and P8), we can formulate a consensus choice function which minimizes sum $\delta(x,X)$ for x belonging not to D but to X.

4.3 Numerical example

Let us assume that for some replicated data after some time period of functioning there are the following versions:

$$R(s_1) = (10011100),$$
$$R(s_2) = (11100110),$$
$$R(s_3) = (11000111),$$
$$R(s_4) = (11100011),$$
$$R(s_5) = (00100111),$$
$$R(s_6) = (11010011),$$
$$R(s_7) = (10111101).$$

The consensus of above versions satisfying postulates P1-P5 determined by function C_1 (defined in section 4.1.) is the sequence (11000111), while the consensus satisfying postulates P2-P7 determined by function C_2 is the sequence (11100111). The sequence (11110111) is a consensus satisfying postulates P4,P5 and P8.

5   Algorithms for consensus choice

In this section we present 2 algorithms: the first determines a consensus specified by a C_7 function, and the second algorithm determines a consensus specified by a C_8 function. For this purpose we assume that the structure of set D is Hamming distance function [4], and the length of binary sequences is equal n. Thus for $x,y \in D$

$$\delta(x, y) = \sum_{i=1}^{n} |x[i] \oplus y[i]|$$

where $a \oplus b = 0$ if $a=b$ and $a \oplus b = 1$ if $a \neq b$ for $a,b \in \{0,1\}$.

Let X be a set of m binary sequences of length n, and $\alpha = \sum_{x \in X} x$ be the arithmetical sum of these sequences, such that $\alpha[i] = \sum_{x \in X} x[i]$ for $i=1,2,...,m$.

The first algorithm determines a sequence $u = (u_1, \dots u_n)$ which minimizes the sum $\delta(x,X)$.

Procedure 1. Determining a consensus u satisfying postulate P7.
given: set X consisting of m binary sequences of length n
result: sequence $u = (u_1,\dots,u_n)$ minimizing $\delta(x,X)$

```
begin
        for i:=1 to n do
        count α;
        if α[i] = m/2 then u[i]:= random else
        if α[i] < m/2 then u[i] := 0 else u[i] := 1
end
```

Notice that this algorithm can be performed in time of $O(mn)$.

Determining a consensus specified by a C_8 function is a NP-complete problem [11], for which we present below a heuristic algorithm.

Procedure 2. Determining a consensus u satisfying postulate P8.
given: set X consisting of m binary sequences of length n
result: sequence $u = (u_1,\dots u_n)$ minimizing $\delta^2(x,X)$

```
begin
        count u using  procedure 1;
        s:=δ²(u,X);
        v:=u;
        for i:=1 to n do
          begin
                v[i] := v[i]⊕1;
                count δ²(v,X);
                if δ²(v,X)< s then s:= δ²(v,X)
                else v[i]:= v[i]⊕1
          end;
          u:=v
end
```

The computational complexity of *procedure 2* is also $O(mn)$.

If *procedure* 1 determines more than 1 sequence minimizing sum $\delta(v,X)$ then they can create an initial population for using a genetic algorithm for minimizing sum $\delta^2(v,X)$ [20].

References

1.   Arrow K.J. (1963): *Social Choice and Individual Values*. Wiley New York.
2.   Batchelder W.H., Romney A.K. (1986): The statistical analysis of a general Condorcet model for dichotomous choice situations, in *Information pooling and group decision making*, ed. by B. Frofman and G. Owen, JAP Press, pp. 103-112.
3.   Bazzi R.A., Neiger G., Peterson G.L (1997): On the use of registers in achieving wait-free consensus. *Distributed Computing* 10, pp. 117-127.

4. Blahut R.E. (1984): *Theory and Practice of Error Control Codes.* Addison–Wesley.
5. Bogart K.P. (1973): Preference structure I: Distance between transitive preference relations. *J. of Math. Sociology* 3, pp. 455–470.
6. Buretta M. (1997): Using transaction–based and transaction–consistent asynchronous replication. http://www–4.ibm.com/software/data/pubs/papers.
7. Ceri S., Pelagatti G. (1984): *Distributed Databases, Principle and Systems.* McGraw–Hill.
8. Chandra T.D., Hadzilacos V., Toueg S. (1996): The weakest failure detector for solving consensus, *J. ACM* 43, pp. 685-722.
9. Coulouris G, Dollimore J., Kindberg T. (1999): *Distributed systems, concepts and design.* WNT Warsaw.
10. Daniłowicz C., Nguyen N.T. (1988): Consensus–based partition in the space of ordered partitions. *Patter Recogn.* 21, pp. 269–273.
11. Daniłowicz C., Nguyen N.T. (1992): *Methods for choice of representation of ordered partitions and coverings.* Monographs, Wrocław University of Technology.
12. Daniłowicz C., Nguyen N.T. (2000): Consensus as a tool for resolving inconsistency of replicated data in distributed database systems. Technical Reports, series: PRE, No. 29, Wrocław Univ. of Technology.
13. Day W.H.E. (1984): Extremes in the complexity of computing metric distance between partitions. *IEEE Trans. on Pattern Analysis and Machine Intell.* 6, pp. 69–73.
14. Day W.H.E. (1988): Consensus methods as tools for data analysis. In *Classification and Related Methods for Data Analysis,* ed. by H.H. Bock, North–Holland, pp. 312–324.
15. Ephrati E., Rosenschein J.S (1998): Deriving consensus in multiagent systems, *Artificial Intelligence* 87, pp. 21-74.
16. Fishburn P.C. (1977): Condorset social choice functions. *SIAM J. App. Math.* 33, pp. 469–489.
17. Kemeny J.G. (1959): Mathematics without numbers. *Daedalus* 88, pp. 577–591.
18. Kumar A., Malik K. (1996): Optimizing the cost of hierarchical quorum consensus. *Acta Informatica* 33, pp. 255–275.
19. Lipski W., Marek W. (1986): *Combinatorial Analysis.* WTN Warsaw.
20. Michalewicz Z. (1996): *Genetic algorithms + data structures = evolution programs.* WTN Warsaw.
21. Nguyen N.T. (1989): *Methods for set representation choice.* Ph.D. Thesis, Wrocław University of Technology.
22. Nguyen N.T. (1994): The information retrieval model based on the theory of choice of objects set representation, in: *Information Systems Architecture and Technology ISAT'94, Proceedings of the 16th International Scientific School ISAT,* ed. by M. Bazewicz, Wrocław Univ. of Technology, pp. 297-303.
23. Nguyen N.T. (1998): The axiom approach to the experts opinions representation choice problem, in *Proceedings of the 13th International Conference on System Science,* ed. by Z. Bubnicki, Wrocław University of Technology, pp. 224–229.
24. Nguyen N.T. (1999): A computer-based multiagent system for building and updating models of dynamic populations located in distributed environments, in *Proceeding of 5th International Conference on Computer in Medicine,* ed. by E. Kącki, Lódź University of Technology, pp. 133-138.
25. Nguyen N.T. (2000): Consensus methods for resolving conflict situations in distributed information systems. Technical Reports, series: SPR, No. 29, Wrocław University of Technology.
26. Nguyen N.T. (2000): The analysis of consensus choice postulates in solving inconsistency of replicated data. Technical Reports, series: SPR, No. 30, Wrocław University of Technology.

27. Nguyen N.T., Katarzyniak R. (1999): Determining consensus problem in temporal data-bases supporting modal time, in *Information Systems Architecture and Technology, Proceedings of the 21th International Scientific School ISAT*, ed. by A. Grzech, Wrocław University of Technology, pp. 222-227.
28. Ozsu T.M. (1991): *Principles of Distributed Database Systems.* Prentice–Hall.
29. Pawlak Z. (1998): An inquiry into anatomy of conflicts. *Journal of Information Sciences* 108, pp. 65-78
30. Pham H. (1998): Optimal cost design of replicated data in distributed database systems. *International Journal of System Science* 29, pp. 795–804.

A Strategy for Partial Evaluation of Views

Parke Godfrey and Jarek Gryz

York University, Toronto, Canada

Abstract. Database applications and environments such as mediation over heterogeneous database sources and data warehousing for decision support lead to complex queries. Queries are often nested, defined over views, and may involve unions. In certain cases, one might want to "remove" pieces (*sub-queries* or *sub-views*) from such queries. Some sub-views may be effectively cached, or may be materialized views. Some may be known to evaluate empty, through reasoning over the integrity constraints. Some may match protected queries, which for security cannot be evaluated.

We introduce an evaluation strategy called *tuple-tagging* for queries defined over views that efficiently "removes" marked sub-views. This differs from the approach of *rewriting* the query so that the sub-views to be removed are effectively gone, and then evaluating the rewritten query. With the tuple tagging evaluation, no rewrite of the original query is necessary.

1 Introduction

1.1 Motivation and Objectives

Many current database applications and environments, as mediation over heterogeneous database sources and data warehousing for decision support, incur complex queries. Queries are often nested, defined over previously defined views, and may involve unions. (A special type of such queries called *fusion queries*, which are self-joins of views defined over unions, was discussed in [25]). This is a necessity in mediation, as views in the meta-schema are defined to combine data from disparate sources. In these environments, view definition maintenance is of paramount importance.

There are many reasons why one might want to "remove" pieces (*sub-queries*) from a given query. Let us call a "sub-query" an *unfolding*, as the query can be *unfolded* via view definition into more specific sub-queries. These reasons include the following.

1. Some unfoldings of the query may be effectively cached from previous queries [5, 9], or may be materialized views [16] themselves.
2. Some unfoldings may be known to evaluate empty, by reasoning over the integrity constraints [1, 3].
3. Some unfoldings may match protected queries, which for security cannot be evaluated for all users [22].
4. Some unfoldings may be subsumed by previously asked queries, so are not of interest.

338

5. An unfolding shared by two queries in an **except** (difference) operation can be removed from both queries *before* the operation is carried out.

What does it mean to remove unfoldings from a query? The modified query should not subsume—and thus when evaluated should never evaluate—the removed unfoldings, but should subsume "everything" else of the original query.

In case 1, one might want to separate out certain unfoldings, because they can be evaluated much less expensively, and in a networked, distributed environment be evaluated locally. Then, a "remainder query" can be evaluated independently to find the remaining answers [5]. If the remainder query is significantly less expensive to evaluate than the original, this is an optimization. In case 2, the unfoldings are free to evaluate, since it is known in advance that they must evaluate empty. In case 3, when some unfoldings are protected, it does not mean that the "rest" of the query cannot be safely evaluated. In case 4, when a user is asking a series of queries, he or she may just be interested in the stream of answers returned. So any previously seen answers are no longer of interest. In case 5, **except** queries might be optimized by this technique.

Consider the following example.

Example 1. Let there be six relations defined in the database **DB**:
- **Departments**(did, address),
- **Institutes**(did, address)
- **Faculty**(eid, did, rank),
- **Staff**(eid, did, position),
- **Health_Ins**(eid, premium, provider), and
- **Life_ins**(eid, premium, provider).

There are also three views defined in terms of these relations.

create view	*create view*	*create view*
Academic_Units as	**Employees** as	**Benefits** as
(*select* did, address	(*select* eid, did	(*select* eid, premium, provider
from **Departments**)	*from* **Faculty**)	*from* **Life_Ins**)
union	union	union
(*select* did, address	(*select* eid, did	(*select* eid, premium, provider
from **Institutes**)	*from* **Staff**)	*from* **Health_ins**)

Define query Q as follows.

Q: *select* E.eid
    from **Academic Units** A, **Employees** E, **Benefits** B
    where A.did=E.did and E.eid=B.eid and B.provider="Blue Cross"

Query Q can be represented as a parse tree of its relational algebra representation, which is an AND/OR tree, as shown in Figure 1. (We ignore for brevity explicit representation of project and select operations.) Evaluating the query—in the order of operations as specified in its relational algebra representation—is equivalent to materializing all nodes of the query tree. This type of evaluation (and representation) is referred to as *bottom-up*.

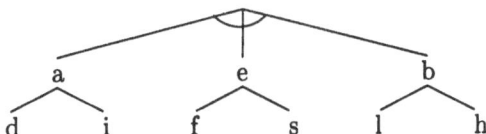

Fig. 1. The AND/OR tree representation of the original query of Example 1.

Now assume that the the following query $\mathcal{F}$ has been asked before and its result is stored in cache.

$\mathcal{F}$: *select* E.eid
   from **Departments** D, **Faculty** F, **Life_Ins** L
   where D.did=F.did and F.eid=L.eid and L.provider= "Blue Cross"

Equivalently, we can assume that this formula represents a materialized view or that it matches a protected query whose answers should not be displayed. If $\mathcal{F}$ is a protected query, then the join expression it computes should not be evaluated. Thus, it has to be eliminated from the query. Otherwise, if $\mathcal{F}$ is a cached query or a materialized view, it may still be beneficial to "remove" it from the query. We call the result of this a *discounted query*.

One way to achieve this is to rewrite $\mathcal{Q}$ as a union of joins over base tables, then to remove the join represented by $\mathcal{F}$ (which then is explicitly present), and finally to evaluate the remaining join expressions. This may be very inefficient, however. The number of join expressions that remain to be evaluated may be exponential in the size of the collection of view definitions. Furthermore, we have shown in [11] that such an evaluation plan (which is often called *top-down*) may require evaluating the same joins many times, and incur the expense that a given tuple may be computed many times (whenever the projected parts of base tables overlap significantly). A seemingly more efficient evaluation plan for the discounted query can be devised by rewriting the query so that the number of operations (unions and joins) is minimized. (See Figure 2.) As a side effect of this approach, the redundancy in join evaluation, as well as redundancy in answer computation, is reduced. To obtain such rewrites, however, is **NP**-*hard*. Furthermore, such redundancy is not entirely eliminated: for example, the join **Institutes** ⋈ **Faculty** is computed twice (implicitly in the left sub-tree and explicitly in the right sub-tree). One can verify that there is no rewrite of the query tree that removes the join **Departments** ⋈ **Faculty** ⋈ **Life_Ins** and yet guarantees at the same time that there is no redundancy in the computation of other joins. Thus, the "optimized" query can sometimes cost more to evaluate than the original query; our experimental results show (see Section 4) that this is, indeed, the case for this example.

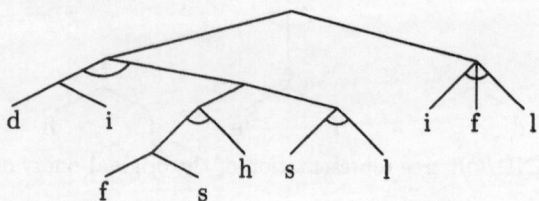

Fig. 2. The AND/OR tree representation of the modified query of Example 1.

We present a new strategy for partial evaluation of queries defined over views, which we call *tuple-tagging*, which offers many advantages over explicit query rewrites.

- Tuple-tagging is easily implemented at the *logical level*, and can be accomplished by rewriting the SQL expression of the query.
- The technique is *modular*: it can be implemented independently of other optimization stages (in particular, of traditional relational database query optimization) to work in conjunction with the other stages.
- Tuple-tagging is *not* an algebraic rewrite of the query: it preserves the query tree *as is*, and thus scales up for complex queries.
- The tuple-tagging is interleaved with query evaluation. Thus, reliable heuristics can be devised and employed to decide step-wise whether a given "optimization" step should be applied.

The paper is organized as follows. Section 2 presents a formal framework for *discounted queries*. (Section 2 can be skipped on the first reading.) Section 3 presents a tuple-tagging technique for evaluating discounted queries. An overview of experimental results over a TPC/D benchmark database in DB2 is presented in Section 4. Section 5 concludes with issues and future work.

1.2 Related Work

There is a substantial body of research in rewrite-based query optimization [4, 6, 7, 19]. The techniques discussed in literature have all considered rewriting a query into a logically *equivalent* form. This is a different goal than ours. We are interested in generating and efficiently evaluating a query or view from which unfoldings have been removed. Thus, the resulting query is *not* equivalent to the original query.

The problem we address is also different from the problem of answering queries using materialized views [2, 14, 16, 20]. In that problem, the goal is to *replace* sub-queries of a query by views (or other queries) to generate a query that is equivalent, or contained by, the original query. Again, our goal is to *remove*—or more precisely to *avoid evaluating*—parts of a query for optimization or security reasons.

The work that is most closely related is [15], in which the authors consider queries that involve nested union operations. They propose a technique for rewriting such queries when it is known that some of the joins evaluated as part of the query are empty. The technique applies only to a simple class of queries, however, and no complexity issues were addressed.

Another research area related to our problem is *multiple query optimization* [21]. The goal here is to optimize evaluation of a set of queries, rather than a single query. Since the queries in the set are arbitrary, they may not be related in any structured way to allow use of the techniques that we propose in this paper. The techniques developed for multiple query optimization are focused towards finding and reusing common subexpressions across collections of queries, and are heuristics-based.

The problem of query tree rewrites for the purpose of optimization has also been considered in the context of deductive databases with recursion. In [12], the problem of detecting and eliminating redundant subgoal occurrences in proof trees generated by programs in the presence of functional dependencies is discussed. In [13], the residue method of [1] is extended to recursive queries.

We investigated the computational complexity of query rewrites in [10]. We showed that the optimal rewrite of a query is NP-hard. We also identified a special class of queries and unfoldings for which rewrites result is a simpler query, thus always providing an optimization.

2 Discounted Queries

In this section, we formally define the notion of an *unfolding* and a *discounted query*. For preciseness, we use the notation of Datalog [24]. We will write a query as a set of atoms, to be interpreted as a conjunction of the atoms. For instance, $\{a, e, b\}$ represents the query of Example 1.[1] Some of the atoms may be intensional; that is, they are written with view predicates defined over base table predicates and, perhaps, other views.

We provide a formal definition for an *unfolding* of a query.

Definition 1. Given query sets $\mathcal{Q}$ and $\mathcal{U}$, call $\mathcal{U}$ a *1-step unfolding* of query set $\mathcal{Q}$ with respect to database **DB** *iff*, given some $q_i \in \mathcal{Q}$ and a rule $\langle a \leftarrow b_1, \ldots, b_n. \rangle$ defining a view for a, such that $q_i\theta \equiv a\theta$ (for *most general unifier* θ [17]), then

$$\mathcal{U} = (\mathcal{Q} - \{q_i\} \cup \{b_1, \ldots, b_n\})\theta$$

Denote this by $\mathcal{U} \leq^1 \mathcal{Q}$. Call $\mathcal{U}_1$ simply an *unfolding* of $\mathcal{Q}$, written as $\mathcal{U}_1 \leq \mathcal{Q}$, *iff* there is some finite collection of query sets $\mathcal{U}_1, \ldots, \mathcal{U}_k$ such that $\mathcal{U}_1 \leq^1 \ldots \leq^1 \mathcal{U}_k \leq^1 \mathcal{Q}$.

---

[1] We present only "propositional" examples for simplicity's sake. They can be extended in a obvious way to queries with the variables made explicit.

An unfolding $\mathcal{U}$ is called *extensional iff*, for every $q_i \in \mathcal{U}$, atom q_i refers to a base table. Call the unfolding *intensional* otherwise (in other words, some of the atoms refer to views).

Example 2. The views of Example 1 can be represented in simplified Datalog (where letters represent atoms) as:

$$a \leftarrow d. \qquad e \leftarrow f. \qquad b \leftarrow l.$$
$$a \leftarrow i. \qquad e \leftarrow s. \qquad b \leftarrow h.$$

Since b in the query $\mathcal{Q}$ can be unfolded into l using a single rule $\langle b \leftarrow l. \rangle$, then $\{a, e, l\}$ is one of the 1-step unfoldings of $\mathcal{Q}$.

Since all of the atoms in unfolding $\mathcal{F}$ of $\mathcal{Q}$ (d, f, and l) are extensional, it is an extensional unfoldings of $\mathcal{Q}$.

It is easy to see how an unfolding's AND/OR tree can be "inscribed" in the query's AND/OR tree. The atoms of an unfolding can be *marked* in the query's tree as shown in Figure 3 for unfoldings $\mathcal{F} = \{d, f, l\}$ (1) and, say, $\mathcal{G} = \{i, s, b\}$ (2).

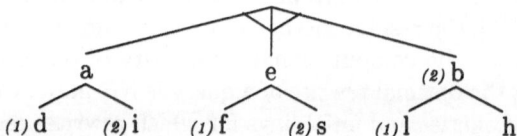

Fig. 3. AND/OR tree of Example 1 with two unfoldings marked.

A query is considered to be equivalent to the union of all its extensional unfoldings. Define **unfolds** $(\mathcal{Q})$ to be the set of all such extensional unfoldings of $\mathcal{Q}$. We can now define the concept of a *discounted query*, which is to represent the query with some of its unfoldings "removed" (or *discounted*).

Definition 2. Given a query set $\mathcal{Q}$ and unfoldings $\mathcal{U}_1, \ldots, \mathcal{U}_k$ of $\mathcal{Q}$, then the expression $\mathcal{Q} \backslash \{\mathcal{U}_1, \ldots, \mathcal{U}_k\}$ is a *discounted query*. We define its meaning to be:

$$\mathbf{unfolds}\,(\mathcal{Q} \backslash \{\mathcal{U}_1, \ldots, \mathcal{U}_k\}) = \mathbf{unfolds}\,(\mathcal{Q}) - (\bigcup_{i=1}^{k} \mathbf{unfolds}\,(\mathcal{U}_i))$$

We call $\mathcal{U}_1, \ldots, \mathcal{U}_k$ the *unfoldings-to-discount*, and the tuples in the answer sets of these unfoldings the *tuples-to-discount*.

Example 3. Consider again the query $\mathcal{Q}$ of Example 1. Since **unfolds**$(\mathcal{Q}) = \{\{d,f,l\}, \{d,f,h\}, \{d,s,l\}, \{d,s,h\}, \{i,f,l\}, \{i,f,h\}, \{i,s,l\}, \{i,s,h\}\}$, and **unfolds**$(\mathcal{F})$ $= \{\{d,f,l\}\}$, then **unfolds**$(\mathcal{Q} \backslash \{\mathcal{F}\}) = \{\{d,f,h\}, \{d,s,l\}, \{d,s,h\}, \{i,f,l\}, \{i,f,h\},$ $\{i,s,l\}, \{i,s,h\}\}$. Similarly, for the unfolding $\mathcal{G} = \{i,s,b\}$ in Figure 3, we have **unfolds**$(\mathcal{G}) = \{\{i,s,l\}, \{i,s,h\}\}$ and **unfolds**$(\mathcal{Q} \backslash \{\mathcal{G}\}) = \{\{d,f,h\}, \{d,f,l\}, \{d,s,l\},$ $\{d,s,h\}, \{i,f,l\}, \{i,f,h\}\}$. Last, **unfolds**$(\mathcal{Q} \backslash \{\mathcal{F}, \mathcal{G}\}) = \{\{d,f,h\}, \{d,s,l\}, \{d,s,h\},$ $\{i,f,l\}, \{i,f,h\}\}$.

We discuss more formally the semantics of discounted queries in [8].

3 The Tuple-Tagging Evaluation Strategy

3.1 Overview

Our strategy is a bottom-up materialization strategy for the query tree with the union and join operations *modified* to account for the discounted unfoldings. The strategy ensures two things:

- that tuples resulting from an unfolding-to-discount do not contribute to the answer set of the discounted query; and
- any join represented by an unfolding-to-discount is never fully evaluated.

The tuples resulting from an unfolding-to-discount can be removed either during or after the actual query evaluation. To ensure the second property and thus to gain optimization, we need somehow to avoid evaluating the unfoldings-to-discount; that is, to prevent those tuples from being materialized *during* query evaluation.

Our proposed method, *tuple-tagging*, is to keep extra information in the temporary tables created during the materialization of the query tree. In essence, each table will have an extra column for each unfolding-to-discount. The domain of these *tag* columns is boolean. The value of a tag column for a given tuple is *true* when that tuple is derived from the corresponding unfolding-to-discount; it is *false* otherwise. During each union or join operation (which creates a new temporary table), these tag columns' values must be maintained properly.

Example 4. Consider query Q of Example 1. Query $\mathcal{F}$, which represents the unfolding-to-discount, is a join of **Departments**, **Faculty** and **Life Ins**. For each of these tables, a new column $C_{\mathcal{F}}$ is added and its values initialized to *true*. Similarly, for tables **Institutes**, **Staff**, and **Health Ins** which are unioned with the above tables, the same column is added and its values initialized to *false*.

By keeping this derivation information for each tuple during evaluation, we can easily ensure the first property from above. After evaluation of the query, select those tuples which have all *false* values in the tag columns (and also project away the tag columns). We shall be able further to use the tag columns—and ultimately satisfy our second property—to determine during a join operation which tuples should be joined, and which should not be (because the resulting tuple would be "from" an unfolding-to-discount). The computation saved will primarily depend on the size of the *true* section in the table.

We present the evaluation strategy in two versions. The simpler version ensures only the first property; that is, the final answer set contains no tuples that arise solely from unfoldings-to-discount. The strategy is useful in the case when unfoldings are removed for security reasons. It does little, however, to optimize query evaluation: gross savings are equal to the difference in the cost of writing back the results of the original query versus the cost of writing back the results of the discounted query (which can sometimes be significantly smaller). These savings can only be substantial when query results are sent over a network. The second version removes the tuples-to-discount *during* query evaluation, as soon as is possible. This strategy can reduce the cost of query evaluation. Both versions of the algorithm require modifying the union and join operations. This is what we define next.

3.2   The Modified Union Operation

We assume that the query tree contains only union and join nodes (that is, all other operations are implicit). Furthermore, without loss of generality, we assume the the tree is binary. We refer to one child of any branch (non-leaf) node $\mathcal{N}$ in a binary query tree as $\mathcal{L}_{\mathcal{N}}$ (for *left* child), and the other as $\mathcal{R}_{\mathcal{N}}$ (for *right* child). We assume that any leaf $\mathcal{N}$ in the query tree has a corresponding table in the database; that is, the answer set for $\mathcal{N}$ is derivable from some table (perhaps temporary) in the database via selects and projections. Call $\mathcal{N}$'s table (with any selects and projections implicit) $\mathbf{T}_{\mathcal{N}}$.

To handle discounted queries, we modify the traditional algorithm for bottom-up query evaluation. This involves replacing the union and join operations with specialized versions, which handle and exploit the tag columns for the unfoldings-to-discount, as discussed above. Given discounted query $\mathcal{Q}\backslash\{\mathcal{U}_1, \ldots, \mathcal{U}_k\}$, we introduce new columns, $\mathbf{C}_{\mathcal{U}_i}$, for $i \in \{1, \ldots, k\}$, as the tag columns corresponding to the unfoldings-to-discount (as described in Example 4).

We assume for any well-formed query tree that the tables to be unioned at any union step are union-compatible. With our addition of tag columns, this could now be violated. The two tables to be unioned may not be union-compatible over the tag columns. Thus, we need to modify the union step first to make the tables union-compatible by adding any tag columns that are needed. Algorithm 1 shows this. This is the only way in which we need to modify the union step.

Note that Algorithm 1 can be efficiently implemented in SQL by adding tag columns and initializing their values not before, but *during* the execution of the union operator. As we show in Section 4, this adds very little overhead to the cost of the query execution.

3.3   The Modified Join Operation

We must assign the correct values to tag columns of joined tables. If a tuple results from the join of one tuple which was derived under a given unfolding-to-discount $\mathcal{U}$ (hence the value of its $\mathbf{C}_{\mathcal{U}}$ is *true*), and a second tuple which was not (hence the value of its $\mathbf{C}_{\mathcal{U}}$ is *false*), then the resulting tuple is *not* in the answer set of $\mathcal{U}$. So $\mathbf{C}_{\mathcal{U}}$ for the resulting tuple should have the value *false*. Only when both tuples being joined were derived under $\mathcal{U}$ should the resulting tuple's column $\mathbf{C}_{\mathcal{U}}$ be set to *true*. Thus, tags are *conjunctively* combined.

% *Add new tag columns on a need-by basis.*
For each $\mathcal{U}_i$
    For $\{\mathcal{A}, \mathcal{B}\} = \{\mathcal{L}_{\mathcal{N}}, \mathcal{R}_{\mathcal{N}}\}$
        If $\mathcal{A} \in \mathcal{U}_i$ then
            Add column $\mathbf{C}_{\mathcal{U}_i}$ to $\mathbf{T}_{\mathcal{A}}$.
            Instantiate all values of $\mathbf{C}_{\mathcal{U}_i}$ in $\mathbf{T}_{\mathcal{A}}$ to *true*.

% *Make union-compatible.*
For each $\mathcal{U}_i$
    For $\{\mathcal{A}, \mathcal{B}\} = \{\mathcal{L}_{\mathcal{N}}, \mathcal{R}_{\mathcal{N}}\}$
        If $\mathbf{C}_{\mathcal{U}_i}$ belongs to $\mathbf{T}_{\mathcal{A}}$ but not to $\mathbf{T}_{\mathcal{B}}$ then
            Add column $\mathbf{C}_{\mathcal{U}_i}$ to $\mathbf{T}_{\mathcal{B}}$.
            Instantiate all values of $\mathbf{C}_{\mathcal{U}_i}$ in $\mathbf{T}_{\mathcal{B}}$ to *false*.

% *Union the two tables.*
Union $\mathbf{T}_{\mathcal{L}_{\mathcal{N}}}$ and $\mathbf{T}_{\mathcal{R}_{\mathcal{N}}}$ to create $\mathbf{T}_{\mathcal{N}}$.

Algorithm 1. The Modified Union Operation

Let $\mathcal{N}$ be a join node in a query tree for which the children are $\mathcal{L}_{\mathcal{N}}$ and $\mathcal{R}_{\mathcal{N}}$ and let $\mathcal{U}$ be an unfoldings-to-discount with the tag column $\mathbf{C}_{\mathcal{U}}$ in both tables $\mathbf{T}_{\mathcal{L}_{\mathcal{N}}}$ and $\mathbf{T}_{\mathcal{R}_{\mathcal{N}}}$. The modified join operation executed at node $\mathcal{N}$ is modified by adding the following assignment statement[2] for each unfolding-to-discount $\mathcal{U}$:

$$(\mathbf{T}_{\mathcal{L}_{\mathcal{N}}}.\mathbf{C}_{\mathcal{U}} \wedge \mathbf{T}_{\mathcal{R}_{\mathcal{N}}}.\mathbf{C}_{\mathcal{U}}) \text{ as } \mathbf{C}_{\mathcal{U}}$$

Example 5. Consider the final join of the query of Example 1. The three joined tables, **Academic Units, Employees, Benefits** will each contain an extra column, $\mathbf{C}_{\mathcal{F}}$, storing the values for the unfolding-to-discount $\mathcal{F}$. This column has been introduced during the execution of the union operations (as described in Algorithm 1). The query with the modified join operation is as follows.

    select E.eid, (A.$\mathbf{C}_{\mathcal{F}}$ AND E.$\mathbf{C}_{\mathcal{F}}$ AND B.$\mathbf{C}_{\mathcal{F}}$) as $\mathbf{C}_{\mathcal{F}}$
    from **Academic Units** A, **Employees** E, **Benefits** B
    where A.did=E.did and E.eid=B.eid and B.provider="Blue Cross"

The modified union and join operations have no influence (except for adding extra columns) on the final answer set of a query. Their only purpose is to keep the trace information about the unfoldings-to-discount via the tag columns. The last step of the tuple-tagging algorithm in its first version then

---

[2] The **as** statement (as per the SQL'92 standards [18]) perform the requisite logical *ands* between tag columns and introduces the tag columns back into the new table.

consists in using this information to select only the tuples that are known to be derivable from some unfolding other than an unfolding-to-discount. To ensure this, it is sufficient to select the tuples that have the value *false* for all their tag columns.

3.4 Optimization

As stated in Section 3.1, removing tuples-to-discount from the final query answer set according to the optimization described above does not, in general, improve efficiency of query evaluation. For complex queries, however, such removal can be executed *during* query evaluation; that is, before the final answer set is produced. In other words, we can push some of the selects for *false* over the tag columns further down in the query tree. This constitutes the tuple-tagging algorithm in its second version. Consider the following example.

Example 6. Let the query be as in Example 1 and the unfolding-to-discount be $\mathcal{G} = \{i, s, b\}$ (marked as *(2)* in Figure 3). Thus, all tuples in the join **Intitutes ⋈ Staff ⋈ Benefits** should be removed from the query's answer set. Let us assume that the final join of the query **Academic_Units ⋈ Employees ⋈ Benefits** is executed as specified in the query tree (that is, left to right). Consider the result of evaluating **Academic_Units ⋈ Employees**. Some tuples in the result of that join will have the value *true* for the column $C_\mathcal{G}$. Now, *all* tuples in the table for **Benefits** have the value *true* for that column (because the table is a part of the unfolding-to-discount $\mathcal{G}$). Thus, all of the tuples marked *true* in the result of the join **Academic_Units ⋈ Employees** will remain *true* after the join with **Benefits**, hence will be removed from the final query answer set.[3] If so, they can be eliminated as soon as **Academic_Units ⋈ Employees** is evaluated. Note that this provides optimization because the size of one of the tables in the input to the final join decreases. The gross savings achieved through this optimization can be estimated to the cost of the join of the result of **Institutes ⋈ Staff** with **Benefits**.

We introduce the notion of a *closing* of an unfolding-to-discount by a node in a query tree.

Definition 3. Unfolding-to-discount $\mathcal{U}$ is *closed* by node $\mathcal{N}$ with respect to binary query tree **QT** if all tuple marked *true* in $\mathbf{T}_\mathcal{N}$ contribute to all and only tuples of $\mathcal{U}$.

Thus, the node representing the join of **Academic_Units ⋈ Employees** is a closing node of unfolding-to-discount $\mathcal{G}$ in Example 6. Of course, the root of a query tree is a closing node for all unfoldings-to-discount. Since there may be several closing nodes for a given unfolding, it is useful to identify the

---

[3] In the final tuple-tagging query plan, we would not even need to add a tag column $C_\mathcal{G}$ to **Benefits** for this very reason.

first one (in the sequence of operations specified by the query tree) in order to eliminate tuples-to-discount as soon as possible. Again, the condition for this property is simple. If $\mathcal{N}$ is a closing node for $\mathcal{U}$ and $\mathcal{U}$ does not have a closing node in the subtree rooted at $\mathcal{N}$, then $\mathcal{N}$ is the first of the closing nodes for $\mathcal{U}$. The tuple-tagging algorithm can utilize (as described in Example 6) the existence of closing nodes not only to eliminate unfoldings-to-discount, but also to provide optimization. Our experimental results confirm that this is indeed the case.

4 Performance Analysis

We ran three sets of experiments to evaluate the tuple-tagging technique.[4] We used TPC/D benchmark database of size 100MB for our experiments. installed on DB2 with Windows-NT. (For details on this benchmark, please see [23].)

The purpose of the first experiment was to measure the overhead of adding and manipulating tags. The query is designed in such a way that no optimization in query execution time can possibly be achieved by using tags. This is done by making the root the closing node for an unfolding-to-discount and minimizing the size of the answer set (thus making sure that there is no benefit in writing less data back to a disk). Indeed, query execution time for the discounted query was larger than that for the original query; the good news is that the difference is negligible: 0.29%. Once the size of the answer becomes substantial, tuple-tagging begins to optimize. By increasing the size of the answer set, the discounted query provides optimization in query execution time over the original query: 17.5 seconds vs. 25.6 seconds.

The purpose of the second experiment was to compare tuple-tagging with two other techniques for removing unfolding from a query: top-down query evaluation; and an explicit rewrite of a query tree to minimize algebraic form. Tuple-tagging outperforms the other two techniques by a respectable margin. In fact, both the top-down approach and the explicit query rewrite approach add substantial overhead to the cost of evaluating discounted queries. As we conjectured in Section 1, this is due to the introduction of redundancy in join evaluation for both techniques. On the other hand, both of the discounted queries evaluated under the tuple-tagging strategy provide modest optimization over the original query. This is still achieved only through the reduction of the size of the answer set, and not through reduction of the sizes of the joined tables.

The last experiment provides a crucial test for the technique. We designed a query in which a closing node for an unfolding-to-discount is below the root of the query tree. This means that all tuples marked as *true* in the table representing the closing node can be eliminated before the next join is

---

[4] Due to space limitations, we present only a brief overview of the experiments.

executed, thus reducing the cost of that last join. Indeed, the reduction of the execution cost for this query was 25.7%.

5 Conclusions

We introduced a new framework in which a query is represented as a collection of selected unfoldings of the query and a *discounted query*, which represents the query with those unfoldings "removed". The selected unfoldings may be removed for security reasons, or because their answers are readily available (through caching or materialized views). We presented an efficient evaluation strategy for discounted queries called tuple-tagging. We showed through experiments that a discounted query can be, in general, evaluated more efficiently than the query itself. The experiments also suggested that rewrite techniques, which seem to be an intuitive approach to removing unfoldings from a query, may perform worse than the evaluation of the original query, and much worse than the tuple tagging approach. Thus the discounting framework and the tuple-tagging algorithm offer a viable approach to optimization of queries which employ views.

There are numerous issues to explore with respect to optimization of queries over views. This type of optimization is orthogonal to other optimization techniques, and so can be directly used in conjunction with existing optimizers. It would be beneficial to identify the types of interaction with the traditional query optimizer that could increase overall optimization. Currently tuple-tagging is done in a prior stage, and optimization is applied over the resulting queries. We also need to understand better the various cost tradeoffs in tuple-tagging, and how best to balance them.

References

1. Chakravarthy U., Grant J., and Minker J. (1990) Logic-based approach to semantic query optimization. *ACM TODS*, 15(2):162–207
2. Chaudhuri S., Krishnamurthy R. et al. (1995) Optimizing queries with materialized views. In *Proceedings of the 11th ICDE*, 190–200
3. Cheng Q., Gryz J. et al. (1999) Implementation of two semantic query optimization techniques in DB2 universal database. In *Proceedings of the 25th VLDB*, Edinburgh, Scotland
4. Cherniack M. and Zdonik S. (1996) Rule languages and internal algebras for rule-based optimizers. In *Proc. SIGMOD*, 401–412
5. Dar S., Franklin M. et al. (1996) Semantic data caching and replacement. In *Proceedings of 22nd VLDB*, 330–341
6. Das D. and Batory D. (1995) Prairie: A rule specification framework for query optimizers. In *Proceedings of ICDE*, 201–210
7. Freytag J. (1987) A rule-based view of query optimization. In *SIGMOD Proceedings*, 173–180

8. Godfrey P. and Gryz J. (1996) A framework for intensional query optimization. In *Proceedings of DDLP'96*, 57–68
9. Godfrey P. and Gryz J. (1999) Answering queries by semantic caches. In *Proceedings of 10th DEXA*, 485–498
10. Godfrey P. and Gryz J. (1999) View disassembly. In *Proceedings of 7th ICDT*, 417–434
11. Godfrey P., Gryz J., and Minker J. (1996) Semantic query optimization for bottom-up evaluation. In Ras Z. and Michalewicz M., editors, *Proc. of the 9th. ISMIS*, 561–571
12. Lakshmanan L.V.S. and Hernandez H.J. (1991) Structural query optimization: a uniform framework for semantic query optimization in deductive databases. In *Proc. PODS*, 102–114
13. Lakshmanan L.V.S. and Missaoui R. (1995) Pushing semantics inside recursion: A general framework for semantic optimization of recursive queries. In *Proc. ICDE*, 211–220
14. Larson P.-A. and Yang H. (1985) Computing queries from derived relations. In *Proc. of 11th VLDB*, 259–269
15. Lee S., Henschen L.J., and Qadah G. (1991) Semantic query reformulation in deductive databases. In *Proc. ICDE*, 232–239
16. Levy A.Y., Mendelzon A.O. et al. (1995) Answering queries using views. In *Proc. PODS*, 95–104
17. Lloyd J. (1987) *Foundations of Logic Programming*. Springer–Verlag, second edition
18. Melton J. and Simon A.R. (1993) *Understanding the New SQL: A Complete Guide*. Morgan Kaufmann, San Mateo, California
19. Pirahesh H., Hellerstein J.M., and Hasan W. (1992) Extensible/rule based query rewrite optimization in Starburst. In *Proc. SIGMOD*, 39–48
20. Qian X. (1996) Query folding. In *Proceedings of the 12th ICDE*, 48–55
21. Sellis T. and Ghosh S. (1990) On the multiple-query optimization problem. *TKDE*, 2(2):262–266
22. Thuraisingham B. and Ford W. (1995) Security constraint processing in a multilevel secure distributed database management system. *TKDE*, 7(2):274–293
23. Transaction Processing Performance Council. (1998) 777 No. First Street, Suite 600, San Jose, CA 95112-6311, www.tpc.org. *TPC Benchmark^{TM} D*, 1.3.1 edition
24. Ullman J.D. (1988) *Principles of Database and Knowledge-Base Systems*. Principles of Computer Science Series. Computer Science Press, Rockville, Maryland 20850
25. Yernani R., Papakonstantinou Y. et al. (1998) Fusion queries over internet databases. In *Proceedings of the 6th EDBT*, 57–71

Approximate Answers in Databases of Labeled Objects

Tadeusz Pankowski

Chair of Control, Robotics and Computer Science,

Poznań University of Technology, Poland

pankowsk@sol.put.poznan.pl

Abstract: We discuss some problems concerning approximate answering to queries in databases of labeled objects representing semistructured data. An approximate answer is an answer corresponding to a relaxed version of the query. The relaxation is obtained by means of replacement of equality relations by a partial ordering or pre-ordering relations (in "child semantics" and "neighbor semantics"), or by using generalized query instead of the original one. Some novel theorems relevant to the problem are formulated.

Keywords: approximate answers, semistructured data, labeled objects, partial ordering

1 Introduction

In conventional databases, a query written in a formal query language is accepted, evaluated against a database, and the complete set of data satisfying the query (the answer set) is returned. In some systems, however, (e.g. in cooperative database systems [8,9,10,12,15], or in multilevel database [4,10]) this query/answer paradigm is augmented to allow the system to relax a query (e.g. when a query fails or if access privileges of the user are too low). Then an approximate answer may be provided. Relaxation of a query may consist in rewriting it into a set of more general queries [7,8,15].

In [15] we have discussed semantics of approximate answers in the context of relational databases. In this paper, we extend these considerations to labeled objects, which represent semistructured data. Semistructured data is data that has no absolute schema fixed in advance, its structure is irregular, incomplete, heterogeneous, and often not fully known [1,2,16,17]. Such data arises mainly in two situations: (1) when data is stored in sources that do not require a rigid structure (such as the World-Wide- -Web), and (2) when data is integrated from heterogeneous sources (especially when new sources are frequently added). It is commonly agreed, that data models and query languages designed for well-structured data are inappropriate in such environments.

We discuss approximate answers through relaxation of semantics of the underlying query language. In particular, we propose a "weaker" interpretation of the symbol "=" in atomic formulas. Instead of the equality, the symbol might be interpreted as a partial pre-ordering relation (in "child semantics" or in "neighbor semantics"). Therefore, we introduce subsumption between labeled objects. This allows us to introduce subsumption on database queries. Thus, instead of evaluating original query, a subsuming (more general) query may be evaluated by the system. Such approach is of special importance, when access to data occurring in the original query is restricted to the user or when data represent semantically ambiguous information from heterogeneous databases [10]. In order to resolve semantic heterogeneity, generalization of data may be applied. As the result of the generalization, data heterogeneous at a low level of abstraction become homogenous at higher level. Thus, in the process of query evaluation, if the exact answer does not exist, we can use data from different levels of generalization in order to obtain a non-empty approximate answer.

The paper is organized as follows. In Section 2 a method for modeling and querying semistructured data, by means of labeled objects, is discussed. Partial pre-ordering relations on labeled objects are defined in Section 3. Next, in Section 4, we discuss three approaches to approximate answering. They are based on relaxed (approximate) semantics using the fact that labeled objects may be partially pre-ordered. Section 5 concludes the paper.

2 Databases of labeled objects

In comparison to classical approaches, databases storing semistructured data are schemaless. In such databases, there is no separate schema describing data structures. Instead, data are kept together with labels supporting the interpretation of data. The most popular model for representing semistructured data by means of labeled object is the Object Exchange Model (OEM) [2,17]. In [13,16], we have proposed an extended variant of OEM, the PLO (Partially Labeled Objects) data model, in which partial labeling is allowed. In this paper, we restrict ourselves to objects which are totally labeled, and which states are atomic constants and disjunctive or conjunctive sets of identifiers.

Definition 1. Let **D** be a set of *atomic constants*, **OID** = **AID** $\cup$ **SID** $\cup$ **TID** be a set of *object identifiers* (where **AID**, **SID** and **TID** are sets of *atomic*, *set* and *tuple object identifiers*, respectively), and **L** be a set of *labels*. *Labeled objects* are defined as follows:

1. If $i \in$ **AID**, $L \in$ **L** and $a \in$ **D**, then (i, L, a) is *an atomic labeled object*.

2. If $i \in \mathbf{SID}$, $L \in \mathbf{L}$ and $\{i_1, ..., i_n\}$ is a finite subset of **OID**, then $(i, L, \{i_1, ..., i_n\})$ is a *set labeled object*; $\{i_1, ..., i_n\}$ is referred to as *disjunctive* set of identifiers.

3. If $i \in \mathbf{TID}$, $L \in \mathbf{L}$ and $\{i_1, ..., i_n\}$ is a finite subset of **OID**, then $(i, L, [i_1, ..., i_n])$ is *a tuple labeled object*; $[i_1, ..., i_n]$ is referred to as *conjunctive* set of identifiers.. ∎

According to the definition above, every labeled object is a triple of the form $(i, L, \mathrm{val}(i))$, where i is a unique *object identifier*, L is a *label* of the object (the label express the meaning of the object, every object has exactly one label), and $\mathrm{val}(i)$ determines *object state*, and $\mathrm{val}(i)$ is either an atomic constant or a finite set of object identifiers.

A set **O** of labeled objects is *consistent* if for every identifier occurring in **O** there is a labeled object in **O** with this identifier.

Example 1. The following set of labeled objects is consistent:

```
1   Store      [2, 3]
2       Address   'Warsaw'
3       Parts      {4, 5}
4           Part       [6, 7]
6               Name 'Pentium III'
7               Price      300
5           Part       'CDx34'
8   Store      [9, 10]
9       Address   [11, 12]
11          City       'Poznań'
12          Street     'Chopin'
10      Parts   {13}
13          Part       'wheel' ∎
```

In the above example, $(3, \mathrm{Parts}, \{4, 5\})$ is a set labeled object (or a disjunctive labeled object). Its state enumerates references to objects being components of the object. The labeled object $(4, \mathrm{Part}, [6, 7])$ is a tuple object (or a conjunctive object). Its state consists of references to objects constituting the description of the object.

Query languages for labeled objects are based on notion of *paths* [2,17]. For the PLO data model we have developed a query language PathCal (*Path Calculus*) which semantics is described by means of algebraic operations on path and sets of paths [16].

A paths in PathCal is a sequence $(i_1, i_2, ..., i_n)$, $n \geq 1$, of distinct identifiers such that $i_{k+1} \in \mathrm{val}(i_k)$, $k = 1, 2, ..., n\text{-}1$, i.e. the successor belongs to the state of its predecessor. A set of paths may be determined by a path expression. For example, the path expression Store.Address determines the set of paths $\{(1, 2), (8, 9)\}$, since

1 is identifier of an object labeled by Store, 2 is identifier of an object labeled by Address, and $2 \in \text{val}(1) = [2, 3]$.

The path expression Store.Address* "closes" the set $\{(1, 2), (8, 9)\}$. The closure consists of all paths with prefixes belonging to the closed set. Thus, the value of the expression Store.Address* is the set $\{(1, 2), (8, 9), (8, 9, 11), (8, 9, 12)\}$.

Store, Store.Address and Store.Address* are examples of set-of-paths terms – their values are sets of paths. They are used to build formulas. For example Store.Addres(v) is a formula true for all v from the set $\{(1, 2), (8, 9)\}$. We will say that this formula determines the set $\{(1, 2), (8, 9)\}$. The complex formula Store.Addres(v) $\wedge$ v = 'Warsaw' determines the set $\{(1, 2)\}$ because v = 'Warsaw' is true if val(last(v)) = 'Warsaw'. We assume that expressions of the form $\{v\}$, where v is a path variable, is also a set-of-path term. Moreover, existential and universal quantifiers are allowed in formulas, as well as logical connectives.

A query is a set-of-path term of the form $\{v \mid \varphi\}$, where v is a path variable free in the formula φ (φ is qualifier of the query).

Example 2. The query returns stores located in Warsaw:

$$\{x \mid \text{Store}(x) \wedge \exists v \{x\}.\text{Address*}(v) \wedge v = \text{'Warsaw'}\}*.$$

Considering the following two possible valuations of variables

$[x/1, v/(1, 2)]$, val(last(v)) = 'Warsaw',
$[x/8, v/(8, 9, 11)]$, val(last(v)) = 'Poznań,

we can see that only for the first of them the qualifiers of the query is true. So the answer to the query (after the closure) consists of the following set of labeled objects:

1	Store		[2, 3]
2		Address	'Warsaw'
3		Parts	$\{4, 5\}$
4		Part	[6, 7]
6			Name 'Pentium III'
7			Price 300
5		Part	'CDx34' ∎

In the above examples we have used the exact semantics of the equality symbol "=" for comparing states of objects, and of identity symbol "= =" for comparing object identifiers, while evaluating formulas. This semantics is defined in the following definition by means of the satisfaction relation.

Definition 2. Let ω be a valuation of variables, a be an atomic constant, v be a path variable, and p be a path. The satisfaction relation $\models$ for (atomic) formulas is defined as follows:

$\omega \models v = a \Leftrightarrow \text{val(last}(\omega(v))) = a;$

$\omega \models v = p \Leftrightarrow \text{val}(\text{last}(\omega(v))) = \text{val}(\text{last}(p))$,

$\omega \models v == p \Leftrightarrow \text{last}(\omega(v)) = \text{last}(p)$. ∎

The satisfaction relation for composed formulas is defined as usual [11,14,16].

3 Partial ordering on labeled objects

In order to define approximate answers to queries formulated against databases of labeled objects, we define partial pre-ordering relation on these objects. We will use three well-known partial ordering relations, which have been used in the study of the semantics of programs [18], feature structures [6], and value-oriented complex objects [3,5,13,16]. The orderings are: partial ordering for disjunctive sets, $\leq^{\#}$ (Smyth' ordering), partial ordering for conjunctive sets, $\leq^{S}$ (Hoare's ordering), and partial ordering for convex sets, $\leq^{+}$ (Plotkin's ordering), which combines the two previous, i.e. $X \leq^{+} Y \Leftrightarrow X \leq^{\#} Y \wedge X \leq^{S} Y$. Note, that according to the Definition 1 states of set objects are disjunctive sets whereas states of tuple objects are conjunctive sets.

Theorem 1. Let on **D** and **L** be defined partial ordering relations $\leq^{D}$ and $\leq^{L}$, respectively. Let a and a' denote atomic constants (states of atomic objects), i and i' object identifiers, s and s' states of set objects, t and t' states of tuple objects. Then the binary relation, $\leq$, on states of labeled objects, defined in the following recursive way, is a partial pre-ordering relation, i.e. it is reflexive and transitive but not anti-symmetric:

$\alpha \leq \alpha' = $ **case** (α, α') **of**

$(a, a') : a \leq^{D} a'$

$(s, s') : \forall i' \in s'. \exists i \in s. i \leq i'$ // partial ordering on disjunctive sets

$(t, t') : \forall i \in t. \exists i' \in t'. i \leq i'$ // partial ordering on conjunctive sets

$(a, i) : a \leq \text{val}(i)$

$(a, s) : \forall i \in s. a \leq i$

$(a, t) : \exists i \in t. a \leq i$

$(i, a) : \text{val}(i) \leq a$

$(i, s) : \forall i' \in s. i \leq i'$

$(i, t) : \exists i' \in t. i \leq i'$

$(s, a) : \exists i \in s. i \leq a$

$(s, i) : \exists i' \in s. i' \leq i$

$(s, t) : \exists i \in s. \exists i' \in t. i \leq i'$

$(t, a) : \forall i \in t. i \leq a$

$(t, i) : \forall i' \in t. i' \leq i$

$(t, s) : \forall i \in t. \forall i' \in t. i \leq i'$

endcase,

where partial pre-ordering on labeled objects and object identifiers is:

$$(i, L, \text{val}(i)) \leq (i', L', \text{val}(i')) \Leftrightarrow i \leq i' \Leftrightarrow L \leq^L L' \wedge \text{val}(i) \leq \text{val}(i').$$

and

$$L \leq^L L' \Rightarrow \{x \mid L(x)\} \leq^+ \{x \mid L'(x)\}. \ \blacksquare$$

Let $o = (i, L, \text{val}(i))$, $o' = (i', L', \text{val}(i'))$. Further on, if $o \leq o'$, we will say that o is more general than o', or that o' is more specific than o; similarly for object identifiers and labels.

4 Approximate answers

In the context of cooperative and multilevel databases, many researches have been interested in approximate answering [7,8,15]. In [15] we described the application of "child" and "neighbor" semantics to approximate answering in relational databases. Now, we discuss this semantics for labeled objects. We will use the partial pre-ordering relation specified in Theorem 1.

4. 1 Child semantics

In the child semantics satisfaction of atomic formulas in exact semantics (Definition 2), is reformulated in the following way:

$\omega \models_0 v = a \quad \Leftrightarrow a \leq \text{val}(\text{last}(\omega(v)));$

$\omega \models_0 v = p \quad \Leftrightarrow \text{val}(\text{last}(p)) \leq \text{val}(\text{last}(\omega(v)));$

$\omega \models_0 v = = p \Leftrightarrow \text{last}(p) \leq \text{last}(\omega(v));$

Intuitively, if the formula φ is satisfied by a valuation ω, then φ is also satisfied by any valuation more specific than ω.

Example 3. Let us assume that 'Poland' < 'Warsaw' and 'Poland' < 'Poznań' are constraints in the system. Then the query:

$$\{x \mid \text{Store}(x) \wedge \exists v \ \{x\}.\text{Address}*(v) \wedge v = \text{'Poland'}\}*.$$

returns stores located in Poland. Note that by using the exact semantics (Definition 3), we obtain the empty set as the answer. However, if we follow the child semantics, we have:

$\omega = [x/1, v/(1, 2)]$, $\text{val}(\text{last}(1, 2)) = \text{'Warsaw'}$, 'Poland' $\leq$ 'Warsaw',
$\omega = [x/8, v/(8, 9, 11)]$, $\text{val}(\text{last}(8, 9, 11)) = \text{'Poznań, 'Poland'} \leq \text{'Warsaw'}$.

So, the answer is $\{1, 8\}*$. $\blacksquare$

Example 4. The following query

$$\{v \mid \text{Store}(x) \wedge \exists\, v\, \{x\}.\text{Parts}.\text{Part}(v) \wedge v = \text{'Pentium III'}\}*$$

is intended to retrieve stores with 'Pentium III'.

The following valuations are possible:

$\omega = [x/1,\ v/(1, 3, 4)]$, val(last(1, 3, 4)) = [6, 7], 'Pentium III' $\leq$ [6, 7],
$\omega = [x/1,\ v/(1, 3, 5)]$, val(last(1, 3, 5)) = 'CDx34',
$\omega = [x/8,\ v/(8, 10, 13)]$, val(last(8, 10, 13)) = 'wheel'.

So, the answer consists of $\{1\}*$.

Note, that for the query:

$$\{v \mid \text{Store}(x) \wedge \exists\, v\, \{x\}.\text{Parts}(v) \wedge v = \text{'Pentium III'}\},$$

and for the valuation $\omega = [x/1,\ v/(1, 3)]$, val(last(1, 3)) = $\{4, 5\}$, we obtain the condition 'Pentium III' $\leq \{4, 5\}$ that is not true.

However, looking for computer parts, we can formulate the query:

$$\{v \mid \text{Store}(x) \wedge \exists\, v\, \{x\}.\text{Parts}(v) \wedge v = \text{'Computer part'}\}.$$

For the valuation $\omega = [x/1,\ v/(1, 3)]$, val(last(1, 3)) = $\{4, 5\}$, and we have the true formula 'Computer part' $\leq \{4, 5\}$, since the two following relations are true:

'Computer part' $\leq$ val(4) = [6, 7],
'Computer part' $\leq$ val(5) = 'CDx34'. ∎

4.2 Neighbor semantics

In the neighbor semantics we try to match the given entity not only with its child, but also with neighbors in the taxonomy hierarchy. The neighbor must be at least as specific as the given entity. We assume that there are taxonomy hierarchies in the set of atomic constants. An example of such hierarchy is in Fig 1.

H:

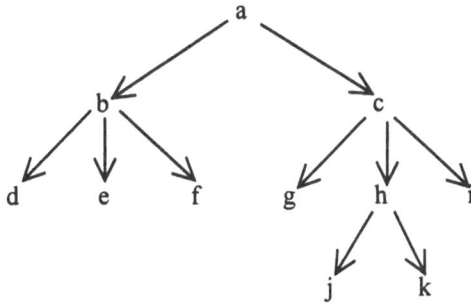

Fig. 1. A taxonomy hierarchy of atomic constants

In order to define the neighbor semantic, for every element (vertex) of the hierarchy taxonomy **H** we define its depth:

$depth(a) = 0$, if a is a root,

$depth(a) = depth(a') + 1$, if a' is the parent of a.

For two elements a and a' belonging to the same paths, $a \leq a'$, the *distance* between them is given by the function:

$dist(a, a') = depth(a') - depth(a)$.

For every $a \in \mathbf{H}$, the set of *ancestors* of a, of degree not greater than k, is:

$anc^k(a) = \{a' \in \mathbf{H} \mid dist(a', a) \leq k\}$.

The *meet* $(\otimes)$ of $a, a' \in \mathbf{H}$ is their parent, i.e. $a \otimes a' = a''$ if a'' is the parent of a and a' (the greatest lower bound of a and a' in the means of the lattice theory).

The following binary relation will be used in definition of the neighbor semantics:

$$a \leq_k a' \Leftrightarrow depth(a) \leq depth(a') \wedge a \otimes a' \in anc^k(a).$$

Intuitively, if $a \leq_k a'$ then a' is a neighbor of degree not greater than k of a. Note that for $k = 0$, we have the child relationship. The following theorem can be proven [15].

Theorem 2. Let $(\mathbf{H}, \leq)$ be a partially ordered and tree structured set of concepts. Then the binary relation $\leq_k$ is a partial pre-orderig relation on **H**. ∎

For the hierarchy in Fig. 1, we have e.g.: $e \leq_1 x$ for $x \in \{d, e, f\}$ and $e \leq_2 x$ for every $x \in \{d, e, f, g, h, i, j, k\}$.

Rules for satisfaction of atomic formulas in the neighbor semantics are:

$\omega \models_k v = a \quad \Leftrightarrow a \leq_k val(last(\omega(v)))$;

$\omega \models_k v = p \quad\quad \Leftrightarrow val(last(p)) \leq_k val(last(\omega(v)))$;

$\omega \models_k v = = p \Leftrightarrow last(p) \leq_k last(\omega(v))$.

Example 5. The following query

$$\{v \mid Store(x) \wedge \exists v (x).Parts.Part*(v) \wedge v = \text{'Pentium II'}\}*$$

is intended to retrieve stores with 'Pentium II'.

Using exact $(\models)$ or child $(\models_0)$ relations of satisfaction of formulas, the query produces the empty answer. However, assuming that in a hierarchy **H** we have: 'Pentium' < 'Pentium II' and 'Pentium' < 'Pentium III', we can use $\models_1$. So, we obtain:

$\omega = [x/1, v/(1, 3, 4, 6)]$, $val(last(1, 3, 4, 6)) = $ 'Pentium III', 'Pentium II' $\leq_1$ 'Pentium III'. Thus, the answer consists of $\{1\}*$. ∎

4. 3 Subsumption on conjunctive queries

Partial ordering on atomic constraints, labels and partial pre-ordering on labeled objects will be used to define generalized queries.

We define a partial pre-ordering relation $\leq^E$ on conjunctive expressions of the data manipulation language:

$\alpha \leq^E \alpha'$ $\Leftrightarrow \alpha \leq \alpha'$, if α and α' are constants,

$L \leq^E L'$ $\Leftrightarrow L \leq^L L'$,

$P.L \leq^E P'.L'$ $\Leftrightarrow P \leq^E P' \wedge L \leq^L L'$,

$P* \leq^E P'$ $\Leftrightarrow P \leq^E P'$,

$v \leq^E v'$ $\Leftrightarrow v = v'$, or the are formulas $P(v)$, $P'(v')$ such that $P \leq^E P'$,

$\{v\} \leq^E \{v'\}$ $\Leftrightarrow v \leq^E v'$,

$\wedge(\varphi_1, ..., \varphi_n) \leq^E \wedge(\psi_1, ..., \psi_{n+k}) \Leftrightarrow \forall i, 1 \leq i \leq n, \varphi_i \leq^E \psi_i$.

$\exists \underline{x} \, \varphi \leq^E \exists \underline{y} \, \psi \Leftrightarrow \forall x \in \underline{x} \, \exists y \in \underline{y} \, (x \leq^E y) \wedge \varphi \leq^E \psi$.

$\{v \mid \varphi\} \leq^E \{v' \mid \varphi'\} \Leftrightarrow v \leq^E v' \wedge \varphi \leq^E \varphi'$.

Example 6. The following set of labeled objects is a generalization of this from Example 1:

```
101    Store1 [102, 103]
102        Address1    'Warsaw'
103        Parts1      'Computer parts'
104    Store1 [105, 106]
105        Address1    'Poznań'
106        Parts1      'Car parts',
```

since

$101 \leq 1$, $104 \leq 8$, $[102, 103] \leq [2, 3]$, Address1 $\leq^L$ Address, Parts1 $\leq^L$ Parts,

'Computer parts' $\leq \{4,5\}$, $[105,106] \leq [9, 10]$, 'Poznań' $\leq [11, 12]$,

'Car parts' $\leq \{13\}$.

Thus, the following query

$$\{v \mid Store(x) \wedge \exists \, v \, \{x\}.Parts(v) \wedge v = \text{'Pentium III'}\}*,$$

returning $\{1\}*$, can be generalized to the query

$$\{w \mid Store1(y) \wedge \exists \, w \, \{y\}.Parts1(w) \wedge w = \text{'Computer part'}\}*$$

which returns $\{101\}*$. ∎

Theorem 3. Let q, q' be conjunctive queries returning ans(q) and ans(q'), respectively. Then:

$$q \leq^E q' \Rightarrow \text{ans}(q) \leq^{\#} \text{ans}(q').$$

Proof: The theorem follows from the fact that conjunctive queries are monotonic.

∎

5 Conclusions

In the paper the problems of approximate answering to queries within databases of labeled objects, representing semistuctured data, have been discussed. Approximate answering make the systems easy to use and more informative, and it is useful or necessary at least in the two following cases:

1. The exact answer to a query is empty and the taxonomic organization of some basic concepts allows us to use one of the relaxed semantics.

2. A multilevel organization of database is used in order to resolve semantic heterogeneity or to achieve database security. The multilevel organization of labeled objects is created according to recursive generalization of atomic constants, labels and objects reflecting the semantics of data.

To address the problems we have defined partial ordering and partial pre-ordering relations both on database concepts and on database language expressions. We have formulated novel theorems concerning the problem. Some other problems, which are under further investigations, address explanation of how and why approximate answers were derived. Without an explanation it is hard to estimate usefulness of the answer.

References

1. Abiteboul S., *Querying semistructured data*, Proc. of the International Conference on Database Theory ICDT'97, 1997, pp. 1-17.

2. Abiteboul S., Quass D., McHugh L., Widom J., Weiner J.L., *The Lorel query language for semistructured data*, Technical Report, Department of Computer Science, Stanford University, 1996

3. Bancilhon F., Khoshafian S., *A calculus for complex objects*, Journal of Computer and System Sciences, No. 38, 1989, pp. 326-340.

4. Bilski T., Pankowski T., Stokłosa J., *Database security*, Proc. Information Systems Architecture and Technology ISAT'98, 1998, Wrocław, pp. 135-142

5. Buneman O. P., Davidson S.B., Waters A., *A semantics for complex objects and approximate answers*, Journal of Computer and System Sciences, No. 43, 1991, pp. 170-218.

6. Carpenter B., *The Logic of Typed Feature Structures*, Cambridge University Press, 1992.

7. Chu W.W., Chen Q., *Neighborhood and Associative Query Answering*, Journal of Intelligent Systems, 1, 1992, pp. 355-382.

8. Gaasterland T., Godfrey P., Minker J., *An overview of cooperative answering*, Journal of Intelligent Information Systems 1(2), 1992, pp. 123-157.

9. Godfrey P., Minker J., Novik L., *An Architecture for a Cooperative Database System*, Applications of Databases, (eds.: W. Litwin, T. Risch), Lecture Notes in Computer Science 819, 1994, pp. 2-24.

10. Han J. *et al.*, *Dealing with Semantic Heterogeneity by Generalization-Based Data Mining Techniques*, Cooperative Information Systems. Trends and Directions, Academic Press, 1998, pp. 207-231.

11. Lloyd J.W., *Foundations of Logic Programming*, Springer-Verlag, Berlin, 1987.

12. Minock M.J., Chu W.W., *Explanation for Cooperative Information Systems*, Foundation of Intelligent Systems, (eds.: Z.W. Raś, M. Michalewicz), Lecture Notes in Artificial Intelligence 1079, 1996, pp. 264-273.

13. Pankowski T., *Powerdomain of Path for Representing Object Structures*, Fundamenta Informaticae 33(2), 1998, pp. 121-148.

14. Pankowski T., *Foundations of Databases*, Scientific Publishing PWN, Warszawa, 1992 (in Polish).

15. Pankowski T., *Semantics of approximate answers in cooperative database systems*, Proc. of Int. Conf. on Computational Intelligence on Modeling, Control and Automaton, CIMCA'99, Vienna, February 17-19, 1999, pp. 260-265.

16. Pankowski T., *Database model of partially labeled objects*, Rozprawy Nr 354, Wydawnictwo Politechniki Poznańskiej, Poznań, 2000 (in Polish).

17. Quass D., Rajaraman A., Sagiv Y., Ullman J., Widom J., *Querying Semistructured Heterogenous Information*, Proc. of International Conference on Deductive and Object-Oriented Databases, DOOD95, LNiCS 1013, pp.319-344, 1995.

18. Smyth M.B., *Power Domains*, Journal of Computer and System Sciences, Vol 16, 1978, pp. 23-36.

Author Index